The Photographer's and Artist's Guide
to High-Quality Digital Output

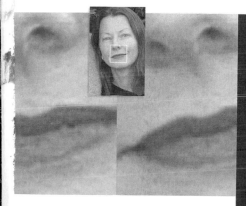

MASTERING

Digital
Printing

With Digital Techniques for:

- Photography
- Digital Printing
- Machine Art
- Hybrid Process
- Giclées!

Harald Johnson

Mastering Digital Printing

Credits: Senior Editor, Mark Garvey; Production Editor, Rodney Wilson; Copyeditor, Jill Batistick; Proofreader, Karen Annett; Technical Editor, C. David Tobie; Cover Design and Interior Design and Layout, Chad Planner, *Pop Design Works*; Indexer, Kevin Broccoli, *Broccoli Information Management*.

Publisher: Andy Shafran

COVER PHOTO CREDITS

Front Cover

TOP RIGHT: *French Farm 1*, © 2001 Ry Smith

BOTTOM RIGHT: *La Paz*, © 2001 Ileana Frómeta Grillo

BOTTOM LEFT: *Big Wave 1*, © 2001 Harald Johnson

TOP LEFT: © 2002 Harald Johnson

Back Cover

BOTTOM LEFT: HP Deskjet 5550 photo reprinted with permission from Hewlett-Packard Company; EPSON Stylus Pro 7600/9600 photo reprinted with permission from Epson America, Inc.

TOP LEFT: Nikon Coolpix 4300 photo courtesy of Nikon, Inc. Nikon and Coolpix are registered trademarks of Nikon Inc. © 2002. All rights reserved.

CHAPTER INTRO PHOTO CREDITS

Chapter 1: from *Welcome to the Breakers!* © 2001 Harald Johnson

Chapter 2: Courtesy of Martin Juergens

Chapter 3: Courtesy of Durst-Dice America, LLC

Chapter 4: *The Fountain*, © 2001 Carol Pentleton

Chapter 5: Courtesy of GretagMacbeth

Chapter 6: © 2000 Mark H. McCormick-Goodhart

Chapter 7: Courtesy of Teri Brudnak

Chapter 8: by Harald Johnson

Chapter 9: *North of the Pier* © 2001 Harald Johnson

Chapter 10: Photo by Dick Faller/New Media Arts

Chapter 11: Courtesy of Paul Roark

Library of Congress Catalog Number: 2002113693

ISBN 1-929685-65-3

5 4 3 2 1

Educational facilities, companies, and organizations interested in multiple copies or licensing of this book should contact the publisher for quantity discount information. Training manuals, CD-ROMs, and portions of this book are also available individually or can be tailored for specific needs.

MUSKA&LIPMAN Muska & Lipman Publishing ■ 2645 Erie Avenue, Suite 41 ■ Cincinnati, Ohio 45208
www.muskalipman.com ■ publisher@muskalipman.com

About the Author

Harald Johnson has been immersed in the world of commercial and fine-art imaging and printing for more than 25 years. A lifelong photographer and an award-winning digital and commercial artist and designer, he is the head of his own marketing communications agency, and has worked with many blue-chip artists as well as galleries and corporate clients throughout the United States.

Harald was introduced to digital imaging workflows in 1988 and has never looked back. He is the creator and moderator of Yahoo's *digital-fineart*, the world's largest online discussion group on the subject of digital fine art and digital printing. He is also the creator of DP&I.com (www.dpandi.com), the digital printing and imaging resource for photographers and digital/traditional artists.

Dedication

To my wife, Lynn, for all your support, partnership, and patience.

Acknowledgments

Trust me—books are much harder to write and publish than you think. Although the author is at the center of the storm, the contributions of many others are required to create the final product you are holding in your hands.

First, I thank the people who gave the idea for this book its early energy: fellow writer Gregory Georges, my old friend and confidant Richard Marks, fellow country dweller Bill Van Doren, and publisher Andy Shafran, who had the courage—and the smarts—to run with it. (I also thank Mark Garvey, Rodney Wilson, Sherri Schwartz, Kathy O'Hara, and the rest of the Muska & Lipman team plus book designer Chad Planner for all their professional and enthusiastic help.)

Further, I called on many experts and information sources in writing this book. Some who deserve singling out include the following: Steve Boulter, Patrick Brennan, Michael Collette, David Coons, Jed DeYoung and Stephen Pond's book *Inkjet Technology and Product Development Strategies*, John Doe, Jack Duganne, David Hamre, Mac Holbert, Joseph Holmes, Ileana, JD Jarvis, Martin Juergens and his report *Preservation of Ink Jet Hardcopies*, Dorothy Simpson Krause, Sally Larsen, Bonny Lhotka, Joy Turner Luke, Mark McCormick-Goodhart, Graham Nash, Karin Schminke, John Shaw, Steve Upton, Barbara Vogt and her paper *Stability Issues and Test Methods for Ink Jet Materials*, Charles Wehrenberg, and Henry Wilhelm and his landmark book *The Permanence and Care of Color Photographs*. For those others I've surely missed, remind me, and I'll make it up to you.

I also want to thank my expert readers who kept me from looking too foolish: Eric Everett, Robert Krawitz, Dr. David Matz, Robert Rex, John Thompson, C. David Tobie, and Dr. Ray Work III. And, an extra-special nod goes to the book's ever-knowledgeable Technical Editor, C. David Tobie.

More thanks go to all the product and brand managers, PR managers and outside PR reps, and owners of the companies who supplied me with information, material, and encouragement. Special thanks to: Amy Agnew (Weber Shanwick/HP), Nicole Andergard (Extensis), Anjali Ariathurai (Adobe Systems), Royce and Chris Bair (inkjetART), Jane Bolhorst (Walt & Co./Epson America), Debra Boring (Auto FX Software), Joanna Bruno (Porter-Novelli/HP), David Burkwall (Continuous Ink Systems), Bruce Butler (MacDermid ColorSpan), Halie Crocker (Alexander Ogilvy/Xerox), Chris Cudzilo and Ron Simkins (LexJet Direct), Will Curtis (Roland DGA), Karen Ernst (Digital Art Supplies), Ryan Fosegan (Durst-Dice America), Ted Ginsburg (Legion Paper), Sandy Gramley (HP), Michele Gray (Edelman PR/Fuji), Jennifer Gurien (Walt & Co./Epson America), Shivaun Korfanta (HP), John Jatinen (Epson America), Anders Jonsson (BrightCube), Lisa Jorgensen (Porter Novelli/HP), Patrick Kersey (Roland DGA), Bruce Leaf (iProof Systems), Brian Levey (ColorVision), Norm Levy (MediaStreet), Hyung Lim (LizardTech), Shannon Lyman (Lexmark), Merritt Mazzera (Walt & Co./Epson America), Bob McCurdy (GTI Graphic Technology), Bob McIntosh (Monaco Systems), John Mills (WeInk), Andrea Mulligan (Olympus America), John Nollendorfs (Lincoln Ink & Paper), Melanie Notkin (Celartem Technology), Fabia Ochoa (Epson America), Mike Pelletier (Improved Technologies), Parker Plaisted (Epson America), Chip Pryor (Pictorico), Liz Quinlisk (GretagMacbeth), R&J Group (ILFORD Imaging), Kelli Ramirez (Océ/LightJet), Will Reeb (Wacom Technology), Robert Rex (Crane & Co.), Aaron

Salik (Talas), Steve Saltman (American Imaging Corp.), Gregory Schern (Inkjet Goodies), Kristine Snyder (Epson America), Wade Steverson (Imaging Technologies), Min Tak (Dentsu Communications/Pictorico, Celartem), Karen Thomas PR (Image-Edit & Art, Olympus), C. David Tobie (Design Cooperative), Steve Upton (CHROMiX), Lara Vacante (Adobe Systems), Kylie Ware (Walt & Co./Epson America), Gwyn Weisberg (Adobe Systems), Patti Williams and Michael Flippin (I.T. Strategies), Diana York (Hawk Mountain Art Papers), and Brian Zimmer (ILFORD Imaging). Again, any omissions are inadvertent.

I want to acknowledge the many and varied online discussion lists that I follow (see Appendix). They have provided me with ideas, inspiration, and a connection to thousands of creative and thoughtful people around the world. Speaking of inspiration, much appreciation goes to the many photographers, artists, and printmakers who contributed their images and their stories to this book.

And finally, I want to thank my life partner, Lynn, for supporting me and for putting up with my long absence.

Contents

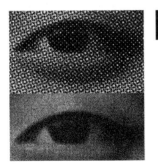

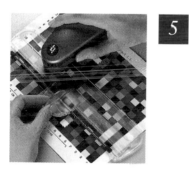

PART II: THE MAIN EVENT: INKJET PRINTING

PART III: BEYOND THE BASICS

PART IV: GALLERY SHOWCASE

APPENDIX: RESOURCES

Foreword

In early 1989, I was facing two upcoming art shows—one in New York and one in Tokyo—of large format prints of my photographic images. The task was daunting: 50 images in an edition of 25 and each printed at 30 2 40." My humble darkroom was clearly not up to such a task, not to mention the fact that the negatives for many of the key images had been forever lost during a shipment from San Francisco to Los Angeles. What to do? Whenever faced with a problem, I have only had to turn around and find that the answer is staring me right in the face. The same was true on this occasion.

With the help of my longtime friend, R. Mac Holbert, we were able to meet the challenge of finding a way to output digital images that would: (1) print in B&W as well as in color, (2) print on a wide variety of papers, (3) print at a resolution that approached that of photography, and (4) be permanent.

By using custom software programs and printing with an IRIS printer on nontraditional substrates, we finally succeeded, and the resulting shows of my images in New York, Tokyo, and Los Angeles were not only widely acclaimed, but the worlds of photography and art were introduced to a new printmaking model.

Few innovations are the result of one person's efforts. In our case, this was especially true. Without the help of John Bilotta, Charles Wehrenberg, Steve Boulter, David Coons, Jack Duganne, Al Luccesse, Mike Pelletier, Henry Wilhelm, Susan Nash, and Ruthanne Holbert, Nash Editions—which we officially opened in July 1991 as the world's first professional, digital printmaking studio—never would have become a reality.

The digital revolution rolls along. The people, the tools, and the materials continue to evolve. I applaud Harald Johnson's efforts to provide a comprehensive guidebook to digital imaging and to chronicle the past, the present, and the future of this exciting medium.

Graham Nash

Nash Editions

Introduction

I remember very clearly how it happened.

I had just entered the art gallery on South Dixie Highway in West Palm Beach on an extended trip to Florida. The local newspaper had promised new photographic work by artist John Paul Caponigro, son of famous landscape photographer Paul Caponigro. John Paul's digital composites of landscape elements and images of floating rocks were fascinating, but it was the style of the limited-edition prints that really caught my eye. They were rich and velvety, not like the cold and hard photographic prints I was used to. There was something special about these prints, although I couldn't put my finger on what it was.

When I found myself standing next to the artist, I asked him how he produced them, and he explained that they were digital prints or *giclées*. I only followed about half of what he was saying, but the memory of those vivid and luscious prints stayed with me. Soon, I started seeing more of digital printing. I went to outdoor art festivals, and there were artists and photographers selling their digital prints. I went to galleries, and there they were again. Ads in magazines mentioned them; the art Web sites had them. The signs were clear enough: I had to find out more about digital printing.

In addition to photographing South Florida's beaches —one of my favorite subjects—that winter, I started my research. During a trip to the West Coast, I got in some more exploring. In Los Angeles, I visited photo galleries and saw wonderful inkjet panoramics by German filmmaker Wim Wenders and gorgeous flower blowups by Harold Feinstein. I also visited the print studio of Jack Duganne, who first coined the term *giclée* (see Chapter 1 for more). In Seattle and Vancouver I saw even more examples. The range of subjects and artistic techniques was all over the board, but the common thread was the digital imaging and printing process. I was hooked.

Now back in Virginia, where I normally live, I got busy. I had a group of my best 35mm transparencies scanned (this was before I bought my first digital camera) and started printing my images with different printmakers around the United States. I also bought a desktop inkjet printer and started doing my own prints.

I now regularly produce a wide range of digital prints that I've sold to hotels, exhibited in several real-world and online galleries, and used for commercial contract proofing. In general, I've absorbed digital printing into my creative life.

Through my interest in learning about and printing my own imagery in this digital way, I discovered that I was not alone. There are literally tens of thousands of photographers, artists, and other types of imagemakers who are looking for the answers to the same questions I had. They want to know how to create and produce their images and their art by using the new digital technologies that are changing our lives. If you're one of those people, you've come to the right place!

Whom This Book is For

Written for photographers, digital and traditional artists, printmakers, art educators, and art marketers, *Mastering Digital Printing* is the first in-depth reference to the new world of digital printing for photography and fine art. Whether you're an amateur, a serious hobbyist, or an aspiring or even veteran professional, if you're interested in spreading your creative wings and learning more about this powerful art medium, this book is for you.

What You'll Find in This Book

This book is about nothing less than a revolution. A revolution that, although barely a dozen years old, has enabled photographers and artists the world over to create and produce their work in a way that has never been available to them before: with high-quality digital printing.

Part overview and part how-to, *Mastering Digital Printing* not only walks you through a complete, step-by-step workflow for making a great inkjet print, but also it covers the pluses and minuses of using the print technologies of digital photoprint and photo process, dye sublimation, and electrophotography (color lasers).

You'll learn about the following: how to pick the right inkjet printer; how to choose inks and papers; color management, print permanence, RIPs, and self-printing versus using a professional printmaker; the difference between original prints and reproductions; wide-format versus desktop printers; and advanced printing and image-editing techniques.

Other special features include the following: an inspiring Gallery Showcase of the best of digitally imaged and printed art and photography; an extensive resource section listing digital suppliers and digital-friendly galleries, art shows, and contests; plenty of sidebars, charts, diagrams, and photos illustrating the book's text; and the first accurate history of digital fine-art printmaking as well as the true origin of the term *giclée*.

Let this book be your trusted guide as you explore the exciting world of digital printing!

Note: Although this book discusses techniques for and uses images created on both Macintosh and PC/Windows platforms, the majority of the screen-shot images were created on a Macintosh, and they may look somewhat different from what you see depending on your computer setup. You'll also notice that the book's figures and illustrations show different types of interfaces and dialog boxes depending on the operating system and software versions used. I like variety!

How This Book is Organized

Mastering Digital Printing is divided into four parts. These parts are further subdivided into eleven chapters, the Gallery Showcase, and the Appendix:

Part I: Digital Printing Basics

- Chapter 1: "Navigating the Digital Landscape." This chapter puts digital printing into context and gives you a basic understanding of its role in the printmaking process. You'll learn the history of digital fine-art printing and the term *giclée*, along with an analysis of the different types of prints. We then explore the reasons for going digital, and who's "doin' the digital." The question of digital's acceptance is tackled next, and the chapter wraps up with the advantages and disadvantages of printing material yourself or sending it out, plus the crucial difference between a reproduction and an original print.

- Chapter 2: "Understanding Digital Printing." You'll learn about the components of a digital image and how digital prints are made. I cover pixels, bit depth, resolution, halftones, contones, and dithers. We go over the elements of a basic digital system, including options for computers, monitors, scanners, digital cameras, and graphics tablets. You'll even see two, actual system setups—one by a photographer and one by a digital artist. The chapter closes with an overview of printer drivers, PostScript, and RIPs.

- Chapter 3: "Comparing Digital Printing Technologies." This is the chapter that shows you the differences among the four major types of digital printing. It's not just about inkjets! I also cover digital photoprint and photo process, dye sublimation, and electrophotography (laser printers). How each technology works is explained along with the advantages and disadvantages of using each. There are also plenty of visual examples to help you make up your mind.

- Chapter 4: "Creating and Processing the Image." You'll learn all about how to input the image via non-camera scanning, camera scanning, or digital drawing and painting. The next step is image editing, and I discuss all the major software with examples of each. An image-editing workflow is then described with step-by-step instructions. The chapter concludes with a discussion of file formats, image compression, and file transport, storage, and archiving/asset management.

- Chapter 5: "Understanding and Managing Color." This is one of the least-understood digital-printing subjects, and we jump right in with a complete explanation of color basics and color spaces. Next is a thorough overview of color management including monitor matching and printer profiling. Finally, I cover all the main ways to get the color you want using printer settings, the transfer function, image-editing adjustments, printer profiles and soft-proofing, and RIPs.

- Chapter 6: "Not Fade Away: Print Permanence." The classic song title serves as a perfect backdrop for this controversial subject. We start by asking (and answering) the main question: How long is long enough? I explain the meaning of image stability and print permanence and describe the major factors that contribute to its failure. A complete analysis of permanence standards, tests, and claims follows, including the major testing organizations. The chapter ends with explanations of how you can do your own permanence testing, how to maximize the permanence of your own prints, and why all this matters.

Part II: The Main Event: Inkjet Printing

■ Chapter 7: "Picking an Inkjet Printer." Inkjet printers are the output devices of choice for many photographers and traditional and digital artists, and we dive right in by asking nine important questions that form the backbone of this chapter: (1) "Can I Use It to Print...?" (2) "Which Inkjet Technology?" (3) "What's the Print Quality?" (4) "What Different Paper and Inks Can I Use?" (5) "How Permanent Are the Prints?" (6) "Speed: How Long Does It Take to Print...?" (7) "How Easy to Set Up and Connect? How Big? How Noisy?" (8) "What About Printer Software, Drivers, and RIPs?" and (9) "What Does It Cost?" The chapter closes with a summary of each major inkjet brand.

■ Chapter 8: "Choosing Your Consumables." Consumable supplies are the inks and papers you put through an inkjet printer, and they are important keys to the whole process. We start with inks, and you'll learn about the differences between dye-based and pigment inks as well as the different options for third-party inks and inking systems. Moving to paper, the different types of substrates and coatings are analyzed along with third-party papers and the key paper characteristics. You also find out about alternative media and ways to find the best paper for you. We end with the best ways to match inks to paper.

■ Chapter 9: "Putting It All Together: Making a Great Inkjet Print." In this important chapter, you'll learn the key steps—and pitfalls—of the digital printing process. We start by setting you up with a digital workflow that includes ten specific steps for preparing and outputting a perfect inkjet print. There's even an alternative workflow to show you how to use third-party materials and how to prepare your images for the Web. The chapter concludes with "Finishing and Displaying Your Prints," which includes coatings and how to store and display prints.

Part III: Beyond the Basics

■ Chapter 10: "Print for Pay: Using a Professional Print Service." There are advantages and disadvantages to doing your own printing, and sometimes, it makes sense to farm out some or all of the process. In this chapter, we take a closer look at the role of printmakers and printing services. You'll learn what printmakers do, and why you might want to use one. I cover how to pick an inkjet printmaker, what to look out for, and how the artist/printmaker relationship works. You're also walked through a step-by-step giclée-print workflow. Finally, you'll learn about working with noninkjet providers plus online printing and image-sharing services.

■ Chapter 11: "Special Printing Techniques." Although the majority of people are content—and adequately challenged—to output a decent digital print, there are others who want to push the envelope and go beyond the basics. This is where you find out how to do just that. You'll learn about hybrid printing processes, making books and cards, dye-sublimation transfers, making digital negatives, and printing oversized prints. I follow with a complete section on monochrome options, including converting color and printing to monochrome, using special monochrome inks, and taking advantage of specialized drivers and printers. In the final portion of this chapter, you'll learn about CMYK proof printing and how graphic artists and designers are using it in a commercial context.

Part IV: Gallery Showcase

- "Gallery Showcase." This showcase features artists and images that illustrate the variety of digital imaging and printing being done today. These examples, along with the descriptions of how they were produced, are divided into five categories or types: Photography, Enhanced Photography, Digital Drawing/Painting, Hybrid Process, and Reproduction from Another Medium (Giclée). Enjoy the show!

- "Appendix." Finally, I wrap up the book with one of the most extensive resource sections you'll find anywhere. It lists photographer-artists, print-service providers, equipment, software, and related-service suppliers, suggested reading and information sources, digital-friendly art resources including galleries, showcases, art festivals, workshops, print exchanges, and more.

Keeping the Book's Content Current

Everyone involved with this book has worked hard to make it complete and accurate. However, as we all know, technology waits for no one, especially not for writers and book publishers! Digital printing and imaging is a moving target, and it's hard for anyone to keep up with its dizzying pace of change. This book is a snapshot of the techniques, technologies, products, and models currently available. For updates, corrections, and other information related to the content of the book, feel free to visit:

- www.muskalipman.com/digitalprinting

- www.dpandi.com (DP&I.com—the author's online, digital-printing and imaging resource)

And, if you have any suggestions for additions or changes to revisions of this book, contact the author at: harald@dpandi.com. You may not receive an instant response, but all messages are answered eventually.

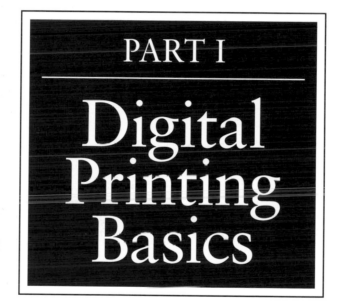

PART I

Digital
Printing
Basics

1

Navigating the Digital Landscape

Like the early explorers who probed the fringes of the known world with their new sextants and square-rigged ships, artists continually experiment with and adopt new technologies, and digital printing is the latest in a long line of artistic innovations. With photographers stepping out of their toxic darkrooms and other artists embracing digital workflows, everyone wants to know more about what digital printing is—and what it isn't. This chapter puts digital printing into context and gives you a basic understanding of its role in the printmaking process.

The Birth of Digital Fine-Art Printing

Sometimes, things just come together in a weird way.

Although artists have been using computers to create and output images for decades (see "Computers, Art, and Printmaking: A Brief History"), things didn't really take off until the paths of six people—a rock star and his best friend, an art publicist, a sales rep, a computer wizard, and a silkscreen printer—unexpectedly intersected in early 1989. As many things do, it all started in California.

Rock musician Graham Nash (of the legendary group Crosby, Stills and Nash) had been quietly collecting photographs for years. On the road with the band, Nash and his best friend, Mac Holbert, who was also CSN's tour manager, would always hit the local galleries and swap meets looking for visual treasures. In the process, Nash amassed a world-class collection of vintage and contemporary photographs.

Nash also took photographs every chance he got, and it was only a matter of time before he caught the computer bug and started scanning and manipulating his images on the computer screen. Of course, this was in the early days (mid '80s), when scanning was crude and printing was even worse. Holbert, who had computerized the band's accounting process early on, was soon helping Nash with his digital experiments. The two could see the potential of

© 1977 Joel Bernstein

Crosby, Stills and Nash in the studio, 1977

working digitally, but a decent print of what they were viewing on the monitor kept eluding them. No photo lab had yet figured out how to print from digital files, and the existing digital printers just weren't up to the task of high-resolution output.

If Nash wanted to start printing and showing his digitally processed B&W images, he was going to have to change gears and move to a new level. He decided to invent a way to do it himself, and to do that, he needed to raise some money—and he needed some help.

Enter Charles Wehrenberg, a San Francisco art publicist and writer. Wehrenberg was a friend of Nash's and a well-known figure in New York and West Coast high-art circles. After he understood that Nash wanted to sell his photo collection to raise money to invest in a way to print digital fine art, Wehrenberg came up with a plan. He arranged for the collection's sale through New York's venerable auction house, Sotheby's. Their PR machine would beat the drum, and Nash would handle the media like the pro he was.

However, Wehrenberg added another twist to the idea. To increase the buzz for the event, he orchestrated a concurrent art show of Nash's own straight photography at the Simon Lowinsky gallery. The show would be held in New York the day before the Sotheby's sale.

The show was scheduled for the following spring (1990), and Nash began pulling together 16 unique portraits taken over many years of touring with the band. However, there was a major problem. Most of the original negatives (and even the prints) had disappeared when Nash sent them to an art director; they never returned. All he had were the contact sheet proofs from which to work, and these were much too small—at least with normal photographic methods—for making the large display prints the gallery wanted.

During his search for high-quality digital output, Nash had discovered Jetgraphix, a design research lab affiliated with UCLA across town from his Encino (Los Angeles) home. Run by former ad agency art director John Bilotta, the studio was a test site for Fuji's experimental, large-format, inkjet printers of the same name (Jetgraphix). Nash was intrigued by the prints Bilotta could make, but the resolution was so low ("dots as big as your head") that when Nash asked if he knew of anything better, Bilotta handed him a sales brochure for something called an IRIS printer. (Another person who received a Bilotta brochure was a serigraph printer named Jack Duganne—more about him shortly.)

Left ©1990 Sally Larsen; right: courtesy of David Coons

Left: Charles Wehrenberg (with cup) and Simon Lowinsky, April 1990; right: David Coons and the IRIS 3024 in a well-air-conditioned room at Disney, 1990

Steve Boulter, the West Coast sales rep for Boston-based IRIS Graphics, had been showing test samples and passing out brochures for their new graphic arts, pre-press proofing machine to anyone he could. Boulter was pushing his company to get the IRIS into the hands of more photographers and artists, but the company didn't see much point to it—they were in the commercial graphics business, not the fine-art business. Boulter, however, believed in his idea, and continued to make the rounds of art studios and businesses involved with art production. One of his big sales at the end of 1988 was to The Walt Disney Company in Burbank, which was using the machine to output hardcopy, color prints in conjunction with their top secret, computer-animation process.

Wehrenberg was already familiar with the IRIS. Artist Richard Lowenberg had shown him some early sample prints, and Wehrenberg liked what he saw—a lot. He called the IRIS company for more information, and they relayed the call to Steve Boulter who happened to be visiting San Francisco. Soon, Boulter was standing at Wehrenberg's dining room table showing off more samples. Impressed all over again, Wehrenberg picked up the phone to call Graham Nash, and he put Boulter on the line to set up a meeting.

Boulter flew to Los Angeles the following week (April 1989), and Nash was equally amazed at the quality of the IRIS prints. He instantly realized that this was the solution to his two-part problem of getting images out of his computer and also making the prints for the Lowinsky show.

However, there was a remaining glitch: how to get the images *into* the IRIS printer. The machine was meant to be hooked up only to large, proprietary, pre-press systems, not home scanners or underpowered Macintosh computers. Boulter knew just the person to solve the problem: David Coons. Coons was a color engineer for Disney, and he was helping the company make the transition from analog to digital animation. (Coons would receive an Academy Award in 1992 for codeveloping Disney's ground-breaking, computer-animation production system.) Coons was also the one in charge of running the new IRIS 3024 printer that Boulter had sold them. Boulter introduced Coons to Nash, and soon, Coons was on the team.

Working off-hours at Disney and using custom software programs that he wrote specifically for the project, Coons scanned and retouched Nash's proof prints, downloaded them to the IRIS, and printed the edition of images onto thick, Arches watercolor paper.

Nash ultimately met his April 24, 1990, deadline for the Lowinsky exhibition, and the following day's sale at Sotheby's brought in $2.17 million, a record for a private photographic collection.

Self Portrait, *Plaza Hotel, New York, by Graham Nash, 1971. Printed by David Coons in September, 1989, as one of the original portfolio prints shown at the Simon Lowinsky gallery in 1990.*

The world's first series of digitally printed, photographic fine art drew crowds and raves in New York and, as the show traveled, in Tokyo and Los Angeles. (A set of those prints later sold at auction at Christie's for $19,500.)

The plan had worked perfectly; digital prints were on the art map.

Even before the show, while Coons was moonlighting at Disney to output the print portfolios, Nash, Boulter, Wehrenberg, Coons, and eventually Holbert were kicking around the idea of setting up a shop to produce these new digital prints on a commercial basis. Coons was already experimenting with non-Nash images, including several for artist Sally Larsen, who was Wehrenberg's wife.

Graham Nash soon bought one of the $126,000 IRIS machines and installed it in July 1990 in the small garage of an old house he owned in nearby Manhattan Beach, a suburb of Los Angeles. By August, Steve Boulter had moved into the top floor of the garage, and David Coons was making the long commute from Burbank each day with nine-track computer tapes of images that needed printing for a new edition of Nash portraits to be shown in Tokyo in November 1990.

Courtesy of Nash Editions

Left: Steve Boulter sits in the new, converted garage studio of Nash Editions, trying to drum up business, August 1990. There was no computer hooked up to the IRIS printer then, only a nine-track tape drive (visible at left of printer); right: Jack Duganne (front) and Mac Holbert at Nash Editions, 1993. Duganne removed the IRIS covers to make them easier to maintain.

Remember serigrapher Jack Duganne? He soon found out about what was going on in Manhattan Beach. It wasn't far from his studio in Santa Monica, so Duganne, who could see the digital writing on the wall, started bringing digital tapes of his art clients' scanned images over for printing. By February 1991, he was printing on the IRIS himself as a Nash Editions' employee. Duganne took to the IRIS quickly, developing new printing procedures and in the process becoming Nash's master printmaker. While there, Duganne also came up with the term "giclée," but more about that later.

The work for outside clients continued to grow, and as Coons and Boulter began to spend less time at the Manhattan Beach studio, it became clear that someone would need to manage this new business enterprise if it were going to succeed. Coons had been running things while Nash and Holbert were on the road with CSN, but when the last tour ended in June 1991, Holbert moved down from his home in Santa Cruz and took over managing the shop. On July 1, 1991, Graham Nash and Mac Holbert officially opened Nash Editions as the world's first professional, digital printmaking studio.

By 1992, three digital printmaking studios (Nash Editions, Harvest Productions, and Cone Editions) were busy on both U.S. coasts. All were using IRIS inkjet technology to make fine-art prints for photographers and artists. Soon, there were a dozen similar shops, then many dozen, then scores. Today, there are anywhere from 2,500 to 5,000 professional printmakers making digital prints for artists the world over.

Courtesy of Nash Editions

However, just as important, and the reason many of you are reading this book, is the fact that there are now many tens of thousands of individual photo-

Mac Holbert (left) and Graham Nash in 1997 at Nash Editions

graphers, artists, and serious hobbyists who are able to print high-quality images in their own homes or offices. No longer constrained by the high costs of traditional printing methods, the production of "artistic" prints has been put in the hands of the artists and imagemakers themselves.

■ ■ ■

The importance of the founding group of Nash, Holbert, Wehrenberg, Boulter, Coons, and Duganne cannot be overstated. They not only laid the technological foundation for digital fine-art printing, but also (and even more importantly) they established its identity and gave it a face. They provided the essential "proof of concept" that the new process needed before it could blossom and evolve.

Without the unique contributions of these six pioneers—the vision and promotability of Graham Nash, the dedication of Mac Holbert, the art world orchestration of Charlie Wehrenberg, the technical wizardry of David Coons, the persistence of Steve Boulter, and the inventiveness of Jack Duganne—the entire digital fine-art printing phenomenon would not be where it is today. They—and the ones who immediately followed, including Maryann and John Doe, and Jon Cone—deserve the credit for creating an industry. All of them opened the door to the promise of digital printing, and the early adopting artists walked right in. Today, that door is swinging wider all the time.

Where Are They Now?

Graham Nash still takes photographs and remains the figurehead of Nash Editions, while Mac Holbert continues to run the day-to-day operations. David Coons and his wife, Susan, opened their own fine-art scanning service (ArtScans) two doors down from Nash Editions in 1993. Steve Boulter is a consultant to the digital imaging industry. Charlie Wehrenberg still lives in San Francisco and continues to work in the art world. Jack Duganne opened his own digital printmaking studio (Duganne Ateliers) in Santa Monica in 1996. John Bilotta is now Nash Edition's master printmaker.

All six remain actively involved with art in general and with digital printmaking in particular.

Computers, Art, and Printmaking: A Brief History

1946
The first large-scale, general-purpose digital computer, the Eniac, is activated at the University of Pennsylvania.

1950
Mathematician Ben Laposky makes "oscillograph" images on screen of cathode-ray tube.

1959
CalComp launches first digital plotter to output computer images to print.

1965
Computer images begin to be exhibited as artwork.

1967
E.A.T. (Experiments in Art and Technology) formed to promote collaborative efforts between artists and engineers.

C.A.V.S., (Center for Advanced Visual Studies), founded by Gyorgy Kepes, opens at M.I.T.

1968
The Machine, as seen at the End of the Mechanical Age exhibition at The Museum of Modern Art, New York.

Some More Beginnings exhibition at the Brooklyn Museum, New York.

Cybernetic Serendipity exhibition at the Institute of Contemporary Arts, London.

1971
Art and Technology exhibition at the Los Angeles County Museum of Art.

1973
First computer "painting" software created at the Xerox Palo Alto Research Center by Richard Shoup.

1976
IBM introduces the 6640, the first continuous-flow inkjet system.

1977
Applicon announces first color continuous-flow inkjet printer.

Siemens launches first piezoelectric inkjet printer.

1981
IBM introduces its first personal computer.

Canon demonstrates its BubbleJet thermal technology.

1984
Apple introduces the Macintosh line of computers.

HP releases first thermal inkjet printer (2225 ThinkJet).

1985
New York master printer Harry Bowers claims to make first digital color photo print.

1987
The IRIS Graphics 3024 inkjet printer is launched for the pre-press proofing industry.

1989
David Coons outputs first IRIS fine-art print (of singer Joni Mitchell) for Graham Nash.

1990
Adobe Systems releases image-editing software Photoshop 1.0, developed by John Knoll and Thomas Knoll.

© 1990 Sally Larsen

Transformer 2 *by Sally Larsen, 1990*

First all-digitally printed, photographic fine-art show (Graham Nash) at the Simon Lowinsky gallery, New York.

Sally Larsen's *Tunnels Point Transformer* is the first digital fine-art print included in the permanent collection of The Metropolitan Museum of Art (New York).

1991
Nash Editions, the world's first digital fine-art printmaking studio, opens for business to the public.

Maryann and John Doe start Harvest Productions, which eventually becomes the largest digital printmaking studio in the world.

Jack Duganne (while at Nash Editions) coins the term "giclée."

1992
Jon Cone's Cone Editions becomes first, U.S. East Coast, IRIS-based digital printmaking studio.

1994
Epson introduces the Stylus Color, the first, desktop, photorealistic inkjet printer.

1997
Formation of the International Association of Fine Art Digital Printmakers (IAFADP).

1998
MacDermid ColorSpan announces its Giclée PrintMakerFA, the first wide-format digital printer created specifically for fine-art market.

IRIS Graphics introduces their 3047G inkjet printer with adjustable head for fine-art market.

Roland DGA releases its Hi-Fi JET, a wide-format, pigmented, six-color printer.

1999
Jon Cone releases his PiezographyBW system for multi-monochromatic printing.

2000
Epson launches the Stylus Photo 2000P, the first desktop printer to use pigmented inks.

2001
Opening of the Beecher Center at The Butler Institute of American Art (Ohio), the first art museum in the United States dedicated to digital art.

010101: Art in Technological Times exhibition at the San Francisco Museum of Modern Art.

BitStreams exhibition at the Whitney Museum of American Art, New York.

Digital: Printmaking Now exhibition at the Brooklyn Museum of Art, New York.

Epson introduces the C80, the first digital printer using pigmented color inks, into the general office market.

2002
IAFADP dissolves and plans to re-form as the "Digital Printmakers Council" (tentative name) within the American Print Alliance.

Lexmark introduces first 4800-dpi desktop inkjet printer (Z65).

Epson unveils first seven-color, pigment-ink desktop inkjet printer (2100/2200).

Epson introduces world's first two-picoliter ink droplet (960).

(Sources: John Bilotta, Steve Boulter; Jon Cone; David Coons; Jack Duganne; Epson America, David Hamre; Mac Holbert, Martin Juergens, *Preservation of Ink Jet Hardcopies*, 1999; Barbara Vogt, *Stability Issues and Test Methods for Ink Jet Materials*, 2001; Marilyn Kushner, *Digital: Printmaking Now*, Brooklyn Museum of Art, 2001; Graham Nash, Mike Pelletier; *The New York Times*; Roland DGA; John Shaw/DPIA; Charles Wehrenberg; Henry Wilhelm)

Defining Digital Printing

Just what is digital printing anyway? The way I like to describe it is by being more specific and using the words "digital art—or fine-art—printing." This phrase defines the boundaries of a complex topic and helps us focus on the subject of this book. So, let's break *digital art printing* into its components. This may seem like an elementary exercise, but it's important to understand the territory we're about to enter.

Digital

Here's the basic concept: *Digital* means using numbers to represent something, and that's exactly what a computer does. A normal image is converted into numerical data (a long string of ones and zeros) that describe or quantify each sample point or "pixel" (short for *pic*ture *el*ement, the basic unit of image information) in terms of certain attributes such as color and intensity. This data can be stored, manipulated, and ultimately transformed with digital printing technologies back into a normally viewed image (see Chapter 2 for an in-depth look at this).

Art

This gets a little tricky. People have been debating the definition of art for thousands of years, and it won't end here. However, we need to put some kind of fence around this, so here's my attempt.

For our purposes, art or fine art (and I use the terms *very* broadly) is created by individual photographers and/or artists—they can be the same or not, and I'll sometimes call the combination "photographer-artists"—even if it's only as a hobby or sideline. Whether it's destined for the walls of the Louvre or the walls of a living room or office, art is meant to be displayed, to be admired—and yes, even to be bought and sold. It's also to provide inspiration and an emotional connection with the artist or the viewer's own thoughts and feelings.

The fields of graphic design, advertising, and marketing communications—commercial imagemaking—are on the edges of this universe, and I'll cover them in a limited way. However, we won't spend much time with the digital printing technologies that produce signs and banners, billboards, event graphics, building wraps, and vehicle signage. The typical client or customer for that type of output is a business that needs to promote a product or service in a high-impact, visual way. Although photographers and artists can—and frequently do—use commercial technologies to create their work, that world is not the focus of this book.

Courtesy of Larry Goldstein Photography, Inc.

Printing

Traditional, analog printing is a mechanical process that uses a physical master or "matrix" for making repeatable prints. Commercial and even traditional fine-art printing presses, for example, use pressure or impact to transfer the image from a carrier, plate, or blanket (the matrix) to the receiving paper. With old-style photography, the negative or a transparency is the matrix through which light travels to expose the print.

Digital fine-art printing is different, however. There is no pressure or impact, and there is no physical matrix. The matrix now sits in the computer in the form of digital data that can be converted repeatedly, and without any variation, into a print by any photographer-artist who self-prints or who uses an outside printing service. (I'm intentionally avoiding all the permutations and variations of computer-to-plate and other forms of commercial digital printing, although there's no reason they can't be used by artists.)

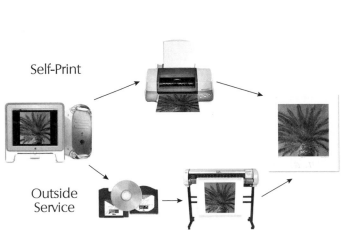

Self-Print

Outside Service

Digital art printing workflow: from digital matrix to hardcopy print

Voila! Digital art printing then simply means *the printing of art by digital processes*. That's it. Sounds rather plain, but as we will soon see, it's not as clear-cut as it seems.

Putting Prints in their Places

The worlds of photography and fine-art printmaking have been historically separated by a kind of psychological barrier. For instance, art exhibitions of fine-art prints don't usually include photographs, and photo exhibits don't also have etchings. In addition, as far as the practitioners themselves go, traditional artists such as painters or printmakers usually are not photographers as well (and vice versa). The techniques and the language of each field have been different—until now.

Computer technology in general, and digital printing in particular, is the big gorilla straddling the fence and spilling over onto the once-separate arenas of photography and fine-art printmaking. The whole field of image and art production is rapidly changing, and if you plan to be an active player in this new world, you have to know something about the old one. It's time for a quick overview to give you some perspective.

Library of Congress, Prints and Photographs Division

Portrait of Alfred, Lord Tennyson *by Julia Margaret Cameron, albumen print, c. 1862-1869*

What's a Print?

Unlike paintings or drawings, prints exist in repeatable, multiple examples. Images are not created directly on paper but with another medium or on another surface (a master or matrix), which then transfers (or in the case of digital, "outputs") the image to paper. You can make more than one impression or example by printing the same image on a new piece of paper. The total number of impressions or prints an artist or photographer makes of one image is frequently called an edition.

Photographic Prints

Photographers have been making prints of their images ever since the pioneering days of the medium. Although Louis Daguerre (1839) and before him Nicéphore Niépce (1829) were able to produce the first, fixed photographs, it was William Henry Fox Talbot's 1840 invention of the Calotype process that allowed photographers to make an unlimited number of positive paper prints from the same negative.

I roughly categorize photographic prints into three technology groups: *black-and-white, color,* and *alternative process.*

Black-and-White Prints

Normal black-and-white (B&W) photography is metallic-silver based. The chemical processing of a silver-halide emulsion that has been exposed to light creates a lasting image made up of tiny bits of silver that absorb, rather than reflect, light. Correctly processed B&W prints on fiber-based paper are essentially permanent; they will last for hundreds of years without image deterioration. "Silver-gelatin print" is the art world description for a normal B&W print.

Color Prints

Although the early photographers had hoped to produce color images from day one—and they partially succeeded but with awkward and time-consuming processes such as Autochrome, dye-transfer, and

Seth Rossman

Traditional B&W developing in a chemical darkroom

tricolor carbro prints—real color photography didn't actually begin until 1935 when Kodak launched its famous Kodachrome transparency film. Then, in 1939, Agfa introduced the first paper for printing from color negatives using the "chromagenic development" (color coupler) method. The basic process is this: The chemical development of a certain type of silver-halide emulsion creates products that react or "couple" with special compounds to form color dyes and a resulting color image. Unlike the metallic-silver prints of B&W, color prints, for the most part, are composed of cyan, magenta, and yellow organic dyes. The main problem with early color prints was their inherent lack of image stability and permanence (see Chapter 6 for more about this). If you have any old family photos dating back from the 1950s through the late 1970s, you know what I mean; they're probably all discolored, faded, and stained by now.

Alternative Process

Fitting somewhere between (or outside, depending on your point of view), B&W and color are the alternative or nontraditional photo print processes. They're "alternative" primarily because they tend to be handmade or use custom techniques that are, in many cases, resurrections—or continuations—of antique methods for printing photographs. Examples include cyanotypes, kallitypes, gum bichromates, platinum and palladium prints, salted paper and albumen prints, van dykes, bromoils, and sepia (or other) chemically toned prints. Many of these are made by contact-printing large negatives (see more in Chapter 11), and most are monochromatic (cyanotypes are blue, which is why they're also called "blue prints").

Polaroid transfer by Marilyn E. Culler

Liquid emulsions, image transfers, and emulsion lifts are alternative printing processes for color photographs.

In some ways, it's been the experimenting with, and acceptance by the art world of, these alternative photo techniques and processes that has led to the current explosion in digital printing by photographer-artists.

Traditional Art Prints

Digital prints are a new wrinkle on the weathered and well-respected face of fine-art prints (also called "fine prints" and "works on paper"). To put digital prints into context, here is a brief run down of the major, traditional, fine-art printmaking methods.

Relief Prints

The artist sketches an image on a wood block or other surface and then cuts away pieces from the surface, leaving only the raised image. Ink is then applied to the surface with a roller and transferred onto paper with a press or by hand-burnishing or rubbing. The recessed, cutaway areas do not receive ink and appear white on the printed image. Relief prints are characterized by bold dark-light contrasts. The

Scenes from the Nineteenth-Century Stage, Dover Publications, Inc., 1977

Figure 1.1 *Woodcut advertising the play* Polaris *in Boston, 1873*

primary relief techniques are *woodcut* (the earliest and most enduring print technique; see Figure 1.1), *wood engraving* (made from the end-grain surface of blocks and offering more precision and detail), and *linocut* (printed from linoleum; well-suited for large areas of contrasting colors).

Intaglio Prints

Intaglio (pronounced "in-tal-yo") comes from the Italian word *intagliare*, meaning "to incise." An image is incised with a pointed tool or "bitten" with acid into a metal plate, usually copper or zinc. The plate is covered with ink and then cleaned so that only the incised grooves hold the ink. The plate and dampened paper are then run through a press to create the print. The intaglio family of printmaking techniques includes the following: *engraving* (an engraved line has a sharp and clean appearance), *drypoint* (results in heavier, softer-looking lines than those in an engraving), *mezzotint* (yields soft tonalities ranging from gray to black), *etching* (results in a characteristically raised surface), and *aquatint* (an etching process yielding a textured and toned image).

Lithography

Invented in 1798, lithography is a "planographic" process that was championed by artists Henri de Toulouse-Lautrec, Rembrandt, Goya, Picasso, Degas, Braque, and Miro. To make a lithograph, the artist uses a greasy medium such as crayon or tusche to create an image on a stone or metal plate. The surface is then dampened with water, which is repelled by the greasy areas, sticking only to the sections of the plate that have not been marked by the artist. Printer's ink is then applied to the plate with a roller. This, in turn, sticks only to the greasy sections, as the water protects the rest of the plate. The stone or plate is then covered with paper and run through a printing press to create the print.

Screenprints (Serigraphy)

This technique was popularized by artists like Andy Warhol who exploited its bold, commercial look. To make a screenprint, an image that has been cut out of a material (paper, fabric, or film) is attached to a piece of tautly stretched mesh. Paint is then forced through the mesh—the "screen"—onto the sheet of paper below by means of a squeegee. The uncovered areas of the screen allow the paint to pass through, while the areas covered by the image shapes do not. For works with more than one color, a separate screen is required for each color.

Monotypes/Monoprints

As their names imply, *monotypes* or *monoprints* (the words are often confused and used interchangeably) are prints that have an edition of a single impression. The artist creates an image on a smooth surface, which is then covered with dampened paper and run through a printing press or rubbed with the back of a spoon, a similar tool, or even the artist's hand.

Digital Prints

Announcing the third, major, fine-art print category—digital prints! Claiming that this is an official classification in a rapidly evolving field is a risky, even foolish, endeavor, but you have to start somewhere, and this is a place to draw a line in the sand. The line can always be moved later! At the very least, we can consider digital printing to be a new tool for photographers and artists who want to expand their artistic options.

© 2001 Harald Johnson

Author's 133-image, digital collage, Welcome to The Breakers!

Although there is no end to the inventiveness of rival terminology—"giclées," "computer prints," "IRIS prints," "inkjets," "digitally rendered prints," "virtual paintings," "digigraphs," "limited editions on canvas," "pigment prints," "pigjets" (do I need to go on?)—let's keep it to one overall term for the moment: digital prints. I define the term as prints resulting from a digital master or matrix.

Of course, artists being artists, all these nice and neat categories are frequently violated. For example, wedding and portrait photographers are famous for coating and embellishing their prints. Kolibri Art Studio, a leading serigraph atelier in Torrance, California, offers both serigraphic and digital printing to artists who will sometimes start with a digital reproduction and add serigraphic embossing, texturizing, or gold-leafing. New York City's Pamplemousse Press creates digital editions that combine IRIS printing with construction and relief techniques. Members of the Digital Atelier printmaking studio love to use digital prints as the base or ground and then add painting, collage, encaustic, and emulsion transfer techniques. (See Chapter 11 for more on this.)

Printing Cousins: Offset and Canvas Transfers

Offset lithography: Although technically not an art print process, offset lithography is frequently used in printing art reproductions, usually only in large editions where economy of scale brings the unit cost down. This is how everyday art posters (as well as brochures, magazines, and newspapers) are printed. The "offset" part of the name comes from the principle of transferring the image from the revolving plate to a rubber blanket before final transfer to the paper (see Figure 1.2). Because of the similarity of terms, and because they both fall under the "planographic" category, fine-art lithographs are sometimes called "original lithographs" to distinguish them from commercial, offset prints.

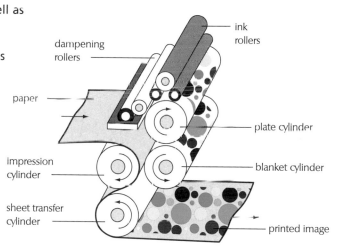

Figure 1.2 *The offset lithography process*

Canvas transfers: Canvas transfers occupy a spot on the art-print pecking order somewhere between offset litho prints/posters and digital prints, and their selling prices reflect this middle rank. This is a mechanical process that "transfers" the top image layer of a preexisting piece of art (usually an offset litho-produced poster) to a new substrate, typically canvas. Canvas transfers are frequently "embellished," with an artist adding highlights or textures by hand as a last step.

Why Go Digital?

Digital imaging and printing have changed the rules of visual communication. Making original prints or reproductions, especially at a large size, used to be costly, cumbersome, or difficult for the individual photographer or artist. No longer. The advantages of digital printing are clear.

Cost

After the initial setup and proofing stage is complete, digital prints can be made on an as-needed basis. This is true print-on-demand. You want one print to test a market or an image? No problem. You want 100? Also no problem. By contrast, conventional nonphotographic, print production methods require the entire print run to be produced all at once. The result is a pile of inventory that probably took a pile of cash to make (also known as the "Now What Do I Do with that Stack of Prints in My Garage?" syndrome).

Consistency

Because digital source files are stored on computer hard disks or other digital storage media, they can be reused over time to produce identical results, assuming the media, inks, and hardware/software have not changed. In theory, the first and last prints in an edition of 100 produced over a ten-year period will look identical.

Storage

Digital art takes little physical room when stored on disk. Digital files can be long-lasting *if* the digital data remains intact and there is a way to read it. In addition, artists working with traditional media can have their completed originals scanned and stored for future use in print editions. Not only does this safeguard the image, but also it allows artists to sell their originals without having to worry about reclaiming them later for reproductions.

Larger Sizes

Size is not much of an issue with digital, especially with wide-format inkjet printers, which come in 40", 50", and even 60" models. Printing on roll paper, the length of an inkjet image is limited only by the printer's software. For even larger prints, images can be "tiled" and assembled in pieces. In addition, the same digital source file can be cropped, blown up or shrunk, and printed in many sizes.

Artistic Control

If you print your own images, you have complete control of the process. You decide on the best machine to use, you select the best paper-and-ink combination, and you decide if you want to run the colors a little heavier on the next print. You have no one else to blame or to praise. You also get the immediate feedback of seeing what's working in print and what's not.

Freedom and Flexibility

Want to print at 4:00 a.m.? Want to change that red to green today, not tomorrow? Using the same image file, a photographer-artist can experiment with different sizes, croppings, or unconventional media. New images, variations, or new editions can be sampled and tested at minimal cost and with no risk, one at a time.

Courtesy of John Livzey Photography

Photographer John Livzey analyzes a digital print in his home studio.

Who's Doing Digital?

Labeling artists has always been a risky proposition, and this is especially true today. The digital revolution (including the Internet) has created opportunities for photographers, artists, and imagemakers to create and distribute their work in ways that were not even dreamed of ten or even five years ago. Although many artists sidestep the traditional channels and categories, it's still useful to attempt some kind of lumping together, if only to allow more understanding of the widespread reach of digital imaging and printing.

Note that art buyers and marketers tend to think in terms of categories—pop art, Old Masters, that sort of thing. It is the same with juried art shows and contests, which by necessity need to categorize entries and awards to keep the whole system of judging art somewhat manageable. So, that being said, here goes my attempt at classifying the *creators* of digital art prints (see Gallery Showcase for some good examples from each group).

Photographers/Imagemakers

The digital wave has definitely broken over the photographic/imagemaking field, and most photographers are riding it (they'll drown if they don't). It's only logical considering that photography was born out of the technological innovations of Niépce, Talbot, Bayard, and Daguerre in the 19th century. Some say that the digital revolution is as important as the invention of color photography, even photography itself. Of course, there will always be the few purists and hold-outs who thumb their noses at technological advances, but if you are reading this book, you are probably not one of them.

Some of the photographers who are emerging from their smelly darkrooms and into the digital light are merely using digital printing to output their existing work with little intervention. Others are playing a more active digital role, either shooting with a digital camera or scanning their film-based images before beginning the work of color correcting, retouching, and improving what they have. The final prints are then made by any of the methods discussed in this book.

Take Seth Rossman, for example. An Indiana-based photographer, he's covered the whole gamut in the last 30 years. He's done everything from combat photography in Vietnam to portraits, advertising, sports, PR, custom lab work, and B&W photo contest printing. He's now a stringer for the Associated Press, who gave him the nudge ("go digital or don't work") to make the transition to digital. He shoots just about everything with his Nikon D1s, and he uses all the major digital output technologies: dye sublimation, inkjet, digital photoprint, and even electrophotography or color laser printing (see the next chapter for a detailed discussion of each, and see the Gallery Showcase for more of Rossman's work).

Left: Photographer Seth Rossman compares inkjet "index prints" from digital images with the view on the screen; right: Fishing, color laser print.

Left: by Marilyn E. Culler; right: by Seth Rossman

Traditional Artists

The painters, watercolorists, and sketch and pastel artists who have taken up digital printing techniques to publish and reproduce their work are currently producing the greatest number of commercially sold, digital fine-art prints. An artist can have a transparency made of his or her original work, take it to a photographer or digital printmaker for direct digital scanning (bypassing the photography step completely), or digitize it with his or her own scanner. The digital file is then typically printed on either paper (watercolors, drawings, or pastels) or canvas (oils or acrylics) to produce an edition.

American painter Craig Forrest is a North Carolina "rural realist." Using photographs as source material, he creates his representational paintings using the methods of pencil drawing, watercolor, drybrush, and, sometimes, egg tempera (dry pigments mixed with distilled water and egg yolk).

Forrest now also makes and sells digital reproductions of his original paintings. He directly scans each painting in sections, stitching the individual pieces together at his computer workstation. He then prints his own limited-edition giclées on an Epson 2000P with its archival pigment inks.

"Being able to do this in my studio has given me the opportunity to make quality reproductions available to collectors who could not afford my originals. With this process, I

Left: Traditional artist Craig Forrest and Kay-Cee are at work in the studio; right: Broom Making, *watercolor, limited edition giclée.*

have total control over my reproductions. I can compare them directly to the original paintings and make adjustments as needed for color matching, saturation, and contrast. Only when I am completely satisfied with the resulting proofs do I commit my images to a production run." (See Gallery Showcase for more of his work.)

Digital Artists

Digital artists are a blurry, hard-to-define kind of group; they are the forward edge of digital fine art. The group includes artists who draw or paint on the computer, who heavily manipulate and alter their photo-based art, who create "machine art" with mathematical formulas or fractals, or who combine traditional and digital techniques to produce new forms of hybrid, mixed-media art. Because their originals exist only in the computer, digital printing is the primary method used to output their work.

These are the artists who are truly partners with the computer, using it as a tool no differently than Monet used a brush. The trick is to create a work that is not too corny or too scientific-looking. This is what used to be called "computer art," but that term is much too imprecise now to cover the amazing range of today's digital artists.

Southern Californian Ileana Frómeta Grillo (known simply as Ileana) is a good example. She uses a digital tablet to draw her images, which she then layers with special backgrounds and textures that she creates. The result is a work that combines a traditional style with modern elements. She uses a desktop inkjet to output in-progress proofs, and she sends the final images to an outside printmaker for wide-format inkjet printing. (See Gallery Showcase for more of her work.)

Left: Hope's Return, limited edition, digital original print; right: Digital artist Ileana with the tools of her trade

Left: © 2000 Ileana Frómeta Grillo; right: courtesy Ileana Frómeta Grillo

Digital reproductions are sometimes indistinguishable from the originals. At a recent art show where Ileana was exhibiting her work, an artist read the sign about digital art, looked around the booth at the framed and unframed canvas pieces, and asked, "Do you have any examples of your digital work?" He was sure that the pieces were oil, oil pastels, acrylic, or something other than digital art produced with a computer and printer.

Gaining Ground: A Question of Acceptance

Artists have been criticized for adopting new technologies since they first rubbed colored dirt on the walls of the caves at Lascaux, France. Oil on canvas was considered heresy by the tempera-on-wooden-panels crowd in the mid-1400s. Photography—and lithography—was blasted as a perversion in the early 19th century. This was also the case with digital technology, which many photographer-artists—the true opportunists that they are—have readily adopted.

Although the digital printing boom includes everyone from aging Baby Boomers who are creating family photo prints in their home offices to professional artists selling fine-art prints through galleries, it is the latter group who are the pioneers and who push the edges of print quality, durability, and acceptability.

It has been a challenging decade in which to gain the public's and the art community's acceptance. First attempts at digital printing were crude and focused on the technology itself. However, art typically expands to absorb new technologies, and after the initial, giddy, "look what I can do" phase, photographers and artists have evolved to the point of focusing on a true artistic goal: moving us with their images.

A watershed event marking the art world's acceptance of digital art was the Whitney Museum of American Art's exhibition in March 2001: *Bitstreams: Exploring the Importance of Digital Technology in American Art*. It was the first Whitney show to focus on the impact of digital media, and, more importantly, it included several digital prints.

Three months later, the Brooklyn Museum of Art staged its *Digital: Printmaking Now* exhibition that ran from June through August, 2001. The second-largest art museum in the U.S. put a huge stamp of approval on digitally created art.

Digital prints (primarily inkjets or giclées) are now part of the permanent collections of New York's Metropolitan Museum of Art, the Museum of Modern Art, the Whitney Museum of American Art, the Corcoran Gallery in Washington, D.C., and the Art Institute of Chicago. Even the Louvre, The Musee D'Orsay, the Hermitage, the National Gallery, and the Library of Congress are now reproducing some of their most important holdings (van Gogh, Matisse, Picasso, Warhol, Seurat, Winslow Homer, Ansel Adams, Man Ray, Walker Evans, Dorothea Lange, Edward Curtis) by way of digital printing.

Chuck Close's inkjet self-portrait stares back at the digerati attending the Brooklyn Museum of Art's exhibition on digital printmaking, August 2001.

Digital printing is not just for the high-art crowd. The proof is in the almost-universal acceptance of digital printing technologies by mini and custom photo labs, online photo services, and by e-commerce businesses who are providing art buyers with high-quality prints that fit somewhere between inexpensive posters and unobtainable originals.

Even art festivals, shows, and contests are getting into the digital act. Although there are still naysayers, more and more of these local and regional events are adding "digital art" or "digital print" categories to their official entry rules.

To be sure, there were questions and problems with digital printing early on. The first IRIS inks were notorious for their ability to fade right off the paper. However, subsequent improvements in ink formulations and in ink/paper matching have ended most of these arguments. The remaining obstacle to the full acceptance of digital print methods today is the faulty perception that this type of art is "mechanical" and, therefore, inferior in some way. Nothing could be further from the truth.

Digital artist Ileana explains her craft at the 2001 Sawdust Art Festival in Laguna Beach, California.

Let's face it—people who are used to slower, more traditional practices sometimes have a hard time adjusting to newer, automated ways of doing things. However, technical methods including automation do not necessarily diminish the value of the creative works aided by them. Besides, Michelangelo used teams of assistants, as did Leonardo DaVinci. Painters such as Caravaggio, Ingres, Velasquez, and Vermeer all used either a *camera obscura* or a *camera lucida* lens system to speed up and improve the initial drafting step in their paintings. In his 2001 book, *Secret Knowledge: Rediscovering the Lost Techniques of the Old Masters*, David Hockney, who himself is one of the world's best-known living artists, makes a solid argument that artists were enthusiastically using lenses and mirrors (the highest of high-tech at the time) in creating their art 400-500 years ago. It's a small step from optics to computers and digital workflows, and Hockney's book has helped open people's eyes to the fact that technology has always been an important part of art creation.

The computer and other digital tools are just that—tools. Used in the hands of a perceptive, talented artist or photographer, a computer is not subordinate to brushes, palette knives, or enlargers. The fact is that the artist's own hand lies heavy on most of the steps in the making of digital art. Using cameras, scanners, digital tablets, and a whole host of image-editing software, photographers and artists have a personal and intense relationship with their images as they guide them through the various stages of creation, manipulation, and printing. The aesthetic decisions are always the artist's. With the exception of machine art, this is not mechanical art; this is imagery that emanates directly from the mind and the soul of the artist.

Digital Decisions

Photographers and artists tend to fall into a couple of large groups when it comes to digital printing. Knowing what these are up front and matching your interests to them can help you better navigate through the digital landscape.

Doing It Yourself Versus Sending It Out

If you want to get involved with digital printing, you must soon make an important decision: do the printing yourself or send it out to a printmaking studio, atelier, or even in a pinch, an online printing service. There are advantages, disadvantages, and consequences to each route. My analysis follows.

Doing Your Own Printing

Some artists love the thought of working with their own printing equipment. Photographers especially, with their tradition of working in a darkroom full of enlargers, timers, and other technical equipment, are a driving force in the growth of "self-printing." Note that the following information applies more to "serious" artists, but an artist at any level can learn from this discussion.

The main *advantages* of photographer-artists printing their own work are as follows:

■ **Personal involvement, flexibility, and full control of the entire process:** It's your printer, your paper, your inks, your everything. You can test, retest, and test again. You can change settings, paper, anything you want, whenever you want. You are in control. Doing it yourself, you can make prints very quickly. You can also fine-tune and output your prints on your schedule, one at a time, or in small quantities.

■ **Once a breakeven point on your initial capital investment is reached, print costs can be less:** After you've locked down your workflow settings and procedures, the extra cost of making additional prints is marginal—only the cost of paper, ink, and overhead is involved.

Photo printmaker C.J. Pressma and his Ritual Site, which he self-printed on a wide-format inkjet, Brooklyn Museum of Art digital printmaking show opening, August 2001

WARNING! Self-printing artists tend to start off printing for themselves, then doing a favor for an artist friend, then buying some more equipment, then taking in a couple more print clients to pay for the equipment, and before you know it, they are in the printmaking business, not the art-making business. That is exactly how many of today's printmakers started.

The *disadvantages* of self-printing are as follows:

■ **Potentially steep learning curve and time commitment to acquire the printmaking craft:** Digital printing is both an art and a craft, and just having the equipment does not guarantee you will know what to do with it. Learning how to work with a new technology takes time, and lots of it. This is time that could be spent doing other things or creating more art.

■ **Upfront investment in hardware, software, and consumables (especially for the larger formats):** Add to that the perpetual, ongoing costs of self-printing that include the following: overhead (rent and utilities), your time or labor (your time is worth something, isn't it?), consumables (paper and inks), maintenance, software/hardware upgrades, and continuing education and training. If you're in the business of art, an accountant would call all of this your "cost of goods sold."

Of course, if you are doing this as a hobby or in your free time, then these obstacles are less of a consideration.

Using an Outside Printmaker or Printing Service

An old saying in the art world goes, "The artist is the eye, the printmaker is the hand." Because printing techniques can be complicated, and considering the traditionally collaborative nature of fine-art printmaking, many photographers and artists use a "print-for-pay" service to create their final work.

Courtesy of Harvest Productions Ltd.

Outside printmakers play a collaborative role in the printing process. Here, digital printing pioneer Maryann Doe (left) of Harvest Productions goes over production details with artist Ernesto Rodriguez. That's an IRIS printer in the background.

The *advantages* of using an outside printmaker include the following:

■ **You work with seasoned printing professionals and take advantage of top-of-the-line technology that is more quickly updated:** An experienced printmaker brings to the table a vast knowledge of materials and artistic approaches that have been tried and tested many times before you walk in the door. Besides helping to guarantee a higher-quality result, a printmaker can act as an aesthetic guide and be a valuable art advisor.

■ **Upfront investment to test the market or your expectations are low:** Depending on the size and the process, an investment of anywhere from $50 to $500 is all that's needed to produce a trial print (unframed). This is a good way for an "emerging artist" to see if his or her work is going to sell or for a photographer to try out a digital photoprint process. A corollary to this is that because your investment is low, you are free to drop a printmaker or service at any point and move on. You haven't lost much.

■ **If you're a professional artist, prints may be more acceptable to galleries or art buyers if produced by a well-known printmaker:** The best printing studios apply a "chop" to every print going out the door. Typically an embossed logo in the print's lower left or right corner, it is a seal of approval indicating that the work has met the printmaker's quality standards. A well-respected printmaker's chop is a marketing tool for the artist; knowledgeable art marketers and buyers will recognize it instantly. The downside is that some—not all—of the more-famous printmakers charge accordingly.

Some *disadvantages* of using an outside printing service are as follows:

- **Loss of some control and flexibility:** The print is in the printmaker's hands, not yours. The final result will depend, in part, on his or her skill level and your ability to communicate what you want. If the printmaker thinks it's good enough, but you don't, you have a problem.

- **Time delays going back and forth:** No matter how good and fast an outside printmaker is, there is still a lot of back-and-forth downtime between artist and printer. Getting to the final, approved proof and to that first, finished print can take weeks or even months.

- **Ongoing, per-print costs are higher:** Using a printing service might not be worth it economically if you are creating large prints for sale and if your prints sell for much less than $500. Run the numbers and see how much profit is left over after the costs for initial setup, prints, coating, "curating," shipping, and framing have been added up. Of course, if your prints are selling for four-figure amounts, this is not a problem!

It is also possible to take *both* paths down the print road. Some artists and photographers using print-for-pay services will make internal proofs on their own equipment to fine-tune their work in progress. This is also handy for the printmakers, who prefer to have a hardcopy proof to look at and work from. On the flip side, some self-printers do the majority of the work themselves, but save the largest or most-complicated pieces for a professional printmaker.

(For more on working with outside printmakers, see Chapter 10.)

Reproductions or Original Prints?

Although there continues to be debate about this, many professionals in the digital art community work with the following definitions: A *digital reproduction* is a multiple print or exact copy of an original work of art that was created by conventional means (painting, drawing, and so on) and then reproduced by using any of the digital print technologies described in this book. A giclée print (see the following "What's in a Name: The Story of Giclée") of an original oil painting, for example, is a digital reproduction. (Not everyone agrees with this definition. Even some of the artists in this book use the term giclée for their original work.)

Seth Rossman

Printmaker Lester Wilson of Greencastle Photo Service, Greencastle, Indiana, checks a reproduction print from his ColorSpan Giclée PrintMaker FA inkjet printer (in background).

What's in a Name: The Story of Giclée

One thing that became apparent to the early digital pioneers was the lack of a proper name to describe the prints they were making. By the close of the 1980s, IRIS printers were installed all over the world and spinning off full-color proofs in commercial printing plants and pre-press shops. These prints were used to check color and get client approvals before starting the main print run. They definitely were *not* meant to last or to be displayed. Most people called them "IRIS prints," "IRIS proofs," or, more simply, "IRISes."

However, this wasn't good enough for the new digital fine-art printmakers, such as Maryann Doe of Harvest Productions and Jack Duganne, who was the first printmaker (after David Coons) at Nash Editions. They wanted to draw a distinction between the beautiful prints they were laboring over and the quickie proofs the commercial printers were cranking out. Just like artist Robert Rauschenberg did when he coined the term "combines" for his new art, they needed a new label, or, in marketing terms, a "brand identity." In other words, the makers of digital art needed a word of their own.

They got their word. In 1991, Duganne had to come up with a print-medium description for a mailer announcing California artist Diane Bartz' upcoming show (see Figure 1.3). He wanted to stay away from words like "computer" or "digital" because of the negative connotations the art world attached to the new medium. Taking a cue from the French word for inkjet (*jet d'encre*), Duganne opened his pocket Larousse and searched for a word that was generic enough to cover most inkjet technologies at the time and hopefully into the future. He focused on the nozzle, which most printers used. In French, that was *gicleur*. Nozzles spray ink, so looking up the French verb for "to spray," he found *gicler*. Turning the verb into a noun made it "giclée," (pronounced "zhee-clay"), which literally means "that which is sprayed." An industry moniker was born.

Bartz Studios is pleased to announce a new and exciting process by which the work of Diane Bartz will be reproduced in a strictly limited edition of less than 50 pieces. Some of our special paintings will be re-created in this new medium through a totally revolutionary digital process called Gicleé by Nash Editions. Gicleé is a French term describing the spraying of ink onto paper. Nash Editions uses the finest archival qual...

Figure 1.3 *From the Bartz Studio newsletter for ArtExpo California, Fall 1991, this is the first known use in print of the word giclée.*

However, the controversy started immediately. Graham Nash and Mac Holbert had come up with "digigraph," which was close to "serigraph" and "photograph." The photographers liked that. On the other hand, the artists and printmakers doing reproductions had adopted "giclée," and the term soon became a synonym for "an art print made on an IRIS inkjet printer."

Today, "giclée" has become established with traditional media artists and some photographers. However, many photographers and other digital artists have not accepted it. Instead, they use labels such as "original digital prints" (my favorite), "inkjet prints," "pigment prints," or "(substitute the name of your print process) prints."

The Giclée Printers Association's Tru Giclée logo

For many artists, the debate over "giclée" continues. Some object to its suggestive, French slang meaning ("to spurt"). Others believe it is still too closely linked to the IRIS printer or to the reproduction market. Still others feel that it is just too silly and pretentious. For many, however, the term has become genericized, like Kleenex, evolving into a broader term that describes any high-quality, digitally produced, fine-art print.

The problem, of course, is that when a term becomes too broad, it loses its ability to describe a specific thing. At that point, it stops being a good marketing label—and make no mistake about it, "giclée" is a marketing term. When everything is a "giclée," the art world gets confused, and the process starts all over again with people coming up with new labels. This is exactly what happened when the Giclée Printers Association (GPA)—a new group formed in 2001—came up with its own standards and term: "Tru Giclée."

The GPA is concerned with reproduction printing only, and its dozen or so printmaker members have approved a short list of printing equipment and materials to bear its logo.

An *original digital print* uses the same output methods, except the original does not exist outside of or apart from the computer. There is still an original, but it's *in* the computer. That is, the "printing matrix" exists only as a digital file. (This is similar to the Print Council of America's definition of traditional printmaking methods where "the impression or print is made directly from the original material by the artist or pursuant to his or her directions; the image does not exist unless it is printed.") Therefore, a print made from a digitally scanned or manipulated photo or from a collage of scanned images is an original digital print, as is a print made from what a digital artist creates with a digital graphics tablet.

Self Portrait *by Sally Larsen; first printed digitally by David Coons in 1990*

These two main divisions represent two different ways of looking at the digital printing process. (Of course, there are other ways, too.) Why is all this nit-picking important? In the art world, the idea of "originality" is carefully considered by many galleries, art festivals, and art buyers. Just as the label "photograph" can affect a work's desirability, acceptance, and price, so too do the labels "reproduction" or "original print."

State of the Art: The Digital Revolution in Art Production

Digital printing has revolutionized the amateur and professional art world. Research company IDC has estimated that more than 15 *billion* digital images will be printed in the United States by 2005. In addition, according to research firm I.T. Strategies, the digital print market is growing at an astonishing rate of 27 percent annually, more than four times as fast as the art market as a whole. This new method of art production, although only a dozen years old, is enabling artists and photographers around the world to create and produce their work on demand, inexpensively, and with superb and consistent quality.

The industry and the technology are still embryonic; there is a lot of change and evolution yet to come. We're only in the month of January in this new art form's calendar, and glimpses of what is on the horizon show a future that is truly astounding. Three-dimensional imaging; lower prices as the market broadens and larger companies enter it; better software, papers and inks; more artist control—we all have a lot to look forward to. As digital artist Bonny Lhotka puts it, "I believe this is the most exciting time to be an artist."

■ ■ ■

Now that you have a high-level view of the digital landscape, it's time to explore the essential, start-up information you'll need before you start printing.

2

Understanding Digital Printing

At its core, digital printing is simple. A binary data stream drives a print engine to render a digital image on an output device. End of story? Not quite. Like any production process, digital printing requires the right tools and the right information to make the right choices. Let's begin at the beginning.

A Digital Primer

Photographers and artists are all image makers, so let's start by looking inside a digital image.

Anatomy of a Digital Image

First things first: Ninety-five percent of all images that photographers and artists end up printing digitally are binary images (also called raster images, pixel-based images, or bitmaps). Confused yet? The term bitmap itself sends some people running for shelter. One reason is that Adobe Photoshop, which is considered the top image-editing software program, has a mode option called "bitmap" that converts an image into the crudest (1-bit) form. That's unfortunate because there's a lot more to bitmaps than that. In fact, bitmaps are the key to the Chamber of Secrets of digital printing.

To put it simply, a bitmapped image is a collection of pixels (*picture elements*) arranged on a rectangular grid (it's a *map* of a bunch of *bits*); see Figure 2.1. As I said in Chapter 1, each pixel can be described or "quantized" in terms of its color and its intensity or value. The more pixels there are and/or the more the depth of information per pixel, the more binary digits (the little ones and zeros that the computer understands) there are, and the more detailed the image (see "Pixels and Bit Depth" for more about this).

That other five percent of digitally printed images are called vector-based or object-oriented images. Instead of a bunch of pixels arranged on a grid, vector graphics are made up of mathematical formulas that describe each object in an image in terms of its outline shape, line weight, fill, and location on the page. Logos, type, and any hard-edged, flat-colored art are

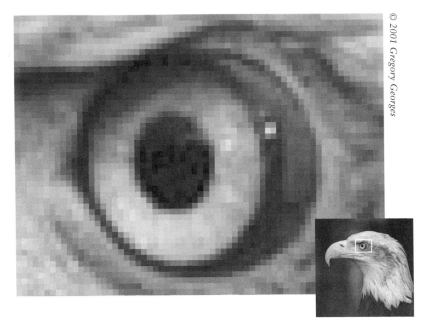

Figure 2.1 *Pixels—the building blocks of all bitmapped images*

perfect for the vector format (see Figure 2.2). That's why vector art often comes from drawing programs such as Adobe Illustrator, Macromedia Freehand, or CorelDRAW.

The problem with vector art is that because it doesn't actually exist except as a formula, there needs to be a way to interpret it and bring it down to earth and onto the printed page. The primary way to do this is through the computer language of Adobe PostScript, which, unfortunately, complicates the digital printing process (see more about PostScript later in this chapter). Alternatively, you can convert the vector graphic into a bitmap through the process of "rasterizing," and you're back in bitmap business.

There are three things you need to know about bitmaps to fully understand the nuances of printing digital images: *pixels and bit depth*, *resolution*, and *halftoning and dithering*. (Color is another issue, but because it's such a huge subject, it gets its own chapter—Chapter 5.) Let's take them one at a time.

Pixels and Bit Depth

Pixels are the basic elements that make up a bitmap image. They are little points that contain information in the form of binary digits or "bits" (ones and zeros—a "0"

Figure 2.2 *Logos are typical vector graphics.*

represents something; a "1" represents nothing or empty space). Bits are the smallest unit of digital information.

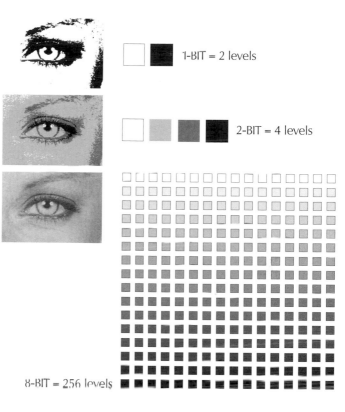

A 1-bit image is the lowliest of all bitmaps. There are only two digits with which to work—a 1 and a 0, which means that each picture element is either on or off, black or white. (I'm keeping this to a simple, one-color example for starters.) However, a 2-bit image is much more detailed. Now you have four possibilities or values for each pixel: 00, 01, 10, and 11 (black, white, and two shades of gray). Keep going, and you see that three bits yield eight values, four bits 16, eight bits 256, and so on (see Figure 2.3). In mathematical terms, this is called the power of two: 2^2 equals four choices (2×2), and 2^8 gives 256 choices ($2\times2\times2\times2\times2\times2\times2\times2$). Generally speaking, a one-color digital image needs to be at least 8-bit (256 tones) to be "photorealistic" or "continuous tone" in appearance.

Figure 2.3
The more bits, the more realistic the image

Digital Equivalents

8 bits=1 byte
1024* bytes=1 kilobyte (KB)
1024 kilobytes=1 megabyte (MB)
1024 megabytes=1 gigabyte (GB)
1024 gigabytes=1 terabyte (TB)
* It's 1024 and not 1000 because of the way the binary system works with its powers of two—in this case, 2^{10}.

So far, we've talked about bits only in terms of black, white, or gray. Because most people work in color, you now have to apply the same thinking *to each color component of the image*. Thus, in a 24-bit (8 bits per color), RGB image, there are 256 possible values of red, 256 of green, and 256 of blue, for a grand total of—are you ready?—16,777,216 possible values, tones, or colors for each pixel (see Figure 2.4). A CMYK color image is described as 32-bit. There is one 8-bit channel for each of the four printing colors: cyan, magenta, yellow, and black (or "K"). There is no more color information with CMYK; it's just allocated differently than with RGB. (For more about color and color models, see Chapter 5.)

Whether an image has one, two, four, eight, or even more bits of information per pixel, per color determines its *bit depth*. The higher the bit depth, the more detailed and realistic the image. (You don't have to stop at eight bits. Current input technology allows for up to 16 bits of information per channel—see Chapter 4 for the pluses and minuses of going "high-bit.")

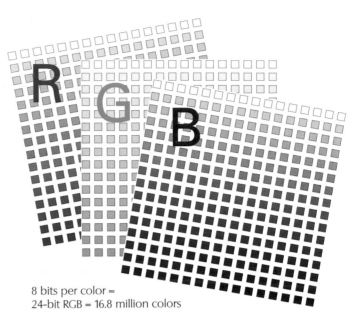

8 bits per color =
24-bit RGB = 16.8 million colors

Figure 2.4 *Color bit depth*

Resolution

This seems to be the single most confusing word in the digital imaging world. It doesn't help that there are different terms and definitions for camera resolution, scanner resolution, monitor resolution, file resolution, and printer resolution. Because this is a book about printing, let's concentrate on the last two: *file* and *printer resolution*.

File or Image Resolution

In basic terms, the resolution of a digital, bitmapped image file is determined by how many pixels there are. If you have a scanned image and can count 72 pixels across (or down) one inch of the image (bitmapped images actually have no physical size until they are viewed, printed, or otherwise rendered into a tangible form; at that point, you can measure them), the resolution is 72 pixels per inch or 72 ppi. Technically, it's pixels per inch (*ppi*) when you're talking about image files, monitors, and cameras; it's dots per inch (*dpi*) when it comes out of a printer.

An image's resolution will determine its quality or the degree of detail and definition. The more pixels you have in a certain amount of space, the higher the quality. The same image scanned at a resolution of 300 ppi instead of 72 ppi looks much different—and better—at the same relative output size (see Figure 2.5).

Of course, there's a downside to more pixels. The higher the ppi and/or the greater the bit depth, the more space the files take up, the slower they are to edit and work with, and the harder they are to print. The goal should always be to have a file that's just big enough for the job, but no bigger.

So what is the best file or image resolution for digital printing? There is no standard rule-of-thumb for all digital devices as there is with commercial offset lithography. In commercial offset lithography, it's well accepted that the ppi-to-lpi ratio (lpi is the screen frequency),

Figure 2.5 *Image resolution affects detail and definition (top: raw scan at 300 ppi; bottom: 72 ppi).*

which is also called the halftone factor, should be somewhere between 1.5 and 2.0. In other words, if you have an image that will be printed as a poster by a commercial print shop, the normal screen frequency would be 150 lpi. Multiply that by 1.5 and you get 225 ppi. Substitute 2.0, and you get 300 ppi. Thus, your best image resolution for *commercial* printing is 225–300 ppi.

However, with most high-quality digital processes (B&W laser printers are an exception), there is no lpi in the same sense as with offset. In the early days of inkjets, some used the 1/3 rule: Take the highest resolution of the printer and divide by 3. For example, an older EPSON with a 720 maximum resolution would require a 240-ppi file for optimal results (the "magic resolution number"). Then, however, EPSON printhead-based printers started coming out with 1440 and then 2880 resolutions. One-third of 2880 is 960 ppi, an absurdly high and unnecessary image resolution. Some photographers and artists still swear by the 240-ppi formula for even the latest models of desktop printers, claiming (correctly) that for EPSONS, the native printhead resolution is still 720, so the 1/3 rule remains in effect. (According to Epson data, the input resolution—the resolution at which data is rasterized—is 720 "dpi" for desktops and 360 "dpi" for wide formats.) However, Epson now recommends 300 ppi *at the size you intend to print* as their new magic number; if you get to 220 or less, you start to see a difference in image quality, and conversely, you won't see much improvement with bitmapped images by going over 300 ppi. (Note that unlike bitmaps, vector art is resolution-independent, which means that you can blow it up or down without any loss of definition or clarity.)

Hewlett-Packard (HP), on the other hand, whose printheads are based on a 600-dpi resolution instead of 720, recommends 150–200 ppi *at final size* for its inkjet printers. They claim that scientists doing satellite photo reproduction for the government on their printers typically find that 125 ppi is adequate.

For continuous-tone printers that don't use halftoning or dithering (digital photoprint and dye sublimation—described in the next chapter), try to have your image resolution match the addressable printer resolution (explained later in this chapter). Most dye sublimation printers are 300 dpi, so make your final image also 300 ppi. This advice is the same for LightJets and Lambdas, which are, respectively, 300 dpi and 400 dpi at their maximum settings; an image resolution of 300 ppi also should work well for them.

For ease of use, I start off with images at 300 ppi, which also means I can print any image commercially without having to change the resolution, and I readjust or resize from there. Chances are that if you are anywhere between 240 to 360 ppi in terms of image resolution, you're going to be fine with most digital print devices, although the best strategy is either to test several resolutions with the intended output device and evaluate the resulting prints or to ask a printmaker for recommendations, if you're using an outside printing service. (For a more complete look at determining the size, scale, and resolution of your digital files—including the use of integer resolution numbers—see Chapter 9.)

Printer Resolution

This is the tough one. We're going to be wading in deep, so pull on your tall boots.

How capable is the printing device in question of reproducing the information in an image? You may have the highest-resolution image imaginable, but if the printer isn't able to output all the fine details on which you've worked so hard, you've wasted your time. There are three main types of printer resolutions with which you should be concerned: *spatial*, *addressable*, and *apparent*.

Spatial Resolution

This is a measure of how finely the image information is grouped for reproduction or rendering by the output device. With the digital imagesetters used in commercial printing, this is where the line screen (or screen frequency) comes into play.

Using the standard 150 lpi as the assumption, the printing dots are arranged in rows that are placed 1/150" apart. The spatial resolution is then 150 lpi. Now output the same image at 85 lpi, and you've lowered the spatial resolution (and reduced the detail of the image). See Figure 2.6 for an exaggerated example.

Figure 2.6
Two spatial resolutions for the same image

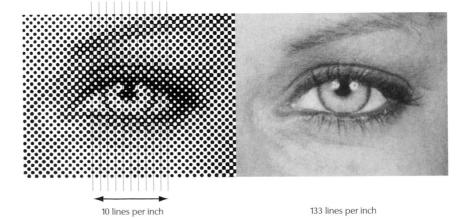

10 lines per inch   133 lines per inch

How Many Ways Can You Say "Resolution"?

- **By pixels per inch and image size:** As long as you know both the intended output size and the ppi, you're set. A 4×5-inch image at 300 ppi is just over five megabytes (MB) in size (at eight bits times three color channels, like all examples in this section), which is about right for printing one of the images in this chapter in a book with all color pages.

- **By pixel array or dimension:** Some people just say, "I've got this 1600×1200 image" (pixels is understood). After you're familiar with certain files sizes, you'll automatically know what a 1600×1200-pixel image (or any other size) will do.

- **By total number of pixels:** Multiply the number of horizontal pixels by the vertical ones, and you've got the total number of pixels or pixel dimension. A 640×480 image totals out at 307,200 pixels or .3 megapixels. With experience, you'll realize that this won't go very far for high-quality reproduction, but it's fine for the Web or for 72-ppi monitor screens.

- **By file size:** Take the total number of pixels, multiply that by 3 (total RGB color bit depth— 24 divided by 8), and you've got the file size in *bytes* (one byte is eight bits). Divide that by one million, and you have the *approximate* final file size in megabytes. Example: 1600×1200 pixels=1,920,000 pixels. 1,920,000×(24/8)=5,760,000 bytes or 5.8 MB (approximately).

- **By single side measure:** Film-recorder users typically refer to the width of the image in pixels. A standard 4K file is one that measures 4,096 pixels horizontally (as already stated, the reason it's not 4,000 pixels is because of the way the binary system works). Because most film-recorder output ends up as standard 35mm transparency film, the other dimension (2,730 pixels) is understood to be in the correct proportion to the first and isn't mentioned. (Read more about film recorders in Chapter 10.)

Addressability

Because lines-per-inch (lpi) is different from dots-per-inch (dpi), we have to shift our thinking to talk about addressable resolution or addressability.

How many little marks is the printer putting down per unit area? Continuing the digital imagesetter example, a 150 lines-per-inch image will probably be output at 2400 or so dots per inch. The addressable resolution of this device is 2400 dpi; the spatial resolution is 150 lpi. The 2400 dots are used to create the 150 lines.

Now, let's move closer to our area of interest. Inkjet and color laser printers have to translate all those nebulous image pixels we learned about into real dots of ink or spots of dyes on paper. This, again, is dpi.

Do you know the story of the blind men and the elephant? Six blind men encountered an elephant for the first time. Each touched a separate part of the beast and then was asked to describe the whole animal. They did so but in very different ways. The elephant was either like a snake, a wall, a spear, a fan, a tree, or a rope—all depending on which blind man spoke.

And so it is with addressability and dpi. Those numbers you see listed on every print device's spec sheet and in every advertisement only give you part of the picture. Each print-device manufacturer talks about it differently.

Take inkjet printers. The EPSON 1280 inkjet printer's maximum resolution is listed as 2880×720 dpi. (Note that virtually all digital-printing devices have multiple modes that allow for more than one resolution setting; naturally, only the maximum is advertised. The smaller the resolution numbers, the faster the printing, but the lower the image quality.) The maximum resolution on the HP 5550 and the Lexmark Z65 is 4800×1200. For the HP 10ps, it's 2400×1200, and for the Canon S900/9000, it also is 2400×1200 dpi.

So, what do all these numbers mean? The 2880 (or 2400 or 4800) refers to the horizontal axis and is the maximum number of colored dots placed in one inch *across* the paper, or in the direction of the printhead's travel (see Figure 2.7). The other number (720 or 1200) is the maximum number of dots the printer can cram into one inch *down* the paper (in the direction of the paper feed, which is controlled by a stepper motor).

Why are the horizontal numbers usually higher? They are higher because it's a lot easier to position the printhead precisely than it is to position the paper precisely. As software developer Robert Krawitz explains it, "The printhead typically doesn't actually lay down a dot every 1/2880th of an inch in one horizontal pass. What happens is that different nozzles on the printhead pass over the same line or row to fill it in. It might require up to eight passes to print all of the intermediate dot positions and complete the row. This interleaving of dots is sometimes referred to as 'weaving.'" (See Figure 2.8 and also Figure 3.39 in Chapter 3 for a detailed view of an Epson printhead.)

Figure 2.7 *Inkjet printers have the high-resolution numbers in the horizontal or printhead-travel direction.*

The theory is the same for the other inkjet brands, although each has its own way to arrive at the maximum resolution numbers. HPs do things like "color layering" to change both horizontal and vertical resolutions. The newest EPSONS (950/960, 2100/2200, 7600, and 9600, as of this writing) were finally able to break through the 720-dpi vertical resolution barrier to 1440 dpi with a finer paper-positioning mechanism, among other things.

What does all this mean? Honestly, not much. Is Canon's 2400×1200 dpi resolution for the S900 really 38 percent higher (as they claim by multiplying the two numbers together) than Epson's 2880×720 for the 1280? Hard to say. I've seen outputs

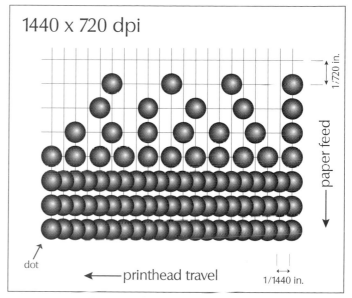

Figure 2.8 *Multi-pass, droplet offsetting or "weaving" is one factor affecting an EPSON's addressable resolution (Note: the dot sizes are representative only).*

from both machines, and I would be hard pressed to say one is that much better than the other, especially when you consider that the human eye cannot resolve details finer than about 500 dpi at a normal, document-viewing distance (which is why laser printers are pegged to 600 dpi resolution).

When you add the issues of bidirectional printing, multiple colors beyond the standard CMYK, variable droplet sizes, and dot layering, you can see why addressable printer resolution is such a can of worms.

When it comes right down to it, the dpi resolution numbers on a spec sheet are irrelevant. They only tell a very small part of the story, just like the blind men's elephant. There are many factors that go into what really counts—the *image quality* a particular printing device is capable of producing. Factors like printer resolution, number of ink colors, the size of the ink droplets, the precise positioning of the drops, how the inkjet nozzles are arranged and fire, and the screening or dithering pattern of the image pixels all come into play (see Chapter 7 for a more complete discussion on how to choose an inkjet printer). My advice: Don't put too much stock in the dpi numbers alone, and don't use them to compare printers of different types or brands. Instead, use addressable resolution only to weigh different models of the same brand—then, at least, you're talking the same language.

Apparent Resolution

Continuous-tone printers such as digital photoprinters and dye-sublimation devices are unique in that their spatial and addressable resolutions are the same. That is, each image pixel ends up being a "device pixel" at the printer end. There is no halftoning, dithering, or screening (see the "Halftones, Contones, and Dithers" section) involved; the full pixel information is output directly to paper. Contone printers are playing a different game on the digital ball field.

Because these types of printers (described in Chapter 3) can list only the relatively lowly 200 ppi, 300 ppi, or at the most, 400 ppi as their addressable resolutions, they've come up with a marketing term—"apparent resolution"—to put them on equal footing with all the inkjets that are claiming much higher numbers.

Using the Océ LightJet 430 digital photoprinter as an example, here's how it works. The LightJet accepts 24-bit, RGB color data. We know that each color is 8-bit, which represents 256 possible values per pixel. The equivalent halftone printing device would need a 16×16 cell to equal that same 256 levels (16×16=256). (If you don't know what a halftone cell is, don't worry; you'll learn about it soon. Just stick with me for now.) So, if you take 300 ppi (one of the LightJet's two resolution settings) and multiply that by 16 (16 cell units per pixel), you get 4800. That's 4800 "dots per inch of apparent resolution." They're not really dots in the same way that inkjets have dots, but that's what they've come up with as a way to do battle with the army of inkjet printers covering the land.

Some inkjets themselves are using "apparent resolution" to compete in the marketplace. Both of the high-end, drum-based, wide-format inkjet printers (IRIS/IXIA and ColorSpan's Giclée PrintMakerFA) have an addressable resolution of 300 dpi, but claim 1800 dpi apparent resolution based on variable-drop technology, the layering of color dots, the layering of additional ink colors, or all three. (You'll learn more about both of these printers in Chapter 3.)

Variable-sized and overlapping dots are clearly visible on an IRIS print on photo glossy paper (40× blowup).

What About Type?

Any type or text that's part of a bitmapped image is no different than the rest of that image, and it will print with the same resolution of the image file. (Note: Although Photoshop versions 6 and 7 now support clean, vector type, you can't print it that way without first going through a PostScript printer or interpreter. You can also perform a file conversion to Portable Document Format (PDF) format and then print from Adobe Acrobat (see more about PostScript and PDFs later in this chapter). Although other factors such as paper surface quality and the kind of printing technology used can definitely have any impact, it's the printer's resolution—addressable, not apparent—that determines the quality of the printed, *bitmapped* type. A high dpi will generally yield higher-quality type with smoother edges while a low dpi produces type with ragged edges (see Figure 2.9).

Figure 2.9 *The type shown is from actual printed samples that were scanned, sharpened, and enlarged identically. From top: Canon S800 inkjet (2400×1200 dpi), IRIS 3047 inkjet (300 dpi), and Lambda 130 digital laser imager (200 ppi). Print technology also makes a difference. The top R (at left) is by Fuji Pictrography (400 dpi); the bottom R is by dye sublimation (300 dpi).*

If you're printing from a drawing or page-layout program, the rules change somewhat. Adobe Illustrator and InDesign (version 1.5 and later) don't require a PostScript interpreter for good-looking type. Other programs, such as Quark XPress, need PostScript font support from a utility program like Adobe Type Manager (ATM) if your operating system doesn't already have PostScript font support built in. In any of these cases, if you're printing through an inkjet's native printer driver, the type quality will still vary with the resolution of the printer. However, as soon as you bring in a PostScript interpreter, things improve significantly (see Figure 2.10).

Figure 2.10 *RIPs (raster image processors) make a difference with type! Each letter X was printed from Adobe Illustrator. Left to right: Lexmark Z53 inkjet at 600 dpi, HP Designjet 20ps inkjet with software RIP, and HP 5MP laser printer (600 dpi) with built-in RIP.*

Viewing Distance

One important factor when thinking about resolution and print quality is the viewing distance, which is how close people are going to be to your print. A perfect example is the ubiquitous billboard that *could* be printed at a high resolution but never is. If you've ever seen a billboard up close, you know that the dots are as big as baseballs. Yet, billboards are perfectly readable at the distance from which they are meant to be viewed.

Billboards take advantage of viewing distance.

The greater the viewing distance, the less information—spatial and addressable resolution—required. The key point here is that you don't need more resolution than you need. Normal people will stand back to view a large image, and they will get close to a small one. It's human nature. Not only are larger dots more acceptable on a large print, but larger prints destined to be viewed from across a room don't necessarily require 300-ppi files. Files with one-half that resolution might work just fine. Besides, as the resolution increases, so does the file size, either geometrically or arithmetically, and no one wants to handle or store a huge file if it's not necessary. You're only burdening yourself, your storage capacity, and your printer (it will slow down as it receives and discards all the extra image information).

Photographers, in particular, do not always factor viewing distance and image size into their considerations. They might expect a digital camera to produce large images with the same sharpness and detail that is found with smaller prints; they also might expect a printer that produces acceptable large prints to make acceptable wallet photos as well. Digital imaging demands the rethinking of previous expectations in these areas.

If you're wondering how to estimate standard viewing distances, photographer Joe Butts gives this formula: $1.5 \times$ the diagonal dimension of the art piece. To calculate the diagonal, it's $a^2 + b^2 = c^2$. For example, to figure the viewing distance for an 8×10, do this math: 8 squared plus 10 squared is 64; add 100 and you have 164 inches. The square root of 164 is 12.806 or rounding it off, 13 inches. When you multiply by 1.5, the viewing distance would be 19.5 inches. Similarly, the normal viewing distance for a large 40×60-inch piece is about 9 feet. You won't see many dots from there!

Halftones, Contones, and Dithers

There are three basic ways to produce continuous-tone images (such as photographs) with any printing process, whether analog or digital: *halftone screening*, *contone imaging*, or *alternative screening (dithers)*.

Halftone Screening

Since the late-19th century, printers have rendered continuous-tone (or "contone") images by using the process of halftoning. Because smooth transitions of grays or colors are impossible to print with analog or even digital devices (remember, all computers and digital printers use binary information that is either on or off, one or zero), images that use halftoning have to be broken down into tiny little dots or spots (I use the two words interchangeably when referring to printing). The darker portions of the image have larger spots with less space between them; the lighter areas have smaller spots with more space to reveal the paper underneath (see Figure 2.11).

Figure 2.11 *Halftones are optical illusions tricking us into thinking we're seeing continuous tones.*

At the right viewing distance, our brains then merge all the spots to give us the impression that what we're seeing is one, smooth image. (Hold the page with the apple farther and farther away to see what I mean.) It's just an optical illusion.

However, by knowing all this, you can affect the coarseness or smoothness of printed images in a number of ways. With digital printing, depending on the capabilities of the device and the software used to drive it, you can vary the following: the number of spots, the size of the spot, the closeness of the spots to each other, and the arrangement of the individual color spots that make up the final image.

Although old-school halftoning utilized the process of photographing images through glass or film screens (hence the terming "screening"), most halftones these days are made digitally. These *amplitude-modulated (AM) screening* halftones are created on digital devices that place dots that are either round, elliptical, or rectangular on a grid-like cell made up of little squares. Each halftone dot is actually made up of clusters of printer dots (sometimes called "device pixels"). The more printer dots in a cell, the bigger the halftone dot, and the darker that cell appears. In addition, the more cell squares (that is, the bigger the grid), the more shades of gray or color that are available.

For example, a 2×2 cell can yield five possible tones (the paper is one) as follows: (See Figure 2.12.)

1. No dots, all you see is the paper

2. One dot, 25% tone

3. Two dots, 50% tone

4. Three dots, 75% tone

5. Four dots, 100% tone
   (solid, no paper showing)

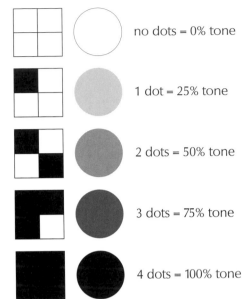

Figure 2.12 *A 2×2 halftone cell can produce five tones.*

This is a simple example. Expand the cell to be, say, 16 squares across, and you now have a lot of tones that can be printed (see Figure 2.13).

Commercial digital printing systems, imagesetters, and some binary, digital desktop printers such as color and B&W lasers use digital halftoning as part of or as their entire image-rendering method.

Contone Imaging

Digital contone imaging, most clearly seen in digital photoprinting and dye-sublimation devices, works differently. Image pixels are still involved, but instead of using halftoning as a middleman to break the various tones in an image apart, contone devices translate the pixel information directly through the printer to the paper. As the image is being rendered, the printer is, in essence, asking each image pixel, "Which color and how much of it?" Therefore, the higher the bit depth, the better the image. Because the printed image is made up of overlapping dyes of each primary color with no spaces between them, the color transitions are very smooth and the resulting images are very photorealistic (see Figure 2.14).

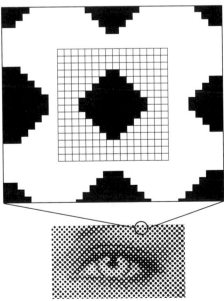

Figure 2.13
A 16×16 halftone cell (center with gridlines), with the halftone dot growing from the center out.

Alternative Screening (Dithers)

Certain branches of digital printing, specifically inkjet and electrophotography, now use a relatively new screening type—*frequency modulated (FM) screening* or *stochastic screening*—to produce near- or at-continuous-tone images where the dots are smaller and more irregular than halftone dots. Nice, regularly shaped, regularly spaced halftone dots are replaced with randomly shaped, irregularly placed ones. If you know what a commercial mezzotint screen looks like, you're close to knowing what alternative screening looks like (see Figure 2.15).

This is where *dithering* comes in. In the dictionary, dithering means "nervously excited or confused." Dithering is simply an alternative to halftoning and is the process of breaking down a continuous-tone image into a bunch of tiny, confused, excited little spots in a stochastic, or random, arrangement. Dithering, sometimes in combination with halftoning, has been successfully implemented by inkjet and color laser printers to output a full range of tones and image detail.

Each printer and printer software manufacturer uses its own dithering method and guards it closely. This is the real secret sauce of digital printing.

HP, for example, combines halftoning with what it calls PhotoREt Color Layering Technology on several of its inkjets. PhotoREt layers the color dots on top of each other and dithers them with *error diffusion*, which is a common dithering method (others include ordered-matrix dithering and threshold dithering). Error diffusion means that the error in creating a specific color—say green, which has to be made up of the only colors the printer has available: cyan, magenta, yellow, and black—is spread to the adjacent dots. If one is too green, the next one over is made less green, and so on. If you stand back and look at

Courtesy of Durst-Dice America, LLC

Figure 2.14 *Contone imaging, in this case with a Durst Lambda, produces photo-realistic images with overlapping dye colors.*

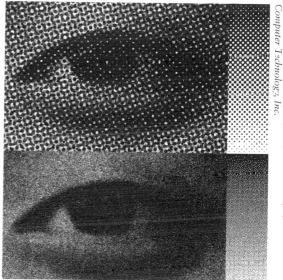

Eyes courtesy of Martin Juergens; panels courtesy of Wasatch Computer Technology, Inc.

Figure 2.15 *A simulation comparing halftone screening (top) with frequency modulated screening (bottom); 30× magnification*

the print, it all balances out, and what you see is green.

Epson also uses its own proprietary algorithms (an algorithm is the mathematical set of instructions the printer software uses to control and precisely place the ink droplets) for error-diffusion-type dithering.

The PiezographyBW software system developed by Jon Cone uses error-diffusion algorithms in conjunction with its own broadband microweave to interweave the various gray inks involved and increase the printer's apparent resolution (theoretically up to 2160 dpi). This unique system works with specific EPSON printers by disabling the printer driver software

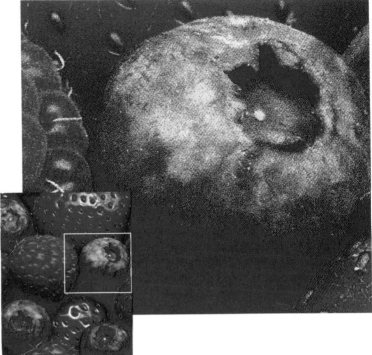

Courtesy of Xerox Network Printers

Figure 2.16 *The Xerox Phaser 7700 color laser printer uses both halftoning and dithering.*

and replacing it with its own. (For more about PiezographyBW software and other multi-monochromatic systems, see Chapter 11.)

Moving away from inkjets, the Xerox Phaser 7700 color laser printer uses a combination of digital halftoning and a special dithering pattern to render the image output (see Figure 2.16).

Why is all this talk about dithers and halftones important? It's important because the type of screen rendering will partially determine the "look" of an image when printed using that particular screening or halftoning technology. This is a big part of what makes up a print's digital signature. When you get experienced enough, you can instantly spot the differences between the specific types of digital output, and you can make your purchase or service choices accordingly.

The bottom line is that when you're at the upper end of digital printing quality, including inkjet and color laser, you've pretty much entered the world of continuous-tone imaging. The dots touch with no space between them, and the four or six (or more) colors are layered next to or on top of each other to blend and form a smooth image. The dividing line between halftones and contones, at least with high-quality, 8-bit digital printing, is starting to disappear.

System Setups

The tools of a digital artist—besides curiosity, thought, feeling, and imagination—include the hardware and software that make it possible to create, process, and, ultimately, output digital prints. In addition to providing a few words about each major equipment category, I will also show you the actual setups of two artists: photographer Larry Berman's PC Digital Darkroom and digital artist Ileana's Mac Digital Studio.

Healthy Hardware: Basic Equipment Setups

Just like socialites in Palm Beach who can never be too rich or too thin, digital artists can never have too much digital horsepower. It's not the printers themselves (if outputting to a desktop printer) that require it; even the newest inkjet printers need only a basic setup. However, when it comes to the large image files that photographers and artists process and inevitably end up with, more is definitely better.

Platforms, Operating Systems, and CPUs

Like fanatical sports team fans, photographers and artists are usually die-hard defenders of either the PC/Windows or Macintosh platform. The fact is, it doesn't make much difference which you go with. Most image-editing programs (but not all) and virtually all high-quality desktop printers run just as well with both. PCs tend to be cheaper and easier to find, and Macs are still preferred with certain niche applications such as pre-press delivery. (I also find it interesting that art galleries invariably use Macs as their office computers; must be something about the cool design!)

Each operating system (OS) software also has its band of adherents. Microsoft Windows reigns supreme on the PC with its many incarnations, and although XP is the latest as of this writing, I know artists who still happily use Windows 95, 98, and 2000 (Windows 2000 is legendary for being rock-solid stable). On the Mac side, the antique OS 7.x can still run the recently discontinued EPSON 3000 inkjet, although most Macophiles are using OS 9.x or OS X. After the image-editing or printer software you're running can no longer work with your old OS, it's time to upgrade it. At that point, many people just opt for a whole new computer, with the latest OS built in.

CPUs and Processing Speed

The central processing unit (CPU) is the heart of your computer. Intel Pentium (3 or 4) and AMD Athlon are two obvious choices for the PC. PowerPC processors (currently G3s and G4s) on the Mac are the only realistic options.

CPUs come in different "clock speeds," which have a big impact on how fast your work gets done as the computer processes all those binary numbers. Get the fastest CPU you can afford unless you like staring at the monitor watching little hourglasses or spinning clocks while your files are processed. PCs are now up to 2 GHz speed, and Macs are over 1 GHz. Note that megahertz or gigahertz ratings should only be used for comparing CPUs in the same family; it doesn't work to compare Pentium speeds with PowerPCs.

System Setup: Photographer

Courtesy of Larry Berman

①
Left Monitor:
Sony 21" 1620HT

Right Monitor:
Gateway 21"

Matrox G400 dual
monitor graphics card

ColorVision Spyder
for calibrating
main monitor

②
Epson Stylus Photo
2000P inkjet printer

③
Wacom ArtZII 6x8"
serial port graphics tablet

④
APC Back-UPS Pro 1000
uninterrupted power supply

⑤
Windows 2000 Pro
P3 550 MHz, 384 MB RAM
Dual 60 GB Maxtor
72000 RPM hard drives

⑥
Polaroid Sprint Scan 4000
35mm film scanner

⑦
Epson Perfection 1640SU
flatbed scanner

Plextor 12x10x32A
CD burner

ZiO! compact flash
card reader for
digital camera files

Netgear through
DS104 hub with
Internet connection
sharing to Win 2000
Pro laptop

Larry Berman's PC Digital Darkroom *Pennsylvania photographer Larry Berman, who has been selling his photography at juried art shows throughout the United States for the past 25 years, originally considered this a power user setup when he purchased it a couple of years ago. He's now planning to upgrade to a higher-chip-speed (2 GHz) and more memory.*

System Setup: Digital Artist

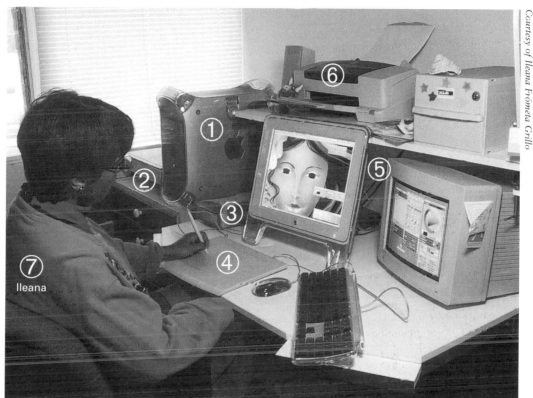

Courtesy of Ileana Frómeta Grillo

① Apple G4 500 Mhz (dual processor) 1 GB RAM 30 GB hard drive Mac OS 9.2

② HP ScanJet 4P 300 dpi scanner

③ Que! Fire 12x10x32 CD-RW External (FireWire)

④ Wacom Intuos ADB 6x8" graphics tablet

⑤ Left Monitor: Apple 15" Studio Display using Apple AGP video card

Right Monitor: Apple 13" using ATI XClaim 3D video card

⑥ Epson Stylus Color 860 inkjet printer

LinkSys EtherFast Cable/DSL Router to connect to Toshiba PCX1100 Cable Modem and the Internet

External Iomega Zip 100

PCI SCSI interface card Assante FriendlyNet 4-port USB hub iMate ADB to USB converter

Canon S-10 2.2MP digital camera with 32 MB SanDisk CompactFlash Media Cards

Ileana's Mac Digital Studio *Digital artist Ileana considers her setup about average for someone expecting to make a living doing fine art on a computer. Her dream setup when the budget and sales allow? Apple G4 Dual Processor (fastest available), 100+ GB hard drive, 2 GB of RAM, a 22" Apple Cinema Display, Apple Titanium G4 laptop so that she can work remotely, a 1200-dpi flatbed scanner, and the latest EPSON, wide-format inkjet printer.*

The best performance will come from using dual processors, and both PCs and Macs support that option. The only problem is that not all software will run on multiprocessors, and conflicts with critical software or drivers can more than offset the speed advantages of a dual-processor system.

RAM

The other big key to processing large image files is Random Access Memory (RAM). These days, RAM is cheap, so buy all you can. Photoshop, especially, is a RAM hog, so load up on it. If you can get and utilize more than 1 GB (1,000 MB) of RAM, get it. You'll be smiling when your work flies off the screen.

An interesting point that digital artist Ileana makes about RAM and her art: Every time she increases the RAM in her computer, she immediately begins to compose larger pieces to take advantage of the improvement, so her work actually changes *because* of the equipment.

Connections

One of the real limitations with older computers is the printer interface or connection. Most contemporary desktop printers, whether inkjet, dye sub, or laser, require a USB or parallel (IEEE-1284) connection. Older computers don't have these, although special cards can be installed for this purpose. When nothing can connect to your computer anymore, that's usually the time to buy a new one.

Hard Drives and Other Storage and Transport

As with RAM and processing speed, large art files require a lot of storage space. It's hard to imagine that I used to work with a 10 MB hard disk, but I did. Now, single file sizes in the 200–500 MB range are not unusual. Because you have to store all those gigantic files somewhere, you should get the largest hard-disk storage capacity you can—40, 60, 80, or even 120 *gigabytes*. You might think about getting multiple hard drives configured in a RAID (Redundant Array of Inexpensive Disks) array for spreading the data across multiple disks. Again, as with RAM, per megabyte storage costs have dropped significantly, so be generous to yourself.

For small-scale or temporary storage (or for file transport), you'll definitely want some kind of removable media system. Iomega Zip 100 MB disks, once the standard for this purpose (remember SyQuest cartridges?), are now almost obsolete because of their limited capacity. Zip 250 MB disks are better, and the newer Iomega Peerless system (10–20 GB!) is better still (see Figure 2.17).

Most file transport these days is done on CD-R or CD-RW disks (650 MB). CD-Rs can be recorded to only once; CD-RWs can

Courtesy of Iomega Corporation

Figure 2.17 *Iomega Peerless base station and disk*

be recorded again and again. DVD (4–9 GB) is coming on strong. You'll either need a built-in CD/DVD writer/reader on the computer (all new computers come with one of the other) or use an external, stand-alone unit.

Displays

Again, bigger is definitely better when it comes to monitors. With the menus and palettes multiplying on the latest image-editing software, screen real estate has become a priceless commodity. Most photographer-artists work on 19–21" screens, but the real trend is to dual monitors (see both of our model setups for examples). One monitor is for the main image, and the other is for all the tools. Mitsubishi, NEC, LaCie, Apple, and Sony make popular models for photographer-artists.

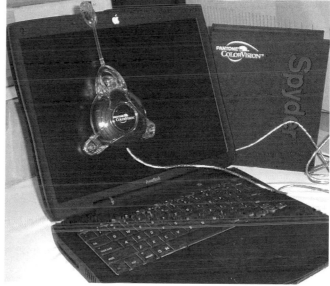

Another trend is to flat-screen, liquid crystal displays (LCDs) and away from the traditional cathode ray tube (CRT) monitors, although some users still maintain that CRTs are better. (Apple has abandoned CRTs almost entirely with its current product line.) Prior concerns about poor color fidelity on LCDs are fading as the quality improves and as more color-profiling devices come online to deal with the new flat-screen monitors (see Figure 2.18).

Figure 2.18 *LCD display with ColorVision Spyder colorimeter attached*

Video Display Cards

Powerful graphics cards are frequently needed to avoid the speed bottlenecks that intense image processing can cause. They are also needed to run sophisticated dual-monitor setups. Matrox, NVIDIA, and AGP make good ones.

Input Devices (Scanners, Digital Cameras, and Graphics Tablets)

Most photographer-artists work with source material in one form or another that needs to end up in the computer. This section discusses the most important options.

Scanners

If you're a film photographer, you'll want a flatbed scanner for reflective art and/or a film scanner for negatives and transparencies. Umax, Microtek, and Epson are good flatbed/combo scanner providers, with Nikon, Imacon, and Polaroid making popular film scanners.

Digital Cameras

Digital cameras are basically little scanners and are becoming a common fixture in digital darkrooms/studios for inputting images for further work. Digital camera files are easily imported into the computer through direct connections or media-card readers.

Graphics Tablets

One of the greatest tools to come along for artists who work digitally is the graphics tablet, which comes in all sizes, shapes, and types. Besides the obvious help with digital painting or drawing, tablets also allow for easier retouching and other kinds of image handwork. The current industry leader is Wacom (see Figure 2.19), although several other manufacturers make competitive products.

See Chapter 4 for much more on scanning, digital cameras, and graphic tablets, as well as image-editing software and techniques.

Internet Connection

This is not really equipment related, but it's becoming more and more necessary for photographers and artists to have a high-speed connection to the Internet. Here's what I use the Internet for: researching art information; browsing and maintaining art-related Web sites; downloading images from stock agencies; sending image files to galleries, colleagues, or outside printmakers; and quickly perusing and contributing to online forums and discussion lists.

Courtesy of Wacom Technology

Figure 2.19 *Wacom's Graphire2 graphics tablet in use*

The more time you spend online, the more frustrating the old 56K-dial-up connection becomes. Cable modems, DSL, and dedicated high-speed lines are the way of the modern, online world.

Color Management

Although there are some exceptions, most photographer-artists are incorporating some type of color management into their workflows. Color management can take many forms: from simple—and free—onboard monitor calibration, to stock or custom profiles, to specialized hardware and software packages costing $5,000 and up. (For an in-depth overview of this important topic, see Chapter 5.)

Printers

Well, that's what this whole book is about, isn't it? No point spoiling the fun at this early stage. Read on.

Printer Drivers, PostScript, and RIPs

This section is primarily for self-printers who print through a computer (photo-direct printers that take media cards don't require computers). If you use an outside printing service, they'll be responsible for knowing all about this, but it can't hurt for you to understand the basics.

Printer Drivers and Printing Software

Before you can print from a drawing, painting, image-editing, or page-layout program, the printer software program, called a *printer driver*, must be correctly installed on the computer. Every print device requires a particular driver for the specific operating system of the computer. (Note that it's your computer's operating system that you match to the printer, not the software application you're using.) You must have the right driver for your printer to support all the printer's features and to tell the print engine how to correctly render the image's digital data. If you change your operating system, you may need to install an updated printer driver, which you can normally download from the printer-manufacturer's Web site.

When you select Print from your application's File menu, you get the print settings dialog box (for Mac OS 9.x) of the printer driver that's already been preselected by you in the Chooser (see Figure 2.20). On a PC, the printer options are available right from the application. If you have a PostScript printing device, you need to use a PostScript driver and select it. (We'll get into more step-by-step, printmaking details in Chapter 9.)

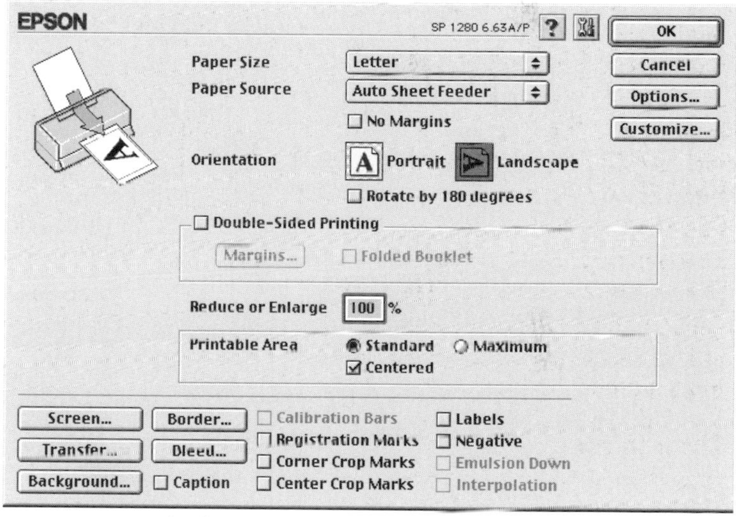

Figure 2.20 *The basic print dialog box for the EPSON 1280*

What Is PostScript?

Adobe PostScript refers to both a page-description language and a processor that interprets PostScript data. PostScript files describe and locate all bitmapped images, vector art, and type on a rectangular page by X and Y coordinates. You can create PostScript files by saving files created in drawing and page-layout programs through a PostScript engine in your imaging application or in a stand-alone application.

Because PostScript is output-device independent, PostScript files are relatively generic, and anyone can deal with them. However, if you're printing PostScript yourself to a specific device, you need to attach PostScript Printer Description (PPD) information to the file so that the output device knows what to do with the file. PPD information includes such things as print resolution, page size, print area, and color rendering instructions. Figure 2.21 shows a PostScript workflow:

Do you need to be worried about PostScript? It depends. If you're creating ads, color separations, or contract proofs destined for the commercial pre-press or printing industry, then yes, you'll need to involve PostScript somewhere in your workflow. In addition, if you're using drawing

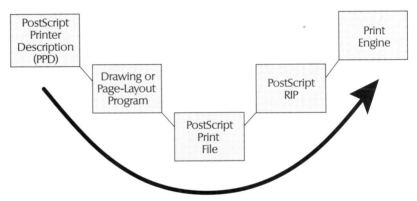

Figure 2.21 *Typical PostScript workflow*

or page-layout programs, have a lot of type, and/or and have your image(s) included as EPS graphics, you'll need a PostScript interpreter to render the graphics correctly.

However, for most art-printing purposes, you may not need to deal with PostScript at all. If you're sending files, even ones with EPS graphics, out to a printmaker, especially one running wide-format devices, they'll undoubtedly have their own PostScript RIP, and because PostScript is device-independent, they should be able to handle any PostScript issues on their end. If you are printing normal bitmapped files to your own non-PostScript printer (which is what most desktop printers are), just use the standard printer drivers. However, if you're dealing with PostScript files or files that have EPS graphics included, you may need to have either a PostScript printer or add a PostScript interpreter to the computer or the printer. You can also use what I like to call the "PDF PostScript RIParound" trick. PDF is a file format that is built on PostScript language. By taking your digital file and going through Adobe Acrobat and its Distiller program, you convert the file into a PDF that will render all EPS elements cleanly (see Figure 2.22).

Figure 2.22 *Left: Bitmapped image, type, and EPS logo printed from QuarkXPress to a non-PostScript inkjet printer using the standard printer driver. Note jagged logo (arrow); right: Same bitmapped image, type, and EPS logo except printed from a PDF version of the same file. Note that the logo cleans up.*

RIPs

A Raster Image Processor (RIP) can give you a significant amount of control over certain aspects of your output. It translates a file's data (bitmap images, vector graphics, and fonts) into a single rasterized (bitmapped) file for printing at the print device's specific resolution.

Actually, all printer drivers act as RIPs, converting a file ("ripping") for printing. Ripping includes telling the printhead where and how to place the dots and remapping the RGB colors to CMYK or whichever subtractive colors are used.

Optional RIPs are available from print device manufacturers or from third-party sources (see Figure 2.23), and they can offer things that the default printer drivers can't. These offerings include more accurate color control, special screening or halftoning, support for more file formats, and the ability to process a file through PostScript. RIPs can be installed in the computer as software, at the printer, or somewhere in between as a hardware device. When a RIP is called on, it takes over the functions of the regular printer driver. This is basically what the PiezographyBW software system described earlier does.

RIPs come in different types ranging from software-only to integrated stand-alone devices. Providers of popular software RIPS include the following: ColorByte (ImagePrint), Compatible Systems (ColorBurst), Epson (StylusRIP), ErgoSoft (PosterPrint), iProof (PowerRIP 2000), LexJet Direct (SpectrumPro/ImagePrint), Onyx (PosterShop), and Wasatch (SoftRIP). Note that Adobe's PressReady was a software PostScript RIP that was aimed at the commercial inkjet-proofing crowd, and it won a following with digital photographer-artists as well. Unfortunately, it was discontinued after 2001.

Another option is to use a dedicated PostScript printer such as the HP 800ps or 5000ps inkjet, which has its own PostScript RIP built right into the device, or one like the HP 10ps/20ps that comes with a bundled software RIP.

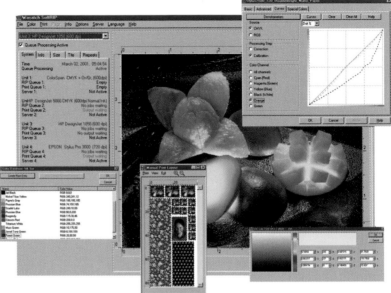

Are All RIPs PostScript Interpreters?

No. However, to take advantage of what PostScript offers (such as the ability to render PostScript files cleanly), many outside RIPs you might consider will

Figure 2.23 *Screen view of the Wasatch SoftRIP*

undoubtedly be PostScript RIPs or, like ImagePrint or SpectrumPro, come in PostScript and non-PostScript versions.

Do I Need a RIP?

As with PostScript, it all depends. For normal desktop printing of bitmapped images, a RIP is not required. But, if you want access to advanced color management with individual ink-limits and channel controls, if your files are very large or complex, if you need to print to unusual output sizes, if you have PostScript elements in your file (plus see PDF workaround above), or if your printing crosses over into the commercial pre-press world at all, then you will want a RIP. Besides, professional-grade PostScript RIPs can handle other advanced features like color separating, trapping, registering, device queuing and faster print spooling, and the layout of multiple images. Printing devices are basically "slaves," and they will only print digital data as they are instructed to do.

There are two other considerations if you're thinking about using a RIP:

■ **Print Quality:** A RIP may or may not give you the same color or image quality. With an EPSON, for example, the printer driver has already been optimized for very small dot placement and smooth image dithering. RIPs override native printer drivers with their own screening or dithering patterns. The only way to know for sure if there's an improvement in print quality is to get feedback from others in your situation or to try out the RIP yourself (demo downloads are available for many).

■ **Cost:** One drawback to RIPs has been that most are expensive, running up to several thousand dollars for a top-end software RIP. However, at the time of this writing, new, non-PostScript RIPs such as ColorByte's ImagePrint 5.0/Desktop Version, LexJet Direct's SpectrumPro (desktop), and ErgoSoft's PosterPrint Photo were coming on the market for $499 to $799. And, there are others supposedly in the pipeline for even less. RIP prices are dropping as manufacturers rush to satisfy the need for RIP alternatives by photographer-artists working digitally.

See Chapters 4, 5, 7, and 11 for more about RIPs.

■ ■ ■

To make informed digital printing decisions, you have to know what the options are. In the next chapter, we'll look at what the major print technologies have to offer.

3

Comparing Digital Printing Technologies

Artists have always experimented with new printmaking materials and techniques, and a list of them would be a long one. However, the process of creating high-quality digital prints has, for the majority of photographers and artists working today, coalesced around four major output methods or technologies: digital photoprint, dye sublimation, electrophotography, and inkjet. To be sure, there are plenty of other digital processes that a photographer-artist can use (electrostatic or "e-stat" from reprographic shops, thermal wax/resin transfer, solvent-based inkjet printing, blueprint reprographics, Indigo Photo-e-Print, and the whole field of digital production printing, to name just a few), but these are either more obscure, more expensive, or too low on the quality scale, so we won't be covering them here in any detail.

Naturally, there are different ways to categorize all these technologies. One is by format size: *narrow* (or desktop) format is anything up to 24 inches in width; *wide* (or large) format is everything 24 inches wide or more. Another way is by drum versus plotter configuration (based on the original CAD plotters used to produce computer-generated charts and graphics). What I've chosen to do in this book is to group them by their logical (in my opinion) imaging characteristics. (Note: Products, brands, and models are current at the time of this writing.)

Snapshot:
Digital Printing

Contone
Digital Photoprint/Photo Process

Wide-Format Digital Photoprint
Format: wide
Maximum output size: 76" × unlimited
Image screening: none
Addressable resolution: 200–400 ppi
Inks/dyes: photo dyes
Media: photo paper
Permanence: up to medium
For self-printing: no
Image quality: excellent

Digital Photo Process
Format: narrow
Maximum output size: 12" × 18"
Image screening: none
Addressable resolution: 300–400 dpi
Inks/dyes: photo dyes/special
Media: photo paper/special paper
Permanence: up to medium
For self-printing: no
Image quality: excellent

Dye Sublimination

Format: desktop
Maximum output size: most 8" × 10"
Image screening: none
Addressable resolution: 300–314 dpi
Inks/dyes: photo dyes
Media: special paper
Permanence: varies
For self-printing: yes
Image quality: very good

Halftone/Dithering
Electrophotography

Color Laser Printers/Copiers
Format: narrow
Maximum output size: 12" × 18"
Image screening: dither/halftone
Addressable resolution: 600–1200 dpi
Inks/dyes: dry toner
Media: normal paper
Permanence: up to long lasting
For self-printing: maybe
Image quality: up to good

Inkjet

Continuous-Flow
Format: wide
Maximum output size: 35" × 47"
Image screening: dither
Addressable resolution: 300 dpi
Inks/dyes: dye inks only
Media: anything flexible
Permanence: long lasting
For self-printing: no
Image quality: can be excellent

Drop-on-Demand
THERMAL
Format: all
Maximum output size: all sizes
Image screening: dither
Addressable resolution: 600–4800 dpi
Inks/dyes: dye/pigment
Media: large range
Permanence: up to long lasting
For self-printing: yes
Image quality: up to excellent

PIEZO
Format: all
Maximum output size: all sizes
Image screening: dither
Addressable resolution: 720–5760 dpi
Inks/dyes: dye/pigment
Media: large range
Permanence: up to long lasting
For self-printing: yes
Image quality: up to excellent

SOLID INK
Format: desktop
Maximum output size: letter/legal
Image screening: dither
Addressable resolution: 1000–1200 dpi
Inks/dyes: solid resin ink
Media: a few options
Permanence: several years maximum
For self-printing: maybe
Image quality: up to good

Digital Photoprint and Photo Process

Until recently, and apart from the IRIS printing process, photographers who wanted actual photographic output (reflective or backlit display) produced from their digital files had to make an intermediate negative or transparency with a film recorder and then use a conventional enlarger to make the final print. However, in 1994, a new type of printer was developed that could print directly from a digital file without the need for the intermediate transparency step. The photo processing industry has never looked back.

I break this category down into two groups: *wide-format digital photoprint* and *digital photo process*.

Wide-Format Digital Photoprint

This is top-of-the-line, continuous-tone photo output, and you'll find the pricey devices for doing this only in photo labs, repro shops, service bureaus, and "imaging centers." (See Chapter 10 for more about how to work with outside print providers.) (I like the term "digital photoprint"; others use words like "laser photo printing," although not all devices use lasers.)

How Does It Work?

Using either three-color lasers (red, green, and blue) or light-emitting diodes (LEDs), these wide-format printers produce extremely high-resolution prints on conventional, light-sensitive, color photo paper that's processed in the normal "wet" photographic manner (using RA-4 chemistry). There is no screening, halftoning, or dithering of the image.

Italy-based Durst invented this category of digital printers, and it now has five models of the Lambda digital laser imager (76, 130, 131, 131 Plus, and Pi50). Using continuous roll feeding, the smallest (Lambda 76) can print a single image up to 31 inches by 164 feet, and the largest (Lambda 130) prints up to 50 inches by 164 feet in one shot. Even larger sizes can be printed in sections or tiles. Two resolution options (200 or 400 dpi) yield an apparent resolution of 4000 dpi. ("Apparent resolution" is explained in Chapter 2.) For color depth, the input is at 24-bit, and output is interpolated to 36-bit using RGB lasers to expose the photographic paper. There are only 600 Lambdas installed around the world, and the price tag ranges from $179,000 (76 Plus) to $325,000 (130 Plus).

Durst, in collaboration with Agfa-Gevaert, recently released their Zeta high-speed, digital laser printer. It's a high-production unit for social and portrait photo labs that specialize in photo package printing. It prints only up to 12 inches wide.

Durst Lambda 130 digital laser imager

The Océ LightJet 430 has a maximum output size of 50×120 inches, and the newer 500XL model can go up to 76 inches wide (the older 5000 model prints to a maximum of 49×97 inches). The spatial/addressable resolution is either 200 dpi or 300 dpi with an apparent resolution of 4000 dpi. As with the Lambda, the input is 24-bit, interpolated to 36-bit output color space (12-bit per RGB color). The LightJet uses three RGB lasers for exposure, and a unique 270-degree internal drum platen for media handling. With a $140,000 price tag, you'll probably prefer to pay about $20 for a single 8×10 and $135 for a 30×40.

Courtesy of Océ Display Graphics Systems

The Océ LightJet 430 photo laser printer

Another high-end, large-format printer is the ZBE Chromira, which uses cool LED lights instead of hot lasers. The print is processed in the normal RA-4 photographic way through a separate processor. There are two models and two sizes, 30 or 50 inches wide, with no limit on length. Yielding 300 ppi resolution, this is another expensive piece of hardware (but less costly than a LightJet or Lambda), so you'll find one only at a photo lab or service bureau.

The Durst Epsilon also uses a LED light source instead of lasers. Printing up to 30 inches wide, it makes use of the same paper and processing as previously described and offers one resolution: 254 dpi.

Advantages of Digital Photoprint

■ Super-high-quality, continuous-tone output

■ No RGB-to-CMYK conversions required (RGB images stay in RGB)

■ No halftoning or dithering required

Disadvantages of Digital Photoprint

■ Limited paper choices (photographic only)

■ Permanence limited by type of paper

■ High print cost

■ Too expensive for self-printers to own

Image/Print Quality for Digital Photoprint

True photographic output is indistinguishable from photographic prints. You can't get much better than that!

Digital Photo Process

Digital photoprinting isn't limited to high-end, large-format devices. In fact, you may not realize it, but most photo labs and photo minilabs today use the same technology to print everything from Grandma's snapshots to professional prints. You rarely see optical enlargers in photo labs anymore.

How Does It Work?

The Fuji Pictrography (models 3500 and 4000II) is a digital printer that uses a unique, single-pass, four-step process (see Figure 3.1). A sheet of photosensitive

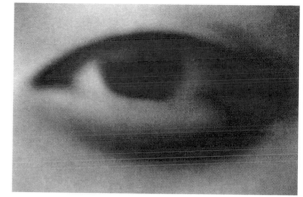

Durst Lambda 76, 30× magnification. The use of this human eye, which includes a range of tones from highlights to shadows, as a visual reference for making image-quality comparisons comes from Martin C. Juergens, a photography conservator, who wrote the report Preservation of Ink Jet Hardcopies, *Rochester Institute of Technology, NY, 1999.*

"donor" paper is exposed to laser diodes (LD). A small amount of water is applied to create the dye image on the donor paper with heat. The dye image is then transferred to the "receiving" paper with a combination of heat and pressure. Finally, the receiving paper, with its transferred dyes, is peeled off and separated from the used donor paper. This is not photographic paper, although Fuji claims the same image permanence. Only special Fuji paper can be used. Two resolutions (267 dpi and 400 dpi) are available with a maximum paper size of 12×18 inches (4000 model only). The Fuji Pictrostat 400 is a printer/copier using the same technology. Both printers are found primarily in photo labs.

Digital minilabs made by Agfa, Noritsu, and Fuji are the standard at many photofinishing labs and the new online processors described in Chapter 10. The Fuji Frontier (see Figure 3.2) was the first digital minilab used for the mass retail market. It's a complete wet-chemistry system that includes a scanner and a modified RA-4 developing unit. You can scan from negatives, transparencies, and prints as well as input directly from CD, Zip, or other digital media. Several different models (330, 350, 370, and 390) are currently installed in photo labs around the world. The largest output is 10×15-inch prints.

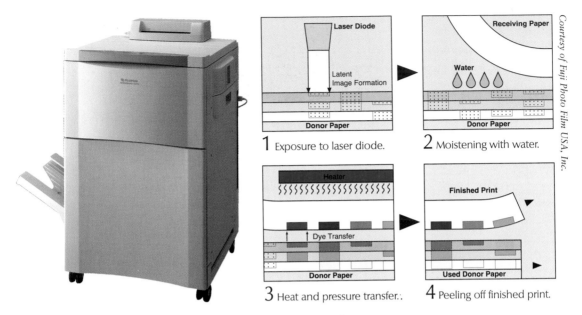

Courtesy of Fuji Photo Film USA, Inc.

1 Exposure to laser diode.   **2** Moistening with water.

3 Heat and pressure transfer.   **4** Peeling off finished print.

Figure 3.1 *The Fuji Pictrography 4000II and its unique four-step printing process*

Advantages of the Digital Photo Process

- High-quality photographic output
- Low-to-medium print cost

Disadvantages of the Digital Photo Process

- Limited paper choices (photographic or special only)

- Depending on model, not practical for self-printers to own

- Maximum size: 10×15 inches (Frontier), 12×18 inches (Pictrography)

Courtesy of Fuji Photo Film USA, Inc.

Figure 3.2 *Fuji Frontier 390 mini photo lab*

Image/Print Quality for the Digital Photo Process

The digital photo process provides true photo-graphic-quality color prints with vivid colors that are sharper than dye sublimation. I have seen photo exhibits hung entirely with Pictro-graphy-made prints, and they were stunning.

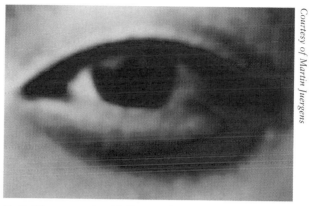

Courtesy of Martin Juergens

Fuji Pictrography (RC paper), 30× magnification

Dye Sublimation

There are two basic flavors of dye sublimation (also called "dye sub" or "thermal dye diffusion"): transfer dye sub and what I call "photo dye sub." The *transfer dye-sub* technology is primarily used in commercial applications to print an image onto a medium and then transfer that image to all kinds of things like T-shirts, mouse pads, hats, name plates, and fabrics (you can read more about this in Chapter 11). *Photo dye sub* is for high-quality photo and digital snapshot printing (and pre-press proofing), which is what most photographer-artists are interested in. (Dye-sub printing has a loyal following among some photographers who prefer dye subs to inkjets.)

How Does It Work?

With dye sublimation, a single-color ribbon containing dye is heated by a special heating head that runs the width of the paper. This head has thousands of tiny elements that, when they heat up, vaporize ("sublimate") the dye at that location. The gaseous dye spot is then absorbed into the surface of the paper. Because the paper receives separate cyan, magenta, yellow, and sometimes black passes of the dye ribbons to make up the final image, the resulting layering of color provides a smooth, seamless image. Photo dye-sub printers have only 300 or so dpi resolution, but they can deliver continuous tone images because of this layering and the way the dyes diffuse or "cloud" into the paper. Some dye subs add a protective layer (a clear UV laminate) as a fourth and final step after the single-color passes.

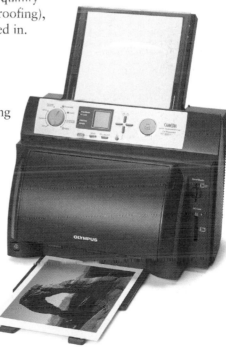

Courtesy of Olympus America, Inc.

Olympus/CAMEDIA P-400 dye-sub printer

Some examples of dye-sub printers include Canon (Powershot CD-200 and CD-300), Kodak (8500, 8660, and 8670PS), Mitsubishi (CP-700 and CP-800), Olympus/CAMEDIA (P-400), Sony (DPP-SV55 and DPP-SV77), and the discontinued Alps line (MD-5000) that combined wax thermal and dye sub in one machine.

Advantages of Dye Sublimation

- Continuous-tone, photographic image quality

- Fast speed on some models; for example, 75 seconds per 8×10 on the Kodak 8500

Disadvantages of Dye Sublimation

- High cost of the larger-format printers

- High cost of consumable supplies

- Limited to special papers (glossy and matte only) and, for desktops, limited to smaller print sizes

Image/Print Quality for Dye Sublimation

Dye sub is photographic quality to the naked eye, with some brands showing a slight pattern of lines or squares under magnification.

Courtesy of Martin Juergens

Kodak Digital Science with CMYK ribbon (RC paper), dye sublimation, and 30× magnification

Electrophotography

Sometimes called "xerography," electrophotography involves the use of laser printers and printer/copiers. We're not talking about run-of-the-mill office copiers; the technology has taken huge leaps in recent years. Traditionally used as proof printers by pre-press departments and production printing operations, color laser printers sometimes double as color copiers but less so all the time with more direct-data input options. They are also used as primary color output devices in graphic arts departments, design studios, and smaller print shops, and, now, by artists—especially photographers. The printing is fast and reasonable, with 8×10 prints averaging under $.50 at retail.

Digital printmaker Jan Steinman says that "many of my artist customers choose color laser prints for the cost. If they're selling them, the higher markup on a laser print compared to inkjet is also very attractive. Laser's 'magazine quality' may not be as good as with inkjet, but for many, it's good enough." Images can be printed on a small range of substrates including matte paper and commercial printing stocks.

How Does It Work?

Many color lasers use hair-thin lasers to etch a latent image onto four rotating drums, one each for the four printing colors (see Figure 3.3). The drums attract electrically charged, dry, plastic-based, pigment toner and then transfer the image to an intermediate transfer belt and then to the paper where it is fused. Other laser printers transfer the toner directly to the paper without the intermediate step.

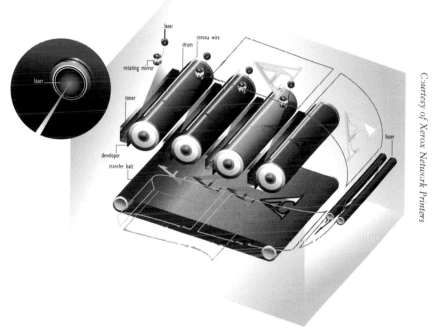

Figure 3.3 *Single-pass, color laser print technology by Xerox*

Older-technology devices image one layer/color at a time; the trend now is to "single pass" printing, which speeds up the process considerably. The Xerox/Tektronix 7700 is a good example. Maximum output size is typically 12×18 inches, and in some printers, laser imaging is replaced with LEDs.

Most color lasers these days offer up to 1200×600 dpi resolution and use their own combinations of stochastic and halftone screening for color rendering. (See Chapter 2 for more about stochastic and halftone screens.) Photographer Seth Rossman loves this type of output. "For photographers, it's an almost perfect medium. I use it in continuous-tone mode, which gives it more of a dithered effect, so no dots."

Some examples of electrophotographic devices include the Xerox Tektronix Phaser line of color laser printers (including the 7700), the Docucolor line, the Canon CLC line of color laser printers, and the Minolta Magicolor line of color laser printers.

Advantages of Electrophotography

- Laser printing widely available as an outside service

- Fast speed

- Low per-print costs

- Long-lasting prints (when pigmented dry toners are used)

Disadvantages of Electrophotography

- Paper selection not as broad as for inkjet, but improving

- Maximum output size limited to 12 × 18 inches

- Some devices too expensive for self-printers to own

Courtesy of Xerox Network Printers

Tektronix Phaser 7700 color printer by Xerox

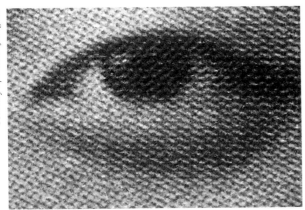

Courtesy of Martin Juergens

Canon CLC color laser printer (bond paper, electrophotographic), 30× magnification

Image/Print Quality for Electrophotography

The image has a raised surface when viewed at an angle, especially on glossy or cast-coated stock, and the colors can be very saturated. Depending on the type of screening, prints under magnification can have a lined or halftone dot look.

Inkjet

Inkjet is the Big Daddy, the current technology of choice for many digital artists and photographers, especially those doing their own printing. The IRIS/IXIA is an inkjet printer, and so are the popular EPSONs, Canons, HPs, and Lexmarks.

Although inkjets have been around since the 1980s in offices and have been used for years to print mailing labels, packages, signage, and other marketing pieces, it wasn't until 1994 and the introduction of the EPSON Stylus Color printer that the whole photorealistic, self-printing boom exploded.

How Does It Work?

Simply described, inkjets use nozzles to spray millions of tiny droplets of ink onto a surface, typically paper. Although earlier devices had an obvious digital signature, the newer printers are so much further along that inkjet images can now be considered continuous tone for all practical purposes.

There are two main types of inkjet technologies: *continuous flow* and *drop-on-demand*, which is further subdivided into thermal, piezoelectric, and solid ink. (We'll go into more detail about inkjet printing in Part II.)

Continuous Flow

Based on the work of Swedish scientist Carl Hellmuth Hertz, continuous-flow inkjet printers shoot a continuous stream of microscopic ink droplets onto a sheet of paper or any other flat surface. The IRIS is a wide-format printer that is no longer made; it's been revamped and is now called the IXIA, pronounced "zia." However, it is the only photo-quality entry in this category, so let's take a closer look at how it works (see Figure 3.4).

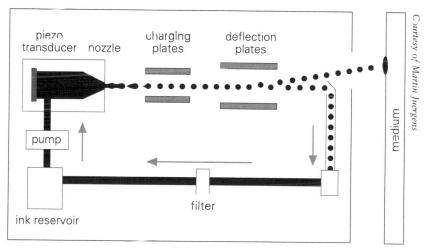

Figure 3.4 *How continuous-flow, inkjet technology works*

A single printhead moves along a rod above the paper that is wrapped around a rotating drum. The printhead encloses four glass nozzles (one for each of the printing colors: cyan, magenta, yellow, and black) that are each connected to a bottle of translucent dye ink. In each head is a tiny vibrating piezoelectric crystal that pushes out a million ink droplets per second. Each droplet is 15 microns in diameter, about the size of a human red blood cell. As the droplets exit the nozzle, some receive an electrostatic charge. Most don't. The charged ink droplets are deflected away from the drum and recycled. But the uncharged ones—our heroes—pass through the deflector and end up hitting the paper to form the image.

Although the IRIS/IXIA has a maximum resolution of only 300 dpi, its apparent resolution is more like 1800 dpi due to its variable droplet size and overlapping dot densities. Images are dithered.

Advantages of Continuous-Flow Inkjet

■ Wide range of media accepted; with an adjustable head height, anything that can be mounted on the drum can be printed on, including handmade and exotic papers

■ Excellent quality for some images including watercolors; synonymous with high-quality, giclée reproduction

Disadvantages of Continuous-Flow Inkjet

■ Limited page size (approx. 35 × 47 inches)

■ Slow print speed (30–60 minutes per print)

■ Can use only dye-based inks

■ Expensive to buy and maintain, therefore higher print costs; time-consuming because of manual paper mounting with drum-based printers

Courtesy of Improved Technologies

The drum-based, IXIA inkjet printer—successor to the IRIS

Image/Print Quality for Continuous Flow

When printed on textured, fine-art paper, IRIS/IXIA prints have a velvety look. Continuous Flow provides near-photographic quality depending on viewing distance and type of substrate used. (See Chapter 7 for more comparisons of inkjet printers.)

Drop-on-Demand

This is the area where the technology advances are coming out at a dizzying pace. The reason it's called drop on-demand is because only the ink droplets that are needed to form the image are produced, one at a time, in contrast to continuous-flow where most of the ink that's sprayed is *not* used. The three main types of drop-on-demand, inkjet printing are *thermal*, *piezo*, and *solid ink*.

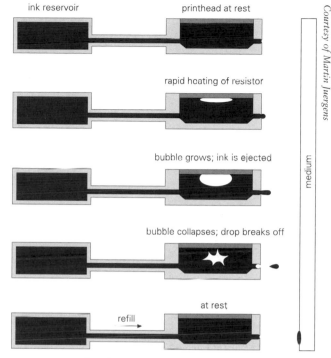

ink reservoir   printhead at rest

rapid heating of resistor

bubble grows; ink is ejected

bubble collapses; drop breaks off

at rest

refill

medium

Figure 3.5 *The thermal-inkjet process*

Thermal

This process, which was invented in 1981 by Canon (the "Bubblejet Printer"), is based on the heating of a resister inside the printhead chamber (see Figure 3.5). As the resister heats up, a vapor bubble surrounded by ink is formed, and the increase in pressure pushes an ink droplet out of the printhead. After the bubble collapses, more ink is drawn in from the ink reservoir, and the cycle repeats.

Wide-format, thermal-inkjet printers come in either drum or plotter formats. The MacDermid ColorSpan Giclée PrintMakerFA (see Figure 3.6) is the only drum-based, thermal-inkjet printer specifically designed for fine-art applications. (ColorSpan makes other more commercial, plotter inkjets that also are used for fine-art output.) It works similarly to the IRIS/IXIA, but with an eight-color printhead carriage moving down the length of a spinning drum with paper attached to it. (The ColorSpan PrintMakerFA recently stopped being produced, but many are still in use.)

Courtesy of MacDermid ColorSpan

Figure 3.6 *The ColorSpan Giclée PrintMakerFA is drum-based with an eight-printhead assembly. Recently discontinued, it's still being used by many digital printmakers.*

Both narrow-format (desktop) and wide-format, thermal plotter printers (also called "bar printers") have printheads that move back and forth on a rail or bar over the paper, which is pushed incrementally after each head pass. Most thermal printheads (one per color, see Figure 3.7) are disposable with replacement periods varying according to the manufacturer; some have to be replaced with each ink change (if they're integrated with the ink supply), and some can last for 10–12 changes (if the ink supply is separate).

Experimental artist Bonny Lhotka (who's known for disassembling her printers to make them better fit her needs) prefers thermal printers because "you can bend them more to do what you want."

The number of inkjet nozzles and their configuration vary with each brand of print device. The Canon S900 has 3,072 nozzles (512 for each of six colors), while the HP Designjets have from 300–500 per color. Typical, maximum thermal resolutions range from 1200×600 dpi to 4800×1200 dpi.

Figure 3.7 *Left: HP's all-in-one print cartridges (black in front, tri-color in back); right: Separate printhead (front) and ink cartridge (back)*

Examples of thermal Inkjet printers include—
Wide-format: HP (Designjet 5000/5000ps,
5500/5500ps), ColorSpan (DisplayMaker
Mach12, DisplayMaker Esprit),
Kodak/ENCAD (NovaJet 880). *Desktop:*
Canon (S800, S820D, S900/9000), HP
(Deskjet 990Cse, 3820, 5550; PhotoSmart
1315, 7350, 7550; Designjet 10ps/20ps/50ps),
Lexmark (Z53, Z55, Z65).

Advantages of Thermal Inkjet

- For the drum-based ColorSpan Giclée, as with the IRIS/IXIA, the range of media types is a big plus; they and the NovaJet 880 have the ability to adjust the head height to accommodate thicker papers.

The Deskjet 5550 is one of HP's new-generation, photo-quality inkjet printers, and it features a top-end resolution of 4800×1200 dpi.

- Some thermal devices print 12 colors; four to six is normal on desktops.

- Desktop thermal printers are widely available.

- Thermal printers are owner-friendly in terms of maintenance.

Disadvantages of Thermal Inkjet

- Time-consuming, manual paper mounting with drum-based printers.

- The 180-degree paper path on some wide-format thermals makes feeding stiff paper difficult.

- Overspraying and "satellite dots" (ink where you don't want it) are more common on thermal printers.

Image/Print Quality for Thermal Inkjet

Thermal-inkjet provides up to photographic quality to the naked eye, depending on printer, ink, and medium. I've seen high-resolution desktop, thermal-inkjet prints on glossy paper that rival any photographic print.

Piezoelectric

When certain kinds of crystals are subjected to an electric field, they undergo mechanical stress; in other words, they expand or contract. This is called the "piezoelectric effect," and it's the key to this popular brand of digital printing, called "piezo" for short. When the crystalline material deflects inside the confined chamber of the printhead, the pressure increases, and a tiny ink droplet shoots out toward the paper (see Figure 3.8). The returning deflection refills the chamber with more ink.

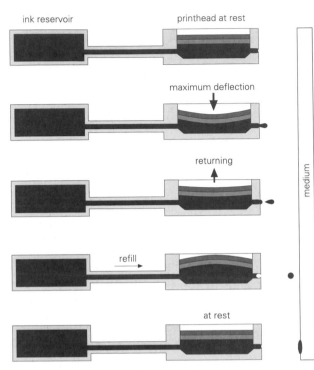

Courtesy of Martin Juergens

ink reservoir   printhead at rest

maximum deflection

returning

refill

at rest

medium

Figure 3.8 *The piezoelectric-inkjet process*

Both the wide-format and desktop models of piezo printers come only in plotter versions with the printhead assembly going back and forth over the paper to create the image. Piezo printheads are typically single units with all colors included; they are a permanent part of the machine and usually need no replacing.

In the desktop category, there's only one piezo player, and that's Epson with its Micro Piezo printheads (see Figure 3.9). With maximum printer resolutions now at 2880 × 1440 dpi and 5760 × 720 dpi, and six- to seven-color inks in dye and pigment versions (the EPSON 2000P was the first desktop pigment-ink printer; now succeeded by the 2100/2200), these are the printers that own a large share of the photographer-artist, self-printing inkjet market.

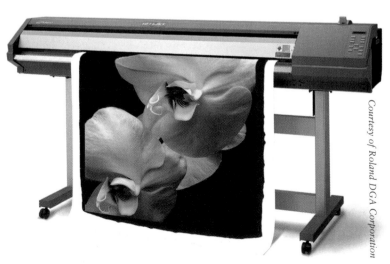

Courtesy of Roland DGA Corporation

Roland's Hi-Fi JET PRO FJ-500 wide-format inkjet

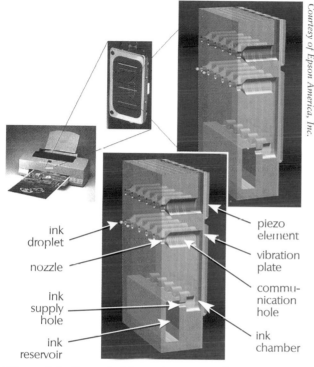

Courtesy of Epson America, Inc.

ink droplet

nozzle

ink supply hole

ink reservoir

piezo element

vibration plate

communication hole

ink chamber

Figure 3.9 *Epson's Micro Piezo printhead*

The configuration and number of inkjet nozzles vary with each printer. For example, office-grade, EPSON inkjets have more black nozzles than color, which creates the faster text printing that those users want. In general, piezo devices have fewer nozzles than thermal ones (the Roland Hi-Fi JET PRO wide-format printer using EPSON printheads has 96 nozzles per color). One theory is that thermal must alternate nozzle firing because of the rapid heating of each chamber, so they need more nozzles than piezo printers to do the same job.

Examples of piezoelectric inkjet printers include—*Wide-format*: EPSON (Stylus Pro 7600, 9600, 10000/10600), Roland (Hi-Fi JET, Hi-Fi JET PRO-V8, HiFi JET PRO II), Kodak/ENCAD (5260), Mutoh (Falcon II), Mimaki (JV4). *Desktop*: EPSON (Stylus C82, Stylus Photo 820, 825/925, 960, 1280, 2200).

Advantages of Piezoelectric

■ Extremely small minimum droplet size (down to two picoliter) and precise dot placement creates very fine image detail.

■ A wide range of media types available.

■ Desktop printers are widely available.

■ Piezo printers are easy to use with standard supplies.

Disadvantages of Piezoelectric

■ At the finest resolutions, printing speeds can be slower compared to thermal.

■ Maintenance and repairs are more difficult and costly with piezos.

■ Metamerism (color shifting in different light) can be a problem with certain pigment-based, piezo inks.

Courtesy of Epson America, Inc.

EPSON Stylus Photo 2200, the first seven-color, pigment-ink, desktop inkjet printer

Image/Print Quality for Piezoelectric

At the higher resolutions and on the right media, no digital signature is apparent; these are true continuous-tone, photographic quality prints. Some claim that the piezo technology produces a sharper, more-controllable ink drop, which results in more vivid and detailed images.

Solid Ink

Formerly called "phase change," solid ink technology is the inkjet oddball, and because Xerox basically owns the technology, they are the main player. The Tektronix/Xerox Phaser 8200, which recently replaced the 860, is a true piezoelectric inkjet, but there are several surprises. First, the pigmented colors come in the form of solid blocks of resin-based inks, although the ink still ends up as a liquid after heating (hence the term "phase change"). These printers also have the affectionate nickname of "crayon printers," from the resemblance of the ink sticks to children's crayons.

Courtesy of Xerox Network Printers

The Tektronix Phaser 8200, solid-ink, color printer by Xerox. At left are the resin-based, solid ColorStix.

Instead of a smaller, reciprocating printhead assembly, there is a single printhead that extends nearly the width of the paper with 88 nozzles in each of four rows (see Figure 3.10). The same piezo substance we've already learned about shoots the ink droplets out as before, but in another twist, the ink doesn't go onto the paper; instead, the ink goes onto a turning offset drum that is kept warm so that the ink doesn't solidify. The drum then transfers (in a single pass) the still-molten ink to the paper under pressure to form the image.

Advantages of Solid Ink Inkjet

- Fast print speed

- Single-pass technology that's more reliable than color laser or inkjet

- Highly saturated images

- Ink is independent of the medium; no absorbing or wicking

Disadvantages of Solid Ink Inkjet

- Output sizes are limited to letter/legal size.

- A little on the high-cost side for purchase by self-printers, but more reasonable than most of the electro-photography devices.

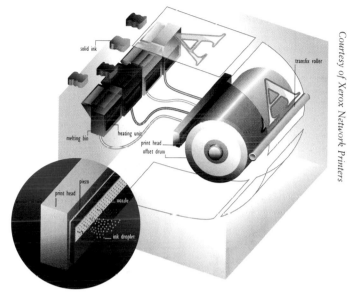

Figure 3.10 *The inner workings of the unique Tektronix Phaser solid-ink printer*

- Image permanence is relatively poor. Xerox claims only "a year or more" with office lighting and "over several years" with dark storage.

Image/Print Quality for Solid Ink

The ink sits on top of the paper, creating a definite relief effect. The colors are brilliant and sharp because the ink drops don't spread or bleed. However, because of that, the effect, even at 1200 dpi, is not always continuous tone. "Near photographic" might describe it better.

■ ■ ■

With all this new, accumulated information about pixels, hardware, and printing technology under our belts, let's move our attention to what it takes to create and process a digital image.

4

Creating and Processing the Image

Art and technology have never been more intertwined than they are now. Digital technology may be the tool, but the act of creation springs from the mind—and heart—of the artist. Let's look at how digital images are created and processed.

Image Input

If printing is close to the last step in the making of digital art, then one of the first steps is inputting or acquiring the image or the image elements. Most photographers and artists work with source material. Photographs, sketches, scans—these are the raw materials that, when combined with a creative vision, end up as an image worth printing.

It's like making a fire. Before the flames can blaze, you've got to go out and gather the wood. If you've spent much time camping, you know that the drier and higher the quality of the wood, the bigger and better the fire.

As with many things digital, the boundary lines between categories are not hard and fast. For example, digital cameras do the same basic thing that scanners do. However, because the digital world has decided that a camera is one thing and a scanner is another, I'll break image input down similarly.

Scanograms

Photograms have been around since the invention of photography, but it seems as though they're being resurrected today through digital imaging and printing. I call them "scanograms." Just lay any semi-flat object on a flatbed scanner and have at it. Leaves, rotting fruit, jellyfish, and seaweed have all been scanned on my trusty Microtek ScanMaker flatbed. However, if you use gooey, dripping, found objects like I have, take photographer/digital artist Joe Butts' advice: To keep the liquid out of your scanner's bed, run a bead of silicon caulk around the glass, creating a trough to hold your liquids. You can keep building up the bead for additional depth if needed. Afterward, the caulk peels right off the glass without requiring too much cleanup.

A "scanogram" made from leaves and manipulated in Photoshop

Non-Camera Scanning

Scanning means sampling a reflective or transparent, flat (or fairly flat) object point by point and turning that information into a usable digital file that can be processed in the computer.

Depending on the type of scanner involved, light generated in the scanner itself is either reflected off or transmitted through a piece of art or film and onto a light sensor, which is actually a grouping of tiny charge-coupled devices (CCDs). The thousands of individual CCD elements, one per image pixel, are either arranged in a grid pattern (area array) or in single or triple rows, called, respectively, linear or trilinear arrays (see Figure 4.1). The light level at each spot is then converted into digital data (our favorite ones and zeroes).

In the context of digital printing, the type and quality of a scan can be critical to the final, printed output. The digital cliché of "garbage in, garbage out" definitely applies here. The main factors to consider for scanning artwork are *resolution*, *sizing and scaling*, *bit depth*, *dynamic range*, *Dmax*, and finally, the *type of scanner* for the job.

Resolution

Most of the sales information for scanners highlights the dpi resolution. Technically, there are no dots in scanning, just samples. It really should be samples per inch (spi) or pixels per inch (ppi), but that battle of terminology has been lost to the scanner industry.

The more CCD elements per unit area, the higher the *optical resolution* of the scanner, and, in general, the more information and detail the scanner is capable of capturing. Flatbed scanners use the same naming system as inkjet printers to trumpet their resolutions: 2400×4800 dpi, for example. In this case, 2400 means the number of CCD elements across the bed of the scanner, while 4800 refers to the other dimension and

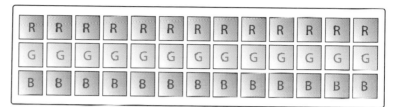

Figure 4.1 *Top: A simplified linear-array CCD. Each pixel element is monochrome; to get color, the whole array is "broomswept" across the art using different filters (RGB); bottom: Trilinear-array CCD. The elements are coated so that each one sees only red, green, or blue.*

is achieved, as with inkjets, by motor stepping. In general, it's the lower number that counts. Film and drum scanners also use dpi, but they usually list only one number, such as 4000 dpi.

Some scanning devices also list an *interpolated resolution*, which is invariably a larger number and is a way to make the resolution appear higher by fudging the pixel data with software. It's usually not a good feature for bitmapped images and should not be a consideration when weighing scanning choices.

At what resolution and how big should the scan be? Good question, and it leads us into the interrelated issues of resolution, sizing, and scaling, which, because the word "resolution" is involved, gets a little complicated.

Scanner Resolution, Sizing, and Scaling

The first thing you have to realize is that the resolution you enter in the scanner's settings box has nothing to do with print size. An image scanned at 300 ppi (or dpi, as most scanners show it) will print at exactly the same size as the same image set for 150 dpi. What *does* affect the final printed size is scanner scaling.

You would think that the resolution setting is the scanning resolution. Not so. It's the combination of the resolution and the scaling or magnification settings that determines the actual *scanning resolution*. Unfortunately, you won't find that number anywhere in the average scanner's settings box (see Figure 4.2). It's hidden away, and you just have to know what you're doing.

Here's how it works:

Let's say you have a 5×5-inch image area you want to scan in normal, color mode. If you select "Millions of Colors" for 24-bit RGB, put 300 dpi in the Resolution field, and 100% in Scaling, you can see in Figure 4.2 that you would end up with a 6.5 MB file that will be output at 5×5 inches in size. So

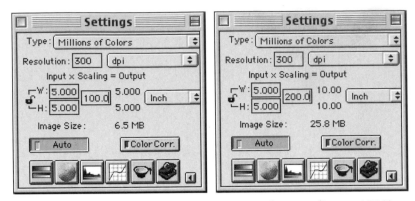

Figure 4.2 *Typical desktop scanner settings box, scaling at 100% (left) and 200% (right)*

far, so good. However, now you want to double the printed size. If you change the resolution setting to 600 dpi, what happens? The output size stays the same (5×5 inches). However, the file size has increased to 25.8 MB. Now try something different. Go back to 300 dpi, and change the scaling setting to 200%. You have the same file size (25.8 MB), but now the output size has changed to 10×10 inches. What has happened is that the scanner itself has calculated a scanning resolution of 600 dpi (300 dpi×200%) for you to end up with a 10×10-inch printed image. The scanner will now capture twice as many pixels so that it can stretch them out over the larger area.

Note that you didn't pick 600 dpi, did you? No, the scanner calculated it (the scaling function is merely a calculator). The danger here is that if you're not careful, you could be asking the scanner to do things it's not capable of doing. For example, assume that your scanner has an optical resolution of 600 dpi. With the same 5×5 area set at 300 dpi, you decide to really make it big and scale it up to 500%, yielding a 25×25-inch output size. Possible? Yes. A good idea? No. Why? Because by doing this, you have let the scanner calculate a scanning resolution of 1500 dpi, which is way beyond the capability of a 600-dpi scanner. You would end up with a blurry, interpolated scan.

So, at what resolution should a scan be made? You have two basic choices:

1. You can scan at your scanner's full optical resolution (making sure you don't exceed 100% scaling), and then resize or resample the image down in Photoshop or another image-editing program (see Chapter 9 for more about resizing and resampling). The only problem with this is that modern scanners have high optical resolutions, and if you scan a large area that way, you'll end up with a gigantic file. An alternative, if your system can even handle it, is to immediately reduce such a scan with your image-editing software to a more reasonable file resolution before saving it to disk. On the plus side, by scanning at a higher resolution, you will help guarantee that you've captured all the digital information there is to capture.

2. You can scan at less than the optical resolution of your scanner but only in integer divisions. Integers are whole numbers (1, 2, 3, 4, and so on), and for reasons that are too complicated to get into here, scanners like it better when resolutions are set to integral divisors of the optical resolution. For a 1200-dpi scanner, the optimal resolutions are 1200, 600, 300 dpi, and so on. If you're like me, then, you'll do most of your bitmapped scans on, say, a 1200-dpi scanner at 300 dpi resolution. If you want to end up with a 150-ppi file, then scan at either 200 or 300 dpi (you always want to scan at or above the final file resolution; you never want to scan at below the intended file resolution and "upsample" the file). In addition, keep in mind this scanning resolution warning: To be safe, scan at 100% scale.

The first rule of thumb of imaging and printing is this: Always work backwards. What that means is you need to consider *all* the possible print sizes and uses for that image and work with *the largest use* in mind. Even if you're preparing to output postage-stamp-size prints, would you ever need to have a larger image for, say, an advertisement in a magazine? If so, you might as well play it safe and scan your original art for that maximum size. You can always repurpose the image files down to smaller sizes later.

My Original's Too Big!

If your original art is too big for your scanner, and you don't want to take a digital or analog photo of it, you're left with one option—scan it in pieces and stitch it back together with an image-editing program like Photoshop. It's a tedious process, but this is exactly what artist Craig Forrest does with his paintings that can reach 22×30 inches. "I have to crop the sectional scans before trying to piece them together in order to allow for the distortion of the edge of my scanner," he explains. "I zoom in on the scans to about 600% and then use the arrow keys on the keyboard to move the images together into alignment, one pixel at a time."

Bit Depth, Dynamic Range, and Dmax

Bit depth is a subject with which we're already familiar, and the same principles apply here. A normal RGB color image will require a minimum 24-bit scan (8 bits of information per RGB color) to reproduce with adequate fidelity. This is the "Millions" scanner setting. However, because some of the scanned bits are invariably corrupted and unusable, using a scanner with a higher bit depth—36 bit, 48 bit, or "Billions"—is a good idea. A 48-bit scanner records 16 bits per color channel, which can be processed as 16 bits or downsampled to 8 bits for further editing (see "High-Bit Bonanza?"). Some swear by these 16-bit images, but others say it's overkill. In addition, increasing the bit depth increases the file size arithmetically.

High-Bit Bonanza?

If 24-bit color scans are good, then 48-bit scans are even better, right? Although this is generally true for scanning, there's a difference of opinion about it when it comes to editing these larger files.

A 24-bit scan means 8 bits per RGB channel (all scanners scan in RGB). Eight bits equates to 256 possible brightness levels per channel (0–255, where 0 is pure black and 255 is bright white). A 48-bit color scan means 16 bits per channel or 65,536 possible values. That's a lot more steps on the digital stairway (see Figure 4.3).

High-bit advocates say that 12- or 16-bit scans are smoother, provide more tonal accuracy, and reduce banding and posterization.

High-bit critics say baloney. Besides the obvious problem that most image-editing software cannot handle 16-bit files fully (Photoshop has many functions unavailable in 16-bit mode), 16-bit files take twice as long to process and use up twice as much hard disk space. In addition, if you're sending your images out to be scanned, you typically pay by the file size, so a 16-bit scan can cost twice as much as the same scan at 8-bits.

Do your own testing and experimenting to decide, but if in doubt, and if you have the storage capacity, scan at high-bit resolution to cover yourself. As scanning expert David Coons says, "Double the file size is a small price to pay for the 256× increase in luminance accuracy you achieve by moving to 16-bits per channel."

Many people get the terms "bit depth" and "dynamic range" confused. Both are important, but they are very different. Think of a stairway: the number of steps is a function of the bit depth (8 bits equals 256 steps), and the height of the entire stairway is the dynamic/density range (see Figure 4.3).

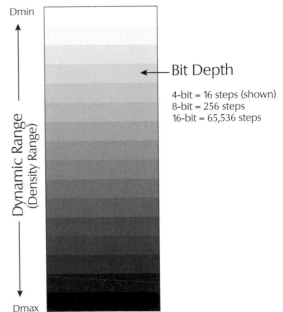

Figure 4.3 *The digital stairway. The number of steps is a function of bit depth; the height of the stairway is the dynamic/density range.*

There are actually two different, but related, types of dynamic range. There's *scene dynamic range*, which is how much tonal information an input process or medium can capture. It usually applies to camera systems, and it's expressed in terms of photographic *exposure value* or *f-stops*. Color reversal film, for example, has a scene dynamic range of 7 f-stops.

Then there's *density range*, which is the difference in density between the lightest and darkest areas of an image. It's the numerical range from the minimum density (Dmin) to the maximum density (Dmax). If the Dmin is 0.3 and the Dmax (also called *optical density*) is 3.9, then the density range is 3.6 D.

Density range applies to digital input devices like scanners, but it can also describe recording material, such as analog film. Reversal film (transparencies), for example, has a wide density range (3.3–3.6 D), but a narrow dynamic range (7 f-stops). Anyone who works with slides quickly realizes that, while the blacks are black and the whites are bright, the shadows and highlights are very compressed. Slides are great for viewing or projecting (which is what they were invented for), but for capturing all the subtle tones in a scene, negative film, with its wider dynamic range but lower density range (2.4 D–3.0 D), is much better. Other types of art also have their own inherent density ranges. Photographic prints have an average range of around 2.1 D; watercolors have even less.

How does all this affect scanning? You need to make sure you consider what type of art you will be scanning before deciding on a scanner to purchase or a service to use. For that purpose, density range and D values are important factors. When dealing with transparencies with very dense blacks, you'll want the widest density range and the highest Dmax you can get. However, with certain kinds of reflective art, it's not as critical, and many low- to mid-priced scanners will do the job. (Unfortunately, because of a lack of standards, advertised density ranges and Dmax specs, as with "resolution" on inkjet printers, serve mostly marketing purposes. Use them to compare scanner models by the same manufacturer, but be leery of any cross-brand comparisons.)

Types of Scanners

There are four basic types of scanners or scanning systems to consider for non-camera image scanning: *flatbed*, *drum*, *film/transparency*, and *Photo CD*.

Snapshot: Non-Camera Scanners

	Flatbed Scanners (Desktop)	Drum Scanners
Media type	reflective and transparency	transparency and reflective
For use with	flat art and film	film and flat art
Art size	up to 12" × 18"	up to 12" × 18"
Optical resolution	600–5000+ dpi	up to 9000+ dpi
Image quality	OK to excellent	excellent
Practical to own?/Cost?	low-to-mid range, yes high-end, no $99–$10K	no $10K–$150K

	Film/Transparency Scanners (Desktop)	Photo CD
Media type	transparency	transparency
For use with	film	film
Art size	35mm to 4" × 5"	35mm to 4" × 5"
Optical resolution	2500–5000+ dpi	2200 dpi(Master) 4400 dpi (Pro)
Image quality	up to excellent	good to excellent
Practical to own?/Cost?	yes $750–$5K	no $10K–$75K

Flatbed Scanners

Flatbeds look like their name implies: flat boxes with a glass plate on which you put the artwork. A moving CCD array travels the length of the bed scanning (either in one pass per RGB color or in an all-in-one pass) as it goes. Earlier flatbeds could scan only reflective art, but the newer generation can do a decent job with transparencies as well; instead of the light coming from under the glass, an adapter or special lid construction allows light to shine from above onto the CCD sensors.

Several manufacturers make a wide range of models for self-scanning with resolutions from 600×1200 dpi to 2400×4800 dpi. Higher-end, commercial flatbeds that can cost tens of thousands of dollars offer resolutions that match drum scanners (more than 5000 dpi). The best of the best of these now use XY technology that has the lens moving along with the CCD array, which supposedly results in more consistent imaging across the entire scanning area.

Examples of flatbed desktop scanners include the following: Agfa (DuoScan models), EPSON (Perfection and Expression), HP (Scanjet), Microtek (ScanMaker), and Umax (Astra and PowerLook). Commercial scanners include Creo (iQSmart and Eversmart), Fujifilm (FineScan), and Microtek. (Note: The products, brands, and models are current at the time of this writing.)

Drum Scanners

It used to be that this was the only way to get a high-resolution scan. Using photomultiplier tubes (PMTs) instead of CCD chips, old-style drum scanners were big, finicky machines that could take up half a room, although newer, desktop models are now available. The artwork, typically a transparency, is attached to a cylinder or drum that spins while a laser beam shines through or on it and activates the sensors. Drum scanners are expensive, slow, and demanding, but they can produce wonderfully large, high-quality images with resolutions that can approach 12000 dpi. However, these outsourced scans aren't cheap. They can be $50–$150 each, depending on the final size.

Although there are plenty of drum scanners around in pre-press shops and service bureaus, there are now lots of cheaper and faster alternatives for photographer-artists.

Major manufacturers include Fuji, Howtek, ICG/Global Graphics, and ScanView.

Film/Transparency Scanners

These specialized desktop scanners have become very popular with photographers and have taken over the position of drum scanners for many wanting high-quality scanning of transparencies or negatives. The light source in many desktop brands is a cold-cathode, mercury fluorescent lamp, or, in other cases, an array of LEDs. Depending on the price, film scanners can handle 35mm up to 4×5-inch sizes. In addition to commercial film scanners like the Durst Sigma, which is a professional, high-speed scanner that can produce a 322-MB file in 34 seconds, most of the high-end, flatbed scanners mentioned in this section can also scan film.

Because film has to be enlarged more than prints, and also because film has a wider density range and more contrast, most film scanners have correspondingly higher optical resolutions. A maximum resolution of 4000 dpi is standard for many desktop film scanners.

A different type of film scanner is made by Denmark's Imacon, and their Flextight models have a unique way to handle the artwork (several models also scan reflective prints). The film is bent in a drum-like shape except there is no drum! There's only air between the sensor and the film, which is held in place by its edges. They call it a virtual drum, and there's no need for the mounting liquids, gels, or tape that drum scanners require. The resolution is high (up to 8000 dpi, non-interpolated), but with a price tag to match.

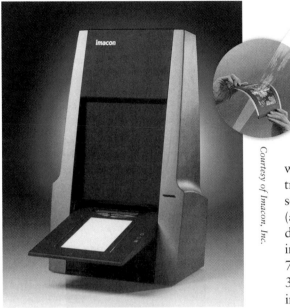

Courtesy of Imacon, Inc.

The Imacon Flextight 848 film (and print) scanner; inset: Imacons use a virtual drum technology that bends the original with a glass-free optical path.

Examples of desktop film scanner manufacturers include Canon (CanoScan models), Imacon (FlexTight), Microtek (ArtixScan), Minolta (Dimage), Nikon (Coolscan), and Polaroid (SprintScan).

Photo CD

Kodak's Photo CD system doesn't get a lot of respect, but it's a good, cost-effective way of scanning film negatives or transparencies. Only offered by photo labs and service bureaus, the regular Photo CD format (also called Master Photo CD) provides five different resolutions for each 35mm-only image: 192×128 pixels, 384×256 pixels, 768×512 pixels, 1536×1024 pixels, and 3072×2048 pixels. The cost is $2–$3 per image. The Pro Photo CD format (a different machine) can handle up to 4×5 images, costs more (about $15–$20 each), and it provides, in addition to the five levels of resolution per image, a sixth one: 6144×4096 pixels at 72 MB each. The two formats can be mixed on the same higher-formatted CD.

The result, as its name implies, is a proprietary Kodak CD Master Disc with an index cover showing all the images in thumbnail view. The CDs hold about 100 Master format images or about 25–30 Pro format ones.

The Photo CD system is a great way to go if you want: good quality at low cost, multiple resolutions of the same image, a permanent archive, and a cute index card showing all the images. The optical resolution of the Master CD is 2200 dpi; for the Pro, it is 4400 dpi.

(Picture CD is a cousin of Photo CD that you can find at every drugstore photo counter. This is primarily used for consumer-level, at-time-of-processing image scans from an entire roll of photographic film. Don't smirk. I have achieved very satisfactory results with photographs shot on color negative film and digitized in this way. As long as you keep the final output size to 4×6" or less (at 300 ppi), the quality is acceptable. In fact, every image of my *Welcome to the Breakers!* digital collage—see Chapter 1—was digitized this way.)

Sending Out for Scans

Not everyone has their own scanner, and even if you do, there will be times when you'll want to send out your images to a scanning service for digitizing. Some of the reasons include the following: you have large-sized artwork and don't want to be bothered scanning it in sections, you don't want to spend the big bucks for a good scanning-camera-back system, or you want a pro to do your scanning and match your colors with minimal proofing.

David Coons, who, with his company ArtScans Studio, is considered by some to be the top fine-art scanning service provider in the world, says, "Anybody just getting started with digital fine-art printing should send out some initial scanning and printing just to get their feet wet, and also to get a sense for what good-quality scanning and printing looks like. When deciding which scanning service to use, make sure the shop is experienced at the kind of work you need. Talk with other artists who are happy with the services they use."

Even if you're doing reproductions through an outside printmaker, realize that, in many cases, they may use a digital scanning service, too.

"Most artists find the printing company first, then either get referred to the scanning service or have the scanning outsourced by the printmaker," Coons explains. "The former provides the artist more freedom to try out different printing services, and the latter keeps them locked in. In fact, some of our printing-company and art-publisher clients don't inform the artists where the scans are done, making us part of their secret recipe."

Bottom: ArtScans Studio co-founders Susan and David Coons are setting up a scan; top: ArtScans staff is examining one of wildlife artist Carol Heiman-Greene's (center) originals.

Camera Scanning

Most cameras use a lens and shutter of some sort, but beyond that, there are lots of possibilities for camera-scanned image input destined for digital printing. Photographers have the most experience in this area because capturing images is already their primary activity, either with analog or digital cameras. Traditional artists, on the other hand, are mainly concerned about digitizing finished artwork, and they tend to rely on outside professionals such as printmakers or photographers. Digital artists pick and choose from the available technologies, and in many cases, use digital cameras and scanners for image capture.

Because photography in general and digital photography in particular are the topics of many worthy books that fill entire libraries, we'll only hit the highlights as they relate to digital printing.

There are two main ways to capture images with what I call "camera scanning": traditional *analog photography* and *direct digital capture*.

Analog Photography

Working with a camera and film used to be the primary way to capture an image. It's still a good alternative, but it's losing ground all the time in the face of the digital onslaught.

For traditional artists reproducing existing artwork, the piece is photographed with a film camera that typically produces a large-format transparency (4×5 or 8×10), which is then scanned on a drum or other high-end scanner. The skill of the photographer in dealing with image squareness, lighting, exposure time, focus, film choice, and more is paramount. Photographing art is an art in and of itself, and it takes a lot of experience and training to do it right.

Advantages of Large-Format Film Scanning

- Predictable workflow, results, and costs.

- Wide density range + large surface area = lots of information.

- Large-format film advocates claim film still has a slight quality edge over the best digital.

There are different ways to go with analog or analog/digital-hybrid camera scanning: shooting with transparency or negative

Courtesy of DaveSmithPhoto.com

Photographer Dave Smith shoots artwork with regular film, which is then scanned. Here, he's using a 35mm camera instead of his normal 425 format.

film and making digital scans of selected frames, shooting with negative film and making prints for scanning (not preferred), or having scans made of the whole roll at the same time as processing. The end result is the same: scanned images ready for digital processing or editing.

Because digital is where you want to end up, why not just start there?

Digital Capture

Digital cameras and scanning backs are all the rage and are gradually replacing their analog ancestors (film cameras). Here are some reasons why:

Advantages of Digital Scanning

■ There's no lag time from exposure to the final image.

■ Digital done correctly is repeatable with no image variation.

■ Because there's no film, you don't have to buy it, store it, or process it.

■ Digital proponents say scanning-back captures (see the "Digital Scanning Backs" section) are sharper, clearer, and show more detail than film.

Although the debate continues over whether film or digital is better for the highest-quality scans, capturing images with either a digital-capable camera or a digital scanning back is a definite trend. Here's a brief summary.

Digital Cameras

Digital cameras or "digicams" are basically little scanners, and all the things we've learned about pixels, file sizes, and resolution apply here as well (in other words, more is better). The main difference is that the cameras in this category are primarily "area array" devices. There is a single, light-sensitive sensor (CCD or complementary metal-oxide semiconductor [CMOS]), which is made up of tiny elements in a checkerboard or mosaic pattern that are individually coated to be sensitive to red, green, or blue light. The sensor is exposed through a lens to the light reflecting off the subject (see Figure 4.4).

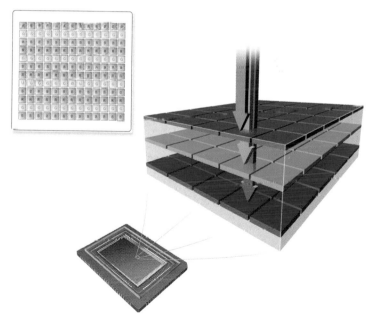

Figure 4.4 *Comparing digital-camera sensor technologies; top left: A simplified CCD area array with striped-array pixel grouping (there are other pixel-grouping patterns, too); lower right: The new Foveon layered chip*

The camera converts the analog signal into binary information, and bingo, you have a digital file. There are single-shot digital cameras that do everything at once and multi-shot ones that take three exposures, one each for red, green, and blue.

At least, that's the way it *has* been. The breakthrough in digital photography that was announced in early 2002 is the Foveon X3 image sensor. Instead of sensing elements that capture only one color at a time, each Foveon chip has three photodetector layers to capture a different color—one each for red, green, and blue (see Figure 4.4). As a light ray sinks into the sensor, first blue, then green, then red is absorbed. So, what's the big deal? The resulting image can be sharper and have a higher resolution. The Foveon chip promises to revolutionize the digital camera industry.

Digicams come in a myriad of styles and types. Pick up a photography magazine or walk into any camera store, and you'll see that there are point-and-shoots, "prosumer," professional, and studio cameras for every possible use and occasion. They are usually categorized and marketed by their maximum resolution in pixel dimensions. For instance, you might see 1600×1200 (that's horizontal by vertical; see "Digicam Resolution Cheat Sheet"). You also might see the CCD size or the maximum number of pixels the camera is capable of capturing, usually rounded off to the closest million-pixel decimal. For example, 1600×1200 pixels equals 1.9 or 2 Megapixels.

You basically get what you pay for, which means that as you spend more, the resolution and CCD size go up, and your ability to process and print larger, higher-quality images increases.

For example, a 2-Megapixel camera like the Nikon Coolpix 775 has a maximum resolution of 1600×1200 pixels. An opened and decompressed file will have a file size of 5.5 MB at 300 ppi, which would yield a good 4×5-inch print but not much more unless you reduce the ppi (cut the ppi to 150 and the print size doubles).

Now, if you jump up to Nikon's Coolpix 5000 (see Figure 4.5), you're dealing with 5 Megapixels, a maximum resolution of 2560×1920, and a file size of 14.1 MB at 300 ppi, all resulting in a 6.4×8.5-inch print (or more if you reduce the ppi).

Courtesy of NikonUSA

Figure 4.5 *Nikon's 5-Megapixel Coolpix 5000 digital camera*

Digicam Resolution Cheat Sheet

VGA *(640×480 pixel = .3 Megapixel):* This is the bottom of the barrel in terms of quality. It's acceptable to use for the Web, but that's about it.

XGA *(1024×768 pixel = .8 Megapixel):* This is a step up but barely usable for printing; it gives about 3×2" at 300 ppi (larger with a lower ppi).

SXGA *(1280×960 pixel = 1.2 Megapixel):* This is better still. It yields about a 3.5-MB file and 4×3" at 300 ppi.

UXGA *(1600×1200 pixel = 1.9 Megapixel):* We're getting there: a 5.5-MB file with 5.3×4" at 300 ppi.

Full *(2048×1536 pixel = 3.2 Megapixel):* We've reached small photo print size: 9 MB and almost 7×5" at 300 ppi.

Full *(2560×1920 pixel = 4.9 Megapixel):* Don't know why they call this "full," too, but we're finally into decent print output with this 14-MB file, which prints almost 9×6" at 300 ppi.

Of course, in the process, you've also spent three times as much for the camera. Other popular digital camera makers include Sony, Canon, HP, Olympus, Epson, Fujifilm and Minolta.

Another important consideration with digital cameras is the type of media handled. Options include CD-RW, floppies, and removable memory cards such as PCMCIA, SD, SmartMedia, or CompactFlash, the last of which is probably the most popular. Some manufacturers, such as Sony with its Memory Stick, use their own proprietary media formats. Memory cards are the equivalent of film—digital film—and you can't have enough of them or have them be too big in terms of storage capacity. Separate card readers accept the removable media and download the files to the computer's desktop.

Most digital cameras will compress the image files and give them to you in JPEG format. Each camera has different quality modes, and the amount of JPEG compression will vary with each setting. The higher the compression, the worse the quality, but the more images the camera can store. Higher-priced digicams will also offer hi-res, uncompressed raw or TIFF files that take up the most space but produce the highest-quality image output. These formats may offer high-bit capture as well. For JPEGs, the best thing to do is immediately convert anything you want to work on into a lossless format like TIFF or PSD (see below for more about file formats).

Some desktop printers (HP PhotoSmart, Canon S820D, and EPSON 825/925) offer direct-to-print options. Bypassing the computer completely, digicam memory cards are inserted into a special slot in the printer, which can offer limited image-editing functions, depending on the printer type.

Convert jpeg (from camera) to TIFF or PSD.

One variation of the single-capture approach includes the high-end, digital camera backs from manufacturers such as Phase One, Leaf, Sinar Bron, and Imacon. These devices are used mostly by professional studio photographers and attach to the backs of medium-format or 4 × 5 cameras. Exposures are instantaneous, so all light sources including flash can be used.

Digital Scanning Backs

Although purists argue that digicams can't equal the quality of a well-exposed, processed, and scanned medium- or large-format piece of film, the ground shifts when you start talking about digital scanning backs. With these devices that typically replace the backs of 4 × 5 cameras with their own inserts or adapters, you're on a different level of quality that either approaches or exceeds large-film formats, depending on who is talking. The BetterLight scanning-back captures I have seen have been stunning: wide dynamic range (BetterLight claims 11+ f-stops), good separation of similar colors, and excellent detail in the highlights and shadows.

Digital scanning backs work just like flatbed scanners, but they are turned up on their sides. They use a stepper motor that varies its speed to change the scanning resolution, and the rows of CCD elements move one line at a time across the image plane to capture it.

Besides the obvious problem that they are not inexpensive ($10K–$25K), there are two other concerns with scanning backs: The subject must be stationary because scan times can reach into the minutes, and the light source must be continuous (incandescent or fluorescent), which means no flashes. Thus, scan backs are rarely employed on location. However, they are well suited for one of their main uses: scanning artwork.

California photographer Ben Blackwell creates digital archives of artwork for the Berkeley Museum of Art. Figure 4.6 shows his setup using a BetterLight Super6K

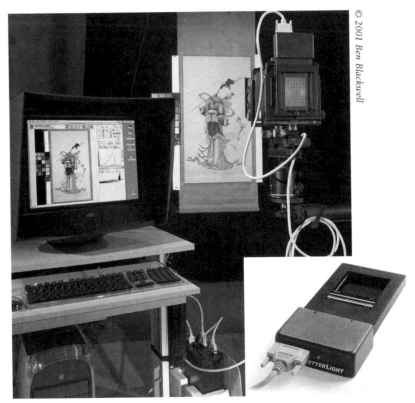

© 2001 Ben Blackwell

Figure 4.6

A BetterLight scanning-back system is used by photographer Ben Blackwell to digitally capture artwork at the Berkeley Museum of Art. The inset shows the Super 6K insert with CCD sensor that moves across the image area.

scanning back on a 4×5 camera. He uses tungsten lights that are bounced into Foam Core towers (10' high×4' feet wide) with the open sides toward the art. Blackwell's files are typically 90–140 MB in size (BetterLight scan sizes can reach 549 MB!), and the images are used for—in addition to archiving—exhibition prints, posters, outdoor banners, publications, and Web sites.

Keep in mind that although digital-scanning-back technology is state of the art, it still takes old-style photographic experience with lighting, focus, and exposure to produce a good digital capture.

Digital Drawing/Painting

This is not really a way to acquire or capture an image; instead, it's a way for artists to creatively input their ideas directly into the computer. It can be done with drawing or painting software applications, image-editing programs, or the many niche programs, plug-ins, and filters that are available.

Let me admit right up front that there is a lot of overlap between this category and the next one, which is image editing. The dividing line where image creation becomes image processing is very fuzzy. Much art is made with a feedback loop of trying something, going back and fixing it, and then trying again. However, that's one of the main advantages of working digitally. Experiments and variations with a computer can be done quickly, and if done appropriately, they're reversible.

One way to get a handle on how digital drawing and painting work is to look at the software used to create it. I'll give a short summary of the major program players along with selected image and interface samples to give you a feel for them. Again, keep in mind that my category dividing lines are not impermeable. Many programs can both create and edit images, and many artists own several types of software and use them all, even in a single image. (See "Snapshot: Image Processing Software" for an overview of the major image-processing software applications, including drawing/painting programs.)

Painter

Corel/Procreate Painter is a digital painting program that simulates traditional media. There are watercolor brushes, oil paint brushes, impasto brushes, and air brushes. There's also dry media such as chalk, oil pastel, and charcoal. There are calligraphy pens and pencils. Then, add all the patterns and paper textures, and you end up with a super-charged natural-media, digital-painting application. It's a complex program that is a little daunting for some, but the results are pretty amazing if you hang in there long enough to learn it.

You can create images from scratch, or you can enhance what you already have, and Painter is completely compatible with Photoshop, so you can exchange layers between the two. Digital artist Ileana, for example, moves back and forth between Painter and Photoshop as she develops her images (see Figure 4.7). Painter also combines well with Photoshop for photo editing, and it works as an image editor, although not as well as Photoshop.

Graphics Tablets

When artists were able to set aside that cute but clunky mouse and replace it with a stylus that allowed the hand and eye to move more naturally in creating lines and shapes, digital drawing and painting took a huge leap forward.

It's such a good idea: a pressure-sensitive pen or stylus moves over an electronic tablet that records the pen's position and action. It's just like writing with a pen on a piece of paper, only the pen never runs out of ink, and the paper never moves. In addition, although the stylus is like a mouse in sampling relative motion (pick it up and position it somewhere else, and the on-screen cursor never moves), it can also record absolute motion (move it to another spot on the tablet, and the cursor moves, too). In addition, it can do things that a simple mouse never dreamed of—like being pressure-sensitive. Wacom's Intuos2 includes a batteryless, cordless pen with 1,024 levels of pressure-sensitivity. Push a little harder and the brush size or the transparency of the stroke changes.

Artist Martha Bradford works with a Wacom Intuos2 9212 graphics tablet (at right) in creating her digital charcoal drawings (see Gallery Showcase for more). Here, she works 1:1 on the fine details of her piece Salt Mist.

The key features to weigh and consider when shopping for a graphics tablet are the following:

1. Size: This is a personal preference. For many, a 425 or 628 tablet is all they need. Others feel cramped with anything smaller than 9212. Larger tablets take up more desk real estate but allow more 1:1 scaling between the monitor and the tablet.

2. Resolution: The more the better because resolution affects the control of the cursor on the monitor. The working range is 1000–2540 dpi, sometimes stated as lpi or lpmm (lines per millimeter).

3. Pressure: The more pressure-sensitivity levels, the more natural and responsive the tablet will feel. A tablet with 512 levels will do the job, but one with 1,024 levels is even better. "Pressure-sensitivity is important," explains artist Martha Bradford, "because I try to make many of my brushstrokes gestural, meaning that starting thin and light, getting thicker and darker, and then finishing thin and light is the effect I'm after, and that comes from pressure-sensitivity."

4. Pen tilt: Pen tilt is a feature that lets the stylus angle change relative to the tablet. Tilt allows for a more flexible and natural drawing style.

5. Compatibility: Almost all high-quality, image creating or editing software is pressure-sensitive-compatible, but check just in case. You may not be able to use a pressure-sensitive tool with a word-processor, for example.

6. Hand-eye coordination: If your hand-eye coordination isn't great, consider one of the newer LCD tablets, such as Wacom's Cintiq interactive models. Instead of drawing on a tablet and watching the monitor, you draw instead right on the monitor/tablet.

7. Versatility: Keep in mind that graphics tablets are not just for painting or drawing. Some artists use them for everything; the only mice they deal with are the ones in the attic.

Figure 4.7 *Corel/Procreate's Painter interface shows some of artist Ileana's progressive steps for* Alice.

CorelDRAW/PhotoPaint

Corel has been developing CorelDRAW since 1987, and it's a big hit as a vector drawing program with PC users (now also for Mac), giving Adobe's Illustrator and Macromedia's Freehand a run for market share, especially in Canada. Primarily used as an illustration/page-layout program, CorelDRAW is now packaged in a suite with Corel PhotoPaint (for image editing and painting) and R.A.V.E. (for creating animations and vector effects for the Web).

Digital artist Carol Pentleton, who also runs the online gallery The Digital Artist, uses CorelDRAW exclusively in the creation of her images. She loves the flexibility, the transparency of use, and the quality of the tools, and her favorite feature is the infinite mutability of fills she can get with the program. Pentleton outputs her series *Levitation* (see Figure 4.8) to IRIS. "I love the color saturation and the smoothness of the transitions of the prints," she says. "The expense is worth it."

Figure 4.8 *Carol Pentleton used CorelDRAW to create* The Fountain *from her* Levitation *series.*

Studio Artist

Synthetik Software's Studio Artist isn't as well known as Painter, but those who use it love it. Based on the idea of a music synthesizer, it's a graphic synthesizer with an unusual interface (see Figure 4.9). One of its great strengths is in letting you take an existing source image and going wild with it. The number of editable controls is astounding, which makes it an experimenter's dream. There are also plenty of brushes and textures for straight digital painting, plus added functions for video processing, morphing, warp animation, and even "intelligent-assisted (auto) painting." One common complaint about images processed in Photoshop is that the various Photoshop effects from common filters and plug-ins become obvious and hackneyed. Studio Artist's approach helps to avoid this problem.

As with other painting programs, Studio Artist is a good companion to Photoshop. Hawaiian artist Diana Jeon likes to start an image in Photoshop, bring it into Studio Artist to add different painted or sketched effects, and then wrap it up in Photoshop for final printing.

Illustrator and Freehand

I put Adobe Illustrator and Macromedia Freehand in the same grouping because they often trade places on most artists' lists for best vector-based, drawing or illustration program (CorelDRAW

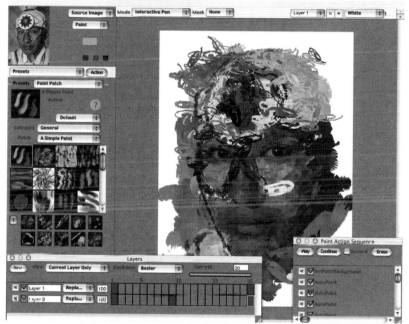

Courtesy of Synthetic Software, Inc.

Figure 4.9 *Synthetic Software's Studio Artist uses a music-synthesizer metaphor. Here, brush effects are added using Paint Patches. The source image is at top, left.*

is the other contender). In fact, my own story is an example. I started off with Illustrator '88 back in—you guessed it—1988. I used it mainly for print graphics, illustrations, logos, and so on. A couple of years later, I found out about Freehand and switched. It seemed that the interface was more natural to my way of doing things. Then I received an offer to upgrade Illustrator. I did the upgrade, and I was pleased with the improvements Adobe had made. Illustrator is what I currently use for my vector-based art (all the drawings and vector art in this book were created with Illustrator).

Digital artists have found good uses for vector-based drawing programs as well, using them in combination with other software. New York artist Howard Berdach works this way. His *Direction Internal* (see Figure 4.10) started off as shapes in Freehand. Brought into Photoshop, the elements were colorized, layered, and then layered some more. "When my images are 'done,'" he says, "they're really just starting points to the next version." Printed output is to both IRIS and EPSON wide-format inkjet printers.

Figure 4.10 *Howard Berdach's* Direction Internal *was created in Freehand and Photoshop.*

The Upgrade Treadmill

You know how it is: As soon as you get comfortable with a version of software—working out the kinks, learning its secrets, paying off the credit card—a new version comes along, and you have to start all over. This is the Upgrade Treadmill, and once you're on it, there's no getting off!

Designers and commercial artists need to upgrade software whenever their clients or everyone else in their industry demands it. Fine artists can usually delay upgrades a little longer, but eventually, either the lure of the new capabilities will win you over, or you'll grow tired of everyone making fun of you.

If tried-and-true programs or procedures work, why the need to change or upgrade? Because the new software is simply irresistible.

3D and Beyond

Everything up to this point in our survey has involved people manipulating computer software to help create art. A final variation goes the next step and merges the worlds of art and mathematics. This is where computer algorithms, with little or no intervention by people, do the work, or as artist Jean-Pierre Hébert explains, "My computers draw, and I watch."

This is "machine art," an apt term I learned from digital printmaker and New Mexico-based artist JD Jarvis. As he explains, "Machine art is the imagery of the computer's soul. What is truly 'digital art' is the work that begins in the mind of the artist with the notion of synthesis. Using all the software tools and all the traditional processes together to make something that we have not yet seen. This is the power and the challenge of working digitally to make Art."

Machine art includes three-dimensional modeling where 3D artists who use programs such as Maya (Alias/Wavefront), Bryce (Corel), Poser (Curious Labs), and LightWave 3D (NewTek) create entire universes that exist only at the interface of the computer software and their imaginations. This is also the world of fractal mathematics and algorithmic art. Using filters (see below), texture and pattern generators, commercial or free software (XenoDream and Fractal ViZion), custom computer coding, scripts, and pure mathematical equations, digital artists spend hours, days, and weeks with precise calculations that are performed by the computer and ultimately rendered into print or other 2D or 3D forms. (Hébert, for example, is well-known for his sand etchings where computer software animates a metal ball that etches itself through fine sand to form abstract designs.) Architectural and engineering CAD applications have reached a point of producing intricate rendered images that also fit this category.

In his work *Guardian* (see Figure 4.11), Jarvis combines automated filters and 3D rendering with digital airbrushing and image editing to create a piece that was finished "when it seemed to be staring back at me, like some sort of guardian."

Plug-ins and Filters

There are dozens and dozens of plug-ins and filters that add to and extend the range of other software. Most are algorithm-based and made for changing, tweaking, and wholesale

Figure 4.11 Guardian, *by JD Jarvis, combines automated filters, 3D rendering, digital airbrushing, and image editing.*

modifying of images. I can't mention them all, but here are some popular ones that work with Photoshop (and most other image editors as well). (Contact information for these plus all the other software makers can be found in the Appendix.)

- *buZZ (Segmentis):* An image-editor plug-in for adding filter effects to images. PC and Mac.

- *Deep Paint (Right Hemisphere):* A powerful paint plug-in for Photoshop that offers 3D lighting and texture control. For PC only.

- *Dream Suite (Auto FX Software):* A visual-enhancement program created to work with images, type, and graphics. Works as both a stand-alone application and Photoshop-compatible plug-in. PC and Mac.

- *Eye Candy (Alien Skin Software):* A collection of more than 20 filters for creating and altering images, text, and backgrounds. PC and Mac.

- *KPT (Corel/Procreate):* A Photoshop and compatible plug-in series of filters for creating image effects. PC and Mac. Trial version bundled with Photoshop 7.

- *Photo/Graphic Edges (Auto FX Software):* A plug-in or stand-alone application that adds edge effects to existing bitmapped images. Full version has 17 volumes with more than 10,000 edges. PC and Mac (see Figure 4.12).

Morning Swim © 1978-2002 Harald Johnson

Figure 4.12 *One of 10,000 edge effects using Auto FX Software's Photo/Graphic Edges program on the author's Morning Swim*

- *VariFocus (Andromeda Software):* A plug-in that lets you focus/defocus features in your image with custom control. PC and Mac. Andromeda has many other interesting plug-ins, too, such as the EtchTone Filter.

Image Editing

After you have the raw materials of an image in your digital workspace, you're ready for image processing or editing. Image editing can be as simple as taking a single image and making sure it's the right size, has the correct file format, and looks about the way you want it to look. However, for many, that's just the beginning. This is where many photographer-artists spend most of their time in creating their complex imagery. Compositing, tessellation, montage, collage—this is where it all happens (see "Montage-Collage"). This is the stage on which much digital art is played out.

Montage-Collage

One of the visual techniques that digital photographer-artists regularly use is montage-collage. I combine the terms here because, with digital, it's so hard to know where one ends and the other begins. If you're looking for definitions, artist John Paul Caponigro, in his book *Adobe Photoshop Master Class*, explains it like this: "In both montage and collage, multiple sources are used to create a single image. In montage, the disparity of the sources is invisible. In collage, the disparity of the sources is visible, sometimes so much so that the whole is fractured into separate elements contained within a single area."

However you define it, advanced image-editing software is absolutely brilliant at it, and this ability alone is worth the price of admission to the world of digital image editing.

It may not match the Caponigro definition, but this digital portrait of Albert Einstein by Jeremy Sutton was turned into a photo montage by using the ArcSoft PhotoMontage 2000 software package. The program uses a library of miniature stock images to create the effect. (For the native version of Sutton's image, see Gallery Showcase.)

Image editing is a full-length subject on its own, so I'll concentrate on only two important aspects of it: *software* and *workflow*. (If you're using a paint program, many image-editing functions are available within that program, although you will still want to consider having a separate image editor, too.)

Image-Editing Software

Snapshot: Image-Processing Software

Program	Maker	Platform	Used for
CorelDRAW/ PhotoPaint	Corel	PC and Mac	DRAW: page layout illustration PhotoPaint: image editing and painting
Freehand	Macromedia	PC and Mac	vector illustrations, print, and Web design
Illustrator	Adobe Systems	PC and Mac	vector illustrations, print, and Web design
Photoshop	Adobe Systems	PC and Mac	image editing, painting, and Web graphics
Photoshop Elements	Adobe Systems	PC and Mac	image editing, photo retouching, and Web graphics
Painter	Corel/Procreate	PC and Mac	painting, and photo and image editing
Paint Shop Pro	Jasc Software	PC only	painting, photo and image editing, and Web graphics
Photo Impact	Ulead	PC only	digital photography, creative design, and Web graphics
Studio Artist	Synthetik Software	Mac only	painting, and photo and image editing

Most photographers and artists use one or more of the advanced image editors. This is not an absolute requirement—you could print an image from a word-processing program if you wanted, but to get the most out of your images and your printing, you'll want to have and use an image editor.

Besides the obvious requirement that you be able to drive a printer from the software—or be able to place the image into another type of program (page-layout, for example) to drive a printer, the other requirements of an image-editing program depend on what you want to do to process or improve your images. Minimum features to look for include the following: layer editing, support for various file and input/output formats, masking, cloning, painting and retouching, Photoshop plug-in compatibility, and color management support.

Here is a summary of the most-popular, image-editing software used to help photographer-artists process and prepare their images for printing.

Photoshop

Adobe's Photoshop is the gold standard of image-editing software for most serious digital photographer-artists. It's the most expensive, the most complex, and for many, the most intimidating piece of software they will ever own.

I was intimidated at first, too. I had Photoshop 2.1 sitting in a corner unused for a couple of years; I was scared to death of it. Then I upgraded to version 5.5 and decided it was time to learn it. Many, many hours later, the veil finally lifted. Now, with version 7, I don't know how I existed without Photoshop. I use it constantly for image editing, and because of that, it's as familiar as an old sweater. Not that I know everything there is to know about it. I don't. I consider Photoshop a lifetime learning experience.

An older version of Adobe Photoshop (5.5) and Curves, its killer feature

What's so great about Photoshop? For one thing, Curves. Curves is a killer feature. This is *the* best way to adjust bitmapped images, and while other image-editing programs may have Curves-like functions, Photoshop excels at it. A second advantage of Photoshop (starting with version 6) is its ability to "soft proof" or show you what an RGB image will look like printed to an inkjet or other digital device (see Chapter 5 for more about this). A final advantage is Photoshop's redundancy. There are many ways to do the same thing, which can be a big plus in terms of flexibility and tailoring the program to your needs.

However, don't be worried if you're not a Photoshop aficionado. Depending on your goals, one of the following software programs may be all that you require.

Photoshop Elements

Adobe's Photoshop Elements is a trimmed down Photoshop for amateur photographers, hobbyists, and mid-range users. It combines image editing, photo retouching, and Web-graphics creation. Although Elements does not have Levels or Curves functions, it does have something that the full version of Photoshop doesn't: Photomerge, which lets you stitch together photographs. Elements is priced the same as Paint Shop Pro, and it sometimes comes bundled with other hardware or software. (One secret that many don't know about Photoshop Elements is that it supports all full-version Photoshop plug-ins that work on RGB images.)

Paint Shop Pro

Paint Shop Pro (PSP) by Jasc Software is a great program for the average-consumer user, especially for the price, which is about a sixth of Photoshop's. You can both create and edit images with it. There are text and drawing tools, photo correction and enhancement tools, and Web design tools. And as with Photoshop, there are layers, adjustment layers, and layer blending modes. It's very Wacom-compatible, and it even has Levels and Curves adjustments. Paint Shop Pro lacks high-bit, CMYK, LAB, and other advanced modes, and it offers only the simplest of color management, but compared to Photoshop, PSP is very easy to use. My main complaint is that it's only for the PC; there's no Mac version.

Jasc Software's Paint Shop Pro is a lower-priced, image-editing alternative to Photoshop.

PhotoImpact

Another easy-to-use, affordable image editor for the amateur user, Ulead's PhotoImpact competes in the market with Paint Shop Pro. Its focus is on digital photography, creative design, and Web graphics. It includes the following for photo work: basic photo correction and enhancement tools, its own version of Levels and Curves, histograms, effects filters, digital watermarking, color management, and image management. For design work, there are all kinds of tools for vector-graphic work, cloning, retouching, masking, selecting, path drawing, and lots of painting tools and effects. It's an impressive package for the money. It's available for PC only.

Image-Editing Workflow

So what do you do with all that great image-editing software? With digital technology, images can be improved to an infinite degree. Almost anything you can imagine, you can do with digital image editing. The trick is knowing when to stop! Although this is not a book about image editing (there are plenty of good ones available), and I will illustrate the key steps in creating, processing, and printing an image in Chapter 9, this is a good point to review a typical, photo-based, image-editing workflow. A paint- or other-based workflow would vary depending on what needs to be done.

Starting with a simple, small image of some hay rolls I took with a digicam, let's take an abbreviated, CliffsNotes tour of how I would edit this image. (Although I'm using Photoshop 7 here, you should be able to take similar actions with other image editors with only slight modifications.)

1. Prep File, Orient, and Crop

Figure 4.13 shows how the original, digicam, 1600×1200-pixel, RGB TIFF image looks when I opened it in Photoshop. I immediately Save As to a new file in PSD format. This now becomes my master working file (never work on an original image). I've already decided that Adobe RGB (1998) is my color working space (see Chapter 5 for more about this and the required monitor calibration), and because the size and resolution (5.3×4 at 300 ppi) are adequate for my modest purpose, I won't change them now (see more on sizing and scaling in Chapter 9).

Figure 4.13 *My original digicam image*

To me, the squareness (orientation) of the image is fine, but it's cropped too loosely; it needs more tension. After changing the name of the Background layer (to Base) to make all the menu items available, I'm ready to crop. Using the Crop tool, I move the four marquee sides to where I want them and press Return/Enter. I now have a 3.5 MB, RGB, 8-bit, 1360×910-pixel, master image at 300 ppi (see Figure 4.14).

Figure 4.14 *Hay rolls, prepped, and cropped*

2. Correct for Global Tone and Color

Now the fun starts. The image looks a little somber to me; it needs some brightness, some snap. I create a Levels Adjustment Layer (I always use Adjustment Layers in case I mess up), and the Levels histogram quickly confirms what I can already see: the tonal range, while not bad, is squeezed a bit; there are no values in the highlights (see Figure 4.15). That's easy enough to fix. I pull the white-point slider to the left to where the values start to rise. This spreads out the tones and increases contrast. To check it, I do a quick copy merge into a new layer (Layer > Option + Merge Visible),

create another Levels layer, and see a nicely redistributed histogram (see Figure 4.16). There are a few gaps showing, but they're minor and should cause no trouble (lots of gaps and/or wide gaps *are* a problem, causing posterization and other evils). The temporary Levels layer disappears when I click Cancel, and I trash the Levels-merge layer.

Figure 4.15 *Levels confirms a lack of highlight values.*

Figure 4.16 *Redistributed tones after making the Levels move— much better!*

In looking at the color, I notice that there seems to be a slight bluish cast overall. I can see it especially on the side of the left hay roll. I confirm this by opening the Info palette and running the cursor over that area; the RGB values are almost equal, which means I've got gray there.

Normally, this is a good thing, but I want the image to be a little warmer, to have golden glow. To fix the color cast, I create another adjustment layer and go into Curves. Keeping the grid big and moving first into the Blue channel, I add a point midway and drag it down a bit. This adds Yellow (Blue and Yellow are complementary colors, so subtracting blue adds yellow). To check, I verify the Info palette again and then toggle the Curve layer's eye icon to alternately hide and show the layer and its effect. I like it (see Figure 4.17).

Figure 4.17 *Curves is good for fixing color casts. Dragging a midway point down in the Blue channel adds yellow.*

3. Make Local Tone/Color Corrections

One thing that's bothered me about this image is that the sky is weak; it needs more drama. It's time to go in and make some bluer sky. First, I need a sky selection. Working in the Base layer, I go to Select > Color Range and play with the eyedroppers until I get a good overall sky selection (see Figure 4.18). It's not perfect, so I zoom in and fine-tune the selection using the Lasso tool and the Shift (add to) and Option (subtract from) keys. After the selection is correct, I save it (Select > Save Selection) so that I can call it up (Select > Load Selection) whenever I need to.

To finish the sky work, I duplicate the Base layer for security, and, working in that layer and with the selection active (the "marching ants" are

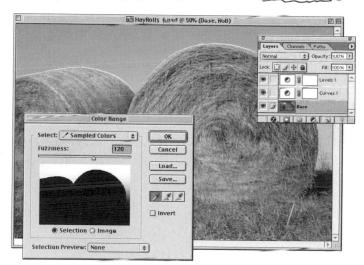

Figure 4.18 *Color Range (left) is a great way to select colors; I used it for the sky.*

moving), I go to the Gradient tool. I could, of course, simply darken the sky with Levels or Curves, but instead, I'm going to trick it up a bit with a gradient. Setting the gradient to Foreground to Transparent, I pick a dark blue beginning point. I then Shift-drag through the selection, and the new blue sky appears like magic (see Figure 4.19). It's perfect, but just to be sure, I hide the selection so that I can see the edges of it without the marching ants.

4. Make Repairs

This is the point at which I like to do basic dust and scratch removal ("dust busting"). Others like to wait until after sharpening. Because the splotchy grass in the foreground is the most obvious repair problem I see, I'm going to use added layers and Copy and Paste procedures to fix it. I could also use Photoshop's Rubber Stamp or Healing Brush tools on a separate repair layer.

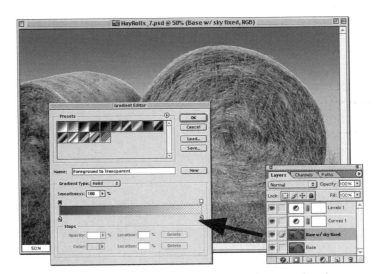

Figure 4.19 *A darker-blue gradient punches up the sky.*

Double-clicking the Lasso tool, I set the Feather for 5 pixels; this will hide the transitions. Next, while in the new Base layer, I hand draw an irregular selection with the Lasso around a good piece of grass. With that selection active, I make a new layer of it (Layer > New > Layer via Copy). Then, I just move the new grass over and cover up a bad spot. I go back to the Base and repeat the same procedure until I have all the bald spots covered with each grass piece on its own layer. The last step is to copy merge all the grass layers together. I rename this new layer Grass Repair, and delete all the individual grass layers (see Figure 4.20). The grass is fixed. There are lots of other flaws that I could repair, but I'll leave those for another time and move on.

Figure 4.20 *Feathered Lasso selections (one is barely visible at bottom) are used to create a merged, grass-repair layer.*

5. Save Master and Project-Specific Versions

At this point, after I've finished editing this master image in its layered, native-file format, it's time to safely store it away. When I'm ready to print, I'll open a copy, flatten to TIFF format, adjust the size and printing resolution, and sharpen. (All this is explained in Chapter 9.)

As I said, this was a whirlwind fix-it tour. Normally, I would have added a few more steps and taken a lot more time. In addition, it's only one version (a personal one at that) of an image-editing workflow; there are any number of ways to arrive at the same result. However, this hopefully gives you some idea of the versatility and power of digital-editing tools.

File Formats, Image Compression, and File Transport, Storage, and Archives

The last steps of image processing require an understanding of file formats and image compression before a final image can be printed, transported, or stored.

File Formats

Image files are stored, shipped, saved, and opened in specific formats. Depending on which platform you're on (PC or Mac) and which version of Photoshop or other major programs you have, there might be up to two-dozen file formats from which to choose. However, for most photographers and artists working with digital printing, there are only a few real choices.

Native Format

If you do a lot of work in Photoshop, the native format (PSD) is the one to use for preliminary work (CDR is CorelDRAW's native format; RIFF is Painter's). It saves all layers, channels, paths, and so on in the most flexible and efficient way. Although some printers may be able to receive data files in a native format, others may not. In addition, native files can get very unwieldy with all the layers and such. Final work destined for printing is usually saved to one of the other formats discussed in the following sections.

TIFF (.tif)

Tagged Image File Format (TIFF) is the standard image file format. Now, starting with Photoshop 6.0, TIFFs have most of the same layers, vector shapes, paths, and channels that exist in the native PSD format. What most people do is store the master, layered PSD file and make a flattened TIFF copy for sending to the printer (yours or anyone else's) or for importing into a page-layout program. TIFFs also compress very nicely and support color-management profiles. Macs and PCs each deal with TIFFs differently; if you're sending your file out for printing, make sure you find out which version they want.

EPS

EPS stands for Encapsulated PostScript, and while on the surface it may seem even better than TIFF because it supports both bitmapped and vector-based art, it's not the best choice for a lot of photographer-artists. As we've already learned, EPS requires a PostScript workflow, either in the form of a PostScript-enabled printer, a RIP, or through the PDF workaround. Graphic designers use EPS files all the time, but usually for importing vector art into page-layout programs that will ultimately be sent to a PostScript imagesetter. If you're placing bitmapped image files into QuarkXPress or InDesign, you're better off using TIFFs, which also process faster than EPS files.

Name that File: File Extensions and Platform Miscommunication

File extensions are those three- or four-digit characters after the dot on file names. The problem is this: Macs don't need them (and until OS X didn't use them at all), and PCs require them. This isn't an issue if you are staying in your own closed-loop world—your computer, your printer. However, as soon as you have to send a file to someone else—a professional printmaker or service bureau, for example—you have to make sure everyone is speaking the same language.

PC users won't be able to recognize a file without the correct file extension. In addition, Macophiles can have the same problem with a PC file depending on its type and name. Thus, the safest thing to do is to consistently name your files correctly right off the bat—eight characters or less before the dot, if possible; all lowercase; no weird characters; and no spaces.

PDF

A PDF (Portable Document Format) file is in reality a PostScript file that has already been pre-interpreted by a RIP. All the fonts and images have been converted to objects that can be seen by anyone with Acrobat Reader, which is free to all. PDF is gradually becoming the standard, transport file format for the commercial pre-press industry, but it can also be used for printing certain types of files if you don't have a PostScript interpreter (see the "PDF PostScript RIParound" technique described in Chapter 2).

To make a PDF, you'll need to use Adobe Acrobat or PDFWriter, if your software program includes it; some applications (such as InDesign) also create PDFs directly. If you're using Acrobat, its Distiller function acts like a PostScript RIP, converting an intermediate PostScript file into a PDF. This is one way to get around having to have a RIP or a PostScript printer if you're printing EPS elements to an inkjet from a page-layout program (again, for a visual example of this, see Figure 2.2 in Chapter 2). The other beauty of PDFs is that the file sizes are tiny when JPEGed or Zipped (see the "Image Compression" section). PDFs are bound to play a larger role in all forms of digital printing in the future.

There are also plenty of other file formats out there, but they're used mostly for specific purposes that usually have little applicability to the digital printing of high-quality bitmapped images. Examples include DCS, a version of EPS; PICT (Mac)/BMP (PC), mainly for internal Mac or PC use; GIF and PNG, primarily for Web compression; and PCX, for limited Windows use.

(For information about color models such as RGB and CMYK, see Chapter 5.)

EXIF

EXIF (Exhangeable Image File Format) is a new JPEG file standard that's based on Epson's P.I.M. idea (see Chapter 5 for more on this). EXIF is growing into a standard file format for digital cameras, and it embeds certain information—such as contrast, saturation, sharpness, and gain control—into the digital camera file used by the newer P.I.M.-enabled printers.

Image Compression

Compression is used primarily to shrink a file's size for transport or storage. With digital art files reaching into the hundreds of megabytes, this is sometimes a necessity, at least for transport. There is normally no reason to compress a file while you're working on it, but if you have to compress, it's critical to understand the difference between the two categories: *lossless* and *lossy*.

The lossless variety compresses without removing any color or pixel data from the file. Lossy removes data. (Obviously, lossless is the way to go whenever possible.) The following are the most common file-format, compression techniques:

LZW

LZW (stands for Lemple-Zif-Welch, in case you're wondering) is a lossless compression process. It's part of the TIFF format (GIF, too) and can be used whenever you're saving a file (it's one of the few TIFF options available prior to Photoshop 6 and 7). It doesn't compress as much as JPEG and is not supported by all output devices or outside service bureaus. Use it sparingly or not at all. Although a LZW-compressed TIFF file will take up about half as much room on your hard drive, keep in mind that it will take significantly longer to save and open the file when using this option.

ZIP (PC) and StuffIt (Mac)

ZIP/Stuffit is another lossless format and also one of the new TIFF options (ZIP) in Photoshop 6 and 7. This is a standard for transporting files (see the "Transporting" section for more). It works best with images containing large areas of a single color.

JPEG

JPEG is the standard lossy format for bitmapped images. You can easily adjust the amount of compression and, with it, the quality of the image. The more you compress, the worse the image gets, eventually showing visible artifacts and breaking up into small image pieces. Amazingly, and as my test in Figure 4.21 shows, even JPEGs set to "Low" can produce useable results, while the "0" (lowest) setting can reduce a file's size more than 94 percent (although you would rarely use this setting because of the poor quality). Keep in mind that JPEG compression (or any compression option except LZW) of TIFF files will make them unopenable to many programs, including older versions of Photoshop.

| TIFF, uncompressed, 680K | JPEG 12 Max., 244K | JPEG 6 Med., 88K | JPEG 3 Low., 60K | JPEG 0 Low, 40K |

Figure 4.21 *The same Royal Palm image fragment with different JPEG compressions. The starting point, a high-resolution TIFF, is at left. As you move to the right, the quality settings get progressively lower, and the file sizes shrink accordingly. It's only at the lowest setting ("0") that the image suffers dramatically.*

In addition, all layers are lost with JPEGs, and PDFs are typically compressed using JPEG (ZIP), although you don't have to use it. This is one reason PDF files are so small.

JPEG2000 is supposedly an improvement on the standard JPEG format, but it's been in the works since 1998, and as of this writing, has still not shown its face to the world.

open jpeg → immediately "SAVE AS" TIFF

CAUTION! *Avoid opening a JPEG file and resaving it in the JPEG format. Depending on the quality setting, you will lose data each time, and if you keep doing it, you could end up with a bowl of digital mush. The best thing to do is open a JPEG and immediately Save As to a TIFF or a native image-editing format.*

(See Chapter 11's "Printing Big!" section for more about using special software and methods for compression and scaling.)

File Transport, Storage, and Archives

The image files that photographers and artists create tend to be large. No, huge is a better word. I can still remember working with files in the late '80s that were in the 5–10 MB range. Those were big files then. Now, I regularly work with files that exceed 200 MB! Files become a problem when you have to take or send them somewhere, like to a printing service, or you want to store or archive them for the future.

Transporting

If you need to get an image file to someone, you really have only three choices: send it electronically (e-mail or FTP), drop it in the mail or call FedEx, or get in the car and take it yourself. If you're sending it electronically, you could use one of the lossless archiving utilities such as StuffIt (Mac) or ZipIt (PC); just make sure that the person on the other end has the same program, or he or she may not be able to open it.

If you're physically sending or taking your files, you have several options. Removable media disks are commonly used to move files around. Depending on the manufacturer and model, you can save up to 100 MB, 250 MB, or even 20 GB per disk. CD-Rs, CD-RWs (650 MB), and DVDs (4.7–9.4 GB) are another great way to transport files. However, if you're sending your files out to print service provider, make sure you talk to them first about acceptable file and transport formats (as well as resolution, color management profiles, and so on).

Storing

All the discussed methods also work for storing your in-progress as well as finished image files. You can either save files onto transportable media and store them somewhere safe, or you can buy auxiliary hard drives and/or tape backup systems to do the same thing. Many digital imagemakers are doing both: using hard drives for primary storage and removable disks like CDs and now DVDs as backups. With data storage space becoming less costly all the time, many power users are now moving to multiple hard drives in a RAID (Redundant Array of Inexpensive Disks) configuration to store their huge files.

Archiving: Managing Your Images

Sometimes, the biggest problem with archiving is not the storage space, but knowing where everything is. This is also called "asset management" or "image management," and there are lots of software products available to help you keep things straight.

For example, Extensis Portfolio (see Figure 4.22) creates a database of assets on your hard drive and helps you catalog and retrieve digital files including images, clip art, movies, audio, and more. You can create previews, digital watermarking, and customizable thumbnails and slide shows. Portfolio can track any image coming into the computer via several types of searching, and you can also access an image catalog from any application with only one keystroke.

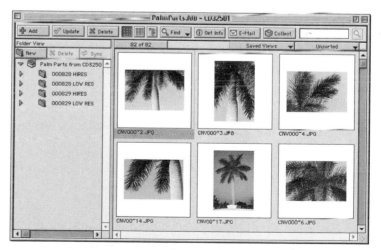

Figure 4.22 *Extensis Portfolio 6 for image management*

Canto Cumulus is another popular, digital asset manager. It differs from Extensis Portfolio in that it catalogs assets (images) based on where they're *from*, not where they reside on the hard drive. This allows you to keep track of images on outside CDs and other removable media. However, Cumulus does not dynamically update the locations of files when they're changed or moved, but it does include powerful search capabilities and multiple-size thumbnail previews.

Photoshop 7's new File Browser is another way to manage images. Although not as powerful as third-party asset-management software, it's easy to work with files directly in the program where you're likely to be using them. File Browser lets you view, sort, and process image files, and you can use it to rename, move, and rotate images.

For the newer Macs (OSX), there is also iPhoto, which is a combination image-importer, browser, and organizer. Currently available as a free download, iPhoto even lets you custom print or order your own rudimentary, coffee-table books (see Chapter 11).

Other lower-priced options for image management are these "picture viewers" or image browsers: ACDSee (ACD Systems), ThumbsPlus (Cerious Software), and IrfanView (shareware). All are PC-only.

■ ■ ■

To fully understand the digital printing process, you have to become an intimate friend of color. It's now time to tackle one of the most important and complex digital subjects of all.

Understanding and Managing Color

Color—and how it affects your printing—is another one of those mysterious, bottomless subject pits. Many people have a hard time wrapping their minds around digital color, so as I've done before, I'll break it down into bite-size pieces.

Color Basics

To understand color, we need a quick course in color theory.

What Is Color?

Color is what happens when our eyes and brains perceive light. Light is a form of electromagnetic energy composed of undulating waves that have peaks and valleys. The shorter the distance between the peaks, the shorter the wavelength and the higher the frequency. The longer the wavelength, the lower the frequency.

The frequency of light waves is measured in nanometers (nm), and the range of visible light extends from about 380–760 nm (see Figure 5.1). Even shorter wavelengths result in ultraviolet (UV) radiation, and that group of wavelengths, which is just over 760 nm, is called infrared.

The full range of visible light is called the visible spectrum, and it's white when all the wavelengths are represented. However, they're usually not all represented when we're talking about color.

Light, and therefore color, comes to photographer-artists working digitally in two different ways: reflective and transmissive. With reflected light, white light is reflected off objects that absorb some of its wavelengths and let others continue on. Our eyes and brains, through the magic of rods and cones, interpret those remaining wavelengths as color. In other words, the color of an image on a piece of paper is what's left over after the paper and the ink have absorbed or subtracted certain wavelengths (see

Figure 5.2). If green and red are absorbed, what we end up seeing is called blue, which is in the 400–500 nm range. If blue and red are absorbed, we see green. If we keep subtracting wavelengths by piling on more dyes or pigments, we end up with black (see Figure 5.3). This is called *subtractive color*, for obvious reasons. (See Chapter 8 for a more in-depth look at color and printing inks.)

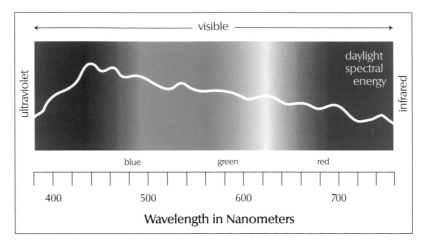

Figure 5.1 *An approximation of the spectral distribution of daylight*

The color resulting from transmissive light, like that coming from a computer monitor, is completely different. As with television screens, traditional cathode-ray-tube (CRT) monitors have "guns" that shoot electron beams toward the inside of the screen where they strike a phosphor coating. When a beam hits a red phosphor, it gets excited and emits light—light that looks red. The same thing happens with the green and blue phosphors. As the voltage of a gun changes, so does the intensity of the light. (Flat-panel, LCD monitors work differently by using filters to either block the light or allow it to pass. There are no electron guns; instead, tiny transistor switches—one each for red, green, and blue—sit in front of each screen spot and control the light through polarization.)

Corresponding to the binary data in the digital file, each pixel on a monitor screen is made up of combinations of red, green, and blue in varying intensities (256 levels in 8-bit mode). All the other secondary colors come from differing combinations and values of the three primary colors. As the intensities (brightness) of the

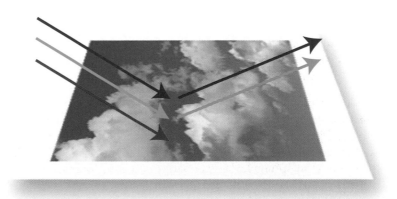

Figure 5.2 *When white light (left) strikes the print, the red is absorbed (subtracted) and the blue and green wavelengths are reflected back from the portion of the sky called cyan.*

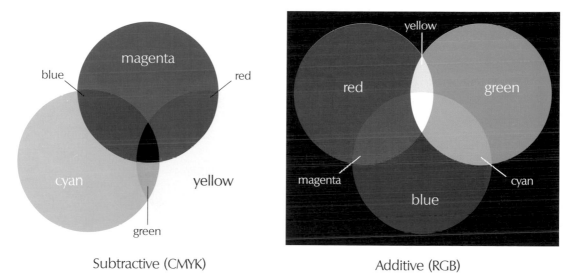

Subtractive (CMYK)   Additive (RGB)

Figure 5.3 *The subtractive primaries (left) and the additive primaries (right). Notice how the primary colors of one type of light become the secondaries of the other type where their primaries overlap.*

individual colored pixels increase, they get lighter. If all the colors are turned on to maximum strength, you end up with white. This is called *additive color* (see Figure 5.3).

One of the problems with color is that it's so subjective. Everybody's eyes and brains are different. For people all over the world to talk about color in the same way, a common language is needed to quantify and discuss it. In 1931, an international group called the Commission Internationale de L'Eclairage (CIE) met in England and developed a method to describe color for the standard observer. This effort resulted in the very powerful tool called color spaces.

Color Spaces

Color spaces (sometimes called color models, although they are technically different things) are crucial to working with and communicating about digital color. They exist to quantify it and to take it out of the subjective; color spaces give names and numbers to colors.

A color space is an abstract, three-dimensional range of colors. Photographer and ProfileCity co-founder Joseph Holmes describes it as something like a football standing on its end with white at the top and black at the bottom. A line drawn top to bottom through the center includes all the grays. The various hues of the visible spectrum wrap around the ball as the colors go from gray on the inside to their most colorful (saturated) on the outside.

Color consultant C. David Tobie uses the analogy of a tent. (I like to think of it as a circus tent because it's so full of bewildering mystery!) The three corners of the tent are attached to the ground with three tent pegs: red, green, and blue. How far you move the pegs out determines the size of the tent or color space. The tent is held up in the center by a pole, which is its gray axis. Raising or lowering the pole changes the gray balance and the *white point*, which is where the pole supports the top of the tent. Colors further away from the pole are more saturated; those that are closer are less saturated.

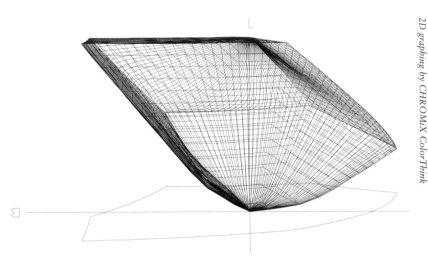

2D graphing by CHROMiX ColorThink

The color space for CMYK printing is distinct and different from the space for RGB monitors or from the scientific space of CIE LAB. One of the important, distinguishing characteristics of each color space is its *color gamut*, which defines the entire range of

Somewhere between a football and a tent, this is a monochrome 3-D representation of the ColorMatch RGB color space.

possible colors in that system (it can also apply to material and devices such as monitors and printers). The bigger or "wider" the gamut, the more colors available. Although most people believe that the gamut of RGB is larger than that of CMYK, color expert Steve Upton of CHROMiX

explains that that's a myth. "I usually describe them as different and use 'a circle drawn over a triangle so they both have portions outside the other' as a description." Figure 5.4 shows how some CMYK colors fall outside the RGB gamut, making them unviewable or "clipped." This is also called being "out-of-gamut," or in color-tent terms, outside the tent.

Here are the three most important color spaces:

LAB

The original CIE color space (XYZ) was adopted in 1931, and it identifies color coordinates in a three-dimensional curved space. It was adapted to become the familiar horseshoe-shaped CIE xyY Chromaticity Diagram (see Figure 5.5) for easier displaying in 2-D space. (*Chromaticity* refers to the

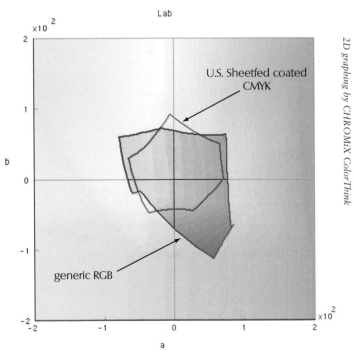

2D graphing by CHROMiX ColorThink

Figure 5.4 *The different gamuts of sample RGB and CMYK color spaces*

color properties of hue and saturation only.)

Between them, "x" and "y" define any color's *hue* and fullness of color or *saturation*. The "y" is a little hard to grasp because it runs perpendicular to the plane of view, and it indicates the lightness or *luminance* of the color. In this sense, the xy diagram is a horizontal section of the color tent.

Because of difficulties with non-uniform color spacing in the XYZ model, improvements were made, and in 1976, the CIE added the LUV and then the now-famous CIE LAB (or just "LAB," also written "Lab") color space. The type of LAB used in color conversions is ICC LAB, which defines three variables in 3-D space: L* (pronounced "L star"), a*, and b* (see Figure 5.6).

L* refers to lightness, ranging from 0 (dark) to 100 (light). a* refers to the red/green axis ranging from -128–127; positive numbers are reddish, and negative ones are greenish. b* refers to the yellow/blue axis also ranging from -128–127; positive numbers are yellowish; negative ones are bluish. Any particular color that you can see can be pinpointed by its three LAB coordinates. For example, a spot of blue sky could be identified as L* = 64, a* = -15, b* = -42. (If you want to get even more color geeky, you'll want to explore the concept of ΔE, spoken as "Delta-E," where each ΔE unit represents the just-noticeable difference between any two LAB colors.)

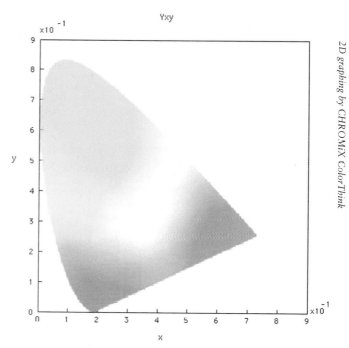

2D graphing by CHROMiX ColorThink

Figure 5.5 *The two-dimensional CIE xyY Chromaticity Diagram*

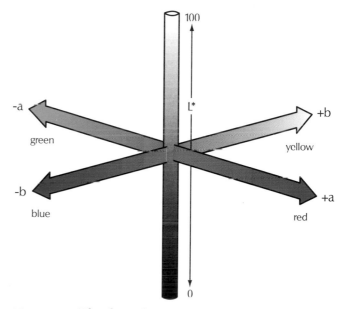

Figure 5.6 *The three dimensional ICC LAB color space*

The LAB color space most closely represents how humans see. It's the one that Photoshop uses for its mode changes. It's the one that color management systems (more details later) generally use as a reference space to relate their input and output behaviors. It's the largest of all the common color spaces, and it includes most of the colors in the RGB and CMYK gamuts. Best of all, LAB is not dependent on any particular device, ink, or process. It just *is*, offering universal color definitions.

Admittedly, it's a little hard to understand LAB, which is why you may not be spending much time there except for some specialized purposes. (It's sometimes used for sharpening images in the Lightness channel.)

RGB

RGB is the dominant color space for digital artists. It's based not only on the viewable colors on a television screen or computer monitor, but also on the fact that red, green, and blue form the basis of the *tristimulas* model of color perception, which scientists have now discovered corresponds to how our nervous systems perceive color.

RGB is the default space for most digital cameras and scanners (*all* scanners scan in RGB; if you're getting CMYK scans, the scanner operator or the software is converting the data), and it's the preferred space for film recorders, digital photoprint, and most desktop inkjets. That last one may surprise you, but even though inkjets must print real inks on real paper in CMYK fashion, they prefer RGB files, and some people actually call them "RGB devices." I wouldn't go that far, but it is true that EPSON printers, for example, are RGB-based, and if you send CMYK information to an EPSON through its normal printer driver, it will first convert the data to RGB and then back again to CMYK for printing! (The use of a CMYK RIP will bypass this workflow.)

RGB is device-*dependent*, which means that the color you end up with depends on the device you send it to or the RGB space you define it in. This is what I call "The Circuit City Phenomenon." Go into any appliance store such as Sears or Circuit City, and pay a visit to the television

department. Stand there in front of the wall of TVs for a moment, and you will instantly understand the problems of working with color. Even though every TV may be set to the same channel, all the screens look different! The same thing happens with digital devices. Some have large color gamuts, and some don't. Some clip colors, and some don't. Fortunately, advanced image editors such as Photoshop help you control some of these uncertainties.

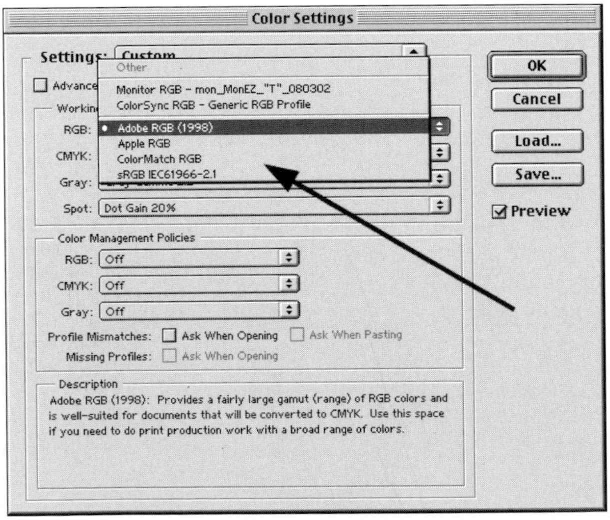

RGB comes in several subvarieties called RGB *working spaces* in Photoshop, which currently recommends only four of them (see Figure 5.7). A working space acts like a color profile either for

Figure 5.7 *The four currently recommended RGB working spaces in Photoshop (version 7.0)*

new documents and their associated color modes or for untagged documents. Although all RGB files are generically called "RGB," when you're actually working on images in Photoshop, you have the option of picking different working spaces for them (starting with Photoshop 6, you no longer have to choose only one). Leaving out the more obscure, from largest gamut to smallest, the main RGB working spaces are these: *Adobe RGB (1998)*, *ColorMatch RGB*, *AppleRGB*, and *sRGB*.

Adobe RGB (1998)

This the largest of the major RGB color working spaces and a good choice for digital artists. It pretty much covers the gamut range of the common CMYK devices, including inkjets, film recorders, and digital photoprinters. You'll rarely be out of gamut with Adobe RGB, yet it's not as unwieldy as the larger LAB space. This working space used to be called SMPTE-240M in Photoshop version 5.0.

ColorMatch RGB

Originally designed for Radius PressView monitors, this is another good working space for the photographer-artist. The color gamut is smaller than for Adobe RGB but larger than the other working spaces in this list. ColorMatch RGB is well accepted by the color industry, so most people know how to handle it. It has been considered the best choice if you plan to do a lot of CMYK commercial printing, although Adobe RGB is gaining ground for this usage.

AppleRGB

This is a holdover from the old Apple 13" Trinitron monitor days (I still have one!). It's gamut is only slightly larger than sRGB. It's not recommended for print, and its other quirk is a very blue white point.

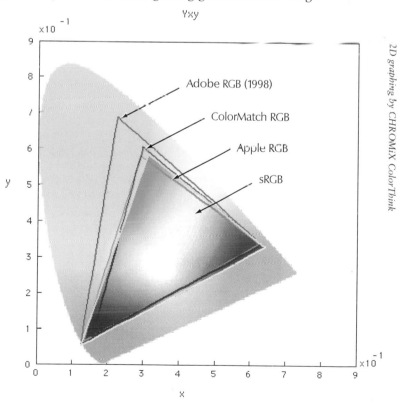

The relative gamuts of the four, major RGB working spaces

sRGB

Even though this is the default working-space setting for Photoshop 6 and 7 and other hardware and software manufacturers, including those making digital cameras, this is the last choice for a color working space. It's mainly for people working with Web images, and it should be avoided by those hoping to output their files to the broadest range of print devices. The color gamut is small, and many deep, saturated colors, especially greens and blues, will be clipped or discarded.

CMYK

CMYK is another device-dependent color space. CMYK is short for Cyan, Magenta, Yellow, and Black ("K"), which are the four, subtractive, process printing colors. Why four instead of three? In theory, CMY (another tristimulus combination) should be enough to make all the colors, but real-world inks aren't pure, and the extra black component is needed to add the snap or depth to the printed image and to solve other print-specific problems.

As Steve Upton points out, all of Photoshop's standard, RGB working spaces will clip 100 percent of press yellow. In addition, most of them will clip the cyans and greens a lot, and sometimes the magentas as well.

Many photographer-artists don't pay enough attention to CMYK, but it's important, especially when you realize that much digital printing is ultimately CMYK-based. In fact, *all* inkjet printers print in CMYK (or CcMmYK, or CMYKOG, or whatever variant). An RGB-to-CMYK conversion is being done somewhere along the line, so it can't hurt to know something about CMYK. This is especially true if you're using a digital, fine-art print service provider. As Diane Trenary, of Renaissance Art Editions in West Palm Beach, Florida, says, "The more you can visually control the results on the front end—on your computer screen—the more satisfied you're going to be on the back end when the piece is printed." By using Photoshop's CMYK preview functions in combination with ICC profiles set up for the type of printing anticipated, you can get a fairly good monitor representation of how things will look in CMYK, without permanently committing yourself to that printing space. This keeps you from being surprised at the final printing step, and it lets you make appropriate image adjustments in advance.

Many color-managed, digital-printing service providers will give you an ICC output profile so that you can preview your image correctly onscreen (see more about ICC profiles later in the chapter). Photoshop also contains some excellent CMYK Press profiles.

CMYK is also the de facto standard of the commercial printing industry, so you will undoubtedly run into CMYK for that reason, too. Anytime you want to create an advertisement, a brochure, or any project that will end up being printed on a commercial press, you (or someone else) will need to convert your images to CMYK.

In Which Color Space Should You Work?

There are many theories about this. Keeping in mind that you'll need to come up with your own answers depending on your needs and goals, here are some recommendations:

1. In general, work and save your master files in one of the larger RGB spaces. You can always *repurpose* a file to a different color space, such as CMYK, as needed.

2. For a specific, all-purpose working space, choose either Adobe RGB or ColorMatch RGB. Experiment with other boutique working spaces if you want, but if you're unsure, stick with the major ones.

3. If you have very specific needs that only involve CMYK printing, and you want tight control of your printing colors, it might be advantageous to work in CMYK. However, if you have *any* inkling of reaching out to other service providers or of other uses for your images, work in the larger RGB spaces. (If you come from an offset printing background as I did, you might feel more comfortable working with CMYK numbers, but my advice is to transition to RGB as quickly as possible.)

4. The same advice goes for sRGB. If you're working exclusively for Web output, sRGB might make sense, but then you wouldn't be reading this book, would you? If there's any possibility of going to print, pick one of the other working spaces.

Tape the following to your monitor until you have it memorized:

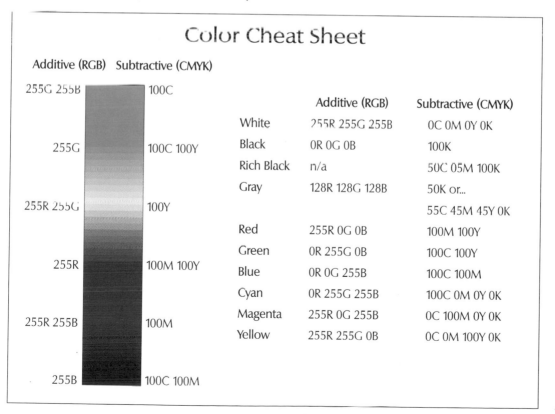

Color Cheat Sheet

Additive (RGB) Subtractive (CMYK)

	Additive (RGB)	Subtractive (CMYK)
White	255R 255G 255B	0C 0M 0Y 0K
Black	0R 0G 0B	100K
Rich Black	n/a	50C 05M 100K
Gray	128R 128G 128B	50K or...
		55C 45M 45Y 0K
Red	255R 0G 0B	100M 100Y
Green	0R 255G 0B	100C 100Y
Blue	0R 0G 255B	100C 100M
Cyan	0R 255G 255B	100C 0M 0Y 0K
Magenta	255R 0G 255B	0C 100M 0Y 0K
Yellow	255R 255G 0B	0C 0M 100Y 0K

255G 255B — 100C
255G — 100C 100Y
255R 255G — 100Y
255R — 100M 100Y
255R 255B — 100M
255B — 100C 100M

Converting from One Space to Another

Chances are, you will have to convert from one color space to another at some point. There are some things to keep in mind when doing so:

1. Convert as few times as possible. Converting color spaces permanently alters a file's color information. Only do it if and when you have to. When you convert from RGB to CMYK, for example, you've forever lost the richer information of RGB—and you can't get it back!

2. If you're using a fine-art, print-service provider that needs to end up with CMYK, have *them* make the RGB-to-CMYK conversion; they'll have more control over the process. Do all your image editing in RGB but use their provided ICC profile to preview on your monitor how it's going to look in CMYK.

3. On the other hand, if you're using page-layout programs to create ads, brochures, and so on for commercial offset printing, do the RGB-to-CMYK conversion yourself (most commercial printers hate receiving RGB files). When in doubt, and if a commercial printer can't or won't give you an ICC profile (and many won't), you can use Photoshop's built-in CMYK profiles, especially the SWOP-standard ones, to get you in the ballpark.

What Is Color Management and Do You Need It?

Color management is one of those terms like health maintenance. Everyone has a vague idea of what it is, and most admit it's important, but few actually understand it.

The crux of the problem is this:

1. Human eyes can see more colors than can be reproduced by digital devices—scanners, cameras, monitors, or printers.

2. The color gamuts of all scanners, cameras, monitors, and printers are different. The color you see depends on the device that's producing it. Monitors can display more colors than can be printed; some printing colors cannot be seen on a monitor.

3. As you move down the art production line from input to onscreen display to final print, the color gamut shrinks (you lose colors).

4. Monitors and printers see color in completely different ways. Monitors use the additive color system; printers use the subtractive. Colors printed on paper look dull and dreary compared to their brighter and more energetic monitor counterparts.

The result of this quadruple threat is that images don't always end up the way you imagine them in your mind or how you see them on the monitor.

The goal, then, behind managing your color is simple enough—WYSIWYP or What You See Is What You Print. Yes, the sky is blue and the grass is green, but is it the blue and the green you intended? Color management is also about detail. For the green grass to show the necessary detail, you need to have lots of accurate shades of green.

Color management in its most generic and simplistic form merely means rendering color across different devices—digicams, scanners, monitors, print devices—in a predictable, repeatable way.

Sometimes you're lucky. You buy a new inkjet printer, you hook it up, and your prints come out looking gorgeous right off, and they continue to do so forever. Yeah, right. The reality is this: An image can pass through many hands and be affected by many variables on its way to final output. These variables include digital cameras, scanners, computer hardware, operating systems, image-editing software, the viewing environment, monitors, and printer software. At any one of those checkpoints, an image can be compromised. Even at the last step of printing, you could be dealing with different inks, paper, and even different printing technologies. A lot can go wrong on an image's path to glory, and, unfortunately, it usually does.

Enter *color management systems* (CMS). A CMS is a software solution to the problems facing all digital imagers. It's a way to smooth out the differences among devices and processes to ensure consistent color all along the art production chain.

Some claim that there's a lot of fuss about nothing here (see "Don't Need No Stinkin' CMS"). All you have to do, they say, is use your experience with image file information plus monitor and printer settings, and simply get familiar with how color A on the monitor relates to color A on the printed piece. If it's different, you either fiddle with your monitor settings or tweak the image file itself until you get a good monitor-to-print match (this is called "reverse proofing").

Don't Need No Stinkin' CMS

Not everyone believes in color management. Color authority Dan Margulis is famous for not toeing the color management line. As he explains, "Someone with a good knowledge of color correction is helped by an accurate monitor display, but it isn't absolutely necessary. During the years I've been teaching my small group courses, four color-blind men have taken the course and have done well, getting better results than some professional photographers who refused to work by the numbers." ("Working by the numbers" means adjusting an image by paying close attention to the actual RGB or CMYK values in Photoshop's Info palette.) In Margulis' advanced classes, he makes the students work part of the time on black-and-white screens just to demonstrate that they have the ability to do so.

Artist Ileana is another nonbeliever. Although she uses Photoshop's built in monitor calibration tools, that's as far as she'll go. Over the years, she has developed her own digital color palette where "this color" on the monitor is known to produce "that color" on a wide-format HP inkjet and on her own EPSON printer. When unexpected results emerge from this process, she will modify the colors in the image (and on the monitor) so that they produce the desired printed color.

Both Margulis and Ileana represent two types of people who may not need third-party color management: those who are very experienced with Photoshop and those who work within a tightly controlled workflow.

There are several problems with this approach. First, it requires a closed-loop system: the same person, the same monitor, the same print device, the same inks, the same paper, the same everything. As soon as you involve other people or other systems (such as with an outside print provider) that aren't identical to yours (and they won't be), your control and predictability is out the window. Second, it takes a lot of time and experience to work "by the numbers" to match digital files to prints. And finally, you can't "soft proof" (accurately preview on the screen) an RGB image without correct calibration and characterization profiles (this has become possible only since Photoshop 6.0).

Welcome to ICC Color Management

In 1993, eight industry vendors, including Adobe Systems, Eastman Kodak, Apple Computer, and Microsoft, formed the International Color Consortium (ICC). Their goal was to create and encourage the use of an open, cross-platform color-management system to make consistent color reproduction a reality. The ICC Color Management System comprises three components:

1. A *device-independent color space*, also known as the *reference color space*: CIE's XYZ and LAB are the two related color spaces chosen by the ICC. XYZ is for monitors, and LAB is for print devices. To get consistent color across different devices, a *transform* (a fancy word for a mathematical process) is needed to convert the colors from one device to the other. It's all about source and destination, such as from monitor to printer. However, what actually happens is that the transformation takes place through an intermediary color space or PCS (profile connection space). That's the role of the CIE color model.

2. *Device profiles* that characterize each device: An ICC device profile—note that the Mac world calls them ICC profiles, and the PC world calls them ICM, but they're really the same thing—is a digital data file that describes a device's capabilities and limitations. It's like an equivalence dictionary. If you characterize (or profile) any input, display, or output device by relating its specific color space values to a known reference space, then any image file moving from one profiled device to another can be rendered so that the image looks the same (has the same values). This can apply to scanners scanning images, monitors displaying images, and printers printing images, and there are ICC profiles for each situation. The profile is actually a fingerprint of the device or process, and it helps each new device in the chain understand what that image is supposed to look like—objectively. In a correctly color-managed system, the same image as viewed through an ICC-savvy application and displayed on two vastly different but ICC-aware monitors will look the same! If you've been around computers for a while, you know that this is an amazing thing, and ICC profiling is an incredibly powerful tool for anyone working digitally.

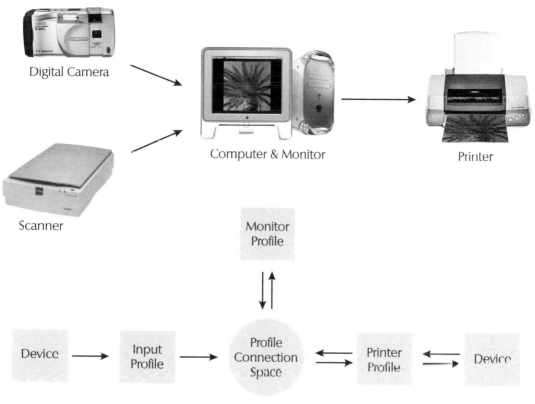

The ICC CMS workflow

3. A *Color Management Module* (CMM) that interprets the device profiles and maps one color gamut to another: CMMs are also called *color engines*, and they use device profiles and *rendering intents* (see "What Is Your Intent?") to map any out-of-gamut colors into a reproducible range of colors by the next device. (As you move down the production line from capture to display to print, the color gamut gets smaller and smaller.)

Apple uses ColorSync as its color architecture, whereas Microsoft uses the comparable Image Color Matching (ICM 2). Both ColorSync and ICM 2 rely on CMMs and ICC-standard device profiles that contain information about how to convert colors from one color space and color gamut into another. Photoshop can use ColorSync or ICM 2 on each platform but by default uses the built-in Adobe ACE color engine for its CMM. This makes highly consistent cross-platform color possible.

What Is Your Intent?

Rendering intents are the guidelines or the rules that color engines follow to handle their color gamut transformations or "mapping." Here are the official ICC definitions with my comments following:

- **Perceptual:** The full gamut of the image is compressed or expanded to fill the gamut of the destination device. Gray balance is preserved but colorimetric (measured color) accuracy might not be. This preserves the visual relationship of all the colors as a single unit. Everything stays relatively the same (including in-gamut colors), but not absolutely the same, so it's a good choice if you've got a lot of out-of-gamut colors.

- **Relative Colorimetric:** The white point (the lightest area) of the actual medium is mapped to the white point of the reference medium. The colors map accordingly. This one changes only the colors that are out-of-gamut, which will by necessity be compressed. This is useful when proofing a commercial printing press on an inkjet printer.

- **Absolute Colorimetric:** The white point of the source profile maps to the white point of the reference illuminant. The colors map accordingly. This allows a proof of dull, gray newsprint to be made on bright white proofing stock. Otherwise, AbCol is just the same as RelCol.

- **Saturation:** The saturation of the pixels in the image is preserved, perhaps at the expense of accuracy in hue and lightness. This is typically used for business-type graphics where vividness is the most important thing; color accuracy takes a back seat. It's not normally recommended, although after Steve Upton suggested giving it a try when I wasn't happy with a profile's saturation, I did and found that certain images gained more punch this way.

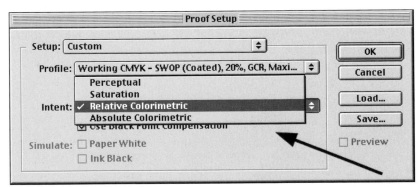

Any of the four ICC rendering intents can be selected in Photoshop.

Instead of using your eyes and brain, which are easily fooled, you should use a color management system that utilizes cold, hard, unbiased numbers. A true CMS follows these steps:

1. Transforms display RGB values to device-independent values (CIE XYZ) using information from the monitor's ICC device profile.

2. Transforms the intermediary CIE display values to CMYK (or its variations) values using information from the printer's ICC device profile(s).

3. Evaluates the color gamut of the source and compares it with the destination and maps the colors according to the chosen rendering intent.

Sounds complicated, yes, but color management systems can handle this and more. A CMS helps you calibrate, characterize, and finally print your images accurately and predictably. It's more than WYSIWYP, it's WYSIWYPET—What You See Is What You Print. Every Time. At least, that's the theory.

To utilize a CMS, you also need to have an ICC-savvy image-creation or image-editing software program. Photoshop is the ultimate ICC-aware software because Adobe, its maker, is a founding member of the ICC. (Adobe Photoshop LE is not ICC-aware, but Photoshop Elements is in a limited way.) Painter, CorelDRAW, PhotoImpact, and Paint Shop Pro are also ICC-aware to varying degrees. You also need an ICC-friendly operating system; with the exception of Windows NT, virtually all modern ones are ICC-friendly.

Assuming that you now believe in color management, let's see how it actually works with our two main areas of device concern—monitors and printers.

Monitor Matching

Good monitor-to-print coordination starts with two related but different processes: *calibration* and *characterization* (which leads to *profiling*). The point of monitor calibration is to bring the screen back to a group of standard settings for *white point* (color temperature of the whitest white), *gamma* (brightness of the midtones), and *black point* (the darkest black the monitor can display). When you calibrate a monitor, you actually change its settings and its behavior, and those new settings are in effect every time you start up the computer. This, in turn, affects how you view and correct your images. If, for example, your monitor is set too bright, then your prints may end up too dark because you erroneously tried to darken them onscreen to look better. That's why monitor calibration is so important.

Monitor characterization and profiling, on the other hand, measure and describe the personality of *that* particular monitor. Profiling doesn't actually change anything; it just keeps track of how the monitor is set up. You calibrate before you profile, although in many instances, both calibration and profiling occur at roughly the same time, especially if you're using third-party software packages.

Monitors should be calibrated and profiled regularly; weekly is a good target. As Pennsylvania digital printmaker Jim Davis explains it, "In the Navy, we had a program called Preventive Maintenance. I take the same basic attitude about monitor calibration. First thing Monday morning, calibrate your monitor. It takes 10 minutes, and then you are set for the week."

A Room with a View?

Color is subjective to start with, and if you're going to be viewing it and making decisions about its rightness or wrongness, you need to reduce the variables in your viewing environment. Here are some tips:

■ Use (or create) a neutral gray for your monitor's desktop color. Extraneous colors will alter your perception of the colors of the image on which you're working.

■ Wear neutral-colored clothes when color correcting an image onscreen. This is not as silly as it sounds. Hard-core digitalists have been known to wear only black turtlenecks and remove all jewelry to make sure the monitor is not reflecting back unwanted colors.

■ Pay attention to everything behind you that can contaminate the image on the screen—no bright lights and no colorful posters of Jamaica.

■ If you just can't control the light in a room, at least make a hood for the monitor to shield it from distracting light and shadows. Black Foam Core material available at any art supply store works great.

■ Make the overall ambient light in the room dim and low. Use rheostats on light fixtures if possible, and adjustable shades or blinds over windows. In fact, the perfect room for viewing images is windowless and painted completely gray. However, that's too depressing for most! If you can't darken your room, consider using an LCD monitor, as they offer a brighter display and can be used effectively with higher levels of ambient lighting.

■ If possible, use a graphics-standard viewing booth and/or lightbox for viewing and evaluating prints. These devices illuminate at an industry standard 5000° Kelvin (also called D5000 or just D50). An excellent viewing booth is the variable-light GTI Soft-View (see Figure 5.8). It provides both transparency viewing (*luminance*) and reflection-copy viewing (*illuminance*) in the same unit, and both can be dimmed or brightened to match the light intensity of the booth to the monitor. It includes viewing masks and also has a solid-state monitor/memory system that records the accumulated lamp life and tells you when it's time to replace them.

■ If a viewing booth is out of the question for evaluating prints, at least try to think about and carefully select the artificial lights for the room. Incandescent tungsten light (regular light bulbs) is the worst choice. It's too heavy on the yellow-orange-red end of the color spectrum. Regular fluorescent tubes ("cool whites") are better, but they have their own quirks, like having spectral spikes in the green and blue ranges and changing color as they warm up and also as they age. A variation is to use "deluxe daylight" or "natural light" fluorescent lamps, such as GE's Chroma 50 or Ott-Lite's SuperD5000, that bring you closer to industry standards. Quartz or tungsten halogen lamps are whiter and preferred by some. (See more about displaying prints and the problem of *metamerism* in later chapters.)

■ Instead of (or in addition to) the standard light of a viewing booth, some prefer to aim for the specific light of the final display environment. Creating prints for gallery display? Consider having a "gallery wall" lit with quartz halogen. Know your prints are heading for an office environment? Set up a fluorescent area for print evaluation.

■ As a last resort for print viewing, find a room with a window (keeping in mind that north daylight contains more blue), and using indirect, midday daylight (no direct sun!), view your print and mark it up with comments and instructions to yourself. Take that back to your monitor and make the changes indicated. Repeat as needed. The obvious problem with this technique is this: it doesn't work at night!

Courtesy of GTI Graphic Technology, Inc.

Figure 5.8 *GTI's Soft-View combination transparency/print viewer at work (on left). Both sets of lights can be independently dimmed to match monitor luminance.*

There are two basic ways to calibrate and profile a monitor: visually, using software alone, or automatically with a measuring tool on either a noncalibrator ("dumb") monitor or on a calibrator ("smart") monitor.

A smart monitor includes its own measuring device, called a colorimeter, that's attached to the screen and wired back into the computer's processor. The instant feedback from the *colorimeter* allows the system to adjust each individual RGB gun as part of the calibration process. The advantage of this system is that color management is automatic; the RGB guns are adjusted for you. The only disadvantage to such a system is the higher cost.

Dumb (noncalibrator) monitors are calibrated through the computer's video board or card and the front panel controls. The card's lookup table (LUT) is altered, which changes the monitor settings. Noncalibrator monitors, which are what most people use, are perfectly capable (especially with third-party help) of being calibrated. The only downside is that because some data has been clipped by the video card, you may see fewer available color values, depending on how far you stray from the monitor's native settings. Some software/hardware packages can compensate for this loss by allowing the user to adjust the color guns through the front panel controls, offering the same level of control as smart monitors at a lower cost.

So What's the Standard?

If monitors should be regularly calibrated to a known standard, the next question is this: To what standard? Although the entire color-viewing industry is based around a white point of D50 (5000K), many digital workers have shifted their monitors to D65, a much cooler color. Although a lot of this is personal preference and also dependent on the monitor and room brightness levels, D50 is too yellow to my eye, and D65 seems to match a D50 viewing light more closely, as strange as that may sound.

Eyeballing It

Every book or article about monitor calibration describes the use of either the Adobe Gamma utility (PC and Mac) or the Apple Monitor Control Panel Calibrator (Mac) for monitor calibrating. Adobe Gamma (not to be confused with the same term for monitor midtone brightness) is a part of Photoshop (other image-editing and profile-building programs have their own versions of this), and it's a straight-forward, wizard-like, visual calibration process, so I'm not going to walk you through it. After a series of steps that include adjusting the monitor for white point, contrast and brightness, and phosphor RGB output levels, you end up with a monitor profile. It's this type of device profile that Photoshop and other ICC-savvy applications must have to display colors correctly on screen.

The main reason I'm giving Adobe Gamma (or similar visual procedures) scant mention is because I don't think it's the best way of calibrating a monitor. It's very dependent on the viewing environment and is easily thrown out of whack because of that. Plus, many people have a hard time evaluating and comparing colors, and that's partly on what these built-in software calibrators rely.

To be sure, eyeballing it is better than no calibration at all, but if you have the option, go with a third-party, instrument-based calibration/profiling system.

Using a Measuring Device

This is the next level of monitor calibration and profiling because it's based on real-world measurements, not just your visual opinion about how good your monitor's display looks.

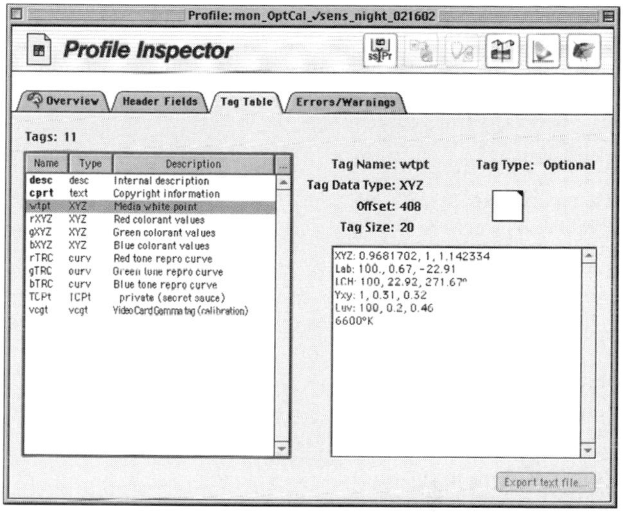

Hardware-based, profile-generating programs do two things for monitor color: (1) calibrate your monitor by automatically measuring test patches and adjusting a combination of the RGB guns and the video board, and (2) create a monitor ICC/ICM profile that

Figure 5.9 *An inside peek at a monitor profile's tags as viewed in the CHROMiX Profile Inspector*

your editing software refers to when displaying images. An ICC *display profile* contains a small group of numerical values in table form for the monitor's white point, gamma, black point, and the balance of the RGB primaries, as well as a set of curves that are downloaded to the video card to adjust the color channels (see Figure 5.9). When a display or monitor profile is correctly stored on your system, any ICC-aware application can use the profile to tweak the onscreen display and make it more objectively accurate. If you also have a printer profile (see the "Printer Profiling" section), that profile can be added to the mix to adjust the display.

What About Input Profiles?

You'll notice that I'm not saying much about input profiles for digicams and scanners. This is officially part of the ICC color management scheme, and it involves scanning a premeasured target and then constructing a profile based on the RGB value differences. In reality, many people don't profile their inputs. The primary reason is that device characterization requires that all variables remain constant. With digital cameras, for example, that means the light cannot change. Clearly, this will never happen except in a controlled, studio environment. With scanners, it means that the settings must always be the same, which is not what most people do with scanners; they're always fiddling with the software to get the best scan they can, as they should.

However, with that said, more and more scanners are supporting proper profiling, and this can save you a lot time in profile tweaking. Thus, if you have a very controlled, consistent workflow with either a scanner, digital camera, or a scanning back, then, yes, you can definitely benefit from an input profile that is passed along with the image. Photographer-artists, however, who don't fall into this category are probably better off learning how to capture a full range of values with neutral graytones and then bringing that image file into a CMS from that point on.

Where is this profile? For OS 9.x Macs, profiles are stored in the ColorSync Profiles folder (System Folder > Preferences > ColorSync Profiles) or located in the ColorSync Profiles folder in the Library folder under OS X. On a PC, the location varies with the operating system: Windows 98 is Windows\System\Color; Windows 2000/ME is Winnt\System32\Spool\Drivers\Color; and Windows XP is Windows\System32\Spool\Drivers\Color.

Now that we know what display profiles are, let's see how they're created with measuring-device systems. Because profiling is such a hot topic, there are lots of companies competing for your color management dollars. Consequently, photographer-artists now working digitally have many more options for hardware-based calibration and profiling systems than ever before. Here are the most popular, costing anywhere from a couple hundred dollars to a few thousand dollars:

MonacoEZcolor 2

MonacoEZcolor 2 is a basic-level software system for creating monitor profiles, input profiles, and printer profiles. It also includes an editing function for tweaking profiles. The ColorWorks utility (included) is an application for editing and printing images if you don't want to use an ICC-savvy, image-editing program.

Monitor profiling can be done visually with onscreen sliders or with the optional MonacoSENSOR, which is a small hardware device (colorimeter) that attaches to your CRT monitor with suction cups (see Figure 5.10). The software displays a series of RGB and neutral color patches on the screen for the sensor to measure. The color patches that are read electronically and interpreted then allow the program to calibrate the monitor and automatically build a monitor profile. EZcolor 2 does not calibrate LCD displays.

Monaco's interface and wizard-like process is clear and very easy to follow. It comes bundled with the sensor or without it.

Monaco has two other more sophisticated (and more expensive) color management options. *MonacoPROOF* is their "advanced" solution; it does everything EZcolor 2 does but adds more output profile options. *MonacoPROFILER* is the professional version. It does even more and adds flat-panel (LCD) display support. Each of these packages also builds printer profiles, which are described later in the chapter.

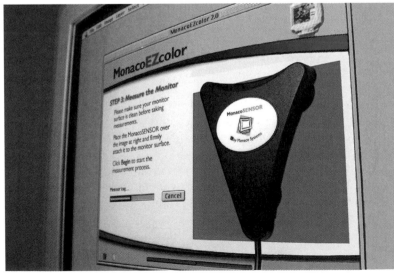

Courtesy of Monaco Systems, Inc.

Figure 5.10 *The colorimeter automatically measures color patches as part of Monaco's display profiling process.*

ColorVision Spyder with PhotoCAL

Pantone ColorVision also makes a suite of color management solutions. Its entry-level system for monitor calibration is Spyder with PhotoCAL. The kit includes a suction-cup colorimeter similar to Monaco's, but it allows both CRT and LCD calibration and the PhotoCAL software on CD.

The PhotoCAL monitor calibration process works through your monitor's control panel, and it's very similar to the Monaco system with a couple of exceptions: (1) There is no visual calibration option, and (2) there's an added step of identifying whether you have separate RGB controls and allowing gun correction if you do.

The next step up for ColorVision monitor calibration is the *Spyder with OptiCAL* version (see Figure 5.11). You can adjust more calibration parameters and also calibrate multiple monitors. There are more targets, a curve adjustment, and special targets for analyzing focus and geometry.

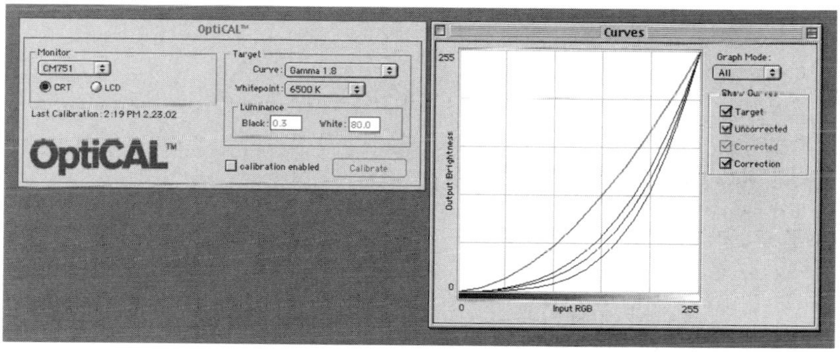

Figure 5.11 *The curves adjustment on ColorVision's OptiCAL monitor calibration solution*

Other monitor-calibration systems include the following:

- **ITEC ColorBlind Prove it!:** Besides offering both visual or instrument calibration options and LCD support, Prove it! follows an iterative (back-and-forth) process; there are lots of steps for fine-tuning gray balance and other monitor parameters, and the software converts your desktop to gray to help color evaluation. There's even a last step of inspecting and editing the profile with curves adjustments.

- **GretagMacbeth ProfileMaker and Eye-One:** *ProfileMaker Professional* is a modular software system for building ICC profiles for all types of input and output devices including monitors, scanners, and printers (see the "Printer Profiling" section). The MeasureTool module allows you to calibrate and profile monitors working with a variety of spectrophotometers; both the Eye-One Pro and the Spectrolino can profile flat-panel and CRT displays. The *Eye-One* system can also build ICC profiles for many input and output devices. Eye-One can be purchased as a Monitor-only device (measuring in transmissive mode) or as an Eye-One Pro device that measures in reflective mode in addition to transmissive. Both (Monitor or Pro) come with Eye-One Match Monitor software for building ICC profiles.

- **ProfileCity ICC Display:** This is a software package for automated calibration and display profiling. The full, bundled version comes with a Chroma 4 colorimeter for CRT calibration; the basic version supports numerous measurement devices. It's simple to use with one-button display profiling.

Spectrophotometers vs. Colorimeters

Instrument-based color management requires a sophisticated color-measurement instrument, and there are two types: *colorimeters* and *spectrophotometers*.

Colorimeters measure light in a few spectral bands with filters and assumptions. They're perfectly adequate for monitor profiling, and they're sometimes bundled with basic-level, profile-building software.

Spectrophotometers, also called "spectros," measure the light spectrum in more detail (36 bands in the GretagMacbeth instruments), and they can detect other problems such as the presence of UV brighteners, metamerism, and other things. Either handheld or adaptable to mounting tables or with suction cups, spectrophotometers can measure reflective prints, and in some cases, monitor displays and transmissive film. They are the color-measuring device of choice for professional profile-generating software and for custom, printer-profile builders. Popular spectrophotometer examples are GretagMacbeth's Eye-One Pro and Spectrolino, and X-Rite's DTP41. They're much more expensive than colorimeters, typically costing thousands instead of hundreds of dollars.

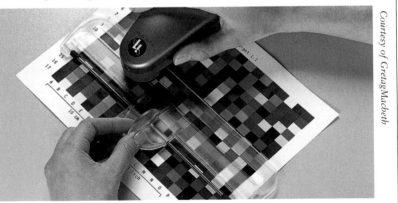

Courtesy of GretagMacbeth

GretagMacbeth's Eye-One Pro spectrophotometer

Printer Profiling

Characterizing (profiling) printers works differently. In a color-managed workflow, this is where *output device* or *printer profiles* (sometimes called *destination profiles*) come into play. However, with printers, you're dealing with an even wider number and range of variables than with monitors. Fortunately, all these variables are taken into account by printing and measuring targets from the device and creating the profiles from those measurements.

Technically, and with another thanks to Steve Upton, here's what happens (skip this if you're already getting bleary-eyed): A target is measured resulting in LAB values. A CMYK>LAB lookup table (LUT) is then calculated, and a LAB>CMYK table is deduced from those values. The only actual color values in the process are the measured LAB values. Many think there is a set of LAB values that begins the process and the resulting measurements are compared to these values, but that's not true—nor is it necessary. Regardless of the original values in the image file, what matters is the formulation for a particular color (LAB>CMYK) or the appearance of a particular formulation (CMYK>LAB).

In any case, you end up with an ICC printer profile that is, as with a display profile, a data file that is organized into header fields and tag tables (see Figure 5.12). The most important things are the lookup tables, which are long lists of numbers that allow the CMM to establish color-equivalence values.

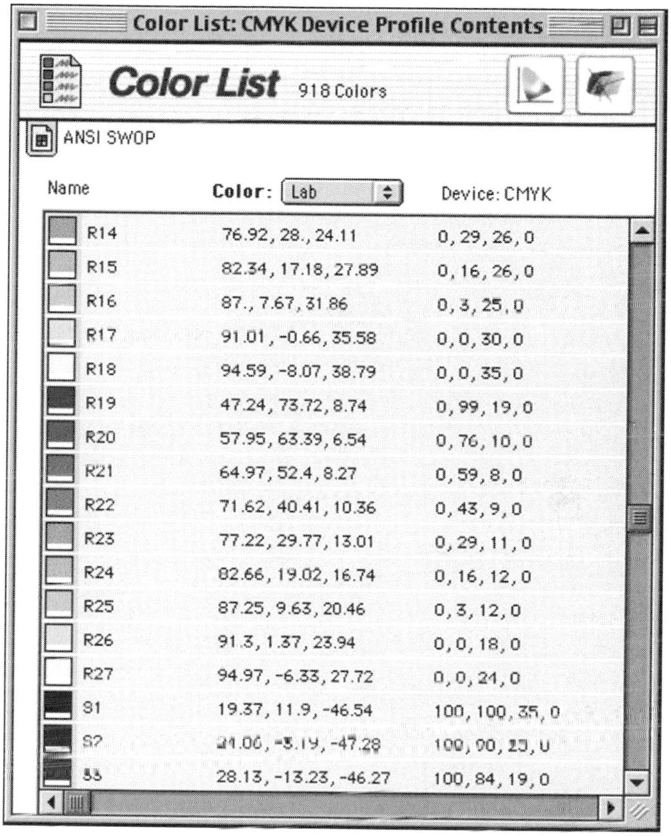

Besides the color translation tables, you'll also find—if you know how and where to look—all kinds of other public and private information about copyright dates, device settings, media white and black points, inks, paper stock, temperature and humidity, screening and resolution, and driver, OS, and application settings.

Using Printer Profiles

A key thing to understand about printer profiling is that it's not the printer that's profiled! Instead, it's the combination of printer resolution and driver settings, ink, and paper. Change

Figure 5.12 *A CHROMiX ColorThink Color List opens up a printer profile to expose the lookup table data.*

one variable, and you need a new profile. That's why it's common for photographer artists to have many different printer profiles, one for each printer/ink/paper combination.

Where do printer profiles go? It depends on the operating system:

Mac OS 9.x—System Folder > ColorSync Profiles

Mac OS X—Library > ColorSync > ColorSync Profiles

Windows 98/ME—\Windows\System\Color

Windows XP—\Windows\System32\Spool\Drivers\Color

Windows NT/2000—\Winnt\System32\Spool\Drivers\Color

Where do profiles come from? There are three main sources: *generic* or *canned*, *custom-made remote*, and *do-it-yourself* with profile-building software. (For information about acquiring and using printer profiles with outside service providers such as photo labs with Fuji Frontiers or printmakers, see Chapter 10.)

Canned Profiles

Canned or generic profiles are just that, generic. They don't take into account *your* unique hardware/software setup or anything that's specific to your workflow. They're only considered starting points to get you in the ballpark of good printing. It's better than nothing, but sometimes, marginally so.

Most canned profiles come from consumables vendors (mainly ink and some paper suppliers), and you basically get what you pay for, meaning that many are free, especially if the supplier is trying to sell you something else. However, you can also buy them for anywhere from $50 to $175 each. The emphasis is on the word *each*. If, for example, you needed a profile for an EPSON 2000P running EPSON OEM inks on Legion Somerset Enhanced paper, that's one profile. If you wanted to switch to Somerset Satin paper, that requires another profile. Somerset Velvet? Yet another. You can see why people collect *lots* of profiles.

Profiles require that you use specific printer settings. You cannot change these settings without invalidating the profile. (You can also adjust or modify profiles.)

As an aside, you may not realize that the built-in Media Type or paper settings on inkjet printers actually invoke canned profiles provided by the manufacturer that are loaded when you install the printer driver. If you have an ICC-aware image-editing or profile-managing program, or if you just look in the computer's system folder that houses them, you can see all the same profiles as those showing in the printer settings dialog box. (See Windows exception at the end of this chapter.)

Generic, third-party, profile providers include the following: Lumijet, MIS, Lyson, Dotworks, and InkjetMall.com. Of course, there's also CHROMiX's ProfileCentral, which is trying to become the "Yahoo" of free, shared profiles. They don't post their own generated profiles but, instead, list the profiles of the other sources so that people have one place to go to find them. ProfileCentral can be used by service providers to post their own profiles and share them with existing customers and to attract new customers. Keep in mind that profiling software contains licensing restrictions; just because you bought the software does not mean you are free to distribute profiles built with it!

Custom-made Remote Profiles

The next step up in profile quality is having someone with professional-grade equipment make you a custom profile. These will be more accurate because they're made specifically for your unique set of variables including inks, paper, environment, driver settings, and so on. It typically works like this: you download a single-page target (see Figure 5.13) and print it out to exact instructions that include printing with uncorrected settings—you want to capture the good *and* the bad about your printer. You send that printed page to the profile maker who then scans it, builds a profile with expensive, spectrophotometer-based profiling gear, and either e-mails or ships it back to you on a CD (or allows you to download it from the Web). You need to carefully record all the printer settings when you make the test print and then use those same settings for all your printing with that profile (which can also be edited or tweaked if needed). Costs vary from $100 to $250. Again, the price is for *each* separate ink/paper/printer combination.

If you don't want to invest the time or money into a profile-making system of your own, and you don't anticipate many printer/ink/paper changes, this can be a good solution. Many claim that custom profiles yield the best results of all the profile options. (To read about my experience using one, see Chapter 9.)

Figure 5.13 *ProfileCity's linearization target, which is used in its two-step method for making custom printer profiles*

Custom, remote profiles can be purchased from providers such as CHROMiX/ColorValet, ProfileCity, InkjetMall.com, and from independent color consultants.

DIY Profiling

As with monitor profiling, you can purchase a third-party, profile-generating package and make your own printer profiles. Profile-making systems either bundle the printer-profile function with monitor calibration or sell it separately. Doing it yourself has the highest start-up cost (several hundred dollars and up is typical), but if you anticipate needing a lot of profiles, and aren't fazed by the learning and experimenting curve, this may be your best choice.

The basic concept is that a reference target with numerous color patches that have known values is output to your print device using the same print settings, ink, and paper as the final prints made with the resulting profile. Those same patches are then measured with either a regular flatbed scanner (low cost but less accurate) or a spectrophotometer (more expensive but more accurate). The variances are recorded by the software in the form of a device profile, which is an ICC printer profile for *that* particular combination of variables.

Printer profiles can also be edited or fine-tuned by most profile-building and profile-managing software programs. Alternatively, you can use adjustment layers in image-editing software to tweak an existing profile (see the "Using Image-Editing Adjustments" section).

Profile Managing

While there are plenty of software tools for building and editing ICC profiles, you won't find many for managing, repairing, evaluating, and graphing them, especially for Windows. ProfileCity's ProfileManager offers profile managing. Mac OS X Version 10.2 Jaguar includes an updated ColorSync Utility that features a few simple profile tools such as profile color-gamut graphing. ColorThink by CHROMiX is a complete toolset (currently for Mac only with a Windows version planned) for handling profiles once they've been created. It's sort of the Norton Utilities for color profile management.

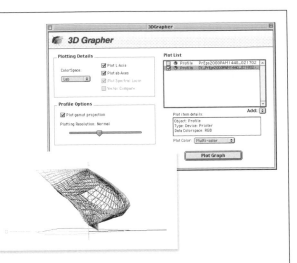

Figure 5.14 *The CHROMiX Grapher tool (now combining 2-D and 3-D graphing in version 2) gives you some great profile perspectives.*

ColorThink contains nine separate but related tools:

- **Profile Manager:** Organizes profiles into a more manageable system. You can enable or disable them in sets.

- **Profile Inspector:** Opens up any ICC-compliant profile and lets you analyze its contents. You'll find overview, header, and tag table information plus any errors or warnings for that particular profile.

- **Profile Medic:** Scans all profile folders on your hard drive and inspects each profile for known problems. It then summarizes the problems and allows you to fix them or leave them alone.

- **Profile Renamer:** All profiles have two names, an internal name that the application sees and an external one that the user sees. This can lead to trouble if you start changing the file names. This tool lets you modify one or both names.

- **Profile Linker:** "Device Link" profiles are a special type of profile that can convert one device's data directly to another's without passing through intermediary profile connection space or PCS. This type of profiling is mostly used with RIPs and commercial applications.

- **Grapher:** In ColorThink version 2, the 2-D and 3-D graphing functions are combined to visually plot the gamut of color space, display, and printer profiles. The 3-D function (see Figure 5.14) lets you see above, below, and all around the profile as you click and rotate it.

- **Color Lists:** Color lists are the long lists of numbers created when profiling software creates a profile. These lists can be imported into ColorThink and viewed, compared, and evaluated.

- **Image Inspector:** Opens images and displays, exports, removes, and embeds ICC profiles.

Monaco EZcolor 2

MonacoEZcolor 2 (the same one used for monitors) has a complex yet ingenious and well-thought-out wizard process for building a printer profile that's similar to the one used for display calibration. After printing out a target employing the same settings, ink, and paper as will be ultimately used, you tape a separate reflective IT8 target (only theirs will work) to the bottom of it, and scan the whole thing on a flatbed scanner. After cropping the scan, you name the profile, and the software builds and stores it. You also have the option of creating a scanner profile at the same time.

MonacoEZcolor 2 also has a full profile-editing function (Edit Printer Profile) that lets you edit their own profiles by making color adjustments to a reference image and then saving those results in the profile. However, remember, editing a profile is a global change. Every image printed with that profile will be affected. Don't use profile editing to tweak single images.

MonacoPROOF does everything EZcolor 2 does but adds the following: linearization and relinearization (for updating profiles as devices drift), curve editing of profiles, interfaces for colorimeters and spectrophotometers, and rotating 3-D gamut displays. *MonacoPROFILER* includes all the previously mentioned features plus digital camera support, PANTONE Hexachrome profiling, neutral balance editing, advanced gamut mapping, and a more robust profile editor. We're talking top-of-the-line color software with a price tag to match.

ColorVision ProfilerPLUS

PANTONE ColorVision's ProfilerPLUS is a Photoshop plug-in for building output profiles with the use of a flatbed scanner as a measuring device. Besides the full version of Photoshop (5.0 or later), ProfilerPLUS will work in RGB mode with Photoshop Elements. Photoshop LE is not supported.

After launching Photoshop and configuring its RGB working space (Adobe RGB 1998 recommended), you start ProfilerPLUS (File > Automate > ProfilerPLUS). You then print a calibration chart and scan it on a flatbed. Bringing up that scan in Photoshop, you select "Build Profile" from a pop-up menu, name the profile, edit as needed, and you're done.

ProfilerPRO is a heftier version of ProfilerPLUS. You can use a scanner, but it's also made to interface with sophisticated spectrophotometers for more accurate results. It also includes ColorVision's *DoctorPRO* utility (also sold separately), which allows you to use Photoshop's own global editing tools for profile editing.

ColorVision's process is much simpler than Monaco's (there's no taping of targets or tricky cropping), and although my first test print with ProfilerPLUS wasn't perfect, adjusting the profile using the software's editing sliders and rebuilding the profile yielded a second print just as good as Monaco's. Each system has its defenders; you'll have to download trials and test them to make up your own mind.

Other printer-profile-making systems include the following:

■ **ITEC ColorBlind Matchbox:** This is a sophisticated profile-builder that includes three products: ColorBlind Matchbox Profiler (for creating ICC profiles for input, display, and printer profiles), ColorBlind Edit (for editing images and profiles), and ColorBlind Spot (for building spot color libraries). A required color-measurement device must be purchased separately.

- **GretagMacbeth ProfileMaker:** Another modular system, ProfileMaker Pro not only includes MeasureTool for device calibration and data measurement, but also ProfileMaker (for printer profile creation), ProfileEditor (for profile enhancement), and ColorPicker (for matching PANTONE and special colors). ProfileMaker lets you measure and create ICC profiles for all types of printers, including multicolor up to seven ink channels.

- **GretagMacbeth Eye-One:** An integrated color-management system with an Eye-One spectrophotometer and Eye-One Match software. It's available in three different packages: Eye-One Monitor (monitor calibration only), Eye-One Pro spectrophotometer and monitor profiling software (scans and measures other color sources), and Eye-One Pro with Eye-One Match (adds input and output profile creation).

- **ProfileCity ICC Print:** There are two separate versions: ICC Print RGB and ICC Print CMYK, and both support spectrophotometer devices (sold separately). ICC Print CMYK offers a range of ink-utilization parameters to control: total ink limit, maximum black, black start, black curve shape, and GCR in grays and colors.

- **Digital Domain Profile Prism:** A lower-cost solution for PCs. Scanner based, Profile Prism includes a 753-patch, reflective 5×7 target, and it generates ICC profiles for digital cameras, scanners, and printers.

Getting the Color You Want

Let's get this out of the way first: The easiest way to obtain adequate print quality is to use the original equipment manufacturer's (OEM) papers, inks, and printer settings. They've already been optimized to work together, and all you have to do is follow the instructions.

However, because most photographers, imagemakers, and artists hope to squeeze the last drops of quality out of their images, they're willing to go a little further to get the color they want.

I'm going to show you five ways to adjust inkjet print color. We'll start off slow and easy with a couple of basic techniques, and then we'll pick up the quality pace.

Using the Printer's Settings

The first thing to try when an inkjet print isn't quite right is go in and adjust the printer's settings. With EPSONs and other popular inkjets, this takes place in the Advanced Settings (or Custom) window in the printer driver interface that's viewable onscreen (see Figure 5.15). This is also where selections for media type, print quality, and color management are made. (Remember that the Media Type or paper pop-up menu is really nothing more than a canned profile specifying the amount of ink to lay down, among other things. You can see this for yourself by test-printing the same image on the same paper but with different Media Type settings chosen.)

All the typical adjustments for brightness, contrast, saturation, and individual color balance are available with moveable sliders. (The sliders instruct the printer driver to adjust ink color percentages, dithering algorithms, and more to change the output.) You can then name and save the settings and call them up later. Other printer brands use similar settings although they may have different names for them.

Figure 5.15
An EPSON Advanced Settings window

One important thing to keep in mind with regard to slider adjustments: You can't always get back to the beginning. Some printer drivers have a cumulative memory. After you've boosted the magenta, the driver may not be able to return to the neutral setting. The ground zero has shifted, which makes predictable color moves very difficult, if not impossible.

Automatic Color Management?

Some manufacturers are starting to develop their own color management solutions. One is Epson with its PRINT Image Matching System (P.I.M.). It's primarily aimed at hobbyist digital camera users and matches the camera to the printer. The EPSON 780, 785FPX, 820, 890, and 1280 were in the first group of printers to support P.I.M. with more being added all the time. Camera manufacturers that support it on their end include Epson, Panasonic, Nikon, Casio, Konica, Minolta, Olympus, Ricoh, Sony, Pentax, Fuji, and Toshiba.

With P.I.M., the digital camera saves information about 14 image-control parameters (color space, color balance, saturation, gamma level, contrast, and so on) with each image in the form of a miniprofile. Only a P.I.M.-compatible printer can use the information for optimizing its output.

As with canned profiles, this is an automatic solution to color management that may work for some people but not for others. For example, P.I.M. works only when cameras are set to Automatic mode.

Using Photoshop's Transfer Function

A little known method of adjusting printed images is by using Photoshop's Transfer function. It's primarily employed (and even then, infrequently) to compensate for dot gain in commercial CMYK printing through page-layout programs and EPS file formats, but it can also work for desktop printing. Instead of changing the image file, a transfer curve is created that applies only as the file is printed, and only if you're printing directly out of Photoshop.

The Transfer button is buried deep in Photoshop's Page Setup (version 6) or Print with Preview (version 7; see Figure 5.16) and works just like a typical Curves dialog box. You can click the graph line and move points up or down, or you can add the precise values in the percentage boxes to the right of the graph. You can adjust the composite image or each color individually.

The main problem with Transfer is that there's no ability to preview the image. You have to try it, make a print, and try again. Because of this limitation, and even more so because it's easy to save the image with a new Transfer curve and not realize it, you should consider this option only if all else fails.

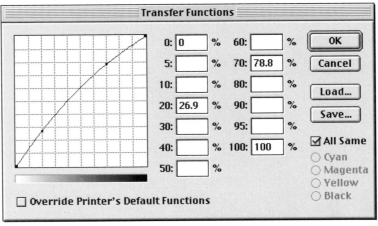

Figure 5.16
Photoshop's Transfer function

Noncolor

An overview of the ins and outs of color wouldn't be complete without talking about the monochromatic rendering of images. I call this noncolor. Noncolor is still color; it's just limited to B&W and grays.

There's a whole secret world of B&W and multi-monochromatic imaging and printing out there. The members are mostly photographers, but anyone can join.

There are several ways to output noncolor, including using Epson's newest seven-color inkjet printers with two black inks.

To learn more about monochromatic printing, see Chapter 11.

Using Image-Editing Adjustments

The color-adjusting controls used with image editing can also nudge the print quality ever so slightly where you want it to go. In my *Pelican Jetty* example in Figure 5.17, I'm using the Color Balance adjustment in Photoshop 7 to get rid of a green cast I picked up somewhere along the way (probably when I left my film camera in the car on a hot Florida day). I could have used Curves to do the same thing.

The beauty of Photoshop adjustment layers is, of course, that they're adjustable (editable). You can make a move, make a print, review it, go back onscreen and adjust the layer, and do it again until you get it right.

Another benefit of adjustment layers, especially if you're seeing the same problem over and over on different images, is that you can easily copy the adjustment layer by itself over to another file—just drag it over. It has now become the adjustment layer of that file, and it's also fully editable. (Alternatively, you can save the adjustment and then load it in the new file. If you're really in production mode, you can also make a Photoshop Action to save time with repeatable steps.) However, as with editing profiles where any changes will affect *all* images in a global fashion, be very careful with this uniform-adjustment approach.

Adjustment layers can also be used in combination with soft-proofing.

Figure 5.17
Image editing with a Color Balance adjustment layer in Photoshop

Using Profiles and Soft-Proofing

As soon as you move out of the comfortable nest of the standard inks and papers recommended by manufacturers, you're on your own. You can play around with settings, adjustment layers, and more until you've pulled all the hair from your head, and you still may not have a print to be proud of for all your trouble. This is where profiles—input and output—come into play. Using profiles should be seriously considered if one of the following is true:

1. You're using non-OEM-recommended, third-party inks.

2. You're using non-OEM-recommended, third-party media (paper).

3. You're just curious and want to see what profiles will do. It can't hurt to create a profile and compare the resulting print to one using your standard settings or other adjustments. It keeps everybody honest!

We now have a set of color standards (ICC) and understandable, affordable tools to implement them. A color-managed workflow with a calibrated monitor and the use of either canned, custom, or do-it-yourself printer profiles can give you accurate, consistent color. It *does* work if you spend the time to understand and work with profile-generating and profile-savvy software. In addition, one of the best ways to implement profile-based color management is with the use of Photoshop's new RGB soft-proofing function.

Soft-proofing RGB files (you could always soft-proof CMYK) is one of the great advancements that Photoshop (beginning with version 6) has brought to digital image editing. No other program offers this feature, and it's a wonderful one, especially if you're a color-management aficionado.

Soft-proofing means proofing an image onscreen with the use of one or more ICC profiles so that you can get an idea of how the image is going to print. The image is viewed through the visual filter of both a monitor profile and a printer profile. Photoshop will change the way the image looks based on these output (and input) profiles.

Soft-proofing works like this (Photoshop 7 on a Mac used for the example):

1. Duplicate the image (Image > Duplicate) for use as a visual reference. This is a temporary image that stays untouched.

2. On the working image, use the Proof Setup dialog box (View > Proof Setup > Custom) to create the proofing space you want (see Figure 5.18). Under Profile, choose an output (printer) profile. The Intent tab lets you pick a rendering intent for converting from document space to proofing space. The Simulate check boxes offer a choice of Paper White and Ink Black. Each option (there are actually three because you can have both unchecked) gives a different rendering of the image. Until you've experimented to discover what works best for you, check Paper White, which uses Absolute Colorimetric for rendering the proof space to the monitor. Don't worry if the image now looks dull and washed out; that's the point—you're getting a preview of how it will print if you didn't do anything to fix it.

3. Now it's time to make your edits to the previewed image. The best way is with adjustment layers, viewing both the reference and new images side by side (see Figure 5.19). (For illustration purposes, I've taken a vertical slice of my *Pelican Jetty* image; you'll be working with the whole image.) In this case, I first beef up the contrast with an RGB S curve and then pull some blue and green from the image with individual channel curves. An improvement starting with Photoshop 6 is that you can now group adjustments into a *layer set*. Just name this grouping with the name of the specific print configuration you're previewing. If you want to output to a different printer or use different inks and papers later, you simply make a different layer set for each purpose. It all stays with the same master file.

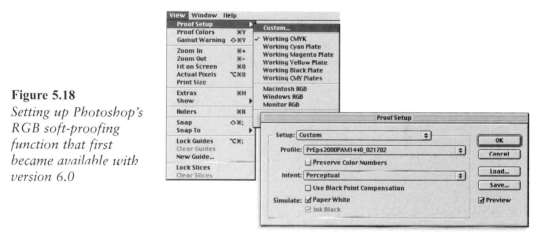

Figure 5.18
Setting up Photoshop's RGB soft-proofing function that first became available with version 6.0

Figure 5.19
Soft-proofing at work: the original, reference RGB image (left) and the new, soft-proofed preview image after a couple of curves are pulled. The shadows still look weak on the preview image, but the actual printing will snap them back.

4. As a last step, view the final image full-screen (use the F key), check for any out-of-gamut colors (View > Gamut Warning), and, if needed, make any last-minute tweaks.

5. Select your ICC printer profile in the Print with Preview window (Show More Options > Color Management; see Figure 5.20). Print it!

A few final notes about soft-proofing in Photoshop:

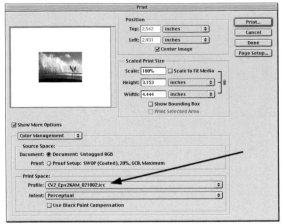

Figure 5.20
Choose your printer profile (Mac) in the Print with Preview (left) dialog box.

■ A special Windows consideration: Individual paper profiles were originally not available with EPSON Windows drivers. People had to either steal them from a Mac driver and add an .icc or .icm extension or download them from third-party sources. Now, with the newer EPSONs like the 2200, the profiles are found on the P.I.M. software as an installation option. Additionally, a limited number of profiles and the Windows P.I.M plug-in can be downloaded from the Epson website.

■ This applies to any profile-managed desktop printing: *Don't double dip your color management!* By that, I mean don't use an ICC profile *and* have the printer driver do its own color adjusting—Print > Custom > Advanced > Color Management. With an EPSON, make sure you select "No Color Adjustment." Failing to do this will lead to unpredictable and usually disastrous results.

■ The validity and quality of this soft-proof process is directly related to how well you've calibrated your monitor. Don't skip—or skimp on—that step.

■ It's important to realize that as great a tool as digital soft-proofing is, you will never match an onscreen preview to a final print exactly. It just isn't going to happen. You can get close—much closer now than ever before—but you still need to understand the limits of your hardware and digital workflow and make allowances for them in your own way.

Using a RIP

Some people swear by raster image processors (RIPs), some swear at them, and the rest just don't understand what all the ruckus is about.

One area where a RIP can be a definite advantage is with color management. Instead of relying on a standard inkjet printer's unseen, "black box" conversions for RGB to CMYK, a good RIP gives you much more power over the output process. For example, here are only a few of the color controls available with LexJet Direct's SpectrumPro RIP (based on ColorByte's ImagePrint) as it bypasses the regular printer driver:

- **System Profile Selection:** This let's you pick a monitor profile (for onscreen display only) plus a printer profile to characterize the color on your output device. You can choose from one of the many ink-paper profiles that ships with the RIP, or you can substitute a profile you've created or purchased from a profiling service.

- **Printer Simulation Profile:** This is a printer profile used to match another printer or press, and it's how you make an inkjet printer become a pre-press proof printer. A RIP provides the best way to do this.

- **Ink Limiting:** With most inkjet printers, the main control you have over ink limiting is with the crude Media Type or paper stock selection (some of the newest printers also have a Color Density or Ink Density slider to help accomplish this). You have only a few choices, and they affect all ink colors across the board. However, with a full-featured RIP, you can specify ink percentages for each ink channel supported by the printer (see Figure 5.21). With this kind of precision, you can avoid not only oversaturating paper stocks with inks, but also color casts at the final output stage.

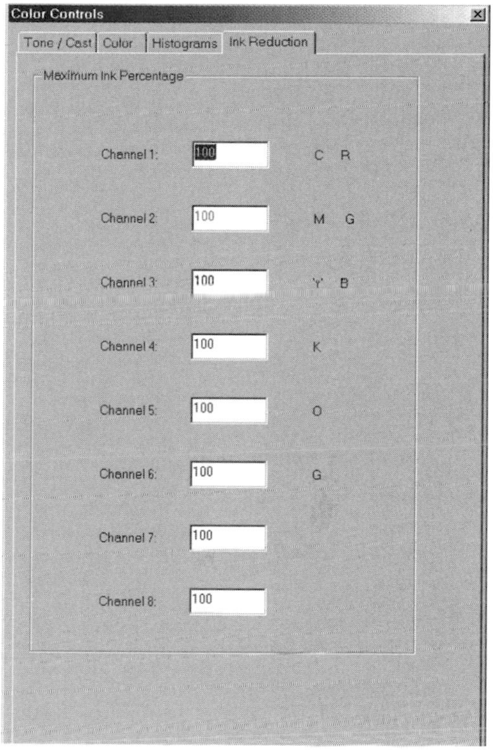

Courtesy of ColorByte Software

Figure 5.21
The SpectrumPro/ImagePrint RIP allows you to set separate ink-channel limits. With an RGB (versus CMYK) workflow, ink limiting with this particular RIP is less important because of the way it separately handles the color and black channels.

Keep in mind that RIPs have been primarily associated with CMYK inkjet proofing and printing in a commercial environment. As one RIP-maker says it, "This is very different from 'pretty picture' color management where you only really need a couple of good ICC profiles to produce predictable, pleasing results." However, the RIP makers are starting to wise up to the booming interest by photographer-artists in high-quality digital output, and you can expect them to continue to offer more options, such as RGB workflows and lower costs, to this growing market. Then, you'll need to decide if a RIP or better color management software and/or more profiles is the best route to getting the color you want.

With a better understanding of color under our belts, it's now time to take a look at one of the most controversial and often-debated topics in the digital printing universe: print permanence.

6

Not Fade Away: Print Permanence

Although substantial improvements in ink and paper manufacturing plus the knowledge gained from controlled testing have brought us to a point where some digital prints can outlast their traditional media counterparts, the whole issue of image stability is still a contentious one.

Anyone who's concerned about print permanence must grapple with two simple questions:

1. How long is permanent?
2. How do I know if a print will actually last that long?

How Long Is Long Enough?

I once innocently asked a well-known watercolorist exhibiting at an art festival why she had only photographic reproduction prints on display next to her originals and not inkjets. She almost tore my head off, fuming that she had lost a good customer when the prints she had sold him had faded in less than a year. For her, that clearly wasn't long enough.

Who Cares?

First, some people don't believe there is a problem. They argue that longevity and permanence are properly the work of conservators, not artists, and that all images fade and deteriorate over time. (Van Gogh's painting Irises, which today hangs in New York's Metropolitan Museum of Art, is badly faded. The original "pink background" that Van Gogh wrote his brother Theo about is now almost snow white.)

Digital artist and printmaker JD Jarvis feels that digital work is held up to more rigorous demands than any other artwork. A gallery owner once worried that his digital prints weren't waterproof. "As if watercolors, photos, and lithos are?" he asked. "I'm making art, not foulweather gear." Although this may be true, most photographer-artists working digitally *are*, nonetheless, concerned about print permanence.

Image-stability researcher Henry Wilhelm (see more about him later in the chapter) brings the point home with a dramatic example. "The entire era of picture taking from 1942 to 1953 when people were using box cameras and Kodak's new Kodacolor print process is lost forever," he explained to me. "There is not one single known print that survives today in reasonable condition; they are *all* severely stained and faded."

Pictures and prints are important to people. Maybe not all of them, but that doesn't mean that *none* of them are! And in the digital age, this becomes even more important because, chances are, the digital files will not survive, but the prints will. "It's always been about the print," says Wilhelm. "And we can actually produce right now, at very low cost, extremely stable photographs and prints in color. Do we want to? Ask anybody, 'Which would you rather have: a longer-lasting print or a shorter-lasting one?' What do you think the answer will be?"

I believe most photographer-artists sensibly want to be confident that the prints they are making—for themselves or for sale or gift to others—will last for a reasonable amount of time under normal conditions. (What the phrases "reasonable amount of time" and "normal conditions" actually mean is, of course, up for grabs.) Although this is not a book about art conservation or preservation, the permanence of prints is an important subject to explore. As digital printing researcher Dr. David Matz says, "Everything will change with time and will change faster under less-friendly conditions. But doesn't it make sense to start with the most stable materials that will change the slowest?"

Family photos have value, but most color prints from the '40s, '50s, and even '60s are now faded or stained. Compare my family's Kodalux print on the left from 1968 with the Kodak B&W print on the right from 1953, which, apart from a slight yellowing on the edges, is otherwise in perfect condition.

The Meaning of Permanence

If we're going to talk about print permanence, we should at least agree on what the phrase means. Unfortunately, that's no easy task. Here are some different ways to define it:

- **Image stability:** The dictionary meaning is "resistance to chemical decomposition," but for the purpose of printing an image, we're talking about what photo conservator Martin Juergens calls "the stability of image-forming substances." These include the inks or dyes (together termed *colorants*) and the paper and coating materials (the *medium*) used to produce the print. It's the inherent stability of not only the colorants and the medium separately, but the ink/medium combination that is vitally important.

- **Archival:** Although ink and paper manufacturers love to throw around the term "archival," there is no uniformly accepted definition of what is archival and what is not. In fact, the word just means that something is in an archive, being stored, but not necessarily monitored or preserved. "Archival" is primarily a conservation term, and there is no upper limit for how long items should be stored. Museums and archives are usually mandated to archive certain objects indefinitely.

- **Lightfast:** Lightfast means resistant to fading. But for how long? The permanence, or fading characteristics, of many pigments used in traditional art materials are well established. In developing test methods for evaluating new materials for lightfastness, an American Society for Testing and Materials (ASTM) subcommittee used some of these historic pigments as controls, and colors rated by the ASTM as "Lightfast I" should last as well as pigments known to have retained their color more than 100 years. (See more about the ASTM's tests below.) However, as permanence researcher Joy Turner Luke explains, ASTM members stress that it's never possible to predict how many years a particular color will last because future display and storage conditions are unknown.

  Other testing organizations (primarily WIR and RIT/IPI; see later) attach usable-life predictions to lightfastness. In essence, they're saying, "Based on certain display or storage assumptions, a print similar to the one tested should last for X years without noticeable fading or should only change this much in terms of its colors or densities." As we will shortly see, there are dangers with this approach.

- **Permanence:** Permanence refers to resistance to *any* physical change, whether it be from light, heat, acids, and so on. As an example, an ink can be lightfast but impermanent because it is prone to fast fading when exposed to ozone. How long is permanent? The U.S. Library of Congress, which is responsible for the care of 123 million cultural artifacts, uses "as long as possible" as its goal for preserving and making available to the public its vast collections.

The Granny Standard

Because there is no accepted time-length standard for image permanence, I thought I'd invent one. Consider this a benchmark, a personal point of reference for determining what is "archival" or "permanent." Here's what I propose:

The Granny, Three-Generation Archival Standard

The standard answers the following question based on this assumption: A pregnant 30-year-old digital artist and fine-art photographer makes a print of her favorite image and frames and displays it proudly in her living room. On her son's 30th birthday, the artist gives him the framed print as a present just after his baby daughter is born. The son hangs the print in his living room then gives it to his daughter on her 30th birthday. It's been 60 years. Question: Has the print lost any of its image quality or experienced any noticeable fading or other deterioration? (It turns out that Granny was pretty smart and kept a duplicate copy in an acid-free envelope stored in a dark, dry dresser drawer all these years. When her granddaughter asked the question, she was able to pull that print out and compare it to the family-heirloom version.)

The Granny Standard—60 years of time that I believe is long enough to be concerned about a print's permanence—provides the following:

- A time frame based on a real-world (albeit somewhat-goofy) scenario that people can understand

- An accepted definition of the term "generation"—the average period (about 30 years) between the birth of one generation and that of the next

(Note: Determining the measuring criteria and the acceptable limits of fading/color shifting is, of course, another issue and covered in the "What Affects Permanence?" section of this chapter.)

Because no one really knows what permanent or archival is, they are relative terms that anyone can claim. In the end, you—the photographer-artist—must decide how long is long enough. You will naturally do so based on your particular situation and set of goals (unless you want to accept my Granny Standard!).

What Affects Permanence?

In addition to the inherent instability of colorants and media—everything disintegrates eventually—there are a whole host of enemies willing and able to do damage to your beautiful prints. No matter which type of digital print technology is used, certain influencing factors can and will affect print permanence. Here are the main culprits to worry about:

Light and UV Radiation

Light negatively affects prints through a complicated combination of processes including photo-oxidation, photo-reduction, photocatalysis, and other photochemical reactions that are not completely understood. However, we're all familiar with one of the results of light striking a print's image: fading. Anyone who has seen a faded poster in a store window knows what this means.

Most light fading occurs in a very narrow band of the light spectrum right on the border where visible light becomes invisible UV radiation (in the 380–400 nm range). UV rays can be very damaging to printed images, in many cases many times more so than visible light. This is the higher-energy end of the spectrum, and regular window glass (or plexiglass) can do a lot to filter the shorter UV wavelengths (see Figure 6.1), but beyond that simple procedure, every material—including inks, dyes, and papers—has its own spectral sensitivity and will be affected by light in a different way. In general, the higher the intensity and the longer the exposure, the worse the damage from light.

Fluorescent and some halogen lamps also emit significant amounts of UV radiation; they can be filtered at the source or, again, with glass or plexiglass (or with UV-protective coatings and sprays, to some extent).

Courtesy of inkjetART.com

Relative Damage of Solar Wavelengths

Figure 6.1 *The benefits of framing inkjet prints behind glass. The print on the left was displayed on a wall for nine months with a standard glass covering in a frame. The one on the right is exactly the same except it was framed without glass. Scientists at the U.S. National Bureau of Standards (NBS) found that UV wavelengths were about three times more damaging than the visible spectrum. The graph at bottom shows the NBS relationship between the wavelength of the radiation and the resulting relative damage. This helps explain why even standard window glass (with a UV cutoff at around 330 nm) is so effective in slowing down fading.*

What Can Happen?

■ Image fading

■ Color-balance changes

■ Yellow stain formation. According to Henry Wilhelm, accelerated light tests can cause light-induced yellow staining on prints that only manifests itself after a period of dark storage. This may or may not occur in normal display conditions.

Temperature

Any student of chemistry knows that as the temperature goes up, chemical reactions speed up as well. Thus, it stands to reason that a photochemical reaction such as light fading will be accelerated by higher temperatures. Studies have found this to be true in general. High humidity also frequently aggravates the situation. Extremely low temperatures, on the other hand, can also be a problem when some materials will become brittle or even crack.

What Can Happen?

■ Rapid color fading

■ Increased yellowing, especially in light or paper-white areas

■ Dye degradation and diffusion

Water and Humidity

Water in its natural form or as moisture in the air can have a big—negative—impact on prints, primarily those made with dye-based inks. Water dripping, spills, water leaks, flood damage—these are just some of the most obvious potential problems. Uncoated IRIS prints are so sensitive to moisture that unknowledgeable framers have ruined them through only their own saliva while talking over them! High humidity can also cause problems and is many times linked with higher temperatures to make things even worse.

What Can Happen?

■ Dye de-aggregation and dye diffusion (bleeding) through the paper

■ Ink migration, smearing, blurring, lateral ink bleeding, and ink spreading (see Figure 6.2)

■ Changes in density and color balance shifts that increase with higher humidity

■ Dark storage print life that decreases with higher humidity

■ "Bronzing" (exhibiting a copper-like sheen) in high-density areas

Figure 6.2
Early generation inkjet inks and media had problems with waterfastness as witnessed by the test shown. Left is the control print, center is a print using a pigmented black ink and immersed in water, right is an immersed print using all dye-based inks. Newer ink-media-coating combinations are better at resisting water damage, although you still need to be careful.

Atmospheric Contaminants

This is a phenomenon that has only recently been recognized, showing up as the infamous "gas fading" problem of a couple years ago (see "The Dreaded Orange Shift"). Not only are air pollutants such as nitrous oxide and sulfur dioxide dangerous for some prints, but ozone levels in possible combination with UV radiation may also cause severe problems. In addition, all of that is exacerbated by open air flow across the face of a print, which is one reason why you want to frame all prints under glass or acrylic (plexiglass). The ironic thing is that air purification systems (particularly those that generate ozone) can actually make matters worse for prints.

What Can Happen?

■ Severe gas fading (some prints turning orange)

■ Gas fading may increase reciprocity failure (see "The Dreaded Orange Shift") in accelerated tests

Bio-Chemical Activity

It's just not safe out there with all the chemicals in printing inks, substrates, or coatings plus those found in the environment or introduced by handling. Add ink impurities and molds that can react with the colorants or media to help destroy a print over time, and you can see how precarious print permanence is.

What Can Happen?

■ Mold formation (especially at relative humidities over 60 percent)

■ Disintegration of paper substrates due to mold growth

■ Chemically induced fading and color-balance shifting

Poor Handling

Folding, creasing, smudging, scraping, fingerprinting, and poor display and storage procedures—all are possible, and all can reduce the permanence of prints.

The Dreaded Orange Shift

The problem of atmospheric contamination was rudely brought to everyone's attention in 2000 by the Orange Shift fiasco. What happened was that some people's prints made on Epson's Premium Glossy Photo Paper (PGPP) inexplicably experienced severe color shifting, turning bright orange, sometimes within 24 hours of being printed! However, this didn't happen to everyone; it was completely dependent on where you lived, what your local atmosphere was like, and whether your prints were covered. It turned out that PGPP was Epson's first paper to use a "microporous" coating to improve image quality. Unfortunately, this coating acted like a sponge, soaking up any ozone or other atmospheric contaminants and speeding up the exchange of gases to the cyan dye in the inks. The cyan rapidly faded, and that left only the yellow and magenta, which combined to produce orange ("differential fading"). (For those who didn't have the problem, the prints were—and continue to be—fine.)

Epson, along with everyone else (photographer Bob Meyer points out that this was *not* just an Epson problem), was caught off-guard by this, and they released a reformulated version of the

paper in December 2000 that supposedly offered improved resistance to the bizarre color shifting. Then, in May 2001, they announced their new, swellable-polymer ColorLife paper to help put the problem behind them.

This situation pointed out the important impact of airflow over the surface of the print. Epson now recommends that for long-term display, people should store all prints in a glass frame, photo album, or plastic sleeve. This is still good, general advice.

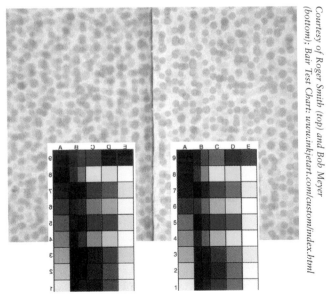

Courtesy of Roger Smith (top) and Bob Meyer (bottom); Bair Test Chart: www.inkjetart.com/custom/index.html

Photographer Bob Meyer has set up a complete Web site (www.meyerweb.net/epson) to chronicle the Orange Shift story. (Keith Krebs has another one at www.p-o-v-image.com/epson.) Meyer's Bair Test Chart images at bottom show an EPSON Premium Glossy Photo Paper print before (left) and after exposure to his "ozone chamber," which involves placing the print at the bottom of an electronic air filter, a known ozone source.

The larger images were taken of a neutral gray patch on a similarly orange-shifted print (plus a control) with a microscope (150× magnification) by Roger Smith at the University of New Brunswick, Canada. Before is on the left; after is on the right. You can clearly see that most of the cyan dots have faded on the right.

Determining Permanence: Standards, Tests, and Claims

With some notable exceptions—when British painter J.M.W. Turner was supposedly accused by paint manufacturer William Winsor for using fugitive pigments, he allegedly responded, "It's your business to make paints; it's my business to use them"—artists, collectors, and curators have been concerned about image permanence for many, many years. According to artist and educator Bruce MacEvoy, English chemist Walter Russell and amateur painter Capt. William de W. Abney published a report in 1888 (*Report on the Action of Light on Watercolors*) that put to rest the debate about whether watercolors faded under certain kinds of light. They did.

Why Test?

As with many areas of human endeavor, knowledge about print permanence can be gained from scientific testing. Just like dropping feathers and apples from tall buildings to investigate the effects of gravity, tests can help explain real-world phenomena if they're carefully constructed and performed under accepted standards. After you have an idea of what can cause the deterioration of a print (the "hypothesis"), you can test for it.

Image-quality researcher Mark McCormick-Goodhart thinks a well-designed test does the following:

■ Provides insight into what we can expect to happen over time

■ Helps to delineate how products compare and what products are best-suited to a particular application

■ Helps end users create appropriate storage and display conditions

Because real-time observation of print deterioration is, for the most part, impractical—the products used to make the print would be off the market by the time the test ended—accelerated tests have been developed to help us out.

Accelerated Testing Standards

The basic idea is simple: By using high-intensity light and any other influencing factors, the tester can speed up what would normally happen to a print over the course of many weeks, months, or years.

Although we have no single, universally accepted testing standard that applies to print permanence, there is a long history of testing methodology that guides today's testers, and several organizations have developed scientific procedures and standards for different kinds of permanence tests. The three most important types are the Blue Wool Lightfastness, American Society for Testing and Materials (ASTM), and ISO/ANSI standards.

Blue Wool Lightfastness Standard References

The Blue Wool Lightfastness Standards were, and still are, aimed at those who work in the textile industry. The European version was introduced by Britain's Society of Dyers and Colourists (SDC) in 1934 and is part of the ISO standards (see below). It gets its name from the dyed blue wool fabric bands or swatches that are used to visually compare fading rates. Much like a litmus test, Blue Wools act as a visual reference and as a timing device for knowing when to end a

lightfastness test (although they have become less important or needed with the introduction of accurate testing instruments that can control exposure times and intensity). There are eight levels or standards, with #8 being essentially permanent and #1 being fugitive (each is roughly twice as light-resistant as the one before; see Figure 6.3). The SDC is experimenting with replacing actual blue wool fabric material with pigmented papers (called "Blue Papers").

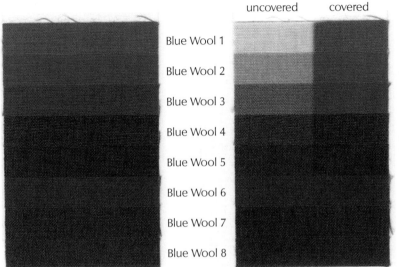

uncovered   covered

Blue Wool 1
Blue Wool 2
Blue Wool 3
Blue Wool 4
Blue Wool 5
Blue Wool 6
Blue Wool 7
Blue Wool 8

Blue Wool references courtesy of TalasOnline.com

Figure 6.3 *ISO Blue Wool references after an actual ten-week, south-window test. Left is before the test; right is after. Test sample is half-covered to keep those references from being exposed to light.*

In the United States, the Blue Wool standards followed a slightly different path of evolution and are based on early twentieth-century testing on the effects of carbon-arc floodlights on theater curtains. This version, which is monitored by the American Association of Textile Chemists and Colorists (AATCC), also has eight levels or standards. The main difference here is that instead of using eight different dyes for each level, the AATCC uses only two dyes, a lightfast one and a fugitive one, and then mixes them to create the different references. This is better in theory, but because the AATCC samples are very close in color visually, many printmakers have a hard time judging the changes and therefore use the European ISO version.

The Blue Wool standards are not just for sheep shearers and textile dyers. As a simple, comparative reference, digital printmakers, especially European ones, are now also using the standards to indicate in general terms how permanent a print is or could be. For example, British artist and giclée printmaker Colin Ruffell refers to his large-format prints achieving "a Blue Wool 6 rating."

ASTM

The ASTM has been in the testing business since the late 1800s, but their work in developing standards for testing art materials is the most relevant for us. The ASTM's D4303 standard describes the basic method to test the lightfastness of artists' paints (oil, acrylic, alkyd, watercolor, and gouache). The standard requires that colors be subjected to a specific amount of irradiation in two

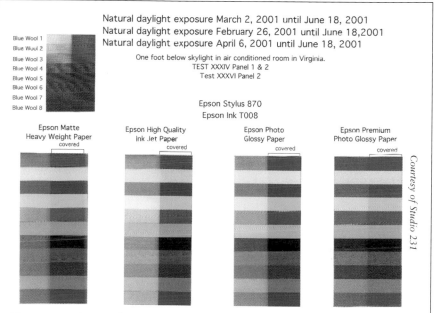

Figure 6.4 *A visual summary of an inkjet test conducted by the ASTM's Joy Turner Luke. This test followed the official ASTM visual reference standard (D5383) including the use of ISO blue wool references.*

Courtesy of Studio 231

tests using different light sources. The test is accelerated to approximate the color changes that can be expected in normal, indoor exposure. Each paint or pigment can then be assigned a lightfastness category based on the difference between samples before and after exposure (by Delta-E, as mentioned in Chapter 5). Walk into any art supply store and pick up a tube of paint. You will see written right on the tube "Lightfastness I" or something similar. That is the result of ASTM testing.

Because D4303 is a complex standard that requires instrument measurements, the ASTM has also developed two simpler ones for the kind of visual testing that more people can do. Standard D5383 describes a method for exposing color samples indoors to sunlight coming through a closed window. Three of the European Blue Wool references (3, 6, and 7) are used as controls for determining when to terminate the test and for evaluating the samples. Three to five outside observers then rate each sample by comparing it to a blue wool reference that shows the same amount of color change (see Figure 6.4). Ratings are categorized as being "fugitive," "inferior," "fair," or "good." Standard D5398 is similar and simpler still because it doesn't required outside observers, and it can be used by any artist to evaluate the lightfastness of his or her own materials.

The ASTM is currently developing lightfastness standards for artists' colored pencils, and some of its members (such as Joy Turner Luke) are pushing for adding inkjet prints to its standards umbrella.

ISO/ANSI

The International Organization for Standardization (ISO) and USA-member-body organization American National Standards Institute (ANSI) have been developing or promoting standards for the testing of everything from toothpaste to photographic film for decades. The first testing methods for comparing the color stabilities of color photographs date back to 1969, and those standards have been updated periodically.

The standards ISO 10977 (1993) and ANSI IT9-9 (1996) deal with color image stability, and they regulate such things as the preparation of test samples, how the tests are to be carried out, how the temperature and humidity are to be controlled, and how the results are to be evaluated. There are two problems with these two standards. First, they don't really address digital output; they're mainly used for traditional color photographs. Second, they do not define endpoints (see "What Are Endpoints, and Why Are They Important?"), and they also do not identify any reference display conditions for projecting a print's lifespan.

An updated standard (ISO 18909) that deals with photographic images is currently being prepared by ANSI/ISO Subcommittee IT9-3 and should be released within the next year or two. Even more importantly, that same committee is working on another set of standards (tentatively titled the "Color Hard Copy Image Stability Standard") that will finally cover digital prints and the effects of environmental pollutants and reciprocity failure (see below). Those new standards will be released in stages over the next several years. According to committee-member David Matz, this latter standard will be a specification and not just a test standard. "Reporting that a value was generated according to the ANSI standard will require that they use specific endpoints for their test, and that the projected lifetime be based on a standard display condition. These two critical conditions still need to be set."

Types of Tests

Permanence tests fall under these broad categories:

Accelerated Versus Real-Time Testing

As we've already learned, accelerated testing exposes a sample to much higher levels of light or whatever is being tested than would occur under normal conditions. This simulates in a short amount of time any deleterious effects, if any, that a print might experience.

Real-time testing, on the other hand, lets the test run over the course of weeks or months or even years under normal display or storage conditions. Individual artists and smaller operations that can afford the space and personpower are doing most of the real-time testing. For many, real-time testing is only practical for investigating short-term effects; however, Henry Wilhelm has been running ongoing, low-level, long-term, moderately accelerated tests on certain photographic materials since 1977.

Accelerated tests are based on the *reciprocity law*, which says that, using light fading as the example, the total amount of fading is equal to the total amount of energy exposure (time × intensity). Doubling the time but halving the intensity would yield the same effect (that is, 10 klux of exposure for one year should equal 1 klux for ten years). That's the theory. However, one of the major problems with accelerated testing is the concept of *reciprocity failure*, which means that the predicted results of high-intensity, short-time exposure do *not* equal the actual results of low-intensity, long-term exposure as they should. In other words, the law doesn't always work.

For example, Wilhelm has reported that accelerated tests of color photographic prints usually produce less overall fading and less yellow stain accumulation than the equivalent light exposure taken over the months or years of normal display. In other words, accelerated tests can *underestimate* (by a factor of 2–4) the amount of print deterioration that will occur during actual, real-world display conditions (see more about this problem under the Wilhelm section later in the chapter).

What Are Normal Display Conditions?

What's normal? It depends on where you are and whom you ask. According to independent researcher Barbara Vogt, the average amount of light an image is exposed to in real life in the United States is about 215 lux (a lux is an illumination measurement equal to one lumen per square meter) with the temperature and humidity at an average of 21° C and 50% RH (relative humidity). The Eastman Kodak Company says that 120 lux is a good, overall estimate for typical home conditions. Henry Wilhelm has adopted 450 lux for 12 hours per day at 75° F and 60% RH to simulate standard, indoor display conditions. David Matz has measured the light levels in his house. One wall (with art) in his living room gets three hours of sunlight each day at an intensity of 50,000 lux; when the sunlight leaves, the room lighting drops to under 2,000 lux. The Montreal Museum of Fine Arts uses 75 lux and 100 lux illumination levels for its exhibits, which it rotates between display and dark storage.

Conclusion? There are no normal display conditions. (See Chapter 9 for more about displaying prints.)

The foyer in this house is lit by a combination of diffused, indirect window light and overhead incandescent spotlights. The midday illumination level at the sailboat painting is around 200 lux.

Comparative Versus Predictive Testing

This is a key testing issue. Is the goal of the test to give results so that different print products can be compared, or is it to give an effective-lifespan prediction for any one print?

A *comparative test* uses a consistent test method and compares how different choices for colorants or media, for example, perform under that test. How long did it take Sample A to lose 30 percent of its density? Sample B? Sample C? Now you can compare all three based on the same criterion. Assuming identical test conditions, you're testing for the relative changes among the samples.

A *predictive test*, on the other hand, uses a consistent test method under a specific set of conditions and projects those results out to a predicted lifetime before a predetermined amount of deterioration would occur. It's a calculated guess of a print's "useful or service life."

Predictive tests are problematic. Because of reciprocity failure and the very likely chance that the test conditions will never be matched exactly, the predicted life-years should be skeptically viewed. "Predicting a printed image's service life is difficult, at best," explains permanence researcher Eric Everett. "Because of the multitude of environmental factors that can work independently or in tandem with UV light, one should be extremely cautious when estimating an image's lightfastness."

One of the criticisms of the Wilhelm test results described later in the chapter is that they are predictive. However, the real problem occurs when people either don't pay attention to the test conditions or mix the two types of tests, trying, for example, to compare the results of a predictive test.

Visual Versus Measurement Testing

The simplest way to test print deterioration is to run different samples under one test and then look at the samples and visually compare them with a control set that wasn't exposed to the test conditions. For a lightfastness test (described later in the chapter), the controls are either covered up next to the test samples, or they're stored out of the light nearby. Visual tests are usually run by individual artists because they're relatively easy to do. You need only line up the samples and visually decide which you like best, or in the case of a lightfastness test, which appear to have faded the least.

Most testing labs and serious testers, however, run instrument-measured tests (using a spectrophotometer, colorimeter, or densitometer). Printed color samples are measured before, during, and after the test is complete. The test ends when either a specified period of time has elapsed or when a specified *endpoint value* is reached (see "What Are Endpoints, and Why Are They Important?"). The measurement values are then computed or graphed for analysis.

What Are Endpoints, and Why Are They Important?

Scientific, instrument-measured tests require endpoints—the point at which a test sample fails and the test ends. The most sophisticated system is Henry Wilhelm's Visually-Weighted Endpoint Criteria Set. Using a spectrophotometer, initial starting densities are recorded on different neutral gray, pure color, and minimum density (paper-white) patches. When repeated measurements of the patches show that one has reached its allowed percentage of change, that patch has reached its endpoint.

The unique thing about this criteria set is that it's visually weighted. Instead of uniform percentages across the board, Wilhelm has used focus groups and other psychometric factors to determine what changes are more acceptable than others. For example, most people will tolerate a Caucasian flesh tone going more red or pink but not more green. In addition, Wilhelm's blue-density change for paper-white patches has a higher limit (.15), which allows the paper to go yellower before failing. Wilhelm colleague Mark McCormick-Goodhart believes that's because the human eye is adapted to campfire light, and we tend to accept— and even prefer—some visual yellowing.

The selection of the endpoints is very important in measured testing. If you want a sample to appear to be more long lasting, all you have to do is increase the endpoint percentage so that it takes longer to reach it. That's why some manufacturers use a 30-percent dye loss change instead of, say, 25 percent. It makes a difference, and explains why it's important to read the fine print on test results.

Dark Fading Tests

The fading of prints occurs under two main types of unrelated conditions: dark storage and light display. *Dark fading* (also called "thermal image degradation" or "dark aging") is usually the result of the inherent instability of the colorants and the media, or because of the effect of other influences such as heat, humidity, and environmental contaminants. Because dark fading can be exacerbated by high temperatures and humidity, this type of test is frequently conducted in high-temperature ovens.

A typical result of dark fading is the formation of yellow stain on color photographic prints. Anyone with family photos that are more than a decade old can attest to this problem. Dark fading is not limited to dark storage, but because it is primarily due to the instability of the materials, it starts the moment the print is made and takes place independently and at the same time as any light-caused fading, if the print is displayed.

Different types of colorants or media will have different dark-fading rates, and the only way to know for sure is to wait for it to happen or to test it.

Light fading is just what it sounds like and is covered next.

Lightfastness Tests

All prints will photodegrade in the presence of light. That means that they undergo a photochemical reaction when exposed to lightwave photons, and they start to deteriorate. The changes can be in the form of fading, darkening, or changing hue (color). The more resistant a print is to this inexorable process, the more lightfast it is.

Light doesn't have to be a high-noon bombardment of Florida sunshine either. Although sunlight or unfiltered fluorescent light tends to accelerate fading more than incandescent light, the weak light from a 75-watt bulb hanging near a print can be enough to fade it into nonexistence. It all depends on the duration and the intensity of the light exposure. High intensity for a short time has the same effect—in theory—as low intensity for a long time. (See reciprocity failure above.)

Because a good test matches the actual display or storage conditions as closely as possible, researcher David Matz envisions a test method that would include three to five conditions that real-word images are likely to see (such as a dimly lit room with no extra image lighting, museum lighting, halogen track lighting, direct sunlight through glass, and so on). Testers would also identify specific illuminants (such as glass-filtered fluorescent, sulfur bulb, glass-filtered xenon arc, unfiltered xenon arc, and so on) and test conditions to best simulate each of these display conditions. This type of all-inclusive test, Matz admits, doesn't yet exist, but it would give the information we really need to make informed decisions.

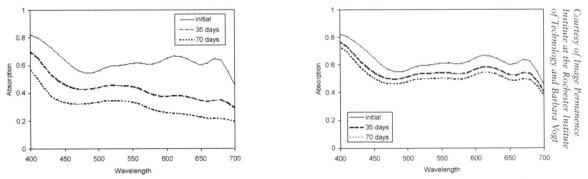

Courtesy of Image Permanence Institute at the Rochester Institute of Technology and Barbara Vogt

These neutral-patch, dye-based ink fading results are from a lightfastness test conducted by researcher Barbara Vogt in 2001. Left: Exposed to 50-klux fluorescent light; right: Exposed to 50-klux light and glass-filtered.

The main problem with lightfast testing is that it may or may not take into account all the other factors that cause prints to fail. Is it really just the light that makes print X fade? Or is it also the humidity, the temperature, the air quality, or some other factors that no one has even discovered yet? Again, Matz recommends performing tests at 75° F and low humidity to separate light affects from humidity affects, but requiring that a humidity test be done separately to isolate and quantify that effect. He also advocates conducting a separate test for sensitivity to known environmental gases and reporting the final test results for a range of display and storage conditions likely to occur.

You can see why this testing business is so tricky.

Other Tests

Other important tests that are currently being carried out or being developed by standards groups include the following:

- Gas fading (for air pollutants, air flow, and ozone)

- Waterfastness (for water-fastness and outdoor durability: the drip test, the pour test, the standing water evaporation test, the standing water plus blotting test, and the water smear test; see Figure 6.5)

- Humidity-fastness

- Fingerprint test (for handling damage)

- Chemical and biological stability (to test resistance to attack by chemicals and biological agents)

Courtesy of Martin Juergens

Figure 6.5

The results of a water-smear test; left: black ink; right: red ink.

Who's Doing the Testing?

There are three kinds of groups doing print permanence testing and making permanence claims: *independent testing organizations and researchers, manufacturers and marketers,* and *photographer-artists* themselves.

Testing Organizations and Independent Researchers

These are the scientists, the university-based, nonprofit, research laboratories, and the independent labs that do the most well-publicized testing of print permanence.

Wilhelm Imaging Research (WIR)

Henry Wilhelm (see Figure 6.6) is the dominant figure in both photographic and now digital print-permanence testing. He wrote the ground-breaking book *The Permanence and Care of Color Photographs* (1993), he is on the key industry standards committees (ANSI/ISO) and panels, and he is a consultant on image permanence to such prestigious institutions as the Museum of Modern Art in New York.

Figure 6.6

Image-stability researcher Henry Wilhelm at the Maine Art Gallery in Kennebunk. Colleague Mark McCormick-Goodhart, who took this photo, explains that "the architectural trend for both homes and galleries seems to be toward higher light levels and natural light using picture windows and skylights. Henry measured the light on this print at about 42,000 lux. That value is higher than what's used in many 'accelerated' aging tests for indoor display conditions!"

WIR is based in the college town of Grinnell, Iowa, and does both independent contract testing on prototype materials for companies as well as generic testing for public consumption. When you see permanence claims made by ink vendors or inkjet printer makers, there's a good chance that WIR did the tests from which the results were drawn.

WIR tests inkjet materials plus other types of digital hardcopy. For its well-known lightfastness testing (see Table 6.1), WIR runs accelerated, measured, predictive testing based on continuous, high-intensity light exposure conducted at 75° F and 60% RH. Using Wilhelm's unique, visually weighted criteria set, the results are then projected out to a reference display condition of 450 lux for 12 hours per day.

WIR has generated a bit of controversy in the past couple of years. Some of the main issues include the following: using predictive "years-of-display" projections that don't take reciprocity failure into account, using higher humidity levels than some ink manufacturers feel appropriate, being surprised by the Orange Shift debacle (although few saw that coming), and the limbo state of WIR's Web site and publicly visible test results that have become the bible of every photographer-artist concerned about print permanence. (I have been assured by WIR that getting the Web site back online has become a major priority, although at this writing, www.wilhelm-research.com was still unavailable.)

On the plus side, WIR is currently changing its testing methods to respond to most of the criticisms to better account for gas fading, reciprocity failures, and humidity-fastness problems. WIR is also widely respected for being scrupulously unbiased and energetic in promoting print-permanence improvements.

IPI/RIT

The Image Permanence Institute (IPI) at the Rochester Institute of Technology (RIT) is a university-based, nonprofit research laboratory in Rochester, New York. It is devoted to scientific research in the preservation of visual and other forms of recorded information. IPI is the world's largest independent lab with this specific scope, and they have sponsors who include the likes of Eastman Kodak Company, 3M Company, Fuji Photo Film Company, and Polaroid Corporation.

The IPI tests for lightfastness (using high-intensity xenon arc and fluorescent) and the effects of pollutants and heat and humidity on photos, inkjet prints, and other imaging media. Normal test conditions used for high-intensity fluorescent tests include exposing color samples for 10 or 14 weeks to 50 klux light with normal airflow. IPI is one of the few facilities in the world equipped to test materials for gas pollutants at different concentrations, temperatures, and humidities. They can study the effects of sulfur dioxide, nitrogen dioxide, hydrogen sulfide, and ozone.

Instead of publicizing any test results as WIR sometimes does, IPI provides them only to the companies that contract for the tests. Those companies—not IPI—are free to draw their own conclusions and use them in their marketing claims. For example, Red River Paper and inkjet ink supplier MIS both promote the longevity of their respective products as tested by RIT/IPI, and they show the results of those tests on their Web sites.

Q-Lab Weathering Research Service

Q-Lab (also known as Q-Panel Lab Products) performs accelerated laboratory light-stability and weathering tests (see Figure 6.7) as well as natural, environmental exposure tests using its Florida and Arizona locations. Q-Lab is ISO Guide 17025-accredited.

Independent Researchers

Independent researchers like Barbara Vogt also conduct scientific testing. For her 2001 thesis at the Department of Image Engineering, University of Applied Science, Cologne, Germany (*Stability Issues and Test Methods for Ink Jet Materials*), Vogt teamed up with the IPI/RIT to conduct a series of accelerated, measured tests on inkjet materials. Her goal was to try to better understand the complex fading behavior of inkjet prints and to demonstrate the difficulties in providing reliable tests.

Figure 6.7 *Eric Everett of Q-Panel Lab Products with two models of their Q-Sun Xenon Arc Test Chambers. Xenon arcs use filters to provide very close simulations of full-spectrum sunlight (UV, visible, and infrared) and sunlight filtered through window glass.*

Using ISO 10977 as her standard, Vogt performed both a lightfastness and an environmental pollution test. One conclusion was that her samples that were printed on two EPSON paper stocks and that "were exposed to air flow showed a significant fade rate, up to three times (cyan dye) faster on the glossy photo paper." This backs up the observation of the Orange Shift problem mentioned earlier. However, perhaps Vogt's main result was that much more work needs to be done and many more tests need to be run to come up with general conclusions about inkjet print stability.

Traditional artist, art educator, and color expert Joy Turner Luke has been doing prototype testing for the ASTM since the 1970s. In her northern-Virginia studio, she conducts skylight (sunlight) tests controlled by ISO blue wool references. She follows the ASTM standard D5383 to the letter (she helped write it) and has been doing inkjet lightfastness testing on her own for six years (see Figure 6.8). In one such test, the skylight version ran for four and a half months, while a companion, room-light test lasted for five years! This was the point at which both tests were visually equivalent, or, in her words, "A picture hanging on the wall in Virginia would begin to lose its vitality in three months, and after five years, it would be as badly faded as the colors that were exposed in the test rack." Keep in mind that this was one test with one set of materials conducted in 1996.

Luke is very interested in inkjet prints and is continuing to test with and to push the ASTM to include them in their standards. However, she thinks dye-based inkjets have a long way to go before they reach the lightfastness levels of traditional fine-art materials. Luke told me recently that she hopes that the different standards-setting groups can put their heads together and come up with universal standards for all art production materials, including digital prints.

Figure 6.8
Permanence researcher Joy Turner Luke in her studio. The top-right inset shows her south-facing, skylight exposure racks (she's holding one of the specimen panels in her hands).

Manufacturers, Vendors, and Distributors

Some manufacturers (Kodak, for example) do their own tests and use the results in promoting their products. Others, like Epson and MIS (who also do some internal testing), contract with independent testers, such as WIR or IPI/RIT, to perform their tests and then use the results in their marketing.

Epson, which was bruised by the infamous Orange Shift problem, is now very careful about its permanence claims. For example, here's the small print about the EPSON 1280 Stylus Photo inkjet printer: "Lightfastness rating of more than 20 years, based on accelerated testing of prints on EPSON Matte Paper-Heavyweight, displayed indoors, under glass. Actual print stability will vary according to image, display conditions, light sensitivity, humidity, and atmospheric conditions. Epson does not guarantee longevity of prints." Jon Cone of InkjetMall.com is less specific and merely claims that their "Piezography BW prints (carbon-pigment B&W prints) should be able to be displayed continuously in proper lighting conditions for well over 100 years."

It's important for photographer-artists to be wary of wonderful-sounding test results and claims from companies that their products will last until the earth stops spinning. These claims can lull you into thinking that you've got nothing to worry about, but you do.

The problem with vendor-sponsored tests and claims, besides an obvious bias, is that they tend to generalize and simplify what is a very complex interaction of separate elements that can contribute to significantly different results depending on the display or storage conditions. There just is no standardized "miles-per-gallon" way to describe print permanence—at least not yet.

Your Mileage May Vary

Just like miles-per-gallon estimates in the auto industry, permanence claims and estimates will vary depending on the specific display or storage conditions any print experiences. Using WIR's lightfastness tests as the model, it's easy to see why this is. The point of print failure (David Matz calls it "the death point") is reached based on the total, cumulative light exposure. The standard way that's figured is by multiplying the lux level by the time of exposure, which yields the total, cumulative amount of light in lux-hours.

Let's say WIR has determined that the death point of a particular ink/paper combination is reached at 100 million lux-hours (that's the equivalent of 30,000 lux over 3,333 hours or 139 24-hour days). Extrapolating the results to WIR's "standard" indoor conditions of 450 lux for 12-hour days, you would end up with a usable print life of 50 years. However, if the intended conditions are more like a museum where 100 lux might be used, then all of a sudden, that same ink/paper combination now becomes a 228-year rating. On the other hand, if the print is going in your south-facing living room where 5,000 lux will hit it each day, the print's lifetime has just shrunk to 4.6 years. Big difference.

One large distributor of inkjet systems and supplies, LexJet Direct, has commissioned the major independent labs to test and verify that the manufacturers' claims are accurate. They basically want to make sure their customers get what they pay for.

I'm not saying that permanence testing is not important or valid—it clearly is. You just need to be smart about it. Use the test results to compare similar products or methods. Don't use them to assure yourself or others that this one particular print will last for X number of years. It may not.

Individual Artist Testing

A lot of photographer-artists do their own "window tests," which involves hanging a print or two in or near a south-facing window and seeing what happens. This isn't as silly as it sounds because a print that can survive a direct attack by sunlight should be able to do the same in a more gentle environment. However, I would suggest a more scientific approach. For example, photographer Paul Roark, an expert on monochromatic inkjet printing, does his own lightfastness tests using a custom-built "fader" and a spectrophotometer. He regularly shares his results (see Figure 6.9) with members of online discussion lists or with anyone who's interested.

Figure 6.9 *A Paul Roark accelerated test comparing two inks and showing fading and color shifting. The top strip is the control for ink #1; the next strip down is the result after 300 hours. Note the warm shifting overall. The bottom two strips show the same test with ink #2.*

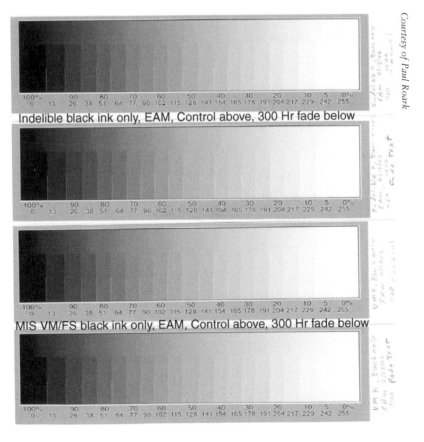

Courtesy of Paul Roark

Photo artist Barry Stein built a fluorescent-fade tester for under $50 that allows him to test with and without a glass filter and to adjust the light level from 20 to 60 klux (see Figure 6.10).

There is no reason why you can't set up your own permanency test to get the most accurate information about *your* materials, methods, and display environments. To find out how, see "How to Do Your Own Permanence Testing" later in this chapter.

Figure 6.10 *Barry Stein's custom-designed, high-intensity, light-testing device—all for under $50*

So How Long Will It Last?

I started off this chapter asking two, simple questions: How long is long enough? How long will it last? That second one is the hardest to answer because there is no one answer and because it all depends. It depends on the specific combination of colorant and media used. Even more so, it depends on the specific storage or display conditions any one print encounters. A basement in Berlin? Your mother's condo in Florida? You see the problem?

Even the best independent permanence tests (see Table 6.1 for the latest published WIR image stability ratings) and manufacturers' claims will only give you a generalized guesstimate of what's going to happen to your prints. There are just too many variables. What is the atmospheric pollution level where the print will be displayed or stored? What is the UV component of the light coming in from the windows? What's the temperature? What's the humidity? These are just some of the influencing factors that will significantly affect the permanence of that print.

One way to get closer to knowing about the longevity of your prints—besides studying test results or waiting around a few decades as your prints age—is to do your own testing to find out.

Table 6.1 *Wilhelm Imaging Research's latest (as of Summer 2002) permanence testing results.*

Predicted "Years of Display" Before Noticeable Fading Occurs with Color Prints

Desktop inkjet printer and inks	Print paper and type of coating	Years of display before noticeable fading occurs[1] (prints framed under glass)
Printer: Canon S800 Photo Printer	Canon Photo Paper Pro PR-101 (microporous coating)	27 years[2]
Ink: Canon BCI-6 (6-ink, dye-based)	Canon Glossy PhotoPaper GP-301 (microporous coating)	6 years[2]
Printer: EPSON Stylus Photo 890, 1280, 870, and 1270	EPSON ColorLife Photo Paper (swellable polymer coating)	26 years
Ink: EPSON inks (6-ink, dye-based)	EPSON Matte Paper-Heavyweight (matte coated paper)	25 years
	EPSON Premium Glossy Photo Paper (v2001) (microporous coating)	9 years[2]
	EPSON Photo Paper (microporous coating)	6 years[2]
Printer: EPSON Stylus Photo 2000P	EPSON Premium Luster Photo Paper (microporous coating)	more than 100 years
Ink: EPSON "Archival" (6-ink, pigmented)	EPSON Premium Semi-Gloss Photo Paper (microporous coating)	more than 100 years
	EPSON Enhanced (Archival) Matte Paper (matte coated paper)	more than 100 years
Printer: Hewlett-Packard PhotoSmart P-1000, 1215, DeskJet 970 series	HP Colorfast Photo Paper (swellable polymer coating)	19 years
Ink: HP #78 (4-ink, dye-based)	HP Premium Plus Photo Paper (swellable polymer coating)	5 years[3]
	HP Premium Photo Paper (swellable polymer coating)	3 years[3]

Desktop inkjet printer and inks	Print paper and type of coating	Years of display before noticeable fading occurs[1] (prints framed under glass)
Printer: Kodak Personal Picture Maker PPM200 (by Lexmark)	Kodak Ultima Picture Paper, High Gloss (swellable polymer coating)	24 years[3]
Ink: Kodak "Photo" (6-ink, dye-based)	Kodak Premium Inkjet Paper, Matte (matte coated paper)	6 years[3]
	Kodak Picture Paper, Soft Gloss (microporous coating)	3 years[2, 3]
Printer: Lexmark Z52 Color Jetprinter **Ink:** Lexmark "Photo" (6-ink, dye-based)	Kodak Premium Picture Paper, High Gloss (swellable polymer coating)	less than 1 year
Traditional Chromogenic Color Prints	Fujicolor Crystal Archive Paper (multilayer gelatin-coated RC photo paper)	60 years[4]
	Kodak Ektacolor Edge 8 Paper (multilayer gelatin-coated RC photo paper)	22 years[4]

[1] Predictions based on accelerated light stability tests conducted at 35 klux with glass-filtered cool white fluorescent illumination at 24° C and 60% RH. Data were extrapolated to display conditions of 450 lux for 12 hours per day using WIR Visually-Weighted Endpoint Criteria Set v2.0 (reciprocity failures are assumed to be zero). [2] Field experience has shown that, as a class of media, microporous papers used with dye-based inks can be very vulnerable to "gas fading" when displayed unframed and/or stored exposed to the open atmosphere where even very low levels of certain air pollutants are present; to a greater or lesser degree, these papers have a pronounced sensitivity to pollutants such as ozone and, in some locations, displayed unframed prints have suffered from extremely rapid image deterioration. [3] These ink/media combinations have poor humidity-fastness and, when stored or displayed in commonly encountered conditions of high relative humidity, over time the prints may suffer from one or more of the following: color balance changes, density changes, lateral ink bleeding, "bronzing" in high density areas, and sticking and ink transfer. [4] Display-life predictions integrated with the manufacturer's Arrhenius dark stability data. Note: An earlier version of this table was included in an article by Anush Yegyazarian entitled, "Fight Photo Fade-Out," *PC World*, July 2001, pp.48-51.

Courtesy of Wilhelm Imaging Research, Inc. (www.wilhelm-research.com)

How to Do Your Own Permanence Testing

There are as many ways to conduct a print permanence test as there are ways to make a print. Let's follow the steps of a simple, actual lightfastness test I recently conducted:

1. **Decide on what you want to test for.** I decide to test the fading of four different papers using the same printer (EPSON 1280) and inks (OEM six-color, dye-based inkset). In addition to one of the specified papers for the 1280 (EPSON ColorLife Photo Paper), I want to also test Hawk Mountain's Osprey, Hahnemuhle Photo Rag (from Digital Art Supplies), and Kodak's Premium Picture Paper to experiment a bit.

Figure 6.11 *The author's fluorescent light-fading test unit*

2. **Select test type, conditions, and testing procedure or standard, if any.** This is actually the most important step, and many people rush through it without much thought. In my case, I'm doing an accelerated, comparative (relative), visual lightfastness test. This will be a timed test, which means that I'll stop it after 100 days of continuous exposure. (One of the key questions is: How long do I run the test? You have two choices: terminate the test when endpoint measurements or visual color changes are reached or when a pre-determined amount of time is up.) I'm not going to control the temperature or humidity, but will just let my normal house conditions prevail. I'll store a duplicate set of target samples in the same room as the references and then compare both at the end of the test.

3. **Set up test conditions and apparatus.** I build a crude light-testing apparatus and install it in a seldom-used bathroom (see Figure 6.11). The light source is two Sylvania Sunstick (full spectrum) fluorescent tubes mounted about six inches from the print surface. To reduce the possibility of any gas fading affecting the results, especially in terms of reciprocity failure, I lay a piece of standard window glass over the target samples. The targets will also get a minimal amount of window light, but it will be minor compared to the test light, which I determine to be 5.5 klux as measured with a photographic light meter.

   Why fluorescents? Although they may not match the spectral distribution of other light sources and display environments, they're cool, cheap, and commonly used. Using tungsten light, xenon arc, or even window light is perfectly fine, but many have found that a fluorescent-light setup is good for inexpensive, controllable, repeatable tests.

4. **Prepare and print the targets.** Using Adobe Illustrator in CMYK mode, I set up a standard target grid (see Figure 6.12). As you can see, it's made up of small patches of different, pure, printing color combinations stepped in 10-percent increments. Note that I include a 0-percent "paper-white" patch as well. Each patch is 1×2 cm., and the overall target image is 11×16 cm. I print each target (along with some real-world images, including

faces) on an 8.5 × 11-inch sheet of each different test paper (noting which is which in the margins). I could print right from Illustrator but, instead, I like to place the file into a CMYK Photoshop file and print from there, turning off color management and picking the paper for my media type and print-space profile. In the end, it doesn't really matter because I'll be comparing the control targets to the printed ones. All the sheets are printed one-after-another, and I let them air-dry overnight. The next day, I arrange

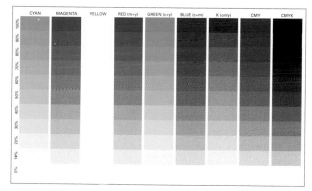

Figure 6.12 *The test target, created in Adobe Illustrator CMYK*

one complete set under the test lights while wrapping the other in acid-free glassine and storing it in a cardboard envelope (for darkness) near the test.

5. **Run the test.** With the targets in place, I turn on the lights. I check in each day and rotate the targets under the lights each week to make sure they all get the same average exposure.

6. **Terminate test and make evaluations.** On the one-hundredth day (the equivalent of 6.7 "Wilhelm Years" at my light intensity), I turn off the lights and take the test samples along with the dark-stored references over to my work area. I place the printed samples in my Soft-View viewing booth and decide which ones look best when compared to their controls (see Figure 6.13). Those that match their controls the closest will have faded the least. I can also compare the printed samples among themselves for a different evaluation. If I'm really feeling energetic, I could instrument-measure or flatbed scan each before and after target and take measurements of a selection of patches using Photoshop's Info palette. Then, I could tabulate the results and determine the numeric conclusions in terms of absolute and also percentage change. Maybe next time!

What have I learned? Of the four ink-paper combinations tested, the ColorLife version held up the best. The fading was minimal, although there was still some. The other samples showed more fading to varying degrees. Because the fading occurred in less than seven projected Wilhelm years, I would have to be very careful with my paper selections for this printer and its dye-based inks.

Remember that this is just one way to do a test. You could, instead, test different inks on the same paper, use a different type of light source (south-facing window, tungsten light, or xenon arc, if you're really ambitious), make the test run longer,

Figure 6.13 *Visually comparing the targets after the lightfastness test is over*

or change any other factors you want. It's *your* test. The whole point is to give you basic information so you can make informed decisions about what material combinations will best meet your needs for certain storage or display conditions. Have fun testing!

How to Maximize Print Permanence

Prints begin deteriorating the moment they're made—some faster, some slower. Whether because of light, temperature, or other factors, your prints are going to degrade. Your goal should be to use your knowledge about materials and processes to make the wisest choices that will improve the permanence of your work. This applies to inkjets, digital photo prints, color lasers, and so on.

Realize that there are three factors that affect print permanence: colorants (inks), medium (paper), and display/storage conditions. To maximize permanence, you need to carefully control all three. If you make prints to sell or give away, you've just lost one leg of the stool because you can't control the conditions where the prints will end up. However, you can do your best with the other two.

Depending on whether you self-print or have someone make prints for you, there are things you can do to extend print permanence (see also Chapter 8 and Chapter 9 for more about inks, paper, framing, and display):

- If relying on outside permanence testing results, make sure you understand what the test conditions and standards were and adjust your expectations accordingly.

- If you have a choice, select/specify long-lasting ("archival") colorants. In general, pigment-based inks produce longer-lasting prints than dye-based ones but tend to have a narrower color gamut. However, over time, we're seeing the pigment inks getting much better in terms of increased color gamut and the dye-based inks becoming more permanent. If you're not already using a pigment-based printer, consider using third-party archival inks. Several vendors supply these inks in either cartridges or in bulk for use in continuous-flow systems. If you're using third-party inks, select an inkset that is primarily pigment-based and study the manufacturer's longevity claims carefully.

- Select/specify archival media (paper). The best papers for inkjet printing in terms of permanence are ones that are made from 100-percent cotton rag and have no acid content. Others can also work, but pay close attention to the pH levels and the presence of buffering agents and optical brighteners.

- Combining the two points just mentioned, select/specify the most long-lasting colorant/media combinations you can. The key is in matching your colorants to your media. Realize that permanence testing is specific to a particular type of ink or dye on a particular type of medium. Don't mix them up and expect the same results.

- Keep prints away from strong light, especially sunlight. (*Never* let one ray of sun strike a print's image.)

■ Display your prints behind glass or plexiglass. This reduces airflow, gas fading, and some UV exposure problems. If using fluorescent lights, filter them with glass or plastic covers to cut down on the UV emissions.

■ If you can't or don't want to display prints—on canvas, for example—behind glass, consider using a coating or spray, which will offer some protection. Keep in mind that coatings add a new element to the chemical interaction of ink and media; under certain circumstances they could even reduce print life.

■ Store your prints in a dark, dry, and cool place; light and moisture are real print killers. Try to minimize temperature and humidity changes; keep them as constant as possible. High temperature and humidity levels can speed up print deterioration, and very low humidity or fluctuating humidity can cause prints to crack or peel. The model conditions are 68° F (20° C) with 30–40-percent relative humidity.

■ Store prints flat in flat files or stackable trays, but not in the open. Dust-free cabinets are even better, and acid-free boxes are best. It's OK to stack prints but separate each print with a sheet of acid-free glassine (available at any art supply store), or use archival envelopes. If you're putting prints into albums, use only archival or acid-free album sheets. Don't use any normal envelopes or sleeves that contain acid or polyvinyl chloride (PVC) for your prints, and never use rubber bands, paper clips, or pressure-sensitive tapes.

■ Don't let prints come in contact with any objects that produce oxidizing agents, solvents, monomers, acids, or other volatile materials. An incident in 2001 illustrates this danger. Photographer Butch Hulett inadvertently put a newly made inkjet print on coated paper on top of an ordinary pillow. He forgot about it, but the next day, he noticed that the print had turned a bright yellow. It was guessed that either the high acid content of the pillow's materials or chemical outgassing of formaldehyde interacted with the paper's coating to cause the problem. "Needless to say," he says, " I decided not to use that pillow for sleeping!" He's now also very careful where he puts his prints.

■ Communicate to and impress upon anyone receiving your prints all of the previous points. You'll save yourself and them a lot of disappointment.

How Permanent Are Digital Files?

Permanence is not only about prints, but also the files that make them. One of the advantages of going digital, people say, is that you can always return to the computer and make another print. That oversimplifies things considerably.

Digital permanence involves two important factors: physical lifespan and obsolescence. Optical disks, CD-Rs, CD-RWs, and DVDs have variable lifespans ranging anywhere from five to fifty years. The more important question is: Will you have a way to read the file in the future? Operating systems, hardware configurations, and software applications are constantly changing. I have a shelf full of SyQuest 44 MB cartridges in my office. Have you seen any SyQuest drives in operation lately?

Artistic Responsibility

Knowing what we now know about the ability of printed images to fade, deteriorate, degrade, and literally become shadows of their original selves, an artist cannot simply shrug off this issue of permanence, or call it "artistic freedom." In my opinion, it is the responsibility of every printmaking photographer-artist to learn about and communicate the particulars of his or her print methods and how they affect a particular print's longevity. To do otherwise is unwise at minimum, and, if prints are being sold, an actual fraud on the buying public and the entire community of other artists.

The answer is simple enough: Anyone selling or distributing print work should include a full disclosure as to the methods and materials used, including paper and inks. In 14 U.S. states, print disclosure is not optional but is set down as law. For example, California's Civil Code (sections 1742–1744.9) requires a "certificate of authenticity" (C of A) that includes "a description of the medium or process, and where pertinent to photographic processes, the material used in producing the multiple…"

There's also a marketing side to this. The excellent Web site www.worldprintmakers.com advises that "by offering the extensive information of the Certificate, printmakers can not only guarantee the authenticity of their work, but also educate their buyers as to just exactly what they are spending their money on. A proper C of A is an additional value-added to a fine-art print insofar as it explains to the client in detail the various factors that intervene in its production and edition. The more details the C of A includes, the more value it contributes to the print."

We've now covered what I consider to be the basics of digital printing. Let's now move to Part II and the subject that everyone is talking about: inkjet.

PART II

The Main Event:
Inkjet
Printing

7

Picking an Inkjet Printer

Inkjet printers are the output devices of choice for many photographers and traditional and digital artists. In Chapter 3, I gave a big-picture overview of the main digital printing technologies. Now, it's time to dive a little deeper and explore the world of inkjets. Whether it's a desktop or a wide-format; if you're looking for your first printer or ready to trade up; no matter if you're planning to self-print or use an outside print service—the more information you have about inkjet printers, the smarter your decision-making will be.

When you go to the grocery store, you take a list. It's the same when shopping for an inkjet printer or an inkjet printmaker. Instead of a list of items, you need to know which questions to ask. So, rather than giving you a rundown of all the printers with a blow-by-blow inventory of features and specifications (with new printers constantly coming onto the market, no book can hope to be up-to-date), I'm going to present you with nine important questions, and ways to think about answering them. Add or subtract questions to suit your situation, and then finalize your own list and start shopping! (The printer brands and models I mention are current as of this writing. For the latest information about inkjet printers, visit www.dpandi.com.)

Can I Use It to Print... ?

The foundation question is: What do you want to do with the printer? It's best if you have an understanding of the type of printing you'll be doing in order to pick the best printer for the job. You may even decide that inkjet is not the best solution for you. If you're looking for "good enough" quality at a lower cost per print, consider color laser, especially for multiple copies. If you want top-end photographic output, and you want it to look, feel, and smell like a chromogenic C-print, then think about using a digital photoprinter (see Chapter 3 for more about these). However, there are plenty of advantages to inkjet, and it's a safe bet that an inkjet printer will meet most, if not all, of your requirements for high-quality digital output.

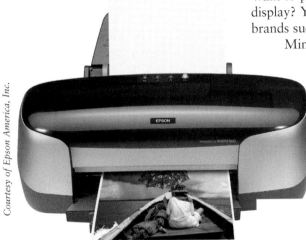

Courtesy of Epson America, Inc.

Want to produce oversized fine-art prints for gallery display? You might consider wide-format printer brands such as ColorSpan, Roland, EPSON, HP, Mimaki, or IRIS/IXIA. Interested in a general, all-purpose, desktop printer that can also do clean text and office graphics? Then HP and Lexmark may be the way to go. Dying to make B&W or quadtone prints? Then consider using one of the older EPSONs that use nonchipped ink cartridges, if you can find them, or one of the newer EPSONs with two black inks. Need durable, water-resistant prints on plain paper? Then, you'll want pigment-based inks, and the EPSON C82/C62 is a good choice at a very reasonable price. Pre-press proofing? Consider a printer with a PostScript RIP such as the HP 10ps/20ps.

The EPSON Stylus Photo 960 desktop inkjet printer, Epson's first dye-based desktop printer has individual ink tanks.

Sometimes, a printer designed for one application is used for another. Take the old EPSON Stylus Color 3000 and the Stylus Pro 5500. Both were created for the pre-press, graphic arts market, but both were immediately "stolen" by commercial and fine-art photographers because of either their reliability (3000) or amazing output quality (5500). The same occurred with the EPSON Stylus C80/C82. It's really an office printer, but digital photographer-artists instantly saw its advantages—high quality, low price, waterproof, pigmented inks—and claimed it for themselves.

What Size Output?

A subset of the "Can I use it to print...?" question is this: What sizes can I print? This is usually a top-level question because you must, at a minimum, have a printer that can handle the largest size you intend to output. In addition, this is where the decision between desktop and wide-format printing is often made.

Desktop

As I've already defined it, desktop (sometimes called "narrow format") means anything *less* than 24 inches. This refers to the media (paper) size and not the physical dimensions of the printer. Practically speaking, the largest common paper size for desktops is 13×19", also called Super B, Super A3, and A3+. (The ancient EPSON 3000—Epson's top-selling printer of all time—is the oddball here. Because of its graphic design heritage, it prints 17×22".) Some people, especially in the UK, like to call the A3+ format "wide-carriage" or, confusingly, "wide-format," but I'll stick with the U.S., industry-standard definition.

Desktops can squeeze more size out of their limited dimensions by turning the image sideways and printing on roll or cut-from-roll stock. Not all desktops can do this, but if you have long panoramics, roll-feeding desktops can be lifesavers. Desktop EPSONs like the Stylus Photo 825/925, 1280, and 2200 are good examples of printers that can provide this function. Keep in mind that the image length on a roll is not unlimited. For instance, on the EPSON Stylus Photo 2200, the maximum printable area is either 13×44" or 13×129", depending on your computer's operating system and the application software. (See more about printing big in Chapter 11.)

Another issue that may be important to you is the ability to make "borderless" prints. Epson introduced this capability (also called "borderfree" or "edge-to-edge" printing") with its newer Stylus Photo printers (currently 820, 825/925, 960, 1280, and 2200). Canon soon followed suit with the S900 and S9000 models. Canons make borderless prints by slightly enlarging the image and over-spraying beyond the edges of the paper.

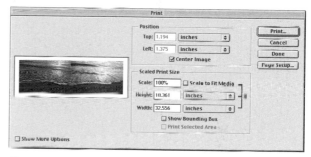

Panoramics can print on roll or cut stock on certain printers. This wide print is ready to go on an EPSON 1280.

Wide-Format Printers

Any printer that can accept media 24" or wider is called "wide-format." Another distinguishing characteristic of wide-formats is that they can generally take both roll and sheet media. Granted, some desktops can also do this (mostly EPSONs), but virtually *all* wide-formats can. (The HP2000/3000CP and 2500/3500CP series, with their problematic sheet feeding functions, and HP's postrelease decision to no longer recommend these machines for sheet-feed printing would be the only notable exception.) The reason is simple: Wide-format printers are designed for high-production environments. Service bureaus, high-volume outputers, professional printmakers—these are the typical users of wide-formats. If you want to print only 4×6-inch snapshots, you could use a wide-format, but unless you wanted thousands of them, it would be overkill—and expensive!

Any outside printmaker you use will undoubtedly have wide-format print devices. Remember that wide-formats can always print a smaller image, but a desktop can't print a larger one (with the exception of panoramics).

Which Inkjet Technology?

As we learned in Chapter 3, there are two broad categories of inkjets: continuous flow and drop-on-demand; the latter group can be divided into three subgroups: thermal, piezoelectric, and solid ink. Does any of this matter? It depends. Although there are those who say that thermal printers are faster than piezos, and others who believe that piezos print sharper than thermals, the fact is, there are enough individual variations among all the printer brands that as soon as a generalization is made, it's proven false when a new printer comes along.

Because most people are unaware of the different inkjet categories, I'll give examples of each in the following sections along with microscopic reference "eye" prints (see Figure 7.1). However, my overall advice is this: Don't get too hung up on these technology types. Be aware of them, but go with the printer that solves your problems best.

Photomicrographs courtesy of Martin Juergens (left) and Roger Smith.

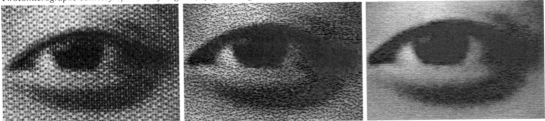

Figure 7.1
Photomicrographic print comparisons. Left: IRIS (continuous flow); middle: HP 990c (thermal); right: EPSON 1280 (piezo).

Continuous Flow

The only option for continuous-flow technology is the drum-based IRIS/IXIA from Improved Technologies. The IRIS itself stopped being manufactured in July 2000, although it's still available as a refurbished device from some resellers. The replacement for the IRIS is the IXIA (pronounced *ZEE-ah*) from Improved Technologies, and it's a souped-up IRIS 3047 with better production capabilities including the following: reduced banding, an improved RIP, better registration, smoother grays, and more consistent repeatability. It can print on virtually any flexible, water-compatible media (it uses four dye-based inks) up to 35.8×46.8". Its main purpose is printing fine art and photography.

Drop-on-Demand

Drop-on-demand is the only technology available for desktop inkjets. With the exception of the less common solid ink printers like the Tektronix/Xerox Phaser 8200, desktop printers are either thermal- or piezoelectric-based. All HPs, Canons, and Lexmarks are thermals, and only Epson makes piezo desktop printers. This is an area where a lot of the research and development dollars are being poured; consequently, this is where you have a good chance of meeting your digital output needs.

Thermal: There are more models of thermal inkjet printers than any other type. Thermal desktops include all the popular HPs, Lexmarks, and Canons. HP and Canon (not Lexmark) also make wide formats, but there are two other manufacturers to consider. MacDermid ColorSpan has several thermal models in its DisplayMaker line, which, although designed more for the signmaking industry, can also output higher-quality imagery. ColorSpan recently discontinued the Giclée PrintMakerFA, an eight-color, dye-based-ink printer that was the only drum-based thermal printer. (The only remaining drum printer for high-quality output is the IRIS/IXIA; all other inkjets are plotters, also called "bar printers" by some.) Kodak/ENCAD makes the popular, flatbed-style NovaJet 880 printer that will accept very thick media, and Kodak had four wide-formats in this category with its 4000-Series printers (now discontinued) and has one remaining, more-specialized thermal printer: the 5260.

The Lexmark Z65, 4800×1200 dpi, 3-picoliter, variable-droplet, four-color Jetprinter

Courtesy of Lexmark International, Inc.

Piezoelectric: Piezos include all the EPSONs, both desktops and wide-formats. The only other piezos are in the wide-format category, and there are several from which to choose. Roland makes six and eight-color, variable-dot, plotter-style printers. Mimaki has three wide-formats in its JV4 line, Mutoh has its Falcon II and Falcon Plus models, and Kodak/ENCAD has its flagship Professional 5260 inkjet printer.

Solid ink: This is the oddball inkjet category. The Tektronix/Xerox Phaser 8200 is a piezoelectric inkjet that uses solid blocks of pigmented, resin-based inks. The image quality is similar to that from color lasers. It's fast, and the colors are brilliant, but the output is not as photorealistic as from most of its inkjet relatives.

Age

Pay attention to the age of the printers you're considering. By this, I don't mean when a particular unit was made, but rather, when a particular printer model was introduced (see Table 7.1). When the EPSON Stylus Photo 2200 was announced in April 2002, it effectively wiped out the demand for the 2000P, which was released in May 2000 (the 2200 was also positioned as a step-up printer for those with 1280s, a printer that appears, at this writing, to be headed for retirement). The same can be said for Canon's S900 and S9000 (the S900 is the smaller-output version of the S9000), which basically replaced the S800 that was announced only the year before. Each of the newer products introduced innovative technology that everyone immediately wanted to have.

I'm not saying that older printers can't do a good job for you; they obviously can. The EPSON Stylus Color 3000 had been around for five years before it was finally discontinued in 2002! It's still a beloved senior citizen in the digital print world and a real workhorse for many photographer-artists even with its limitations (large dot size, no variable dots, and only four ink-colors). However, you may not want to be on the trailing edge of a technology just as a new type of printer is introduced.

Table 7.1

The EPSON Printer Line (as of August 2002)

Model Name[1,2]	Announced	Maximum Resolution (dpi)	# Colors	Smallest Ink-droplet Size[3] (picoliters)	Dye-based or Pigment	Street Price
Consumer Printers						
EPSON Stylus C62	Aug. 26, 2002	5760×720	4 (CMYK)	4	dye	$79
EPSON Stylus C82	Aug. 26, 2002	5760×720	4 (CMYK)	3	pigment	$149
EPSON Stylus C82N	Aug. 26, 2002	5760×720	4 (CMYK)	3	pigment	$349
EPSON Stylus C82WN	Aug. 26, 2002	5760×720	4 (CMYK)	3	pigment	$379
Graphic Printers						
EPSON Stylus Pro 5500	Feb. 12, 2001	2880×720	6 (CMYKcm)	3	pigment	$3,495
EPSON Stylus Pro 7600	May 1, 2002	2880×1440	7 (CcMmYKk)	4	dye or pigment	$2,995
EPSON Stylus Pro 9600	May 1, 2002	2880×1440	7 (CcMmYKk)	4	dye or pigment	$4,995
EPSON Stylus Pro 10000	April 4, 2001	1440×720	6 (CMYKcm)	5	dye or pigment	$9,995
Photo Printers						
EPSON Stylus Photo 820	Oct. 15, 2001	2880×720	6 (CMYKcm)	4	dye	$99
EPSON Stylus Photo 825	August 14, 2002	5760×720	6 (CMYKcm)	4	dye	$199
EPSON Stylus Photo 925	August 14, 2002	5760×720	6 (CMYKcm)	4	dye	$299

Model Name[1,2]	Announced	Maximum Resolution (dpi)	# Colors	Smallest Ink-droplet Size[3] (picoliters)	Dye-based or Pigment	Street Price
EPSON Stylus Photo 960	July 17, 2002	288021440	6 (CcMmYKK)	2	dye	$349
EPSON Stylus Photo 1280	Feb. 12, 2001	28802720	6 (CMYKcm)	4	dye	$499
EPSON Stylus Photo 2200	April 25, 2002	288021440	7 (CcMmYKk) 6 (CcMmYKK)	4	pigment	$699

[1] North American model numbers; models in other world markets may vary; prices and models subject to change.
[2] The C80, /85EPX, 890, 1520, 3000, 2000P, 7000, and 7500 were recently or are in the process of being phased out in 2002.
[3] All printers have variable-sized ink droplets, three sizes per line, except the C62/C82, which has six, and the 825/925, which has eight.

Source: Epson America, Inc.

How do you know when a printer is being replaced? You don't. However, by using some of the clues I've already given, you can bet that any printer that's more than 12–18 months old will soon be on the chopping block. Also be aware of any large price reductions in a printer model; these tend to be used to clear existing stock before a replacement model is announced.

What's the Print Quality?

In a nutshell, any of the newer photo inkjet printers can produce stunning prints. Inkjet output is now as good as—and in some respects, better than—traditional ways of printing images. High-quality, continuous-tone digital printing has finally become a reality. Here are three quality features to pay attention to when picking a printer (there are others as well, but these are three of the most important):

Resolution: As mentioned in Chapter 2, image or print quality is the result of many factors, and each printer OEM highlights different ones to help tell their story. "2400×1200 is nearly 40% higher than 2880×720" (from Canon and Lexmark). "2880×1440 is 44% greater than 2400×1200" (from Epson). "4800×1200: The Ultimate in Resolution" (from Lexmark). You don't need to worry too much about these Battle of the Resolution claims. The difference between 1440 dpi, 2880 dpi, and 4800 dpi is not really discernable by the naked eye, so most newer printers will be more than adequate in terms of resolution.

Number of colors: When possible, go for at least six colors for desktop inkjet printing (some B&W printmakers feel that four is all you need with PiezographyBW or multitone B&W printing). The extra two colors (usually a light cyan and a light magenta for CMYKcm) will smooth out subtle gradations, color blends, and skin tones. Four-color-only printers with lower resolutions tend to show grain in highlight areas. Epson, HP, and Canon all have six-color desktop printers. (Lexmark doesn't, but they feel that it's unnecessary with their highest-resolution printers [Z55 and Z65] and small drop sizes.) The seven-color EPSONs 2200, 7600, and 9600 (CMYKcmk) (see Figure 7.2) have an extra low-density black to reduce graininess and improve the neutrality of grays.

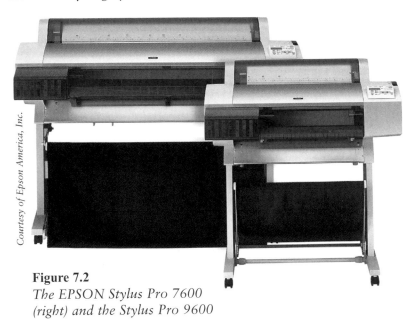

Courtesy of Epson America, Inc.

Figure 7.2
The EPSON Stylus Pro 7600
(right) and the Stylus Pro 9600

Six and seven colors is currently as far as desktops go, but wide-formats go even further. Eight colors are available from Roland (Hi-Fi JET PRO—or six colors including a Hexachrome inkset, CMYKOG, on the Hi-Fi JET), ColorSpan (DisplayMaker Esprit and Giclée PrintMakerFA), Mutoh (Falcon II), and ENCAD (NovaJet 880), and you can get a whopping 12 colors from ColorSpan (DisplayMaker Mach 12 or the Esprit with a 12-color upgrade) and Kodak (Professional 5260). The extra printheads on these devices are often used to double up on the same basic colors, increasing print speed, or they can be used to boost the color gamut by adding extra inks such as orange and green.

Ink droplet sizes: The smaller the drop or dot sizes, the finer the detail and the smoother the color variations. The smallest drop size currently available (at this writing) in the United States is 2 picoliters (a picoliter is a liquid measurement unit) from the new EPSON Stylus Photo 960 desktop (950 in Europe). One thing to keep in mind about dot sizes is this: Uncoated papers are much more forgiving of large dots, which tend to spread or bleed together and create a softer look. That's one reason the EPSON 3000, with its gargantuan 11 picoliter drop size, still produces acceptable prints for many, especially when used on uncoated art and watercolor papers.

Variable drop sizes are a further advancement for increasing fine highlight detail and for optimizing photographic quality. Different brands offer two to eight different drop sizes per line, including IRIS/IXIA, EPSON, Lexmark, Kodak, Roland, and Mimaki. (At this writing, most current EPSONs have three droplet sizes.)

Sample Before You Buy

As part of your research into printers, try to gather actual printed samples for review. For desktops, office super stores will frequently have sample prints available next to the printer on display. Online retailer inkjetART.com offers custom sample prints from several of the inkjets it sells for evaluation/comparison. (InkjetART also has some excellent output comparisons and recommendations on their Web site.)

In addition, most manufacturers will send you sample prints from their various printer models. Narrow your list down to the top few and call their 800 numbers for samples and product brochures. For desktop samples in the United States, call these OEM presales numbers:

Epson: (800) 463-7766

HP: (800) 243-9816

Lexmark: (888) LEXMARK

Canon: (800) OK-CANON

The next step up is to have sample comparison prints made from your own test files. This is usually only done by vendors of the more expensive wide-formats. When printmaker Larry Thomas of Gleedsville Editions in Leesburg, Virginia, was trying to decide on which wide-format printer to buy, he sent the same test image to several different vendors who made prints for him. He then presented the prints to a panel of friends and associates for blind testing and asked them to pick the best one. He went with the printer (a Roland) that produced the winning sample.

What Different Papers and Inks Can I Use?

Some people consider printing merely the final step in a long digital workflow. They're mainly concerned with accurately reproducing on paper what they've worked hard on and now see in front of them on their computer monitors or easels. Others are true printmakers and view the selection of media and ink as an integral part of the creative process. How you locate yourself on this continuum will help determine how important paper and inks are to your decision-making process.

Media

With one exception, all the major desktop OEMs recommend their own specific papers to use with each printer model (the exception is Lexmark, which suggests using Kodak Premium Inkjet or Picture Paper). The reasons are two-fold: (1) The engineers can optimize the print quality for a specific selection of paper and coatings, and (2) they'd like to sell you more of their own paper.

So, if you like the paper selection, you're in good shape; if you don't, well, luckily, many outside companies are now offering high-quality, third-party papers that work well with most inkjet printers. (See Chapter 8 for more about printing papers.)

The widest range of OEM desktop paper choices belongs to Epson, and this is one reason many use their inkjets. They're the only printer company that offers "art" paper including a watercolor paper as a stock item for some of its printers. Both HP and Canon only offer basic choices in "photo papers" in gloss, matte, or satin/luster finishes. (Note: at this writing, Hahnemuhle had just announced a strategic partnership with HP to provide several "HP made by Hahnemuhle" papers.)

Wide-format printers have more media options including artist canvas and the translucent film that artist and fine-art printmaker Steinman favors for his backlit work (see Figure 7.3). The other way to go is to use nonrecommended, third-party papers. Crane, Somerset, Legion, Ilford, Hahnemuhle, Schoellershammer, Pictorico, Hawk Mountain, Red River, DotWorks, and Media Street are only some of the paper makers or distributors offering third-party papers for digital printers. Larger online retailers such as MediaStreet.com and InkjetMall.com also sell high-quality media under their own brand names. Hahnemuhle Photo Rag, for example, is available from MediaStreet as Royal Renaissance. Some wide-format paper is not available for desktop printers. For example, Crane makes a beautiful 100-percent cotton rag

Courtesy of Jan Steinman/Bytesmiths.com

Figure 7.3
Artist and fine-art printmaker Jan Steinman uses translucent film to produce his signature Translesce prints.

paper for Epson (EPSON Smooth/Textured Fine Art Paper by Crane) that is available only as roll stock (24" and wider) for the wide-format models. (The new EPSON Velvet Fine Art Paper is made by Somerset and is available in 13 × 19-inch sheets.)

Another important factor is paper handling. The drum-based inkjets (IRIS/IXIA and the discontinued ColorSpan Giclée PrintMakerFA) are famous for being able to handle very thick media (although their maximum dimensions are limited, and the manual loading and unloading is a major headache—the main reason the Giclée PrintMakerFA is no longer made). I know of an English printmaker who uses an IRIS to print on Arches 640 gsm artist paper (the same paper used for painting).

Wide-format HPs have the opposite problem: They can't handle thick paper because their paper path is not straight; thick, stiff paper has a hard time turning a 180-degree corner. In fact, any paper thicker than a modest 12 mil (a mil is a measurement thickness of 1/1,000 inch) won't work with these HPs. Other printer brands have no trouble with this (the ColorSpan can print on 120 mil), and some, like the ENCAD NovaJet 880, allow you print on rigid media up to 1/2-inch thick, which is the equivalent of 500 mil. Some printers require single-sheet feeding of certain papers while others let you stack up a 100 sheets. Your production needs will determine how important this is to you.

Another niche consideration is whether the printer has the ability to *duplex* (automatically print on both sides of the paper). Several HP Deskjet models can do this.

Inks

We'll go into much more detail about inks in Chapter 8, but here are a few issues that might affect your printer-picking process.

Dye or Pigment?

Most inkjet printers come from the factory preconfigured to run either dye-based or pigment inks. (See Chapter 8 for an in-depth look at these two types of inks.) Desktops come one way or the other, whereas some wide-formats let you switch between the two systems or even run them simultaneously. (With EPSON Stylus Pros 10000/10600, 9600, and 7600, you have to choose between the Photo Dye or the Archival/UltraChrome pigment version when you set up the machine. Several HP Designjets run pigment-based black inks in combination with dye-based colors.)

If you're concerned about print permanence (see the next section in this chapter), you'll want to choose a pigment-based printer or one that can be adapted for third-party pigment inks (some savvy digital printmakers have figured out that they can use a bulk, third-party, pigment ink system on a non-pigment machine and avoid the higher cost of the manufacturer's pigment printer). For dedicated pigment printers for the desktop, your choices are simple and all EPSON: Stylus C82/C62, Stylus Photo 2000P (discontinued), Stylus Photo 2200, or Stylus Pro 5500 (on track to be retired soon). For wide-format, the field opens up considerably with Roland, ENCAD, Mimaki, Mutoh, MacDermid ColorSpan, and Epson all offering several models from which to choose.

Cartridges and Capacities

Out-of-the-box inkjet printers use ink cartridges or tanks to feed the printer, and in general, desktops have small cartridges, whereas the wide-format have larger ink cartridges or tanks, which makes them run longer before ink changing and also helps economize ink costs. At one end of the spectrum, a single desktop ink cartridge might hold as little as 19 milliliters of ink (approximately one half fluid ounce), whereas the

For color, most desktops use foam-filled, multicolor cartridges (left), whereas wide-formats use larger, single-color "bag-in-a-box" carts (110 ml shown at right).

tanks on the Kodak Professional 5260 and the ColorSpan DisplayMaker Mach 12 have a whopping 1-liter (1,000 ml or 28 fluid ounces) capacity.

The way around the high-price and inconvenience of tiny ink cartridges is to use a bulk ink system. These are also called continuous-flow (CFS) or continuous-inking systems (CIS), and they pump bulk ink from large containers to the printer, bypassing those puny cartridges entirely (see the "What Does It Cost?" section and Chapter 8 for more about these). The rub is that the bulk systems work only with certain printers. (Primarily desktops utilize bulk-ink systems; wide-formats normally don't need them because of their larger-capacity ink tanks.)

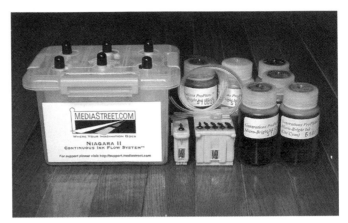

MediaStreet's Niagara II Continuous Ink Flow System

Canon pioneered individual ink cartridges (one cartridge or "tank" per color) for desktops with its S800 and then S900/S9000, but Epson quickly responded with the same idea for the C80 (four tanks) and the 2100/2200 and 950/960 (seven tanks). Whether having separate tanks will actually save you any money (one main benefit cited) depends on your printing; see more about this in the "What Does It Cost?" section of this chapter.

Metamerism

If you're concerned about metamerism (pronounced *me-TAM-er-ism*—somewhat erroneously defined as prints looking different under different types of illumination), you should realize that, in general, dye-based inks will exhibit less of it. It's more the pigmented inks that give many photographer-artists fits, and EPSON's Stylus Photo 2000P probably produced the most obvious examples of this problem. Typically with this printer, the output looks fine under tungsten light, but take the prints over to a window, and they turn green, especially in the more neutral midtones. This is especially disconcerting with skin tones, where that sort of color shift is noticeably unpleasant (to most tastes). Epson acknowledged this deficiency with the archival inks used in the 2000P and released an updated driver in mid-2002 that was a help to some. Epson did even better with the newer 2200/7600/9600 printers by adding a light black ink and also by using reformulated pigment inks (*UltraChrome*) that reduce the greenish tint.

Third-Party Inks

The ability to use third-party inks can be an important consideration (see more about this in the next section). EPSON is the clear favorite in being supported by third-party ink makers. You'll have a harder time finding these inks for HPs, Lexmarks, or Canons. Some of the older EPSON models, such as the 880, 1160, 1270, 3000, 7000, and 9000, don't use the smart-chipped ink cartridges (see Figure 7.4), which makes them easily convertible to third-party ink solutions. (Many of the newer "intelligent," microchipped printers can also accept aftermarket inks and bulk-ink systems, but it usually takes third-party marketers at least six months to a year to come up with workarounds for the printers after they hit the market.)

Another important thing to keep in mind is that the OEMs don't like it when you replace their brand of inks (and media) with an outside source. That's understandable if you consider that they've gone to a lot of trouble to develop the right printer driver settings to match their inks and media for the best results (and the fact that they stand to lose lots of money if you switch to Brand X!). One way to help ensure that you use their consumable supplies—inks, primarily—is to state that you will void the printer's warranty if you stray from the flock.

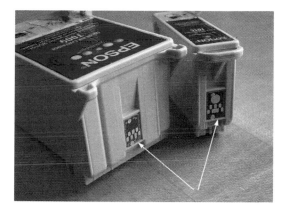

Figure 7.4
Two EPSON smart-chipped ink cartridges. Note the green circuit boards.

How Permanent Are the Prints?

If you've been paying attention so far, you know that that's a trick question. Print permanence is a function of the colorant/media combination and the storage or display conditions. The printer itself is a factor only in that it limits your choices of inks and paper. Depending on who's doing the testing, an EPSON 1280 print using OEM inks on EPSON Matte Paper Heavyweight is supposed to last about 25 years before noticeable fading (under glass). The same thing happens with a Canon S900 print using their inks on Canon Photo Paper Pro. In addition, the same thing happens with the Kodak Personal Picture Maker PPM200 (made by Lexmark) using Kodak inks on Kodak Ultima Picture Paper High Gloss.

However, if you change either the inks or the paper using the same printer, the print permanence situation can vary dramatically. Take that same EPSON 1280 and OEM inkset, make your prints on EPSON Photo Paper, and watch the longevity drop to six years (according to Wilhelm—see Table 6.1 in the previous chapter). Replace the EPSON inks with "archival" aftermarket cartridges, refills, or bulk ink from MIS Associates, for example, and you've roughly doubled (according to MIS) the predicted life of your prints.

Your other option, of course, is to buy a built-in pigmented-ink printer like an EPSON Stylus Photo 2200, the older 2000P, or the C82 (besides the solid ink printers, only Epson currently offers pigmented-based, desktop inkjet output). Depending on the paper used and based on Wilhelm or internal testing, pigmented inks currently offer the most permanent prints available by inkjet printing (more than 100 years predicted by WIR for the 2000P, up to 80 years for the EPSON 2200 on certain fine-art papers, and 70 years for the EPSON C82). Inkjet printers running pigment inks (either OEM or third-party) still have the upper hand in terms of light-fastness before noticeable fading occurs (although some dye-ink/paper combinations last long enough for many). This may seem like a minor issue, but when you look at your prints three, five, or ten years from now, it won't be. (See Chapter 6 for much more about print permanence.)

Courtesy of Hewlett-
Packard Company

Figure 7.5

HP wide-format Designjets 5000/5000ps and 5500/5500ps (shown) come in either dye-based- or pigment-based, UV-ink models.

If you go to wide-format, you instantly have even more pigment-ink options from Roland (Hi-Fi JET, Hi-Fi JET PRO and PRO II), ENCAD (NovaJet 880), Mimaki (JV4), ColorSpan (Displaymaker), HP (Designjet 5000/5000ps, 5500/5500ps; see Figure 7.5), and EPSON, too (10000/10600 and the newer 7600/9600 models).

The bottom line on permanence? Pick your printers carefully if you're interested in print longevity and are looking for third-party rather than built-in solutions. Depending on what you're looking for, there may be ink cartridge refill kits, aftermarket replacement cartridges, and bulk ink systems available. EPSON is the most popular inkjet printer line and the most-supported printer brand by third-party suppliers of specialized inks and media. HP has some third-party support (wide-format only), Canon will undoubtedly have more starting with the popularity of its S900/S9000 printers, and Lexmark, unfortunately, has little. (See Chapter 8 and the Appendix for a list of third-party ink and paper suppliers.)

Speed: How Long Does It Take to Print?

Newcomers to inkjet printing are, at first, enamored by the high-quality prints they can produce. Speed is usually not a primary concern. However, after a few days of watching that printhead going back and forth as the paper slowly emerges at what seems like the rate of a glacial ice flow, speed starts to become more important. It's especially crucial if you're hoping to achieve any sort of production output or run a business by outputting prints for others. The phrase "time is money" is nowhere more appropriate than here. That's why plotter-type, wide-format inkjets usually advertise their speeds in square-feet-per-hour. (You'll note the obvious absence of speed marketing claims by drum-based printers; they can take up to one hour to produce one print!)

One of the selling points for the EPSON Stylus Pro 10000 is that it's about six times faster than the EPSON 9000 series that it replaced, and it's faster than the 9600 model as well. The ColorSpan DisplayMaker Mach 12 is so fast (up to 400 square feet per hour) that it has a special heated-forced-air dryer to dry the ink. The new HP Designjet 5500 even beats that with a top production-mode speed of 569 square feet per hour.

Desktop inkjets, on the other hand, typically advertise the pages-per-minute rate or how many minutes it takes to print an 8×10-inch photo (or a 4×6-inch photo). (See Table 7.2.)

Table 7.2

On Your Marks, Get Set, Go! (Inkjet Printing Speed)

Printer	Print Speed (mins/secs, ppm, sq.ft./hr)
Desktop[1]	
Canon S900/S9000	approx. 60 secs. (8.5 × 11-inch color, default mode using Photo Paper Pro)
EPSON Stylus C80	42 secs. (8 × 10-inch photo, Normal mode); 10 ppm color; 20 ppm black text
EPSON Stylus Photo 820	1 min. 42 secs. (8 × 10-inch photo, Fine mode)
EPSON Stylus Photo 1280	1 min. 50 secs. (8 × 10-inch photo, Fine mode); 9 ppm black text
EPSON Stylus Photo 2200	< 2 mins. (8 × 10-inch photo, Fine mode)
Lexmark Z65	15 ppm color (Draft mode)
HP Photosmart 1315	1.2 ppm color (Best mode)
Wide-Format[2]	
EPSON Stylus Pro 10000	40 sq.ft./hr. (Superfine HS mode; bidirectional)
EPSON Stylus Pro 10000	25 sq.ft./hr. (Superfine mode)
EPSON Stylus Pro 7600/9600	8 sq.ft./hr. (Superfine mode)
Roland Hi-Fi JET	12 sq.ft./hr. (Photo mode HS; high speed)
Roland Hi-Fi JET	8 sq.ft./hr. (Photo mode)
HP Designjet 5000 60 in.	76 sq.ft./hr. (Best quality)
HP Designjet 5000 42 in.	68 sq.ft./hr. (Best quality)

[1] Print speed for desktops is measured either in pages per minute (ppm) or in total time to print a sample photo, usually 4 × 6 or 8 × 10. Keep in mind that the printing/quality mode used for these tests can make a big difference in print speed.

[2] For these sample wide-formats (sq.ft./hr.), each speed is for the highest quality mode(s) available for that printer.

In general, the higher the quality of inkjet output, the slower the print speed. You can check this yourself by simply changing the "quality" (or similar) mode setting on any inkjet printer and timing the same test prints. Many EPSONs also have a High Speed option (in the Advanced dialog box). What this does is change the printer from unidirectional printing to bidirectional; the head now prints in both directions. (Unidirectional printing with EPSONs is always from the parked-head position toward the center of the printer.) This effectively doubles the print speed, but at a slight loss in quality.

These different quality modes become especially important for the wide-formats, which often have to provide higher-speed, lower-quality production output. The Mimaki JV4 Series, for example, has 12 different speed/quality variations for its six printheads.

For the photo-desktop category, the higher-end Lexmarks (Z53, Z55, and Z65), the HP Photosmarts, and the Canon S900/S9000, which is the real speed demon, are all faster than the fastest EPSON Stylus Photo—the 2200. (The EPSON Stylus C82, which is faster still, is considered a consumer printer.)

There are workarounds to slow printing speed (beside buying a faster printer). I've gotten into the habit of having several in-progress projects ready that I can immediately move to while waiting for a slow print—emptying the trash, vacuuming, that sort of thing (it also gets me out of my computer chair). If your printer allows it, you can also take advantage of unattended printing. You load several pieces of paper, press the Print button, and move onto other tasks. Finally, you can print at a lower-quality mode setting. Many photographer-artists report little or no difference in quality when using the next-lower setting.

How Easy to Set Up and Connect? How Big? How Noisy?

The first lesson that all digital printers learn is that, regardless of the marketing hype, digital printing is not a push-button operation. Don't expect magic right out of the box. To be sure, you will get something with your first print, and there will be some—perhaps many—who will be perfectly thrilled and satisfied with no need to explore further. Many others—undoubtedly you, if you've read this far—will need to learn and advance their knowledge to get the kind of superb prints that *are* achievable with inkjet.

Desktop

Size: Size may be a minor issue for some, but if you're living in a one-room apartment and sleeping on a Murphy bed, you probably pay close attention to such things. Although their shapes may vary, letter-size printers all take up about the same amount of desk space. They're approximately 16–17" wide, and the particular configuration of paper support and output tray extensions will determine how much desk depth you need. However, you should count on one entire section of desk devoted to an inkjet printer. Move up to a 13×19-inch printer, and you've increased your width to approximately 24" with only slightly more depth required. Only a few desktop printers don't fit this mold—the HP Designjet 10ps/20ps is huge in comparison; about the size of a copying machine.

Keep in mind that the same printer is sometimes available in two different sizes; only the media handling capacity is different. For instance, the EPSON Stylus Photo 1280 is the larger version of the older 890. The same goes with Canon's S9000 and the S900.

Setup: We've reached the point in desktop inkjet evolution where equipment setup is plug-and-play. Buy any desktop inkjet on the market, and it should be up and running in less than one-half hour. Unpack the box, hook up the printer to your computer, insert the ink cartridges, load the paper, install the printer software (from CD), maybe run a head-alignment check, and you're done.

Compatibility: The first question is this: "Are there drivers for my OS?" You must have printer drivers (or a RIP) that support your computer's current operating system. This can be an important issue depending on where you are on the early-adoption-of-technology scale. For example, after Mac OS X came out, there was only limited driver support at first by Epson for it.

You either had to backtrack to an earlier OS, or keep checking EPSON's Web site to see if the OS X driver for your printer was available for downloading.

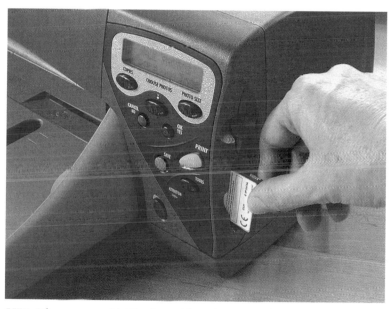

In general, most newer desktops come ready to play with all the usual OSs, both Windows and Mac. Some also support Red Hat Linux (Lexmark was the first inkjet maker to offer printer drivers for the Linux operating system). Again, you can usually download the most recent drivers from the printer OEM's Web site.

HP's Photosmart 1115 takes either CompactFlash or SmartMedia digital camera memory cards for photo-direct printing.

Want to skip the computer all together and go direct-to-print from digital camera memory cards? HP (Photosmart 1115, 1315, 7550), EPSON (Stylus Photo 825/925), Canon (S820D), and Lexmark (P122) all allow this kind of direct-to-print capability. However, realize that most serious photographer-artists are doing significant image editing with Photoshop or other software. They would rarely print raw captures right off a memory card (CompactFlash or SmartMedia). These printers are primarily aimed at hobbyists, although they are perfectly capable of acting like normal printers, too. Just check the specs first.

Connectability (or interface): This means how you physically connect the printer to your computer. Because the printer OEMs want to connect as many printers to as many computers as possible, they all offer the basic options: IEEE 1284 parallel (Windows) and USB (Windows and

Mac). The newest printers also support FireWire ports. If you have an older printer like an EPSON 3000, which only has parallel and Mac serial interfaces, you'll need to add an adapter card, cable, or box to get it to connect to the latest computers. Some, like the Lexmark Z65n, also support an Ethernet Internal 10/100 BaseTx connection for office networking.

Want to print wirelessly from a Palm or other handheld PDA? Need a wireless network solution for multiple laptop printing? EPSON and HP, for the moment, are your main choices. See "Welcome to Wireless" for more.

Noise: All desktops make those characteristic back-and-forth, mechanical sounds when they print. It's a sound you get used to, and for some, it becomes the background noise of their lives! EPSONs and HPs are moderately noisy, whereas the new Canons (S900 and S9000) are noticeably quieter (see Table 7.3).

Wide-Format

Size and setup: As can be expected, wide-format inkjets are bigger and are typically more complicated to set up and use. Drum-based printers like the IXIA are basically big boxes about the size of a very large copying machine—four feet wide and three feet deep. The other plotter-type printers all sit on their own stands, and their widths vary depending on the maximum print area. The EPSON 7600 is 43" wide, the 9600 is 64", and the 10000 is 73". Rolands vary between 78–88" wide, and HPs run anywhere from 60–96" wide. All are about four feet high, including the stand. Add up the printer and stand, plus the space needed for paper loading and output, and any extras like a separate server or RIP station, and you'll probably end up devoting at least a portion of a room to a wide-format printer. However, some wide-format owners, like digital artist and educator Teri Brudnak, are able to maximize space by having their printers on rollers and pushing them up against a wall (see Figure 7.6).

Courtesy of Teri Brudnak

Connectability/compatibility: Most wide-formats have cross-platform OS support (Mac and Windows), although a few do not. There are more connectivity options with wide-formats. Besides standard printer drivers for direct printing, most wide-formats will give you built-in access or expansion slots for parallel, USB, FireWire, and even serial connections, plus internal or external connections (10/100base-T interfaces) for print servers, networks, and RIP drivers.

Even with the added complexities, after you nail down your workflow, wide-format operation is fairly smooth. In terms of noise, wide-format inkjets are only slightly louder than their desktop cousins (see Table 7.3). However, you still have to learn to live with that bzzzz, bzzzz, bzzzz sound!

Figure 7.6
Artist Teri Brudnak and her Roland Hi-Fi JET in her home studio

Table 7.3

Noise Levels of Selected Printers (in Printing Mode)

Printer or Source	Decibel Level (dB)[1]
Canon S900/S9000	37 dB(A)[2]
EPSON 1280	42 dB(A)
HP Photosmart 1115	45 dB
Lexmark Z65	46 dB(A)
HP Deskjet 990c	47 dB
EPSON 5500	47 dB(A)
Lexmark Z55	48 dB(A)
EPSON 7600/9600/10000	50 dB(A)
Roland Hi-Fi JET	<60 dB
ENCAD NovaJet 880	<72 dB(A)
Common Noise Levels	
Quiet whisper	15–20 dB
Airport terminal	55–65 dB
Subway	90 dB
Chickens inside a building	105 dB
Loud rock music	115 dB

[1] A decibel (dB) is the unit used to measure the intensity of sound. Each increase of 6 decibels doubles the noise level. Twenty decibels is not twice as loud as 10 dB, but 10 times as loud. Sound above 130 decibels causes pain.

[2] Because the human ear doesn't respond equally to all frequencies, sound meters use filters to approximate how the ear hears sound. The A weighting filter (dBA) is widely used.

What About Printer Software, Drivers, and RIPs?

In addition to the required printer drivers, inkjet printers now include various software tools to make your printing more efficient (many will also come with bundled third-party software trials and demos). One great new feature of desktop printers is the *ink status monitor*. Lexmark's Ink Levels Indicator counts the number of dots you place and uses that to calculate the remaining ink. HPs use a smart chip on the ink cartridge to monitor how much ink has been used and how much is left. Additionally, smart chips in the HP printheads monitor the amount of ink that flows through the heads plus the status of the printhead's health. The Canon S900/S9000 has a unique optical, low-ink sensor that pops a warning on the screen when an ink tank is getting low.

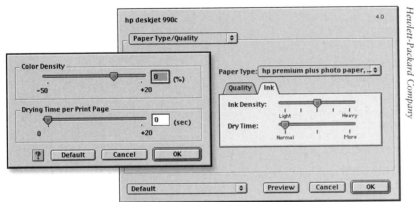

Courtesy of Epson America, Inc. and Hewlett-Packard Company

Figure 7.7
The newer EPSONs and several HPs have controls that allow you to adjust both ink density and drying time between head passes (EPSON at left).

Epson introduced two desktop paper-handling features to the Stylus Photo 2200 in a new Paper configuration dialog box in the printer driver (see Figure 7.7). (HPs have a similar feature.) Instead of being able to use only the Media Type settings for varying the amount of ink going onto the paper with normal printer drivers, the new *Color Density* function allows you to vary the ink density with a simple slider. In addition, taking a cue from the more expensive wide-format printers, a *Drying-Time-per-Print-Head-Pass* function gives you another control of print speed.

RIPs

As mentioned in earlier chapters, you may not need a raster image processor (RIP). RIPs can cost as much or more than the printer itself, so weigh this carefully. In general, if you're primarily printing single, RGB-bitmapped images without PostScript elements, and you're planning to use a desktop inkjet, an optional RIP is not a requirement. If, however, you want to wring the last 10 percent out of the image, a good RIP can help. For example, most RIPs can control very precisely how and where the inks are laid down. Of course, the built-in printer drivers do this, too, but it becomes more important if you use third-party inks and/or nonrecommended papers for which the printer wasn't designed. Setting precise ink limits, defining at what points the light magenta and light cyans come into the image, mixing differing amounts of black with the other colors for dense shadows or "rich blacks"—these are the kinds of things RIPs can sometimes do better than the installed printer driver.

Print Management

Some wide-format printers offer sophisticated usability features to make your printmaking more efficient. For example, the HP Designjet 5000 not only checks the printhead to make sure that all nozzles are firing, but it also tries to recover as many nozzles as it can by priming and cleaning them while printing. In addition, this HP printer goes a step further by identifying which nozzles are not firing and compensating for that in another pass of the printhead. If nozzle number nine isn't working, the printer comes back on the next pass and has neighboring nozzle 54 put down a dot to make sure there is nothing missing.

Similarly, the EPSON Stylus Pro 10000/10600 has proprietary laser technology that scans the surface of the printhead looking for possible nozzle clogging. When detected, the system automatically cleans the head.

The HP 5000/5500 has a fault-tolerant print mode that makes unattended printing a less-risky gamble. You go away for lunch, and the printer does not allow more than one bad print to come out. HP also offers a print accounting function through a unique Web-access interface. It not only tells you the status of all your ink supplies, but it also can track how much ink you're using on any job and how much paper you've used. It even calculates exactly how much media is left on a roll whenever you change rolls, allowing you to swap media as often as you like without having to worry if you're going to run out of paper mid-print.

The EPSON 10000/10600 has its own version of this with the Intelligent Ink Cartridge Technology that can track up to eight different data points for accurate print cost estimates.

Many wide-formats come with their own RIPs, or you can purchase a RIP separately. The EPSON Stylus Pro 10000/10600 comes without a RIP, but you can buy the optional EFI FierySpark Professional software RIP for $2,995. The newer EPSON 9600 has a similar RIP for an additional $1,995. This is a general-purpose graphics RIP for creating Adobe PostScript 3 output for both Mac and Windows. For the other EPSON wide-formats in the Stylus Pro line, there are more than 50 third-party RIPs available for printing everything from fine art to signage.

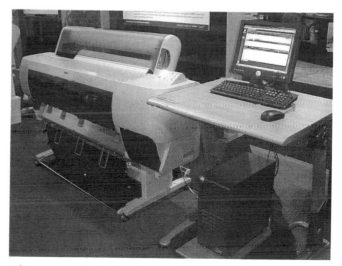

The EPSON Stylus Pro 10000 running the optional EFI FierySpark Professional software RIP

Not everyone uses a RIP for wide-format printing. Colorado-based photographer Tom Andrews, who prints his landscapes on his own EPSON 10000, thinks that "the provided Epson printer driver used with Photoshop is excellent. Because I only print fine-art photographic images, I have no need for a RIP."

Most people don't realize that you can run a sophisticated wide-format printer without a RIP right out of your desktop computer. Teri Brudnak has her Roland Hi-Fi JET connected to her Mac G3 with a simple USB cable. Other wide-format users find it more efficient to set up a dedicated Mac or Windows computer as a network spooler or print server, allowing them to continue image-editing work on their primary computer.

There are also desktop, PostScript inkjet printers (HP 10ps/20ps with a bundled software RIP) that are very appropriate for pre-press graphics output.

What About Service, Repairs, and Warranties?

Just like with cars, you will want to take maintenance and service into account when picking a printer, especially a wide-format. In general, the more money you spend, the more important this becomes. One of the reasons that many printmakers abandoned IRIS printers was the cost and complexity of maintaining the already expensive machines. Printmaker Jan Steinman researched IRIS printers but ultimately bought a 50-inch Roland when he discovered that an IRIS service contract would run him $1,200 per month. (Lynn Lown, another professional printmaker, points out that the cost of a maintenance contract is a good indicator of how much maintenance an average machine will require.)

Being able to do repairs yourself is an area where thermal inkjets have a slight advantage. When an EPSON printhead goes bad, you have two options (after the warranty period): (1) Spend some bucks to have it serviced or replaced at a service center or by an on-call technician, or (2) throw the printer away and buy another. Clearly, if you're paying $99 for a printer, you wouldn't spend $100–$200 for a new printhead. On thermal printers where the head is part of the ink cartridge, that becomes a nonissue—change cartridges and you've changed the heads. Canons have simple-to-replace-by-the-user permanent printheads with their own warranties.

Tech support is one reason to go with an all-OEM solution and *not* to mix different printers, inks, and papers. The manufacturer will help you solve problems when you're using their products. As soon as you don't, fingers start pointing in other directions, and the tech support people are less willing—or able—to help.

All the major desktop printer-makers (Epson, HP, Canon, and Lexmark) offer one-year limited warranties. What this means is that you can exchange a bad printer for a new one if there are any manufacturer's defects, subject, of course, to certain conditions and restrictions. Sending back an EPSON due to ink clogging if you've used third-party inks won't work; that's one of the conditions. Wide-formats go even further in offering next-business-day exchange or on-site service under the standard one-year warranty. They also offer the ability to buy extended warranties and service contracts after that.

What Does It Cost?

You might think that this would be the first question, but I like to bury it down the list. If all the preceding questions bring you to a choice between two printers, then make your decision on price. However, never make a decision about buying or using an inkjet printer solely on cost. You may be getting a good deal, but if the printer doesn't solve your problems, what good is it?

"What Does It Cost?" is also a complex question. There's much more involved than just the cost of the printer.

Desktop

Virtually all desktop inkjet printers cost less than $1,000, most are under $500, and some are under $100. In terms of a low printer-only cost, you really can't go wrong with the lower-end EPSONs, HPs, or Lexmarks. They're practically giving these printers away. Remember, however, that through a marketing strategy called *cost-shifting*, these printer manufacturers make their profit on the consumable supplies: the inks and the media. *That's* where your money will go, so make sure you figure in those costs, too.

Ink: After you realize that ink is the most expensive part of desktop inkjet printing, you'll undoubtedly be looking very carefully at this element. Much has been said about the cost benefits of having a printer that uses individual ink tanks. The argument goes like this: If you print images with a lot of blues, you will obviously run out of cyan ink before one of the other colors. Thus, if you have a printer that uses a combination-color cartridge (plus a separate black one), then you're basically throwing away all the unused ink when the printer indicates it's time to change ink cartridges. It's all or nothing with these combo-color cartridges. The solution would obviously be to have individual ink tanks that could be changed separately as needed, and there are two desktop manufacturers who have picked up on that idea: Canon (S800/S900/S9000; see Figure 7.8) and Epson (2100/2200, 950/960, and C80/C82).

If you look more closely at the problem, you'll see that individual ink tanks may not be any cheaper in the long run. A full set of either Canon or EPSON individual ink cartridges will cost about $72 and $84 (at the time of this writing), respectively (the Canons are six-color; the EPSON 2200 is seven-color). However, if you were to buy a similar six-color combination set of two cartridges (for the EPSON 1280, for example), the total cost is only $52 for both the color and black cartridges. Because the black runs out less frequently, you would only be changing the color cart, which is $30. You would have to buy three color carts before you

Figure 7.8
Canon caught the desktop inkjet world's attention with its individual transparent ink tanks, here shown with the S800 model.

saw any savings from using individual tanks. So, unless you know that you'll be printing a lot of only one color, you may not be that far ahead in the cost game with individual tanks. (There are other considerations besides the cost of inks, but that will have to wait for Chapter 8.)

However, the real savings with desktop inks is by getting rid of the expensive cartridges all together. There are now several bulk-ink delivery systems that allow you to buy and use large, more-economical ink bottles to provide bulk ink to the printer. Unfortunately, not all printers will accept this type of system, which I discuss in more detail in Chapter 8.

Paper: The second important element in figuring ongoing inkjet costs is media. Inkjet paper in cut sheets can run anywhere from $.50–$3.00 each, depending on the size and brand. Zeroing in on the U.S. standard letter size (8.5 × 11"), you should be able to find high-quality paper at well under $1.00 per sheet. OEMs like Canon, who have a very small selection of inkjet media, have expensive paper (Photo Paper Pro) that tends to wipe out any savings from its individual ink cartridges.

One way to save money on paper is to buy it in long rolls. However, the selection for desktops is limited, and it's only practical if you have a roll adapter for your printer (unless you cut your own sheets from the roll and hand-feed them). Wide-formats, on the other hand, are set up for roll media, and that's one way they can economize paper costs. Owners of both have been known to use the wide-format's roll cutter to produce cut sheets as needed for their desktop printers.

Cost per print: Adding these two cost components (ink and media) together brings you to the important "cost per print" (or cost per page). For one example, Epson provides a cost-per-print analysis for the Stylus Photo 2200 (see Table 7.4). As you can see, an 8 × 10-inch glossy print runs $1.25 in consumable costs. Other printer analyses, of course, will vary, but you can use this kind of information to compare different printer/consumable options. (Another way to estimate the true cost of a printer is by Total Cost of Ownership (TCO). The TCO takes into account the printer price, cost per print, and the annual number of pages printed. Add it all up, multiply by three to five years, and you have the Lifetime Printer Cost.)

How does that $1.25 compare to other digital or traditional print costs? My local photo lab charges $9.50 for a single, Fuji Frontier 8 × 10-inch digital print from a digital file, $20 for a LightJet print, and $20 for a traditional enlarger print. Factor in the cost of the printer, and you can see where inkjet printing starts to pay for itself. In addition, using this same kind of information, you will be able to make rational choices among printer vendors.

Wide-Format

Wide-format inkjet printers are *much* more expensive than desktops, running anywhere from $3,000–$30,000. Because wide-formats are widely used by commercial print-service providers who need to keep an eye on the bottom line, a running cost analysis is a standard factor in selecting a wide-format. As with print speeds, ink and media costs are usually figured on a price-per-square-foot basis. Again, I'll use Epson as the sample because they provide a complete breakdown for their wide-format printer line that allows you to see how different media types affect the actual printed-image cost (see Table 7.5). (Some have questioned these cost estimates because they're based on a sample image that has lower ink coverage than most photographer-artists use.)

Table 7.4

Cost Per Print (for EPSON Stylus Photo 2200)

8 × 10-inch Glossy	**$1.25 (ink and paper cost)**
11 × 14-inch Glossy	**$2.50 (ink and paper cost)**[1]

Ink Costs

Each Ink Cartridge	$11.95

Paper Costs (By Size)

Letter (PLPP, PSPP, PGPP)[1]	$0.78–$0.85 per sheet
Borderless PGPP 5 × 7"	$0.45 per sheet
Borderless PGPP 8 × 10"	$0.75 per sheet
4" roll (PGPP, PSPP)	$19.99 per roll; $0.38 per 4 × 6
8.3" roll (PGPP, PLPP)	$47.99 per roll
13" roll (PGPP, PLPP)	$69.99 per roll
Borderless 11 × 14" (PGPP)	$1.50 per sheet
A3, 11.7 × 16.5" (PLPP)	$2.06 per sheet
Super A3, 13 × 19" (PLPP, PGPP, PSPP)	$2.56–$2.85 per sheet

[1] PLPP is Premium Luster Photo Paper; PSPP is Premium Semigloss Photo Paper; PGPP is Premium Glossy Photo Paper.

Source: Epson America, Inc.

Table 7.5

EPSON SP 7600/9600/10000 Printed Image Cost
(in $ Per Square Foot)

EPSON media	EPSON PRINTER/INK			
	SP 7600 UltraChrome	SP 9600 UltraChrome	SP 10000 Photo Dye	SP 10000 Archival
Premium Glossy	1.32	1.15	0.87	1.14
Premium Luster	1.22	1.07	0.87	0.99
Premium Semimatte	1.22	1.07	0.87	0.99
ColorLife Photo Paper Semigloss			0.90	
Photo Glossy	1.11	1.05	0.85	0.97
Glossy Paper HW			1.38	
Photo Semigloss	1.07	0.93	0.74	0.85
Semigloss Paper HW			1.37	
Glossy Paper PW (22×36)	2.13	1.95		1.90
Enhanced Matte	1.09	0.94		0.84
Doubleweight Matte	0.95	0.78	0.74	0.74
Presentation Matte			0.52	
Canvas	2.83	2.70		2.63
Somerset Velvet (sheet 24×30)	3.00	2.89		2.68
Somerset Velvet (roll)	2.33	2.19		1.93^
Fine Art Paper (sheet 24×30)	2.42	2.31		2.10

EPSON media	EPSON PRINTER/INK			
	SP 7600 UltraChrome	SP 9600 UltraChrome	SP 10000 Photo Dye	SP 10000 Archival
Fine Art Paper (roll)	2.43	2.29		2.03
Proofing Paper Comm. Semimatte	1.19	1.02	0.83	0.94
Synthetic Paper	1.34	1.06		0.83
Adhesive Synthetic Paper	1.94	1.80		1.57
Adhesive Vinyl	2.04	1.91	1.66	1.80
Backlight Film	1.38	1.27	1.12	1.29
Tyvek	1.97	1.87	1.74	1.76

All cost per square foot comparisons are based upon the 24×36-inch bicycle image, printed at 720×720 dpi unless otherwise noted. Prices used are EPSON MSRP. SP 7600 based on 24-inch rolls. All others are based on 36-inch rolls.

Source: Epson America, Inc.

Printmaker Jan Steinman has estimated that ink and media cost him about $2–$3 per square foot for the premium-quality media and pigment inks he runs through his Roland Hi-Fi JET. He knows he can reduce his costs to under $1 per square foot by using dye-based inks and cheaper media, but he recognizes that that would be unacceptable for his high-end market.

Like high-ticket office equipment, wide-format printers can also be leased. For a few hundred dollars a month, you can have the latest in technology, and then trade up when you need to. (Of course, if you're interested in the total cost of providing a printmaking service to others, you must also add in basic business expenses such as rent, waste, and overhead, but that's the subject of a different book.)

Artist/printmaker JD Jarvis summed up this whole question of wide-format costs to me recently. "The most expensive solution is not always the best solution," he explained. "I purchased one of the first HP 2500 CP printers when it came out. I continue to be impressed by the output of my system and am rather proud of the cost-effective decisions I made quite a while ago. I will, of course, need to upgrade eventually, and I'll be looking for something more adaptable to a wider range of papers but still in the same purchase and maintenance price range. I am, however, more interested in balance. Balance across the system can out perform anything that has one big, star component."

An Inkjet Summary

A 2002 InfoTrends study shows that 81 percent of people who intend to purchase a digital camera expect to print their digital photos at home, and those are primarily by inkjet. At the other end of the scale, commercial inkjet printing as an industry is projected (by I.T. Strategies) to hit $7.5 billion by 2005. Add everyone in between who is creating and outputting digital art, and there are *a lot* of people involved with inkjet printing.

The days of wondering if inkjet would ever be good enough for high-quality digital output are definitely behind us. Inkjets are helping artists and photographers around the world produce work inexpensively, on-demand, and with great quality. The future for inkjet printers is only going to get rosier—higher resolution, more colors, better and longer-lasting inks, more paper choices, and flatbed wide-format printers. The best is yet to come.

How important is all this talk about inkjet printing equipment? It needs to be kept in perspective. As Santa Fe, New Mexico-based, fine-art digital printmaker Lynn Lown explains, "The printer is like a camera or a musical instrument; the operator is the key. A good printer or artist can make interesting pictures with simple tools. They have the hardware under control and can concentrate on ideas, images, and vision. Of course, that's easy to say."

A View to the Future

At the risk of oversimplifying what is a very deep subject, let me offer a few words about the major inkjet brands and their role in the future of high-quality inkjet printing.

Epson: Epson is the dominant force, or what artist/printmaker Jan Steinman calls the Microsoft of the digital printer world. Fair enough. They are the ones who basically invented photorealistic inkjet printing. They are the leader that everyone else is trying to catch. They're either the first to come out with new technology, or if not, as with individual ink tanks, the quickest to respond with their own solution. Simply put, Epson makes great printers, and you can make great prints using them.

Epson is constantly upping the ante with its new models, and with the introduction of its reasonably priced Stylus Pro 7600 and 9600 models, Epson is starting to bridge the gap between wide-format and desktop printers. One of Epson's main challenges is juggling the diverse needs of both consumer and professional customers, and keeping them all happy.

HP: HP has built a large base of satisfied users for its Deskjet desktops, Photosmart photo-direct printers, and Designjet wide-formats. HPs are solid, reliable performers, but with older technology and little

Courtesy of Hewlett-Packard Company

HP's Deskjet 3820 inkjet printer has a maximum resolution of 4800×1200 dpi.

Printing Packages

A new inkjet printing option that's aimed primarily at professional photographers, photo studios, or art galleries is the turnkey printer package. Here are three systems that combine existing hardware and software into all-in-one solutions:

EPSON Gemini Professional Portrait Printing System: Marketed as an alternative to sending out to traditional photo labs, the Gemini system includes two EPSON Stylus Pro 5500 inkjet printers, a PC server, proprietary software, an uninterrupted power supply, and a touch screen control for the server. The internal modem dials up Epson and orders its own supplies. Interestingly, the package is only available for Mac at this writing. You don't buy it; you lease it ($5,000 initial fee) with a monthly charge depending on the amount of supplies used.

Ilford Studio System: Ilford's version of this concept is its Studio system, which is comprised of *either* an EPSON Stylus Pro 7600 *or* 9600 printer and Ilford RIPSTAR Studio RIP with built-in profiles for Ilford media, which must be purchased separately. The system costs $5,500–$8,900 and includes installation, software, hardware maintenance training, and one year of unlimited technical support.

Brightcube Solution: Brightcube, which also makes inkjet printing media, has an innovative print-on-demand system targeted to frame shops and art galleries. Brightcube Solution includes the following: an online database of downloadable images, a special box that acts as a server/RIP to convert the image and prepare it for printing on Brightcube media, and any of the major wide-format inkjet printers (EPSON, Roland, HP, and ENCAD). You can select an image from the digital database (you pay a "click charge"), and within two minutes, the print is automatically outputting on your printer; all you have to do is load the paper. If you provide your own printer, you only need to purchase the server/RIP ($1,598), or Brightcube can sell or lease you the whole package.

emphasis on fine-art applications, HP has needed to catch up to their Japanese cohorts and bring something new to the table to capture the interest of photographer-artists looking for high-quality digital printing. And, they appear to be doing that. At this writing, HP had announced a $1.2 billion investment in the digital imaging and printing market, and had already released several new desktop printers (Deskjet 5550, 3820, 3420; Photosmart 7150, 7350, 7550) and a new wide-format (Designjet 5500/5500ps). More is sure to come.

Canon: Canon introduced the world to its BubbleJet thermal technology way back in 1981, known to Mac users in the form of the Apple StyleWriter line of printers. Since then, it appeared to be treading digital water. However, with the release of its awesome inkjet duo (the S900 and the S9000) at the beginning of 2002, it's clear that Canon is back in the game. These two printers are the first true rivals to Epson's hegemony in the higher-quality, desktop inkjet field. This new rivalry can only be good for all of us.

Lexmark: Lexmark is the king of the no-nonsense, inexpensive, desktop inkjet printer. However, they've been an innovator all along (first 1200-dpi printer, first sub $100 inkjet printer, first photo-direct printer), and they're slowly attempting to win over photographer-artists as well. In addition, with recent features such as 4800-dpi resolution and variable ink droplets, they have a chance of doing just that (if they would only expand their ink and media options as well).

Roland: Roland has staked out a strong position in the high-quality, wide-format inkjet category. As a favorite brand with many serious photographer-artists, Roland has no current plans to enter the desktop market, but intends, instead, to keep improving their pigment-based printers. Their eight-color, variable-dot, plotter-style inkjet (Hi-Fi JET PRO) is one of the top fine-art inkjets on the market.

ColorSpan: MacDermid ColorSpan's Giclée PrintMakerFA was the first wide-format digital printer created specifically for the fine-art market (in 1998), and there are lots of happy users still spinning its high-quality drum. (Giclée PrintMakerFAs were early and repeated winners of the DIMA Digital Printer Shoot-Outs.) However, that printer is no longer being manufactured, and, like the IRIS/IXIA, represents a printing style (drum-based) that has become less popular over time. ColorSpan also has several very capable plotter-type inkjet printers in its DisplayMaker line, including the Esprit, which has been positioned by ColorSpan to address the needs of fine-art printmakers.

IRIS/IXIA: The IRIS is the printer that started this whole inkjet phenomenon, and it has been reincarnated as the IXIA from Improved Technologies, which is selling the $45,000 devices to fine-art photographers, artists, and printmakers. There are still plenty of IRIS printers in use out there, but as they wear out, printmakers are either trading them in for the newer IXIA or shifting to other styles and brands of inkjet printers.

ENCAD and Kodak: ENCAD, which is now a wholly owned subsidiary of Kodak, has a long history of making wide-format inkjet printers, mostly for the commercial and outdoor signage markets. However, the release of its innovative NovaJet 880 flatbed-style printer and its partnering with Ilford for the 880i flatbed and other printers may be a sign of more interesting things to come. ENCADs are underground favorites of some artists including trendsetter Bonny Lhotka of Digital Atelier, who loves its deep, saturated colors, its inexpensive bulk inks, and the fact that she can run lots of thick media and artwork through it. For its part, Kodak seems to be sticking to the extreme ends of the inkjet spectrum. There's the Personal Picture Maker (made by Lexmark), its only desktop, and then there are the wide-formats led by the remarkable (and expensive at $29,995) Kodak Professional 5260 inkjet printer (now marketed by ENCAD). Both of these leave out most of the middle ground of inkjet users.

Mutoh: Mutoh is primarily known for its wide-format printers used in the point-of-purchase and poster industry. However, they're also targeting the photo/fine-art market, and they have two piezo printers that should be considered: the Falcon II and the Falcon Plus. Both come in three size models, but the Falcon II has the best specs with 2880×1440 dpi maximum resolution, the same printheads that are in the EPSON 10000, and the ability to run both dye and pigment inks in an eight-color configuration.

Mimaki: Another unknown commodity for most photographer-artists, Mimaki makes solid wide-formats, particularly their JV4 line with its three models: JV4-130 (54" wide), JV4-160 (64"), and JV4-180 (75"). Used mostly for commercial signage applications, they are perfectly capable of producing fine-art prints (1440×1440 maximum resolution; see Figure 7.9). Mimakis include some innovative features, such as being able to combine two separate inksets of three different types into 10 printing variations.

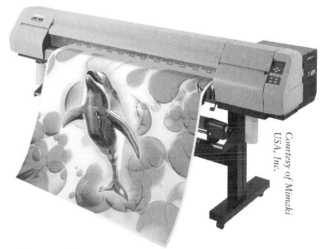

Courtesy of Mimaki USA, Inc.

Figure 7.9
The Mimaki JV4-160 wide-format printer

Welcome to Wireless

Like everything else, inkjet printing is going wireless. Epson and HP are currently the primary desktop players in this game, but that will surely change. Epson offers two different ways to go. The EPSON Stylus C82WN is a C82 with an attached wireless print server. Depending on environmental factors, the range can be up to 300 feet. Although this could be great if your computer is on the porch and the printer is in the basement, this printer's main function is for networked computers, primarily laptops. You could have an office full of busy artists all printing wirelessly to the central printer.

HP has—in addition to a driverless printing workflow through a new Web-file submitter for its Designjet 5500—its own Wireless Print Server wp110 that allows for infrared connectivity from Personal Digital Assistants (PDAs), notebook computers, and other mobile devices to several of its Deskjet (900 series) and all Photosmart inkjets.

Another option is Epson's Print Adapter. Handhelds (PDAs), cell phones, laptops, cars, radios, headsets, and more can now connect to a single printer up to 33 feet away via short-range radio frequency. It's the printer that needs the adapter, and it's only available for EPSON Stylus C80/C82/C62 and EPSON Stylus Photo 820/1280. It's currently only workable for text or low-resolution graphics.

We've been talking a lot about inks and paper for inkjet printing. Let's now get more details on choosing your consumables.

Choosing Your Consumables

Anyone who does a lot of inkjet printing discovers very quickly that the consumable supplies (ink and paper) are important keys to the whole process. Not only are they typically the most expensive aspect of digital printing in the long run, but also they will make or break the quality of your final output.

The Ink Factor

I'm stating the obvious, but it's important to remember that all inkjet printers use ink to form the image—not electrostatically charged toners, not RGB laser lights, not photosensitive dye compounds, but liquid inks. (Solid-ink printers use resin-based inks that turn into liquid after heating, but I won't be covering them here. See Chapter 3 for more information.) The kind of ink is the critical question. There are plenty of choices. (Note: As with printers, this chapter is a snapshot of what's available at the time of this writing. Check with suppliers for their latest products or check www.dpandi.com.

The making of inkjet inks is a complex, scientific undertaking, with modern day alchemists spending their days paying microscopic attention to chemical and physical ink properties such as dispersants, solvents, pH buffers, solubilizing agents, viscosity modifiers, anti-oxidants, biocides, and more. Although making informed choices about which inks to use doesn't require a Ph.D. in chemistry, a certain amount of knowledge is necessary.

Dyes Versus Pigments

Inks are basically composed of two components: a *colorant* and a *vehicle*. The vehicle is a transport medium that holds or contains the colorants, and it's either solvent- or water-based, with water (*aqueous*) being the dominant type for the kind of printing that's the subject of this book. (Solvent-based printers are preferred for various types of commercial and signmaking applications.)

As you learned earlier, the colorant of an ink absorbs certain wavelengths of visible light and reflects others, which are then perceived by our eyes as color. Colorants come in two basic types for inkjet printing: *dyes* and *pigments*. Each has its strengths and weaknesses.

Dye-Based Inks

Dyes, in natural form extracted from animals and plants or man-made, have been used for hundreds, even thousands, of years for coloring things such as textiles. Dyes have these advantages: (1) being easily dissolvable in water, (2) being transparent, and (3) easily providing brilliant, saturated color because they are composed of small, single molecules that refract or scatter very little light.

The first inkjet inks were water-soluble dyes. In fact, some early artists even experimented with running food coloring through their IRIS printers! Dye-based inks are still the dominant type available for inkjet printing. All thermal desktops and most piezos (only Epson currently makes dedicated, pigment desktop printers) come ready-to-print with dye-based inks.

Dye-based inks work very well on uncoated fine-art papers that absorb the ink. The ink droplets also bleed a little and tend to cover up certain printer-based problems such as low-dpi resolution.

The other side of the dye-ink story is that there are also three big disadvantages of using them for printing: (1) poor lightfastness, (2) poor water and humidity fastness, and (3) instability in many environmental gases such as ozone. Anyone with sun-faded upholstery or other dyed fabrics knows the result of these problems firsthand. When the first digital prints were being made on IRIS printers for pre-press proofs, these were nonissues, as the required life of a press proof is measured in days. However, now that inkjet prints are being produced for everything from family heirloom photos to fine-art prints destined for the walls of galleries and museums, print permanence has become vastly more important (see much more about this in Chapter 6).

In terms of lightfastness, dye-based inks are getting better. In 2001, Epson announced their new and improved "photographic dye" inksets. This included a new yellow and light magenta that they claim produces greater lightfastness. These photo-dye inks became available first with the EPSON 1280 desktop and the EPSON 10000 wide-format (dye version), and they were later used with other models as well. Third-party ink suppliers have also gotten on board by producing dye-based color inksets that claim longer display lives than their OEM counterparts (see more about third-party inks later in the chapter). The bottom line is that although the new dye-based inks are better than the original ones, if you're concerned about print longevity, you need to think seriously about pigment inks.

Pigment Inks

Pigment inks are far more complex to manufacture. Unlike dyes, which are made up of single molecules, organic pigments are combinations of thousands of molecules all "stacked up" in a particular order (see Figure 8.1). These super-molecules have very stable chemical bonds and are much larger than their dye counterparts. Whereas a dye molecule might be 1.5–4 nanometers in size (a nanometer is 1/1,000th of a micrometer or a micron, which is 1/1,000th of a millimeter), pigment particles are typically in the .05–.2 micron range. Even though this might seem large in relation to a dye molecule, these pigment particles, which are carefully ground down to microfine sizes, are easily small enough to flow through the smallest 10-micron inkjet orifice that is 50–100 times as large (see Figure 8.1).

Because pigment particles are insoluble in water, they must be carefully dispersed in a vehicle that will deliver them to the paper. One way to do this is with *microencapsulation*, which is how Epson does it with most of its pigment inks (certain black inks use "self-dispersive" technology). Each pigment particle is encased in a resin medium.

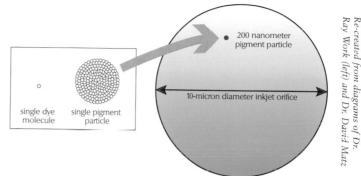

Figure 8.1

A relatively large pigment particle (left) is still very small compared to an inkjet nozzle orifice. Ink researcher David Matz likes to explain it like this: Think of a golf ball falling into a six-foot-diameter cup.

The main advantage of pigment inks is that, in general, they are more stable than dyes. They are significantly more lightfast, and much less sensitive to both humidity and environmental gases. Why? Because of the relationship between surface area and volume, the smaller the particle size, the greater the relative surface area, and the more likely that a photofading agent like light or a chemical attack agent like ozone can reach it. Because pigments are more complex with many more molecular components, light and gases will only reach a small percentage of the colorant particles while leaving the others untouched. The result is that pigments fade more slowly than dyes. They may also fade more evenly without the color-balance shifts that occur more commonly with dyes.

When it comes to humidity sensitivity, again pigments are much better. Because dyes are dissolved to make the ink, the printed colorant can begin to "redissolve" in high humidity and become "mobile," the last thing you want on a print. Pigments don't dissolve in aqueous media, so they don't redissolve when put in high humidity.

However, there's a downside to pigments. The larger particles of pigmented inks cause more light to scatter at the surface, which reduces color range or *color gamut* and makes some colors look weaker or duller. Rich reds are particularly hard to print with some pigments (although researcher David Matz points out that properly made pigment inks printed on a matched medium can result in high color gamut to equal dye systems). Other pigment problems include the following:

■ A greater tendency to *metamerism* (shifting colors under different types of lights—see Chapter 7 for more information). This is a common complaint of the earlier EPSON pigmented printers (such as the 2000P) with neutral tones (also skintones) that turned green under natural daylight. The more recent EPSON printers (2200, 7600, and 9600) with their new UltraChrome inks are designed to reduce this problem.

- Some pigments are *not* recommended for glossy papers because they do not dry completely, do not adhere well, or exhibit what's called *gloss differential*, where one part of the image will look duller than another. Epson does not recommend using their first-generation pigment inks on its Premium Glossy Photo Paper, but does recommend their next-generation DuraBrites and the even-newer UltraChromes for glossy prints. The flip side is that pigments are also not recommended for use on uncoated, fine-art papers like Somerset Velvet or Arches Cold Press; the inks tend to get lost in the paper's fibers and look muddy. Pigments are designed to go on coated papers (see below).

- A related issue with some pigments used on glossy or luster-type papers is smudging or "rub-off," where the ink can smear, especially in darker or black areas. Newer pigment ink formulations have attempted to fix this problem.

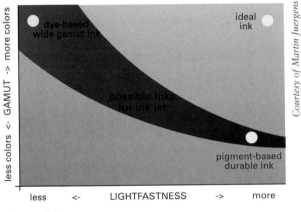

Figure 8.2
The gamut-lightfastness graph for inkjet printing

In theory, the basic trade-off between dyes and pigments is this: Dye-based inks are more "colorful" on a wide range of media but also more prone to show color changes on display, whereas pigment-based inks may offer less color gamut (except on well-matched media) but are more lightfast, humidity fast, and gas fast (see Figure 8.2). In reality, the gap is closing, and ink manufacturers are continually trying to come up with compromise solutions between color gamut and lightfastness.

One solution is by mixing dyes and pigments together for a specific result. For example, third-party ink supplier MediaStreet reformulated its popular Generations brand (G4, G5) pigmented inks to include a black that is 75-percent pigment and 25-percent dye to boost density and richness, which their earlier 100-percent pigment blacks didn't have. (The other colors are all 100-percent pigment, and other Generations inksets still include the 100-percent pigment black.) The only downside to such mixtures is that there can be uneven results when one ink component changes or fades before another. MediaStreet, however, claims that the new hybrid blacks still exceed the same 100 years of display life (tested by Wilhelm Research) as the other colors do, although some printmakers have gone back to using the older, all-pigment black. (Note that multi-monochromatic inksets are handled in a slightly different way: Pigmented black ink is mixed with a clear base stock to create the different gray shades or densities.)

Although several wide-format printers use pigmented OEM ink, the only desktop OEM option for using 100-percent pigment particles as colorants is with Epson. All three versions or generations of its pigmented inks (EPSON Archival, EPSON DuraBrite, and EPSON UltraChrome—see Figure 8.3) are 100-percent pigment-based. Third-party, all-pigment inks include the following: MediaStreet Generations Elite/Outdoor and Standard; MIS Original Archival, Exact Match Archival, and Perpetual Archival; Symphonic Inks; and Indelible Fine Art Inks.

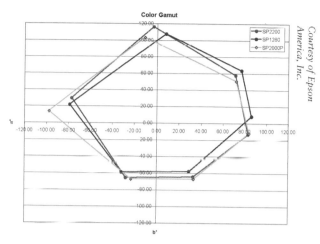

Courtesy of Epson America, Inc.

Figure 8.3

The relative color gamuts of three EPSON inks—two pigmented and one dye-based

The overall trend is definitely to the use of more pigment inks, and many predict that pigments will be the dominant type of ink used for high-quality inkjet printing in the future. Former DuPont ink expert Dr. Ray Work even goes so far as to state that with pigments, "...excellent color gamut and image-quality with long-term durability will make dye-based inks obsolete."

OEM or Third-Party Inks?

All inkjet printer manufacturers (OEMs) have inks they want you to use with their printers, and many desktops come with a starter set of cartridges ("carts") ready for installing and printing. For many people, this is all they want to know about inks, and they are content to use these standard, recommended inks that can usually do a perfectly good job of making prints. After all, the OEMs have carefully researched and developed ink formulations to best match their equipment and their recommended media. For example, thermal inkjets involve the quick heating and cooling of the printhead elements to create the ink droplets. Thus, thermal inks have to be carefully formulated with boiling-point chemistry in mind. Epson's piezo ink technology, on the other hand, is pressure-based, so an ink's boiling point isn't a factor in its formulation. This is one reason why you can't simply switch inks between inkjet technologies.

Thus, while OEMs don't like it when you bypass their ink supplies (and threaten to penalize you for doing so by voiding the printer's warranty), there are some legitimate reasons to consider using third-party inks: *cost, permanence,* and *special uses.*

Warning: Putting third-party inks in your inkjet printer is not without risk. Besides potentially ruining the printer, you may be in violation of the printer's warranty, although the OEM's legal foundation for this is shaky. Check the compatibility of any third-party inks before using them.

Cost: One reason OEMs push their inks is because they make a lot of money on them. Walk into any office superstore and take a good look at the inkjet supplies rack (see Figure 8.4). It will quickly become obvious that all those $35 ink-cartridge packages (plus the paper) are what provide the profit for much of the inkjet printing business. It's the old Gillette business model at work: sell cheap razors but expensive blades.

Figure 8.4

Cartridge inks are a major profit center for the inkjet industry.

Table 8.1

Sample Third-Party Pigment Color Ink Brands

(as of August 2002)

Ink Supplier[1]	Brand	Type	Works well with these papers
M & M Studios	Indelible Fine Art Inks	100% pigment with carbon black	fine art matte only
MediaStreet	Generations ProPhoto 5	100% pigment (black is 75% pigment/25% dye)	(RC) photo paper
	Generations Enhanced 4	100% pigment (black is 75% pigment/25% dye)	various
	Generations Standard 3	all 100% pigment	various
	Generations Elite (Outdoor)	all 100% pigment	various
MIS	Exact Match Archival	fully pigmented	various
	Perpetual Archival	fully pigmented	various
	Original Archival	fully pigmented	various
American Imaging Corp.	Symphonic Inks	all 100% pigment	various

[1] All suppliers listed in the Appendix.

If you feel like you're feeding your printers liquid gold, consider using third-party inks that can reduce your ink bill by as much as 50–75 percent or more. A flourishing mini-industry has developed that provides compatible, non-OEM inks in various ways to consumers who want to save a significant amount of money.

Increased permanence: Certain third-party, dye-based inks are designed to exceed OEM ink permanence. Suppliers such as Lyson, Lumijet, MediaStreet, Inkjet Goodies, Lincoln, and MIS all offer extended-life dye alternatives to OEM inks. Our next stop is pigments. Because only Epson currently makes desktop pigment-ink printers, your only third-party option is to replace the dye-

Manufacturer's permanence claims	Profiles Provided?	Acceptable Printers	Comes In
100 years +	no	select EPSONs	carts and bulk bottles
100 years +	no	various	carts and bulk bottles
100 years +	no	various	carts and bulk bottles
100 years +	no	various	carts and bulk bottles
100 years + testing	no	various	carts and bulk bottles
49 years +	yes, some	select EPSONs	bulk bottles
49 years +	yes, some	select EPSONs	bulk bottles
49 years +	yes, some	select EPSONs	bulk bottles
150–200 years	yes	select EPSONs	bulk bottles

based OEM inks with pigments. Several companies offer pigment inks for this purpose (see Table 8.1).

Specialty uses: There are some applications where the OEM inks just can't do the job as well as third-party inks. Multi-monochromatic B&W printing is a good example. With the exception of Epson's newest seven-color printers that include a light black, it's difficult to get the highest-quality B&W prints out of inkjet printers using stock inks. However, there are numerous third-party solutions that expand the possibilities significantly. Examples include the following: MIS Quadtones, Lumijet Monochrome Plus, Lysonic Quad Blacks and Small Gamuts, and Inkjet

Mall's PiezoTones. (For more about multi-monochromatic specialty printing, see Chapter 11.)

The three main ways of using third-party inks are with *replacement cartridges*, *refill kits*, and *bulk ink systems*.

Replacement Cartridges

Non-OEM replacement cartridges come in rebranded, OEM-compatible cartridges from ink dealers and makers (including MediaStreet, inkjetART.com, Inkjet Goodies, Lumijet, MIS, Lyson, and Lincoln Ink & Paper) for most of the popular inkjet printers in use today. The cartridges are new or recycled, filled with non-OEM inks, and usually a lot cheaper than the real deal. (You can also buy factory-original OEM cartridges from several of these and other suppliers.)

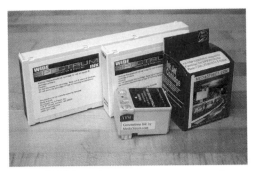

Non-OEM replacement carts come in different shapes and sizes. From left: Lincoln Wide Spectrum 220 ml single-color cart for select wide-format EPSONs, Lincoln Wide Spectrum 110 ml single-color cart, and MediaStreet Generations multicolor cart for EPSON Stylus Photo 1200.

The key issues to consider are these: *match* (How close are they in terms of quality to the OEM inks they're replacing? Are they made to OEM specifications?), *compatibility* (Are they 100-percent compatible with your inkjet printer, and is there a guarantee backing this up?), and *age* (How old is the ink?). In addition, make sure you check to see which printers accept these cartridges.

You can also buy unused, empty cartridges for do-it-yourself filling with the inks of your choice from ink suppliers such as MediaStreet, Inkjet Goodies, and MIS.

Courtesy of inkjetgoodies.com

Figure 8.5
An Inkjet Goodies refill kit for filling your own ink cartridges

Refills

If syringes don't make you cringe, and you don't mind the sometimes-messy and exacting work of refilling cartridges by hand, you might consider one of the refill kits that are sold by companies such as Inkjet Goodies, WeInk.com, and MIS. The Inkjet Goodies kit (see Figure 8.5) includes the following: six 10-cc syringes and blunt needles, six empty cartridges, 12 fill hole plugs, and a full set of Goodies OEM Replacement Ink in 125-ml (4.6 oz) bottles. These are for select EPSON and Canon printers.

MIS takes a slightly different tack with its Inkjet Refill Kits. There are kits for all the major desktop inkjet makers, and each kit's contents varies depending on the cartridge requirements. The main difference with MIS kits is that you refill the existing OEM cartridges. Kits come complete with bottles of ink, syringes, and detailed instructions.

Fooling the Printer

Many of the newer inkjet printers have smart-chipped cartridges with built-in microchips (Epson's are called Intellidge chips). Although they are advertised to help keep track of ink usage, one maybe-not-so-unintended result has been to thwart the use of cartridge refills and third-party inks. However, as soon as each generation of chips appears, entrepreneurs get busy and come up with ways to defeat and fool them.

One invention is the chip reprogrammer or resetter that does the following: (1) allows cartridges to be refilled, (2) makes it possible to use certain bulk ink systems and non-OEM replacement cartridges, and (3) lets you get the last few prints out of a cartridge that would normally be thrown away with some ink remaining (as they are designed to be).

For example, MIS Associates sells three versions of chip resetters:

QB7 Chip Resetter is a self-contained unit with seven small pins that contact to the cartridge chip (see Figure 7.4). When held against the chip for six seconds, the resetter puts the chip back to its electronic FULL setting. This device requires that cartridges be removed from the printer.

F-16 Chip Resetter is a hardware device that connects to the printer (EPSON only). It works without having to lift up the cartridges. It works on Macs and PCs, and it will reset the printer even if the red "out of ink" light is on.

Equalizer Software is the next best method to using the F-16. It's a DOS-based program that will reset the chips without lifting the cartridges. It requires a PC and uses the parallel port on the computer.

MIS even sells a replacement, generic microchip that you can glue onto the cartridge if you damage an original chip.

Bulk Ink Systems

Bulk ink delivery systems—variously called by their popular acronyms CIS, CFS, or CRS—are the latest trend among high-volume printmakers and are popular for two reasons: cost and convenience. The cost savings are obvious; because you buy the ink in bulk, it's cheaper (the systems themselves can cost $100–$300). In addition, because you only need to hook up the system once and then replenish or top off the bottled ink as needed, it's much more convenient than continually having to buy, change, or refill cartridges.

There are only a few manufacturers of these bulk systems, although you will also find them sold under different rebranded names. They all work the same basic way: External, reservoir bottles supply ink to the printer via tubing that then connects to special cartridges that replace the printer's original ones. However, there are some crucial differences among these players.

NoMoreCarts CIS: Continuous Inking Systems of North Carolina originated the commercial bulk-ink system concept with its continuous inking system (CIS) for selected EPSON inkjet printers. As of December 2001, the company stopped selling direct to consumers to concentrate on manufacturing and product support. The NoMoreCarts CIS can be purchased through dealers who offer it either under that name or as a rebranded item such as InkjetArtery from inkjetART.com or LumiFlo Fluidic Ink Delivery System from Lumijet. One key feature of the CIS system is that the cartridge chip for the newer printers always reads full, requires no chip resetter, and can run with any type of computer-printer connection regardless of the platform (Mac or PC) or OS. CIS systems from dealers usually come complete with a set of introductory inks.

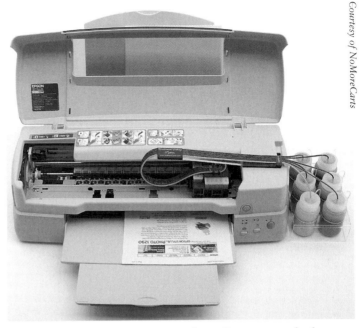

Courtesy of NoMoreCarts

A NoMoreCarts Continuous Inking System attached to an EPSON Stylus Photo 1270

MIS Cobra CFS: Second into the market, ink supplier MIS Associates makes and sells their own Cobra brand Continuous Flow System (CFS) for select EPSON printers. It's very similar to the CIS system, and whereas before it would work only on PCs, the MIS CFS is now also Mac-compatible with the use of the F-16 Chip Resetter. The CFS comes complete with ink and will work with many EPSON inkjets.

MIS will even sell you the parts to make your own CFS system. If you want to make a CFS for a printer that they do not support, this is one way to do it.

Camel Ink Systems CRS: The Camel Continuous Re-Inking System (CRS) has a couple of wrinkles that set it apart. First, it's modular with three components: a CRS module that plugs into the place where the cartridges normally go, a special support arm that keeps the ribbon tubing out of the way of the moving printhead, and the reservoir assembly that holds the inks. Because it's modular, you can use the same reservoir assembly with different ink modules and even combine their system with others. The Camel system is also available for several Canons and especially the S9000. Starter Kits come complete with a set of Ultra-FLO dye-based inks. They are available direct from the manufacturer (weink.com) or from dealers.

MediaStreet Niagara II Continuous Ink Flow System: MediaStreet used to sell the NoMoreCarts system as the Niagara I, but now they're making their own. The Niagara II is the only bulk-ink system that comes preinstalled with filled cartridges ready to go. For systems requiring microchips, the Niagara chips always read full; the chips reset to full every time the printer powers on. The system comes with your choice of Enhanced Generation, Generations ProPhoto, Generations Elite, or Plug-N-Play inks. (See photo in Chapter 7.)

Keep in mind that only specific printer models (mostly EPSONs) are adaptable for bulk-ink-delivery use, depending on the physical design of the printer housing and, more importantly, the method of bypassing the printer's designated ink cartridges. Check with each manufacturer or dealer to make sure your intended printer is on the list.

Third-Party Overview

The use of third-party inks is increasing on some fronts, especially as photographer-artists become more sophisticated and more familiar with digital printing processes. However, you must weigh the disadvantages as well as the advantages. Here are a few observations:

■ *Quality:* With third-party inks, you may or may not get the same quality as you would using the OEM-recommended inks that are made for the printer. OEMs maintain that they are selling printer-ink-media systems, and that you forfeit consistent results and quality if you break that chain. That's why the best third-party inks try to exactly match the OEM's specifications for physical properties (density, viscosity, drying time, surface tension, and so on). The only way to know is to try them and find out for yourself.

Conversely, this is also one advantage of a bulk-ink system. It's reported that there are sometimes differences in color and quality from one OEM ink cartridge to another. Whether it's due to changing ink suppliers or other obscure reasons, the fact is that two seemingly identical ink cartridges bought from the same lot at the same time from the same source can—and sometimes do— vary. A bulk-ink system can mitigate this problem because you buy ink in larger quantities to spread over more prints before a change is needed.

There are other ways around the quality concern. Some people set up bulk-ink systems on their EPSON desktop printers and fill the bottles with cheaper-per-unit ink removed from the larger cartridges used on other printer models. This can only be done with same-generation inks—EPSON 2000P and 9500, for example. A variation on this theme for wide-formats is simply to use larger-capacity cartridges in smaller machines. EPSON 9000 carts will work on an EPSON 7000, even though the cartridges will stick out and look funny. The same procedure will work on the 9600/7600. Going even further, digital artist Bonny Lhotka has been known to open up wide-format ink cartridges and switch the ink-holding bags inside. Always keep in mind that you may risk damaging your printer or voiding the printer's warranty with these kinds of backdoor techniques.

Table 8.2

Sample Third-Party, Dye-Based Color Ink Brands

(as of August 2002)

Ink supplier[1]	Brand	Works well with these papers	Profiles Provided?	Acceptable Printers	Comes in
American Ink Jet	Pinnacle Gold 2	coated	no	various	bulk bottles
	Pinnacle Gold	uncoated	no	various	bulk bottles
Inkjet Goodies	Goodies OEM Replacement	various	no	select EPSONs	bulk bottles
MediaStreet	Plug-N-Play (OEM-compatible inks)	various	no	various	carts & bulk bottles
MIS	factory originals	various	no	various	carts
	aftermarket	various	no	various	bulk bottles
Lincoln	Wide Spectrum	photo gloss photo-semi matte	no no	EPSON 3000, 5000 7000, 9000	carts & bulk bottles
Lumijet	Preservation Series	Preservation media	yes, for Preservation media	select EPSONs	carts
Lyson	Fotonic Photo	Lysonic media	yes, for Lyson media	various	carts & bulk bottles
	Lysonic Archival	Lysonic media	yes, for Lyson media	various	carts & bulk bottles

[1] All suppliers listed in the Appendix

■ *Printer settings and profiles:* Realize that when you use third-party inks, the normal printer settings will no longer work because you've changed the inks for which the manufacturer designed the printer. The same goes for any printer profiles that you've made or bought. Changed the ink? Throw the profiles away. (This can even be a problem with OEM cartridges that vary from one to the next; existing printer profiles may no longer work when this happens.)

- *Availability:* Don't forget that you'll have a harder time finding third-party inks for non-EPSON printers or for the newest ones with smart-chipped ink cartridges. It usually takes third-party ink distributors 12 months or longer to come up with ways to get around the intelligent OEM ink cartridges. Of course, by this time, your one-year warranty will have expired, and you won't be so worried about voiding it.

- *Back-and-forth:* Some third-party inks require that you flush or purge the existing OEM inks from the printhead. This is usually done with cleaning cartridges. This is especially important with third-party inks that are chemically incompatible with the original OEM inks and can damage the printer. Third-party ink makers sell purging or cleaning kits where needed. (Some printmakers make their own home-brewed concoctions.) This obviously causes some ink wastage and limits how many times you'll want to go back and forth between OEM and third-party inks. With desktops, and even more so with wide-format printers where a large amount of ink must be purged from the lines and reservoirs, the best advice is to plan on dedicating the printer to only one type of ink and leaving it that way.

- *Wide-format:* Because the cost of inks is less of an issue for wide-format printers (they economize with larger ink tanks), the need for and use of third-party inks is not as common, although it's still being done. Pennsylvania printmaker Diana York of Hawk Mountain Editions runs two EPSON 9500s with third-party inks, one with Generations 4 and the other with Indelible Fine Art Inks. (Indelibles were first created for the wide-format market but have now migrated to desktops. They're also being tested for other digital print technologies.)

The Medium Is the Message

If inks are the left hand to inkjet printing, then media are the right. You can't have one without the other. Even more so than with inks, the variety available is tremendous. There are coated and uncoated papers, watercolor papers, high-gloss and backlit films, canvas, fabrics, vinyls, plastics, and polyesters. If it can hold ink and be run through an inkjet printer, it's a media candidate for somebody.

However, before you get too excited, let's back up and try to understand how media are made and how they work.

Paper

Media is what you put through a printer. It's what you print on. Because paper is the most common type of media used in inkjet printing, let's study it in more detail. (Nonpaper media are described in the "Alternative Media" section.)

Paper for inkjet printing is composed of three main components: (1) the base or substrate, (2) sizing, if any, and (3) the receptor coating, if any. The *substrate* forms the structure of the paper and determines its thickness, weight, and strength. *Sizing* can be added either internally to the substrate or to its surface to seal or bind the fibers. A *receptor coating* is common on most inkjet papers, and the various coatings now available are what allow photographer-artists to print photorealistic images. (See more about coatings later in the chapter.)

Types of Paper

There are four broad categories of paper about which an inkjet printmaker should know: *bond*, *inkjet*, *fine-art*, and *coated*.

Courtesy of Martin Juergens

Figure 8.6
Ink on uncoated bond paper, 40× magnification, showing wicking and print density loss due to ink penetration, which leads to decrease in image quality

Bond Paper

The plain "bond" paper used in laser printers and copiers in every office around the world is made up, for the most part, of wood pulp, which contains *cellulose* fibers and *lignin*, a natural glue that holds the fibers together. Bond paper is typically sized internally with *rosin* for strength and *calendared* (also spelled *calendered*) or smoothed between two metal rollers. It's not a good choice for inkjet printing except for solid-ink printers and for a couple of the newer inkjets like Epson's C62/C82, which are designed to handle this bottom-of-the-barrel paper medium. Beside poorer image quality due to ink wicking or bleeding (see Figure 8.6), the main problem with bond paper is the presence of the acid-producing rosin sizing and lignin that build up over time and ultimately destroy the paper along with any image printed on it (lignin is what causes newspapers to yellow).

Inkjet Paper

This is the next step up the quality ladder. It's the paper in the office supply stores that costs $10–$12 per ream (500 sheets) instead of $3–5 for plain paper. Inkjet paper is just bond paper improved with external sizing (starches, polymers, and pigments) to make the surface smoother, whiter, and more receptive to inkjet inks. It's fine for letters and charts, but not the best for most high-quality, inkjet output, although, again, certain office inkjets (such as the EPSON C80 line) can print on it.

Fine-Art Paper

These are the beautiful, mouldmade (made on a cylinder mould) art papers that have been lovingly used for decades for watercolors, drawing, and traditional printmaking. They can also be printed on with inkjets, but normally only with dye-based inks. Arches, Rives BFK, and Somerset are three well-known brands, and they typically come in rough, cold-pressed (smoother), and hot-pressed (smoothest) finishes. (See below for *coated* fine-art papers.)

The largest ingredient in paper is cellulose fiber, and it can come from a variety of plant sources including wood (the most common) and cotton. The highest-quality art papers are made from 100-percent cotton-rag content. Cotton fiber contains mostly *alpha cellulose*, the purest form of cellulose, and it's this cotton content that yields highly stable fine-art paper that is more resistant to deterioration than wood-based paper. There is also no rosin sizing or lignin (and hence no acid-forming compounds), but, instead, alkaline buffering agents like calcium carbonate are used to raise the paper's pH level. The surface of fine-art paper is sometimes sized with starches or gelatins.

Printing on fine-art papers can be a challenge for a couple of reasons. First, these special papers can be full of loose fibers and dust that can clog the feeding mechanism and the delicate, inkjet printheads. (Some printmakers actually vacuum—or roll with a tacky roller—each sheet before printing.) If a paper is especially nonuniform or wavy, it can cause "head strikes" (the printhead strikes the paper surface), which could seriously damage the printer. In addition, many art papers have deckle (rough or torn) edges that can be damaged or cause damage. Digital artist Karin Schminke, a member of the Digital Atelier printmaking group, covers deckle edges with removable tape or tapes a strip of acetate to the back of the paper to hold the edges flat.

Coated Inkjet Paper

This is where most of the action is for inkjet printing. Coated papers, which can include versions of the fine-art papers previously mentioned, have a *receptor coating* added to the paper's surface (see Figure 8.7) to better receive the inks and render the image. This coating can contain a whole host of substances such as alumina, silica, clay, titanium dioxide, calcium carbonates, and various polymers. Coatings are specifically designed to enhance a desired effect like better image quality, better binding with the ink, higher-color gamut, less ink bleeding into the substrate, greater brightness, and so on. The coating can also change the surface finish of the paper to be more glossy, matte, or anything in between.

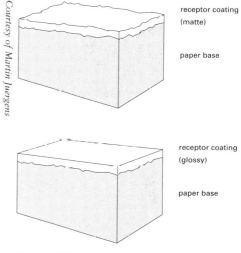

Courtesy of Martin Juergens

receptor coating (matte)

paper base

receptor coating (glossy)

paper base

Figure 8.7
The receptor coating is finished to create a matte (top) or glossy (or other) surface texture.

A variation of the 100-percent-cotton, fine-art paper also shares space on the coated inkjet paper shelves. The variation is *Sulphite paper*. Instead of using cotton fibers, which are naturally high in alpha cellulose as the source material, Sulphite papers use standard wood pulp that is refined using sulfite acid. After buffering agents are added, you end up with a 100-percent, alpha cellulose paper that is pH neutral. Call it the poor man's cotton-fiber paper. Examples include Hahnemuhle German Etching and Torchon, Legion Photo Gloss, Photo Matte, and Photo Silk.

There are so many coated inkjet papers available now, it's hard even to keep track of the categories for organizing them. However, that won't keep me from trying.

One way that suppliers like to classify coated papers is with the terms "photo paper" and "fine-art paper." Photo papers tend to have a resin-coated (RC) component structure (see below) and a glossy or semiglossy finish just as their traditional counterparts have. Fine-art papers frequently resemble watercolor paper. However, there is really little reason to limit your thinking to only these two categories. There are plenty of crossover choices that don't fit neatly into either camp.

Another way to classify paper is by finish or surface texture type: glossy, matte, satin, and so on. This, however, tells you very little about the type of paper and its appropriateness for use with different inks or printers.

Instead, I categorize papers by the coating technology: *microporous, swellable polymer*, or *matte coated*, plus the misnamed *resin coated*. These help tell you what you can and cannot do with a particular paper.

- *Microporous:* A relatively new solution to the problem of inkjets printing faster than the ink can dry, microporous coatings contain small, inorganic particles of either alumina or silica to create voids or pores in the coating. The ink is absorbed into these pores, which results in fast-drying, but also allows the ink to come into contact with air. This may have contributed to the Orange Shift problem described earlier, which is why all microporous prints made with dye-based inks should be displayed or stored covered or framed behind glass or plexiglass. Microporous papers produce excellent image quality, and they usually have a glossy or luster finish. OEM examples include the following: EPSON Premium Glossy Photo Paper, EPSON Premium Luster Photo Paper, EPSON Semi-Gloss Photo Paper, Canon Photo Paper Pro, and Kodak Picture Paper Soft Gloss. Third-party sources (see below) include the following: BrightCube ProPhoto Gloss and ProPhoto Silk, Legion Photo Gloss and Photo Silk, Lumijet Ultra Gloss, and Lyson Professional Photo Gloss. These papers can work with either dye-based inks or pigment inks depending on the particular brand.

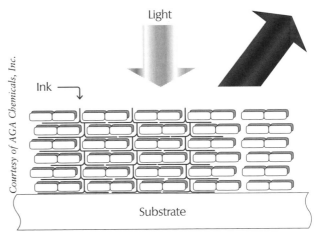

Figure 8.8

Pictorico's ceramic coating works by ink being absorbed quickly into the straight, uniform inkwells; reflected light does not scatter.

A variation or subset of the microporous coating is the *microceramic* coating (see Figure 8.8). The Asahi Glass Company of Japan has developed a proprietary ceramic coating technology on which the entire Pictorico inkjet media line is based. The unique feature of their coating is a monodirectional layer of highly uniform, ultrafine ceramic particles (technically, alumina sol particles suspended in a silica gel). The ink dries virtually on contact as it's pulled into the ink wells between the particles. There's very little ink bleed, and the images are sharp and also resistant to smudging (although sometimes sensitive to scratching). However, like other microporous coatings, microceramics are prone to environmental contaminants, and should be similarly displayed or stored covered or framed. These can be printed with dyes or pigments.

Another paper in this category is ILFORD's Galerie Smooth Gloss and Smooth Pearl, which have their own "microceramic" coatings.

- *Swellable polymer:* Water-receptive polymer coatings for printing papers have been around since the early 1990s, but their use was limited. All that changed when people needed to find a way to reduce the fading caused by ozone and other atmospheric contaminants. Swellable polymer is a nonporous coating made with organic polymers that swell up to surround the ink after it hits the paper. Only a very thin layer of ink is then open to direct air exposure; the rest is protected. Examples include the following: EPSON ColorLife Photo Paper, HP Colorfast Photo Paper, Kodak Ultima Picture Paper High Gloss, and ILFORD Galerie Classic Gloss and Classic Pearl. The finishes of these papers tend to be either glossy or satiny, and the image quality is excellent, although they can be negatively affected by high humidity and contact with water. They are for dye-based inks only.

- *Matte coated:* Matte-coated papers, which have a dull but smooth- or textured-looking finish, are coated with aluminum or silicium oxides to give them high shadow density, a large color gamut, and good water-fastness. They also resist fading from air contact better than the microporous papers with dye-based inks. OEM examples include the following: EPSON Matte Paper-Heavyweight, EPSON Enhanced Matte (formerly Archival Matte), EPSON Smooth Fine Art Paper, EPSON Textured Fine Art Paper, and Kodak Premium Inkjet Paper Matte. Third-party matte papers include the following: Crane Museo, Legion Photo Matte, MediaStreet Glacier Photo Matte, and Red River Denali Matte and Premium Matte. They are for dye-based and pigment inks.

- *Resin Coated (RC):* This is not a coating but a different way that papers are constructed. RC papers have been around for a long time; they are well-known in the photographic world and have now migrated to inkjets as well. Typically, a standard substrate is sandwiched between two layers of polyethylene, and one of the receptor coatings described above is then applied on top (see Figure 8.9). It's the inkjet receptive layer that determines the printing performance of the paper. The in-between polyethylene layer acts as a barrier and helps reduce wrinkling that could result from heavy ink coverage. Many microporous- and swellable-coated inkjet papers aimed at photographers are in fact, RCs. They include the following: MediaStreet Generations ProPhoto Gloss and ProPhoto Luster, Legion Photo Silk, Pictorico Photo Gallery Glossy Paper, ILFORD Galerie Classic Gloss and Classic Pearl, Red River Polar Gloss, Luminos Glossy, and Pearl RC, and BrightCube Gloss, Semi-Matte, Duet Gloss, and Xtreme Gamut Gloss. The goal of many of these papers is to look and feel the same as a traditional photo print. Although not always appropriate for pigment inks, some RCs are specially designed to accept them. Check for compatibility.

receptor coating

polyethylene

paper base

polyethylene

Courtesy of Martin Juergens

Figure 8.9
The structure of RC paper for inkjet printing

The Finest of Coated Fine Art

If office bond paper is the worst paper to choose for inkjet printing, then what's the best? Obviously, the criteria will vary depending on your particular goals and whether you're interested in photo or fine-art paper, but if 100-percent cotton is any indicator, here are the very finest of today's *coated*, inkjet printing papers for fine art: (Note: Many of these are third-party papers; see the next section for more information.)

BrightCube Eclipse Satine: This two-sided paper is 100-percent cotton fiber, acid-free, and pH neutral. It comes in two weights (190 gsm and 300 gsm) in both rolls and sheets. The Bright White version has optical brighteners; Soft White does not. It is used for both dyes and pigment inks.

Crane Museo: Made by the oldest continuously run paper mill in the United States, which also happens to make the currency paper for the U.S. Treasury, Museo is 100-percent cotton, buffered with calcium carbonate, acid-free, made with Artesian well water, and contains no optical brighteners. It comes in two weights with a pH of 7.9–8.5.

Epson: Made for Epson by Crane, *EPSON Textured Fine Art* and *EPSON Smooth Fine Art* are available only in rolls or large sheets for wide-format. They're very similar to Crane's Museo and are also 100-percent cotton and acid- and optical-brightener free. There are two available finishes: cold press matte (ETFA) and hot press matte (ESFA). There's also a new *Somerset Velvet for EPSON* that's 100-percent cotton, acid-free, and available in 255 gsm rolls and a whopping 505 gsm in cut sheets; it is used for EPSON Archival and UltraChrome pigment inks.

Hahnemuhle: Hahnemuhle is a German paper mill that's been producing fine-art papers for more than 400 years. Their *Photo Rag* and *William Turner* papers are 100-percent cotton rag, acid-free, and with neutral pH. They usually come in two weights and work with both dye-base and pigment inks. I've had IRIS prints made on William Turner, and they were gorgeous printed on this slightly creamy paper.

Hawk Mountain Art Papers: Located in Leesport, Pennsylvania, Hawk Mountain is a small papermaker of coated, bright-white, fine-art inkjet papers named after birds of prey, specifically raptors: *Goshawk, Osprey, Peregrine, Merlin, Condor, Talon, Aerie,* and *Kestrel.* All their papers are mouldmade from archival 100-percent cotton, are acid-free, and are manufactured to their specifications in the United States. Each has a unique surface finish, and most are 250 gsm and 15 mil.

ILFORD Inkjet Fine Art: For artists and photographers, Inkjet Fine Art Paper is 100-percent cotton rag, acid-free, and with a neutral pH balance. It has a matte surface and comes in a 190 gsm weight. It is used for dye-based inks.

Legion: *Concorde Rag* is mouldmade in France, has a neutral pH, and is a 100-percent cotton rag that's creamy white with a vellum finish. In a whiter version, it's a stock paper for Roland wide-format printers and works with both dye and pigment inks. *Somerset Photo Enhanced,* introduced in 1999, is the same mouldmade paper from the St. Cuthberts paper mill in Somerset, England, as the immensely popular Somerset Velvet art paper except it's coated on one side for inkjet printing. It comes in two finishes: velvet and textured. It's 100-percent cotton fiber, acid-free, and radiant white in color. It can be used for both dye and pigment inks.

Schoellershammer: Schoellershammer is another German paper mill, and #10 Velvet and Linen (which looks like canvas, but with a unique linen herringbone pattern) are two of their best, coated, fine-art papers for inkjets. Both are 100-percent cotton rag, bright white, and come in two weights: 225 gsm and 300 gsm. They are used for dyes and pigments.

Legion Paper, the exclusive marketer of some of the finest art and digital printing papers including the entire Somerset line, currently has seven papers in its Digital Art Paper group for inkjet printing.

Courtesy of Legion Paper

How much do these premium fine-art papers cost? (I know you're wondering.) As an example, Crane Museo (250 gsm) goes for about $1.45 per letter-sized sheet and $20 per 35x47 inch sheet (365 gsm).

Deciding on Paper

Choosing among all the different types of papers for inkjet printing can be either an exhilarating or exhausting experience. The assortment available has become bewildering. Where do you start? With the recommended printer papers.

Printer Paper

Just like with inks, desktop inkjet printer manufacturers (with Lexmark as the lone exception) market their own lines of papers. In terms of choice, this is where Epson clearly excels. No one else even comes close to offering the range of inkjet media that Epson does. In fact, they are the only printer OEM that has, not just one, but more than four different fine-art papers on its product list.

So, again, as with inks, the question is this: Do you stick with the recommended media of the printer maker, or do you experiment with the smorgasbord of third-party choices that awaits you? Again, the answer is this: It all depends. If you're happy with the recommended papers, you can be confident that they will be optimally designed for the printer's inks and printing technology. The permanence of those combinations will have been researched and well advertised. In most cases, you know what you're getting.

However, what if you want to spread your wings a little to see what's on the other side of the door? It's time to open that door.

Third-Party Paper

The first thing to acknowledge is that printer OEMs discourage you from using non-recommended papers. The rationale is the same as it is with inks: (1) They lose money if you buy your paper elsewhere, and (2) they lose control of the performance of their product because you are now introducing an unknown element to it. OEM-branded papers are designed to work in conjunction with OEM printers, drivers, and inks in a coordinated system.

Because there are no smart chips embedded in papers (yet), you are free to use and print on whatever you can find, within reason. Of course, some papers will work better than others depending on your needs. What follows are the key factors and characteristics you should be aware of (and questions to ask) when going paper hunting, whether for OEM or third-party brands:

Key Paper Characteristics

Size: As I mentioned in Chapter 7, size is one of the primary factors in deciding among inkjet printers. Most of the finer inkjet papers come in normal, commercial print sizes: 8.5×11, 11×17, 13×19, and so on. These sizes are based on those used in the United States for standard office paper products (see Table 8.3). (Printers made for Europe or other parts of the world come in different sizes and match the paper sizes of that area.) Some paper suppliers will also list standard photographic paper sizes (4×6, 8×10, 11×14, and so on).

Don't forget that most papers, including some of the very finest, come in sheets *and* rolls. Rolls are not just for wide-format printers, but also for desktops. Digital Art Supplies carries a complete line of eight-inch wide rolls of high-quality papers from Hahnemuhle, Schoellershammer, and others. Rolls work well for people who not only need to print with roll-fed media but also for those who want the flexibility to cut their own sizes. Printers of panoramic images do this regularly.

Color: In most cases, you want to print on white paper because that's the color that will distort ink colors the least. However, there's white, and then there's white. If the white is too white, it will seem cold. Too beige, and it will be dull and dreary. Again, it's a matter of personal preference. Papers have their characteristic colors, and people gravitate to them accordingly.

Weight: The standard measurement of paper weight for inkjet papers is grams per square meter (gsm). This is more accurate than the Imperial system that measures paper by its "basis weight," or the weight in pounds of 500 sheets of standard size, usually 17×22". Knowing a paper's weight is only partially useful information. A much more important thing to know is a paper's thickness, which is not necessarily related to its weight. Within one brand of paper, heavier weights may be thicker, but Brand X of one weight may be thicker than Brand Y with the same weight.

Caliper (thickness): Caliper or thickness is a more useful paper measurement because each printer model prints best with papers of a certain thickness range (and have a maximum thickness they will print). A paper's caliper is measured in mils (one mil is 1/1,000th of an inch), and it is determined by the substrate composition, the additives, and the coating. Some papers have different calipers for sheets and rolls. Legion Concorde Rag, for example, is 11 mil for sheets and 17.5 mil for rolls.

Table 8.3

Standard Paper Sizes

U.S. Name	U.S. Size	Metric Equivalent
A (letter)	8.5 × 11 inches	216 × 279 mm
Legal	8.5 × 14 inches	216 × 356 mm
B (ledger)	11 × 17 inches	279 × 432 mm
Super B/Super A3	13 × 19 inches	330 × 483 mm
C	17 × 22 inches	432 × 559 mm
D	22 × 34 inches	559 × 864 mm

Metric Name	Metric Size	U.S. Equivalent
A5	148 × 210 mm	5.8 × 8.3 inches
A4	210 × 297 mm	8.3 × 11.7 inches
A3	297 × 420 mm	11.7 × 16.5 inches
A3+	329 × 483 mm	13 × 19 inches
A2	420 × 594 mm	16.5 × 23.4 inches
A1	594 × 841 mm	23.4 × 33.1 inches

Substrate: How is the paper made? What is the substrate material? Wood pulp? Cotton-rag content? Plastic or other synthetics? RC? This is the starting point for knowing about a type of paper.

Coating: Although this was already covered, it bears repeating. (Note: "Coating" in this context refers to the precoating on the paper when you buy it. If you're considering any postprinting coatings or sprays, see Chapter 9.) It's *very* important to match the paper coating to your inks and printer type. Quality and handling issues such as *Dmax* (the maximum density reading possible at the highest black ink levels; depends on the type of inks used), ink puddling, smearing, scuffing, flaking, wicking, and excessive dot gain (ink spreading) are all affected by the type—or lack—of the appropriate paper coating (see Figure 8.10).

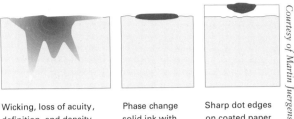

Wicking, loss of acuity, definition, and density on uncoated paper

Phase change solid ink with sharp edges

Sharp dot edges on coated paper

Courtesy of Martin Juergens

Figure 8.10
Ink-substrate interaction

Finish: This is the surface texture. The range is high gloss to very rough with all kinds of pearls, satins, lusters (equivalent to the photographic "E" surface), mattes, and more in between. People tend to have strong feelings about their paper finishes. Color consultant C. David Tobie says it well when he states it this way: "Paper is like religion or politics; you will have little success preaching matte to the glossy crowd, or vice versa. Celebrate diversity."

pH: You want papers that are pH-neutral (pH 7) or a little alkaline. Acidic paper is a ticking time bomb; it will self-destruct sooner or later. Look for papers that say "acid-free" and hope they mean it. Acid-free means either that no acids were added to the paper (as with 100-percent cotton) or that any acids used in a wood-pulp-based paper have been removed or neutralized. It's best if you can find out the actual pH level, which is what Crane does in its paper specs: 7.9–8.5. If they advertise it, that's a good indicator that it's safe.

Brightness: Brightness is usually given, if at all, in terms of a rating scale of 1–100, with 100 being the brightest. Keep in mind that some papers achieve a higher brightness by adding optical brighteners.

Opacity: This becomes an issue with thinner papers, and you see this measurement on many from Epson plus a few third-party suppliers (Legion Photo Silk). Opacity means how much "show-through"—how much you can see the image underneath when stacked—there is. It's measured with a simple meter; the higher the opacity figure up to 100, the more opaque the paper. The most common usage where opacity is important is in the making of specialty books and albums.

Optical brighteners: Optical brighteners (OBs) are commonly used in the paper, textile, and detergent industries. As the name implies, they're also added to inkjet printing papers and coatings to make them whiter and brighter. The way OBs work is by absorbing UV radiation and fluorescing (reemitting as visible light). A common OB is titanium dioxide, which is added to the paper's outer receptor coating. You can tell if a paper has OBs added by turning on a portable "black light" in a dark room and running it over the paper. If OBs are present, the paper will appear to glow while a non-optical-brightened paper will appear dark or "optically dead" because no light is reflected. (This gets more complicated with a 100-percent cotton paper that has no OBs added to its coating but may have OBs in the substrate if the original cotton trimmings contain optical brighteners.)

It's unclear what long-term effects OBs have on print permanence. Some believe that they can possibly contribute to print deterioration, but others disagree, saying first that not all OBs are the same. All standard EPSON papers have optical brighteners to improve whiteness and to inhibit the yellowing of the paper, according to Epson. BrightCube maintains that the worst that could happen is that a bright white paper will end up being less white (yellower) as the brightener loses its ability to fluoresce over time.

Permanence/lightfastness: As we already know, print permanence is the result of the interaction of inks, paper, and display or storage conditions. You cannot pick only a paper and have any idea as to its permanence. You need to know the other parts of the equation. Most paper suppliers include permanence ratings in their paper specs or marketing material. Make sure you read the fine print carefully to see how those projections are determined. (See Chapter 6 for more about print permanence.)

Free profiles provided? In addition to what ink suppliers provide, some paper vendors or manufacturers also furnish generic or canned printer profiles for their papers. For example, Crane, Legion Paper, and Pictorico all offer OEM-ink-based ICC profiles for several desktop inkjet printers. BrightCube has ICC profiles by EPSON pigment (only) printer type, Dotworks offers a wide range of Epson inkjet profiles for their private-label papers, and ILFORD lists recommended printer settings on its Web site for EPSON, HP, Canon, and Lexmark inkjets.

Two-sided? Most people print on just one side of the paper, but there are times when printing on both sides (also called "duplexing") is a real bonus. Portfolios, brochures, greeting cards, postcards, and digital books—these are all natural uses for two-sided printing. However, in such cases, you need a dual-sided, dual-coated paper to print on. (Be careful if you think you can just print on a single-sided paper and not worry about the back. Some papers from Epson, Kodak, and others, have advertising or logos printed on the back.) Examples include the following: BrightCube's Eclipse Satine and Duet Gloss (see Figure 8.11), Hahnemuhle Photo Rag Duo, Lumijet Matte Double Sided, Red River Denali Matte Two, Pictorico Premium DualSide Photo, Dotworks FS2 (a good bookmaking stock), and EPSON Double-Sided Matte. (See Chapter 11 for more about printing books.)

Figure 8.11
BrightCube's Anders Jonsson shows off double-sided Eclipse Satine.

Note that *all* coated inkjet papers are automatically coated on both sides. The printing side has a receptor coating, and the opposite side has a water coating to ensure stability and paper flatness. Dual-sided paper, on the other hand, has an inkjet receptor coating on *both* sides. The thing to recognize is that most inkjet receptive coatings are fragile and easily scuffable. When using a two-sided paper, you must take extra care in handling the sheets.

There are very few inkjets that can automatically duplex print (you can do it manually by turning the paper over and feeding it back through). One is the Tektronix/Xerox Phaser 8200 solid ink printer where the paper is fed back through the machine on a different paper path. Several HP Deskjets can also do it with special two-sided printing modules that hold and then automatically pull the paper back to print the reverse side.

Cost: I've already described ink and media costs in Chapter 7, but I'll mention another cost-saver here. One trick that experienced printmakers have learned is to do the testing, color balancing, and other preliminary work on similar, but cheaper, paper. Then, when they're ready, they pull out the good stuff.

For example, I might proof images on EPSON Archival/Enhanced Matte ($1.00 per 13 × 19-inch sheet) and then make my final prints on Crane Museo ($3.60 per sheet). I find that the same Photoshop curves and settings work with both papers for most of the inks I'm using.

The Paper Name Game

Trying to sift through all the various types and names of printing paper can be a challenging task. It's made even harder when you realize that the same paper can have different, rebranded marketing names depending on who is selling it. Hahnemuhle, in particular, is famous for this. For example, consider the following:

Hahnemuhle German Etching = Lumijet Classic Velour = Lyson Standard Fine Art = MediaStreet Royal Plush = ConeTech Orwell.

Sometimes, it's common knowledge when it's the same paper, but many times, as with Lumijet, Lyson, MediaStreet, and ConeTech (InkjetMall), it's not. You just have to know. (For an informative database of papers and equivalent paper names, go to the Files section of the online discussion list at http://groups.yahoo.com/group/DigitalBlackandWhiteThePrint, run by Antonis Ricos and Martin Wesley.)

Alternative Media

I've concentrated on normal paper in this chapter because it's the most common type of media. However, there are many alternatives to paper for inkjet printing. Handmade? Sandpaper? Aluminum foil? Old house-painter drop cloths? (Don't laugh, artist Bonny Lhotka has developed an entire process to clean, prep, and finally print on them.) Open your mind to the possibilities—but at the same time, be forewarned about the possible fatal dangers to your printer whenever you put nonrecommended media through it. (See more about special printing techniques in Chapter 11.)

Canvas: One of the primary media choices for artists working with canvas originals and printing giclée reproductions is canvas. Canvas, of course, has been around for hundreds of years as an artist medium, but now, specially treated canvas is also available for inkjet printing. Different canvases have different coatings, different weaves or textures, and come either on rolls for wide-format printers or in cut sheets for desktops. For example, Fredrix, the oldest (since 1868) and largest maker of artist canvas in the United States, also has a line of PrintCanvas products. These are 100-percent cotton or cotton/poly blends, and they come in either cut sheets or bulk rolls. Other inkjet canvas suppliers (of their own or rebranded canvas) include the following: Legion Paper, LexJet Direct, Hahnemuhle, Luminos, BrightCube, Bulldog Products, and Parrot

Digigraphic. Epson also carries a 100-percent cotton canvas, but it only comes in wide-format rolls. All are used for dye-based or pigment inks.

Exotic papers: There are lots of specialty papers available for inkjet printing. Paper vendor Digital Art Supplies carries an entire stock of handmade Japanese papers and even has a sampler pack devoted to them. With names like Harukaze, Kinwashi, and Yanagi, you are actually printing on mixtures of hemp, kozo, bamboo, or straw (see Figure 8.12). Different from the Japanese papers found at art supply stores, these are specially treated for inkjet printing.

Red River Paper carries Silver and Gold Metallic papers that yield an unusual effect when printed with dye-based (only) inks.

Specialty films and plastics: Although they are normal materials for sign and display print shops, backlit films, vinyls, polycarbonates, and decal media are coming under the scrutiny of photographer-artists who want to print on something different. Clear or translucent films, for example, can be used to make digital negatives, positive films for screen printing, and the kind of window art we saw in Chapter 7.

Figure 8.12
Kinwashi, a Japanese handmade paper from Digital Art Supplies is treated for inkjet use. It contains 90-percent Manila hemp and 10-percent kozo.

Epson has its own mini line of specialty media that includes inkjet transparency film, white gloss film, and back light film in rolls for reverse printing with dye and pigment inks.

Pictorico's Photo Gallery Hi-Gloss White Film, used for photo reproduction, is made entirely with DuPont Melinex polyester film as the substrate (it's also coated with ceramic particles). LexJet Direct also has a Melinex Photo product that is tear and water resistant, and with the look and feel—and price—of regular photo paper. LexJet carries this film plus many more specialty inkjet media for photographers and wide-format inkjet printmakers.

Dotworks' RDG gloss and RDL luster media are resin-coated polyester film. In addition to having impressive print longevity, and greater color gamut and black depth than generally available on paper stock, these media have the advantage of not buckling in humid conditions, making the matting of large prints easier. Both dye and pigment inks are supported.

Consultant Dr. Ray Work has come up with a Cibachrome-like solution for digital photographic output. It's an all-synthetic sandwich comprised of a base of 8-mil DuPont Melinex polyester film with a microporous inkjet coating, pigment colorants that form the image, and a laminated Teflon topcoat. There is no paper. There's also nothing to degrade, and, because there's no contact with the air, there are no gas fading problems.

Interestingly, there is another claim to a "digital Cibachrome," and that's by John Nollendorfs of Lincoln Ink & Paper. His version uses Wide-Spectrum dye-based inks printed on UltraStable UltraGloss paper topped with a swellable-polymer coating.

DuPont Tyvek: Tyvek is a spun-bonded polyolefin (a hydrocarbon polymer like polyethylene). Known mostly as a wrap in home construction and for FedEx and Priority Mail Paks—I also used to design paper jackets with it back in the days of disco—Tyvek is gaining popularity with adventurous digital printmakers willing to search it out and deal with certain shortcomings like image fragility. Artist JD Jarvis has been inkjet printing on it for years. Jarvis admits that it's been a struggle to convince collectors and gallery staff to accept it, but he has had large pieces printed on Tyvek hung vertically in galleries by hooks and bungy cords. "My feeling is that new tools beget new materials, and maybe even new ways to display art," he explains. "Art in general is about innovation, and I maintain that digital artists, at this point, should be the most willing to innovate with any and all new materials, images, and display modes." Tyvek is available from digital supplier Azon.

A related product available from LexJet Direct is called WallPro Inkjet Wallpaper. You simply print, add a protective coating, and apply it to any wall with standard wallpaper paste. It works with thermal and piezo inkjet printers, and it's waterproof with pigmented inks.

Textiles and fabrics: Inkjet printing on textiles and fabrics has come a long way, and very quickly. In addition to the well-established use of digital printing on banners and flags in commercial settings, there is a new trend brewing for printing directly on fabrics for more utilitarian uses like home decor textiles and clothing.

The first use of this textile printing technology was (and still is) to produce samples and "strike-offs" quickly and cheaply without having to go through the traditionally complicated and expensive process of cutting screens and so on. This can be very important when you realize that 95 percent of fabric designs never make it into production. California company DigiFab sells a range of treated fabrics plus the special RIP software needed for special textile applications like step-and-repeats and textile color management, which is slightly different from the one used with paper. Up to now, this effort has been aimed at wide-format printmakers, but DigiFab realizes that this whole phenomenon is evolving so that individuals can use their own inkjet printers to print on smaller pieces of fabric for personal use. (A variation of inkjet printing on fabrics is the use of dye-sublimation transfers, which is described in more detail in Chapter 11.)

German company 3P InkJet Textiles shows off its digitally printed silk fabric at the Digital Printing & Imaging Association's 2002 trade show.

Finding Paper

Where do you find all these wonderful printing papers? With the crazy quilt of paper mills, converters, manufacturers, importers, coaters, suppliers, distributors, repackagers, dealers, and so on, it would be almost impossible to come up with a comprehensive list of *all* the papers and their sources (although Antonis Ricos has tried with his ambitious paper database mentioned earlier). However, there are two good ways to track down the media of your dreams: start at the top and at the bottom. By the top, I mean go to the major manufacturer/distributor Web sites (I've listed them in the Appendix) and research the features and specs of an entire product line. Then, you can go to the bottom of the food chain—retailers and dealers—and see what they have to offer and for how much.

Because papers are so personal, it's always best to sample them yourself before deciding on a larger order. One of the best ways to try out different papers is to order sample packs; most major paper brands offer them. If, however, the goal is to evaluate different paper brand samples, then go to the dealers that carry more than one brand. For example, Digital Art Supplies has "A Bit of (Almost) Everything Multipack" with samples from various brands and mills all in one box. They also have themed multipacks like "11×17 Strictly Hahnemuhle." It's a great way to touch, feel, and try out different inkjet papers.

Matching Ink to Paper

If there is one lesson to take away from this chapter, it's this: You must carefully match your inks and media to get the best and the most permanent inkjet output. Think of it as a system; everything has to work together. Some points to remember include the following:

- If you want to print on uncoated fine-art paper, use dye-based inks; pigments will look muddier. However, be aware that the dye inks may fade more quickly.

- Use pigment inks on coated papers; use dyes on both coated and uncoated papers. Check the paper specifications carefully for compatibility.

- Use pigment inks if you require maximum print permanence.

- If you want to use pigment inks on glossy or semiglossy papers, carefully check for ink/paper compatibility. The paper may require a protective coating or spray.

- Although dye inks can usually produce brighter colors, pigments on carefully matched media can come very close to dyes in terms of color gamut.

Courtesy of ILFORD Imaging USA

ILFORD's Galerie series of professional inkjet photo papers is designed to be compatible with specific types of inks and printers.

- Pigments, in general, tend to exhibit more metamerism, although newer pigment inks, especially the new UltraChromes from Epson, have reduced the problem.

As soon as the ink hits the paper, a chain of events takes place, and you want to understand and control the resulting physical and chemical interactions as much as possible.

You *may* have a better chance of achieving this goal with the consumables recommended by the printer manufacturer. As I've already said, companies like Epson have spent a great deal of time and money to come up with a complete system of inks, papers, and printers that optimizes print quality.

You can, of course, stray from the herd if you choose (taking into account certain restrictions like smart-chipped ink cartridges). Third-party providers of inks and papers have also done their homework, and they offer many compatible products that compare favorably with—and are sometimes better than—the OEMs'. However, you will have to spend your own time and money to do the research needed to prove this to yourself (one of the reasons you're probably reading this book!).

The bottom line for consumables is this: Inkjet printing has finally evolved to the stage where photographer-artists can now choose a specific printer, inkset, and medium to produce the kind of output or look they have in their mind's eye. You just have to make the right choices to make the perfect match.

■■■

Enough background information; let's make a print!

9

Putting It All Together: Making a Great Inkjet Print

I can't give you instant, hard-earned experience in the digital trenches, but I can illuminate the key steps—and pitfalls—of the digital printing process. Ready to print? (Note: These are the basic steps for self-printing on a desktop inkjet printer; if you plan to use an outside printmaker or a printing service, see Chapter 10.)

Setting Up a Workflow

I love the word "workflow." It's not in any of my dictionaries, but it communicates a very clear idea: a specific method or procedure of doing some work. In our case, the work is making an inkjet print.

However, before we begin, I will make certain assumptions: (1) that you have or have access to an inkjet printer and know the basics of how it works; (2) that you have scanned in, captured, or otherwise created a digital image file (see Chapter 4); (3) that you are using Photoshop or another advanced image-editor (see Chapter 4); and (4) that you have a reasonably calibrated monitor (see Chapter 5). You don't absolutely *have* to have all these, but it will make what follows a little more understandable if you do.

Making a Print: Step-by-Step

I'm going to take you through the steps of printing one of my photo-based, digital images. It's called *North of the Pier*, and it won an award in the Museum of Computer Art's 2001 digital art competition (see Figure 9.1). I call what I will end up with an *original print*; if you're more interested in making reproduction prints, the same, basic workflow would apply (see "A Giclée Workflow" in Chapter 10).

The printer used in this first section is the older and somewhat quirky EPSON Stylus Photo 2000P (I'll switch printers and consumables in the "A Third-Party Alternative" section later). The 2000P is a six-color, piezo, desktop, inkjet printer. The pigment inks and the watercolor paper are OEM from EPSON. I am not pushing this printer model (it's being phased out by EPSON in any case) or brand over any others. I just didn't want this to be too easy; there have been many reported challenges of getting the best prints out of an EPSON 2000P.

For this print, I won't be using a RIP, but will be using both printer settings and, as a second option, a self-made printer profile. (I'll use a custom-made profile later in the chapter.) I'll be working on a Mac (G4) with the older Photoshop 6 to mix things up a little, but the same basic principles and procedures apply to Windows workers with only a few minor changes, which I'll note as we go along.

As I walk you through my printing procedure, keep in mind that this is only one way of doing it. Use this workflow as a base or a point of reference; don't hesitate to change it to suit your own way of working. These steps are not carved in stone, even for me. I will sometimes change their order just for fun, or to see if there are any creative possibilities to discover.

The steps in my inkjet printmaking workflow are as follows:

1. Plan Your Print

2. Prep Your File

3. Edit the Image

4. Save a Print-Specific Version

5. Flatten, Size, Scale, Res, and Sharpen

6. Select and Load Paper

7. Select Printer Settings or Profile

8. Make a Test Print (or two or three...)

9. Make Adjustments and More Test Prints

10. Make the Final Print(s)

© 2001 Harald Johnson

Figure 9.1
Our test image: North of the Pier

Step 1: Plan Your Print

Just like tailors who measure twice and cut once, I spend a lot of time planning out my prints in advance. This may be less fun than jumping in and starting to image-edit, but believe me, you will save yourself a lot of headaches if you take your time with this step.

After I've decided on my image and the rough print size, I make a full-size mock-up. This is the best way to see if what you're planning is really going to work. The old-fashioned way is simply to cut down or tape together pieces of white poster board to equal the exact finished size of the print. (If you have an extra piece of the actual paper you'll be using, that's even better.) Then, cut out various-sized blocks of a colored paper to match the image size. I like to try out different sizes, taping them to the white backing piece. This is a very easy and good way to get a sense of a print's borders and proportions.

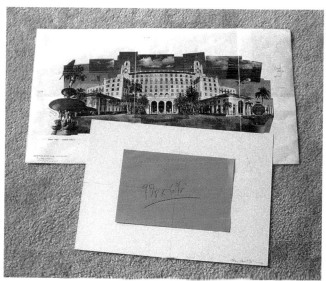

Full-sized mock-ups, done with either blocks of color or low-res versions of the actual image, are good ways to evaluate the size and proportions of a print.

A more-sophisticated variation for making a mock-up is to output your actual image in a low-resolution format. For larger sizes, you may need to *tile* the image. You can do this with most page-layout and drawing programs or even in Photoshop if you add reference grid lines. I sometimes make a tiled, B&W mock-up with my office laser printer. The image can then be taped together and attached to the print-backing sheet to evaluate the overall effect.

Again, the purpose of this important step is to have a 100-percent-size mock-up of your intended print that you live with for a while. I like to tack them up in different locations around my house over the course of several days. Whenever I walk by, I stop and make a mental note. When I'm satisfied with the image and print size, I'm ready for Step 2.

Step 2: Prep Your File

Working in Photoshop 6.0.1, I verify my Color Settings RGB Working Space as Adobe RGB (1998). I also check my monitor calibration settings or calibrate the monitor with one of the measured-calibration systems described in Chapter 5.

I organize my computer desktop with the appropriate folders and prepare to work on the file. Because this particular image was scanned to a regular Kodak Photo CD at the time of processing the color negative camera film, I go to the CD, open the 3072×2048 pixel version of the file to

8-bit RGB and save it to a new file name at 300 ppi, my standard resolution (I will be changing it later). The new "north_LYRS_300" file (see Figure 9.2) is 18 MB, the largest file size available in the regular Photo CD format. I know from experience and in working with my mock-ups that this will be enough for the print size I'll be making. If I want a much larger print, I could rescan the color negative (the Pro Photo CD format would give me a 72-MB file).

Figure 9.2
The original renamed scan and a newly created folder for organizing the files

Step 3: Edit the Image

I covered this in Chapter 4, but I'm going to hit the highlights again, especially because it's a different image with different requirements.

The first thing I usually do is check the *squareness* and the *cropping* of the image. In this case, it's easy to see that it's unsquare when I pull down a guide to the horizon line. It's running downhill a bit, so I rotate it visually back to where I want it (Edit > Transform > Rotate). This creates gaps at the edges and corners, so I crop in to eliminate them. I try not to do any severe cropping at this early stage because I might want to change my mind later. It's best to only crop out the obvious flaws now and do a final crop for visual effect at the end of the image-editing process.

Figure 9.3
The base image with five adjustment layers to achieve the desired effect

Now I start the creative work. I've already determined that I want a surreal landscape, so I begin experimenting and adding *adjustment layers* (see Figure 9.3) to create the overall tone and color effect I'm looking for. (This is why I added "LYRS" to the file's name; it reminds me that this is the master layered file.) I start with an extreme hue shift that gives me the purple foliage and the golden sky. I then add more adjustment layers using different color channels, layer masks, gradients, opacities, and a special 50% gray layer in Overlay blending mode to punch up the clouds.

I finish the editing by going over the entire image at 200% view, removing dust spots and repairing holes and defects in the foliage.

Figure 9.4 shows my final edited image next to the "before" version.

Figure 9.4 *Before (left) and after image editing*

Step 4: Save a Print-Specific Version

After I have a finished, edited master file tucked safely away on my hard disk and on a backup CD stored in my wife's safety deposit box at the bank (you think I'm kidding?), I now make a print specific version to continue my work. Using the Save As command, I create a new file, adding to its name the destination printer—_EP2K—or a project name or whatever makes the most sense. I also remove the "LYRS" from the file name to help differentiate this new file from the master, layered file. See Figure 9.5 to see how my project folder now looks.

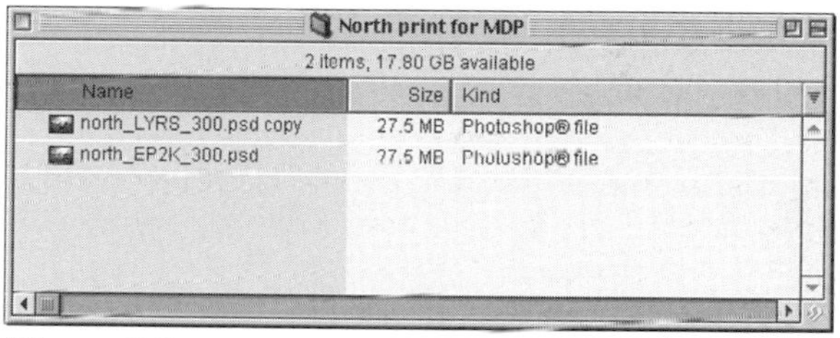

Figure 9.5
Work folder with the original layered file and the new print-specific file before flattening

Step 5: Flatten, Size, Scale, Res, and Sharpen

Flatten: The first thing I like to do with my new print-specific file is to get rid of all the preliminary layers that take up a lot of palette real estate. This helps me see things more clearly as I move into the next phases of production, and it also reduces the file size.

Because I'll be printing directly out of Photoshop, I could choose to leave the file in the PSD format and simply flatten all the layers into one (Layer > Flatten Image), or I could Save As to TIFF format, which flattens the file. Because there's always a chance of adding a layer tweak

Figure 9.6
Flattened file in PSD format

or adjustment here or there, I like to use the flattened PSD file format (see Figure 9.6). If you are sending the file to someone else for printing, they'll want a flattened TIFF.

Size, Scale, and Resolution: This is where a lot of people get tripped up or confused. I covered the idea of printer resolution a little in Chapter 2 and again in Chapter 4, but now is the time to make sure you understand these important and complementary issues.

There are two basic ways to size or scale an image for printing:

1. Have your image-editing software or printer driver do it. In Photoshop, this takes place in Print Options (version 6) or Print with Preview (version 7) where you can specify a scale percentage. You can do the same thing in File > Page Setup (Mac) or File > Page Setup > Properties > Graphics (Windows). With EPSON printer drivers, there is a Reduce or Enlarge by percentage function on either of these screens. Other printer brands have similar ways of doing this. Based on my tests, this method produces similar quality results as the resizing procedure described next, although there is occasionally some degradation when scaling *up* with the driver.

2. Use your image-editing software to scale (resize) or resample the image to the appropriate size.

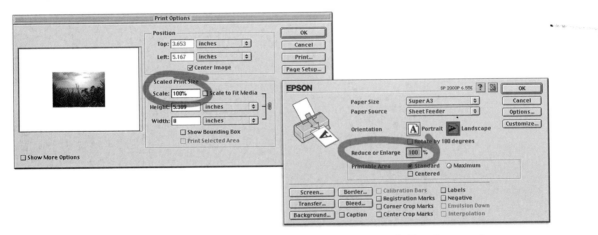

Images can be scaled or sized through the Print Options/Print with Preview or the Page Setup screens.

Let me clarify the crucial differences between Photoshop's methods for sizing or scaling the image.

In Photoshop's Image Size dialog box (Image > Image Size), you are confronted with a perplexing array of settings and options (see Figure 9.7).

The top portion is titled *Pixel Dimensions*, and it merely measures the number of pixels across (Width) and the number down (Height). The number of pixels determines the amount of information or detail contained in the image; more is better.

The next section down is titled *Document Size*, and this is where the critical decisions about image size and resolution are made. In addition, the key to how this section works is the little check box at the bottom called *Resample Image*. By either checking or unchecking that box, you are committing yourself to either *resampling* or *resizing*, and they are very different things. Let me explain the impact of this important choice.

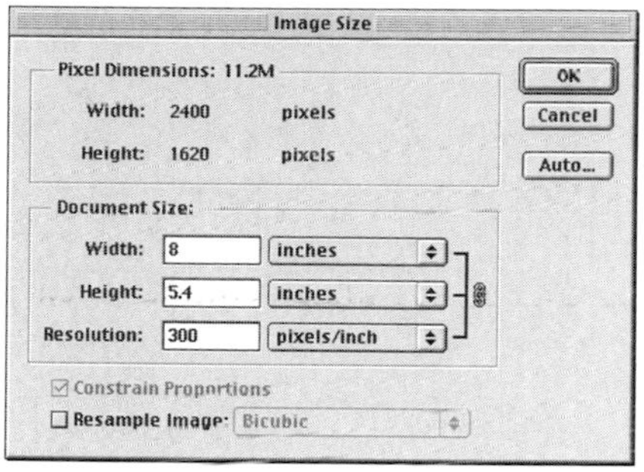

With the Resample box *checked*, you are *resampling* or *interpolating* the pixel information in the image to reach a desired height and width while at the same time maintaining a fixed resolution. You are adding or deleting pixels depending on whether you are going up in size (*upsampling* or *resampling up*) or down (*downsampling*). Either way, realize that you are changing the pixel information and, therefore, the image itself. (The Interpolation Method—Bicubic, Bilinear, or Nearest Neighbor—determines *how* the new pixels are created.) This action *always* degrades the image to some degree, usually resulting in the loss of sharpness and detail. I try to avoid this whenever I can, although it's sometimes not possible.

Figure 9.7
Photoshop's important Image Size dialog box.

If you *uncheck* the Resample box, there is now a direct correlation among height, width, and resolution. If you change one, the others change, too. However, in this case—and this is the important point—*you are not changing any pixel data!* You can prove this to yourself by changing the Resolution number while keeping an eye on the Pixel Dimensions; they won't budge. In essence, what you are doing is taking the same number of pixels and spreading them over a larger or smaller amount of space. You are only *resizing* the image, and because you're not actually printing pixels but dots, the printer driver's (or RIP's) dithering or screening method will try to cover up the differences, usually successfully.

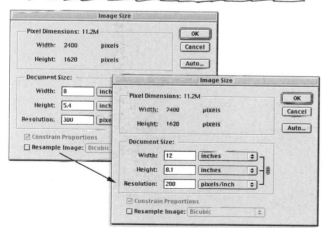

Figure 9.8
With Resample Image unchecked, decreasing the resolution from 300 ppi to 200 ppi increases the print size without affecting the pixel information.

Following this latter method with my image, if I have Resample Image unchecked and change the Resolution from 300 ppi to, say, 200 ppi, the Document Size reading has now magically changed from 8×5.4" to 12×8.1" (see Figure 9.8). In other words, the image is now larger in size because I lowered the image's file resolution. Conversely, I could shrink the image by increasing the resolution. However, again, this works only with the Resample Image box *unchecked*.

Don't be too concerned about even numbers for the resolution. If it takes 243 ppi to get the image to the right size, so be it. I have tested the theory of using only integer (whole number) divisions as the printer resolution (180, 240, and 360 dpi for EPSONs), and I've found virtually no improvement in inkjet print quality on the EPSONs and HPs I've tried it on. (A lot depends on the type of output. For normal bitmapped images, I've seen no difference between odd and even resolutions. I have seen a *slight* difference with images containing angled straight lines, but only with EPSONs, not HPs.) I've even done

Author's test image for evaluating whole-number or odd-even printer resolutions

what I call a Double-Whammy Test: taking a 243-ppi image and shrinking it down to 82 percent in Print Options/Print with Preview and then comparing the result with a 300 ppi version of the same image (mathematically, they both end up at the same size). The result? No difference. Thus, in general, use 300 ppi, 243 ppi, 307 ppi, or whatever you want to get you to the size you need.

Figure 9.9

A resaved 254-ppi version of the image (bottom) and how the file folder currently looks

This is also a good time to make any final cropping to the image to optimize the visual effect. Because I've already made a rough decision about the size I want the image to be based on my earlier mock-ups, I fiddle with the Document Size Resolution numbers until I reach my desired print size. I end up at 9.449×6.378" at 254 ppi. I save the file at this new size and change the file's name accordingly (see Figure 9.9).

Sharpen: Now for the last part of this step: *sharpening*. There are many ways to sharpen an image—and I have yet to meet an image that didn't need it— including using Photoshop's standard unsharp masking filter (Filter > Sharpen > Unsharp Mask), using what's called the High Pass/Hard Light method, sharpening the L (Lightness) channel in Lab Color mode (keeping in mind that there is some degree of quality loss every time a file is moved into or out of Lab), or using special software, plug-ins, or procedures (such as sharpening only in 10-percent increments). For this image, I decide to use standard RGB sharpening but with a filter fade effect.

To use the Fade Unsharp Mask method, I make a duplicate image layer and start experimenting with the Unsharp Mask filter (see Figure 9.10). Because the image already has a substantial amount of film grain, I beef up the Threshold setting. This protects the big flat areas like the

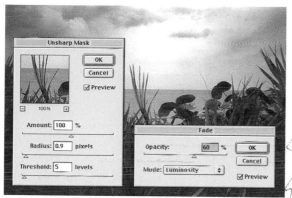

clouds and sky because Photoshop only sharpens the edges that have more contrast. I end up with sharpness settings of 100/.9/5.

Then I do a trick: Before I take any other action, I go into Fade Unsharp Mask (Edit > Fade Unsharp Mask), adjust my opacity, in this case to 60 percent, and change the Mode to Luminosity (see Figure 9.10). After I click OK, the fade feature is no longer available, which is why I made the duplicate layer. This method yields results similar to sharpening the L channel in Lab, but without the image and layer loss. (You could also come at it a different way by changing the duplicate layer's blending mode to Luminosity, sharpening it, and adjusting that layer's opacity.)

Figure 9.10

Final sharpening with the Fade Unsharp Mask method. left; The Unsharp Mask filter; right: Using the Fade command

Speaking of layers...because I've now introduced a new one, I'll need to flatten the file again. Most print-service providers want to work with single-layer flattened files (usually in TIFF format) only.

After sharpening, it's always a good idea to go over and check the image again carefully, usually at 100–200% view or more. Sharpening tends to add artifacts and to exaggerate any repair work.

Step 6: Select and Load Paper

I can't tell you how many times I've tried to print a file only to realize that I forgot to load the paper first. That's why I put this step here.

I'll be using EPSON's Watercolor Paper-Radiant White in 13 × 19-inch sheets. It's designed for use with the 2000P (and 7500 and 9500), and I like its textured matte surface as well as the 11.5-mil thickness (190 gsm). After I turn on the printer (another essential step!), I load the paper so that it's leaning against the back paper support with the printing side in the correct orientation (another stupid mistake I've made). See Figure 9.11. Certain papers

Figure 9.11

Single-sided coated paper has a front and a back, but sometimes it's hard to tell which is which. The printing front side is usually whiter and either smoother or rougher. You can print (effectively) only on the front of coated-one-side paper.

can be loaded only one sheet at a time, and because this is one of them, I load a single sheet. (If I'm going to be running thinner proof paper first, I can sometimes load up more sheets at once.)

Proofing paper: If I anticipate a lot of trouble, or if I'm using a very expensive paper stock, I might run my first tests on proofing paper, which only means that it costs less. Because the EPSON Watercolor Paper-Radiant White is a moderately priced paper (about $1.25 a sheet in the 13×19 size), I choose to skip the special proofing paper and print right on the real stuff. However, I'm still not one to throw my money away if I can help it, so I have a compromise solution: I cut the paper in half so that I can get two test prints out of each sheet. (If I were really pinching pennies, I'd cut the sheet into quarters.) Because my image is only about 9.5×6.5", it will fit nicely on a half-sheet of 13×19-inch paper. All I have to do is set up a new 13×9.5-inch size in Page Setup > Customize (see Figure 9.12). (In Windows, it's

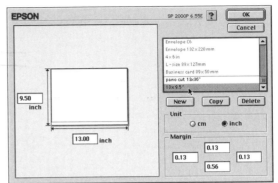

Figure 9.12
The EPSON Customize (Mac) or User Defined (Windows) screen lets you create unique paper sizes for different purposes such as my half-sheet proofs.

Page Setup > Properties > Paper > Custom.) The new size now appears on the Paper Size list. If the image were larger, I could scale it down to fit just for this testing stage. Alternatively, I could pick a paper with similar characteristics in 8.5×11-inch format and use that. The whole point is to use less-expensive paper to proof and to see if you're even in the ballpark with the image.

Step 7: Select Printer Settings or Profile

Because I've selected OEM inks and paper for the first variation of this print, I should be able to use the standard printer settings to get the quality I'm looking for, but I have a sneaky suspicion that I may need a little extra help. That's why I've added to this chapter information about using special printer profiles.

Before I do anything, I have to select my printer. On a Mac, I go to the Chooser and choose the 2000P that's connected to my G4 with a USB cable. I can then access the printer's settings through the Page Setup screen. In Windows, I would go to File > Page Setup where I select the printer under Name and then click Properties to access the printer settings.

Using the Printer's Settings

Whichever way I get there, I now need to select the basic settings. Using the Mac Photoshop Page Setup screen as the reference (see Figure 9.13), I first select the Paper size (Super A3, which is 13×19") and then the Paper Source (Sheet Feeder). (If I were printing on a roll, I'd pick Roll Paper.) Because I'll be printing in Landscape mode, I change that setting under Orientation. I leave everything else as is and click OK.

Print Options/Print with Preview: Now I move to Photoshop's (Mac) Print Options (Print with Preview in version 7) box (see Figure 9.13). (Note that I could have accessed Page Setup directly from Print Options as well.) In Windows, you click Properties to move to the next layer of printer settings.

In Print Options/Print with Preview, I can view a mini version of how the image will look on the print. This is a great last-minute check to see if the sizing and proportions are OK. Seeing this reminds me that I'll need to trim off the left and right edges to make the print's borders even.

I first check Center Image and uncheck Bounding Box in Scaled Print Size. This is also where I could change the image's scaling or sizing, but I've already taken care of that as described in Step 5.

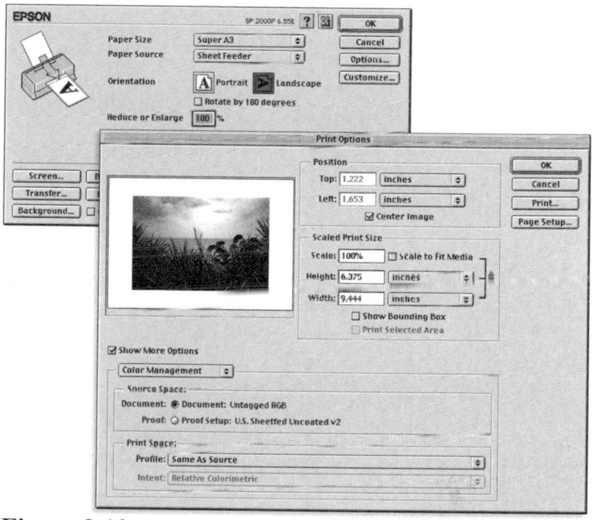

Now we get into the important Color Management section of Print Options/Print with Preview (see Figure 9.13). Checking Show More Options to open up the box, I make sure the first pop-up menu is set for Color Management and the Source Space is set for Document, in this case, as untagged RGB. (Realize that not embedding a profile in your file means that if your RGB workspace is ever changed, or if the file is opened in another computer with different settings, the color may be interpreted incorrectly.) Moving down to Print Space, I select Same As Source from the Profile pop-up menu. I do this because I'm using the printer's settings; if I were using a printer profile (as I will below), then I would select it here. I click OK and close the Print Options box.

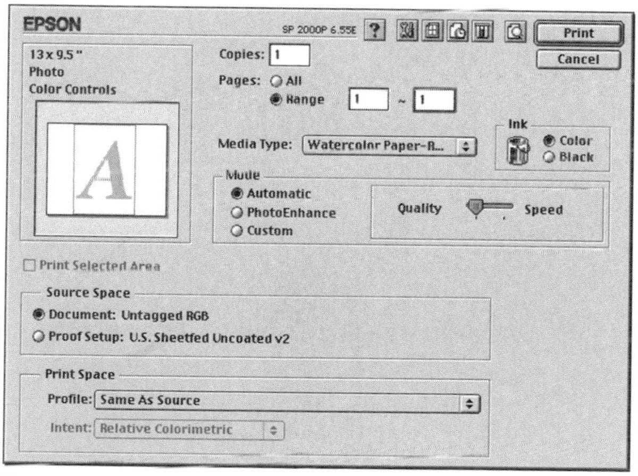

Print: For the last stage, I select Print from the File menu, which opens up the general printer settings dialog box (see Figure 9.14). I check the basics at the top (number of copies, pages, and color ink) and pick my paper under Media Type. (With Windows, the Media Type and Mode settings are under Properties > Device Options.)

Figure 9.13

Top: The typical EPSON Page Setup screen (Mac) from Photoshop. Other applications might call it Print Setup or similar; bottom: Photoshop's Print Options (version 6; it's called Print with Preview in version 7) dialog box shows the image on a custom page size for proofing and with the Color Management section opened at bottom.

Figure 9.14

The initial printer driver screen as accessed from Photoshop

Media Type Settings, Ink Output, and Dot Gain

The Media Type setting on an EPSON inkjet printer (it's called Paper Type or other names on different printers) determines, among other things, the amount of ink coverage or "ink laydown." This crosses over into the arcane world of *dot gain*, which is the tendency of ink dots to grow in size as they interact with different types of paper. Fibrous papers or more porous coatings set the stage for higher dot gain as the ink spreads, wicks, or bleeds into the paper. The opposite occurs on harder-coated or glossy paper surfaces where the ink tends to sit on top without much bleeding, spreading, or dot gain. The end result is that if the ink laydown or dot gain is not matched to the paper, prints can end up looking dark and muddy, or conversely, light and wimpy.

There are many sophisticated ways to control dot gain, including Photoshop's Dot Gain setting and Dot Gain Curves, but one of the easiest adjustments to make on a print that is coming out too light or too dark is to simply change the Media Type setting, which acts as a kind of dot-gain controller. (An alternative with the newest EPSONs and also some HPs is to use the Color Density or Ink Density sliders. See Figure 7.7 back in Chapter 7.)

The Print Quality—or resolution—setting will also affect the amount of ink laydown. In general, the higher the resolution, the more ink will be used, although it's *not* true that doubling the dpi will double the amount of ink coverage. I've done tests, and the increase in total ink density from 360 to 720 to 1440 dpi is marginal, unless printing with no color adjustment, as is done for profiling targets.

Figure 9.15 shows what the same test-strip image looks like printed on the same paper with only the Media Type settings changed. One caveat here is that because Media Type settings include a whole package of image-quality features, changing these settings can affect other things—such as color rendition—in addition to ink coverage.

Figure 9.15

The same test strip of RGB black (0R, 0G, 0B) in equal gradient steps printed with an EPSON 1280 on the same paper (EPSON Premium Glossy Photo Paper) at 1440 dpi with exactly the same settings, except that the Media Type was changed for each. From left, the selections are Matte Paper Heavyweight, Premium Glossy Photo Paper, Photo Quality Ink Jet Paper, Plain Paper, Photo Paper, and Ink Jet Back Light Film. The Matte Paper Heavyweight setting applied the least amount of ink, and the

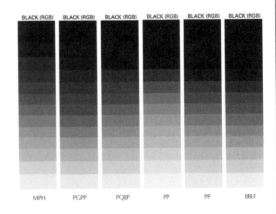

Photo Paper or Ink Jet Back Light Film settings applied the most. Although color shifts were theoretically controlled by using a consistent No Color Adjustment setting, you can see how each setting changed the colors on a supposedly neutral black image.

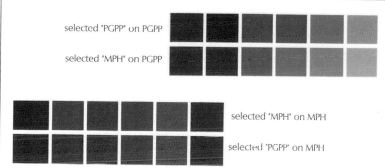

selected "PGPP" on PGPP

selected "MPH" on PGPP

selected "MPH" on MPH

selected "PGPP" on MPH

Target patches courtesy of ColorVision, Inc.

Figure 9.16
Using a porous Media Type setting like Matte Paper Heavyweight on a glossy stock will usually result in lighter ink coverage (top pair). Why? Because inks tends to sink into MPH, and the setting compensates for this by applying less ink. The reverse is also true when Premium Glossy Photo Paper is selected but printed on Matte Paper Heavyweight (bottom pair).

Although you can't always predict the results of changing Media Types without testing them yourself, a rule of thumb that usually holds true is that a setting for porous paper will yield *lighter* ink coverage on a glossy stock, and a glossy setting will do the reverse and yield *darker* ink output on a porous paper (see Figure 9.16).

The bottom line to all this Media Type fiddling is that sometimes the wrong settings can produce the right results! See Figure 9.17.

Figure 9.17
Sometimes it's right to pick the wrong setting! Here, the same image was printed with an EPSON 1280 on the same paper (EPSON Photo Quality Glossy Film) at 1440 dpi with only the Media Type settings changed. From left, the settings are Photo Quality Glossy Film, Photo Quality Ink Jet Paper, and Ink Jet Back Light Film. The far-left image has the correct setting for the paper used, but I personally prefer the far-right "wrong" setting. Although it's grainier, the colors are punchier and more pleasing to my eye. You'll also note that it's reversed, but that's easily fixed with the "Flip Horizontal" check box that becomes active when you select this setting.

Because I want to see first if I'm even close with this print, I start off with the simplest settings in the Mode section: Automatic and Quality (which changes the resolution to 720 dpi). This will hand over everything to the printer driver, and I'll know soon enough if this is the right decision or not.

The last thing I do in this box is confirm the Source Space and Print Space that were already selected in Print Options and should not have changed.

I'm ready to make my first print.

Using a Printer Profile

An even better option to using the onboard printer settings is to use a printer profile. It can be one you create yourself with a profile software package as described in Chapter 5, or it can be a purchased custom profile. Because I feel like I'm going to be close with this image, I choose the DIY Profile route.

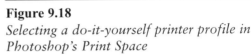

Figure 9.18
Selecting a do-it-yourself printer profile in Photoshop's Print Space

I had already made a scanner-based profile for this combination of inks and paper with ColorVision's ProfilerPLUS software, and I am ready to give it a try. I select the profile in the Print Space section of the main printer driver screen and prepare to make a test print (see Figure 9.18). Obviously, if you plan to use a printer profile but haven't made one, now is the time.

Step 8: Make a Test Print (or two or three...)

The moment of truth—and an exciting one it is—comes with that first print out of the printer.

Figure 9.19
It's a good idea to keep records of test-printing settings.

This is almost never the final print, but it serves as the reference benchmark for all subsequent adjustments. I'll make several more as needed.

A big part of printing is keeping track of what you've done so you can take your experience to improve the next prints down the line. That's why I take the time to pull out a blank legal pad and jot down all the specifications, settings, and decisions I've made up to this point (see Figure 9.19).

With Printer Settings

I'll try one test print with each basic printer setting option to see where I am and to illustrate how the settings work. (Although the settings and modes mentioned below are specific to this printer driver, other drivers will have similar settings with different names.)

What follows are three preset printing options on this particular EPSON printer driver. Other drivers and brands will have their own preset options to choose from to solve common problems, such as improving improperly exposed or low-resolution images. Although these are only stock solutions, they can be quite effective when used appropriately. They are a good place to start, especially if you are a novice digital printmaker.

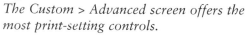

Figure 9.20
The Custom > Advanced screen offers the most print-setting controls.

Automatic mode: The first print I make is with the Automatic printer settings. I have to be honest—it looks pretty awful. The colors are very weak, and it's too blue overall. Next.

Photo Enhanced mode: My second print is with Photo Enhance mode with Nature selected in the nearby pop-up menu. This print is much better; more like what I'm seeing on my monitor. If I were in a hurry or less discerning, I would accept it. However, I know I can do better.

Custom mode: Selecting Custom > Advanced gains you access to a new dialog box and a new level of printer setting controls (see Figure 9.20). Without going into all the variations, I'll just concentrate on the one that allows the most fine-tuning with printer settings. That's with Color Controls selected in the Color Management section. This opens all the various sliders for customizing the brightness, contrast, saturation, and color ink levels. My first attempt with all the settings at zero gives me a washed-out print that looks worse than the previous one. However, I'll work on that in the next step.

Figure 9.21
The key to using printer profiles is to not also use the driver's color management. The print on the right is the result of the correct "No Color Adjustment" shown above; the print on the left used Color Controls in addition to the printer profile.

With a Printer Profile

To establish a baseline, I make an initial print using the printer profile but being very careful to use no other color management (see Figure 9.21). From the Print dialog box, I choose Custom > Advanced > Color Management > No Color Adjustment. Then, in the Print box, I go to Print Space and select the printer profile as shown earlier in Figure 9.14. I make the print and am pleasantly surprised by how good it is. A little tweaking should do it.

Step 9: Make Adjustments and More Test Prints

You'll notice that I didn't say in this heading "Make Adjustments and *One More Print*." I suppose it would be possible to make only one round of adjustments, then one more print, and be done. I just know that it's never happened to me! I usually go through lots of rounds of adjusting, printing, readjusting, reprinting, and so on. That's why it's important to take notes and to consistently number the prints as soon as they come out of the printer.

Using Advanced Printer Settings

By adjusting the sliders and experimenting with other options like Gamma in the Custom > Advanced mode, I was, after about eight attempts, able to produce a print that I liked. (Glad I cut that paper down!) The final image has a soft quality that I expected with the pigmented inks on a textured watercolor paper like this. Figure 9.22 shows the before and after, scanned from the actual prints.

Figure 9.22
This is the before (left) and after ... after several test prints adjusting printer settings.

If you're using printer settings, and after you've found your ideal combination of settings, you need to lock them in. The easiest way is with the Save Settings button—or its equivalent—that lets you name and save them for future use.

Adjusting a Printer Profile

If the number of test prints is any indication, using a printer profile for *this* image and *this* printer/ink/media combination is the better way to go. The first print was already good, but never being satisfied, I make three more prints, each time adding an adjustment layer to make a subtle move (see Figure 9.23). The fourth and final print is less contrasty, smoother, and richer; it's what I'm looking for.

I have now gone through two rounds of reduced-size test-printing using two different methods. Evaluating all my prints in a daylight environment, I pick the best test print (one that used my do-it-yourself printer profile) as the final proof, and I check my notes for which settings were used to make it. (Although the EPSON 2000P is infamous for producing prints exhibiting metamerism, this print seems hardly affected, primarily due to the lack of neutral-colored midtones.) As a safety measure, I transfer all the setting information to the border of the test print itself (see Figure 9.24).

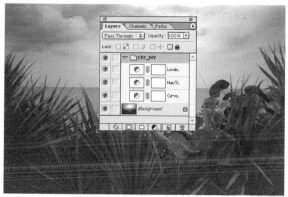

Figure 9.23
Three adjustment layers, grouped in a layer set named for the printer profile, make this print the best so far.

I have one more thing to do before making the final prints. Using the same settings as my approved test, I go back to the file, change the paper size, reload a sheet of 13 × 19-inch paper, and I make another print at full size. It matches the other proofs perfectly. I use the traditional printmaking term—*bon à tirer*, which means "good to print" in French—and write it on the final proof as a reminder. (If you use an outside printmaker, they will undoubtedly ask you to similarly sign off on the approved test print so that they can use it as a guide against which all the final prints must conform.)

I'm ready to go.

Step 10: Make the Final Print(s)

Final prints require more planning. Test prints are disposable (or make great gift cards), but depending on how many of the real thing you'll now be printing at once, you need to think through this last step *before* you start:

- How long do the prints need to dry before they can be stacked or stored? (I'll let them air dry for several hours; glossy paper can take up to 24 hours or more.)

- How many are you doing and how will you store them? Do you have an envelope or box that's big enough? (The original box the paper came is the perfect storage container.)

- How will you keep the prints from being damaged or soiled while handling? Do you have a clean work table? Do you have cotton photo-darkroom gloves to wear? Do you have a good way—compressed air, for example—to clean off surface dust or dirt?

Figure 9.24
All important test notes are transferred to the border of the final proof print.

- Do you need to do any coating, spraying, or other type of finishing of the prints? How, when, and where will that be done?

- Are you signing and numbering the prints? When? How?

These are just some of the obvious questions that need answers; you will undoubtedly have more. In my case, because I'm only making one print for framing (and one extra as a backup), I have my drying table, acid-free glassine cover sheets (available at any art supply store), empty paper storage box, and gloves ready.

With everything in place, I reopen my final digital file, inspect and load the paper, do a quick check of the EPSON StatusMonitor to make sure I have enough ink remaining for the job, verify all my settings, and press the Print button.

As soon as the print comes out of the printer, I pick it up at the edges and carefully inspect it. It's perfect, and it goes to the drying area to lay flat while I return to the computer and print a backup copy.

A few hours later, I blow off any accumulated dust, and separate the two prints with slip sheets of glassine. To protect the edges as well as the prints in general, I put them in the empty paper box they came in. This will keep them away from air circulation and light, and in general, keep them safe and sound until I'm ready to move to the final step: finishing and framing, explained in more detail later in this chapter.

After the final prints are safely stored away, I congratulate myself for making a great inkjet print. You should do the same.

A Third-Party Alternative

Some people prefer to break the rules a little and use third-party materials. The following describes just such an alternative.

Here's my setup: EPSON Stylus Photo 1280 printer, NoMoreCarts bulk ink system, Symphonic pigmented inks, and Crane Museo paper (100-percent cotton, 250 gsm) in 13×19-inch size. You'll note that I'm still using pigment inks. I could, of course, test the dye-based inks that come with the 1280, which is acknowledged as one of the best photorealistic inkjet printers, but I want to do a pigments-to-pigments comparison with the same image.

All the other pieces of the puzzle have been changed. I'm pushing the envelope a little!

The same basic steps apply as described earlier in the chapter; I'll note only the changes and additions:

Step 7: Select Printer Settings/Profile

Printer settings: To set a benchmark, I want to see how the onboard printer settings will fare. As outlined previously, I use Custom > Advanced settings but switch to Matte Paper Heavyweight as the Media Type selection because this is what Crane recommends for its Museo paper. I try several different combinations of settings.

Generic profile: For my next attempt, I try two ICC profiles (EPSON 1280 and EPSON 2000P) downloaded from the Crane Web site. I know that this is not the correct thing to do because these generic profiles are meant to be used only with the OEM inks, but I want to see for myself.

Custom profile: Finally, because they're the next step up in quality over scanner-based profiles, I want to see what a custom-made, spectrophotometer-based profile can do. I contract with color workflow and profiling consultant C. David Tobie to build me one. He e-mails me a profiling target (see Figure 9.25), and I print it out on the intended paper using the preferred Matte Paper Heavyweight Media Type setting. I'm careful to choose No Color Adjustment in the Custom > Advance section. After making sure that the target print is clean with no printing flaws, I send it back to him for profile building. A few days later, he e-mails me

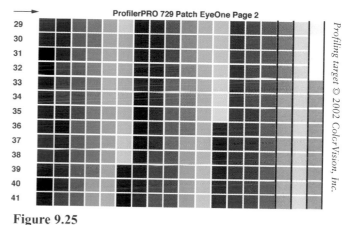

Figure 9.25
Portion of a ColorVision ProfilerPRO profiling target file. I printed this with the same settings to be used for the final prints and sent it off for a custom-made, spectrophotometer-based profile.

the profile, named as I requested. It's a small file (392K), and I put it in my ColorSync Profiles folder. I'm ready to print. (Please note that licensing restrictions apply to the distribution of ICC profiles; follow the terms of any profiling software you purchase.)

Steps 8 and 9: Make Test Prints

With printer settings: Using my money-saving technique of cutting the Museo paper in half, I make several prints trying different automatic and also slider-control settings. The results were terrible to barely acceptable, but I expect this because I'm using nonrecommended inks and paper for this printer.

With generic profiles: I did no better with the two downloaded, generic profiles. Again, this was expected.

With the custom profile: Bingo! My first print using the custom-made profile is nothing short of wonderful. The colors are rich, and the tones are smooth. It's excellent. I also try printing with different rendering intents (*Perceptual* was the default used) and find that *Saturation* does an equally good job. *Relative Colorimetric* is a little lighter and weaker, and *Absolute Colorimetric* is a little too blue.

Then I take it one more step. Using Photoshop's soft-proofing feature (View > Proof Setup > Custom), I tweak the image with a couple of adjustment layers, and make a final test print. It's breathtaking and even better than the prior prints, which I thought were already excellent. Time to quit.

Step 10: Make the Final Print(s)

I load the full-sized 13 × 19-inch paper, and, using the same custom profile, I make two final prints. They're gorgeous.

The final results? Although this test is specific to the image used, I am very pleased with the prints from both the original and the third-party workflow. However, the prize would have to go to the prints using the custom-made profile; they are truly astounding. (To make sure I wasn't dreaming, I did a quick test: I switched the paper back to the EPSON Watercolor Paper-Radiant White and reprinted the last version of the image. The results were also excellent; the colors were a bit more saturated and with more contrast.)

The final results: The top two images are the same before-and-after scanned prints (using Advanced Printer Settings) as in Figure 9.22. The bottom two are prints made with the custom profile. At left is the first print, and at right is a print made using adjustment layers after soft-proofing in Photoshop.

Obviously, I could have done more testing, using, for example, a custom-made profile for the EPSON 2000P prints on watercolor paper, or making my own DIY profile with the third-party inks and papers on the EPSON 1280. However, I'm satisfied that I covered the major bases, and I'm more than satisfied with the final prints made.

Finishing and Displaying Your Prints

You've output one or more great digital prints. Now what? It's time to finish them in a way that protects and preserves them, and to show them off for the world to see.

Print Aesthetics

Because digital printing is a new art process, many wonder if the age-old rules of traditional printmaking apply to it. Canadian photographer Alan Scharf introduced me to the question of *print aesthetics*, and it's a good one. Should a digitally printed photograph look different from one printed in a darkroom? Is glossy paper or fine-art paper more appropriate? Should prints have square-cut edges or deckled ones? Plain borders, printed borders, or no borders? Over-matted or float-mounted when framed or no frame at all?

A Web Workflow

Because so many digital images end up on the Internet, here is a short workflow for preparing images for the Web. (My thanks to digital photographer and artist Web-designer Larry Berman at www.BermanGraphics.com for these 10 basic Photoshop steps.)

1. Convert to an uncompressed format, preferably PSD.

2. Crop and do your image adjustments, such as curves, levels, cloning out dust, and so on. (Larry works at 100%.)

3. Resize to 72 ppi at whatever your long-pixel dimension is going to be. Be consistent. If you are preparing a series of images for a Web site, make them all the same long-pixel dimensions.

4. Add a single pixel stroke (Edit > Stroke in Photoshop). If the page is going to be black, make the stroke white; if the page is white, make the stroke black. That will let the dark areas stand out from a black page or the light areas stand out from a white page. Choose "inside" for the placement of the stroke, or it won't show.

5. Add a drop shadow if desired. This only works on a white or light-colored background, and the shadow should be right and bottom.

6. Add your copyright as a text layer. If you have a Web site, use that URL as the copyright so that you can be found later.

7. Select the background layer and add unsharp masking.

8. Save and use the long-pixel dimensions as part of the file name to differentiate it from the full-size image in step one.

9. File > Save For Web. (Larry uses a setting of 40 for a progressive JPEG.)

10. For each image, you now have a full-sized uncompressed file, a resized version with active layers uncompressed, and the JPEG for the Web.

An example of a Larry Berman Web image complete with a white stroke and a URL copyright

Courtesy of Larry Berman

This is a good workflow, and the only added suggestions I have are these: (1) I also add the compression setting (such as nordstrom_300x_50q.jpg) to the file name, and (2) instead of always using a consistent JPEG setting, and depending on the situation, I sometimes try to hit a certain file size range. I adjust the setting accordingly until I have it. With experience, I can do it in one or two tries.

One advantage of the digital printing revolution is that there are now many different looks available—everything from muted prints that evoke watercolors to glossy photographic prints and beyond. Artist and printmaker JD Jarvis believes that digital printing cries out for new approaches. "When it comes to printing or displaying digital art, think in nontraditional terms. Explore new materials and ways of displaying the work. In the long run, we stand to gain more credibility with the fine-arts world by thinking outside the box it has created."

Curating Prints

"Curating" means different things to different people, but in the context of printing, I like to define it as the preparation, care, and handling of prints after they emerge from the printer. The major subactivities that come under curating are: *finishing*, *coating*, and *framing*.

This home installation shows the author's photo-based image Big Wave 1 printed by Duganne Ateliers. It's an IRIS print on fine-art paper with four torn edges float-mounted in an antique frame. The decorator in charge of the project loved the hybrid look.

Finishing

Edge deckling: Although some artists such as Karin Schminke print directly onto fine-art paper with deckled edges (she has a special technique using removable tape plus strips of acetate taped to the back of the print), most artists prefer to tear the edges to give a deckled effect *after* printing. This takes some practice, but it's a skill that can be picked up. Here's Jack Duganne's explanation for tearing the edges of a print: "Punch the front of the paper (where you want the tear to be) with a pin so that you can see the holes through the back of the paper. Turn the paper over and, lining up the holes made on the other side, tear against a straight edge, pulling the paper that you want to remove against it and keeping the pressure against the edge with a downward pulling motion. After the tears are made, just smooth the torn paper down with a rounded device like a spoon or piece of rubbing bone, and—voila!—a perfect deckled edge!"

I've found that with some paper stocks, it works well to use short tears (rather than one long one), even ripping toward the straight edge at varying angles to get a different look. Different edge thicknesses will also create different tears. Some like to wet the paper with a brush or Q-tip, but I find that unnecessary. Best to practice on scraps of paper first. Then, when you're ready, move to the real print, take a deep breath, and start tearing.

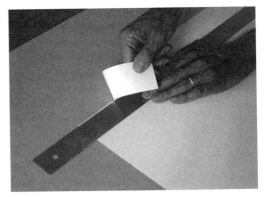

Tear prints from the back to create a ragged edge.

Signing and numbering: If you're producing an edition, you'll probably want to sign and number your prints. There are no hard-and-fast rules, although it's traditional for the signature and date to go on the right under the image, and for the edition number (if any) to go on the left. The title can go in the center. This only works if there's an empty border to sign on. If not, and the print is matted, you can sign and number the mat.

If it's a limited edition, you'll write the number as a fraction: the first number (the numerator) is the number of the print; the second number (the denominator) is the full number of the edition. Like this: 15/50 or 1/250.

As for the mechanics of signing, it's conventional to sign art prints in pencil, although that obviously won't work with glossy and other nonporous media. In that case, everything from Sharpies, gold or silver pens, or other permanent marking pens are used. Some hardcore digitalists who are concerned with "differential permanence" have been known to use pens filled with the actual black ink from their printing inksets.

There's an entire movement of photographer-artists who are opposed to the principle of artificial limited editions when applied to digital prints that, in theory, can be produced endlessly without any image loss. These artists produce *open editions* and sign and number sequentially only. It's a personal choice.

Embellishing: Embellishing means taking a digital print and adding hand brush strokes, glitter, textures, or other artistic flourishes and enhancements to give the print a more custom look. Artist Ray Bliss Rich uses sumi ink for his sumi-e brushwork on inkjet prints made with an EPSON 2000P. Canvas-print embellishing is frequently done with acrylic or oil paints over a solvent-based protective coating. The largest print-for-pay shops use staff assistants to embellish their artists' prints (see Figure 9.26).

Figure 9.26
A staff artist embellishes a giclée print at Harvest Productions.

Coating

The decision of whether to coat a digital print is completely dependent on how the print is made. The original IRIS prints were (and still are) treated with a light, water-resistant, protective coating. There are lots of war stories of printmakers who have had IRIS prints ruined merely from the moisture or spit coming from their mouths while talking near them!

When is coating needed? The main print enemies that coatings protect against are these: moisture, UV light damage, atmospheric contaminants, biochemical activity (molds and such), and abrasion or marring. If you can avoid these problems, and you're using long-lasting inks, especially pigment inks, that are well-matched to the medium or paper, you probably don't need to coat your (paper) prints. This is especially true if they're destined to end up under glass in a frame. If, however, you're (1) printing on canvas that won't be framed under glass, (2) using certain pigment inks that tend to smear or smudge on glossy media, or (3) using dyes that could end up in a vulnerable storage and display environment, think about coating your prints.

Coatings can also be used to punch-up or add depth to the color intensity of inkjet inks, especially pigmented ones that sometimes have a reduced color gamut. This is a well-known technique to increasing the Dmax of an inkjet print's dark shadows.

Types of coatings: Coatings (also called *overcoats* or *topcoats*) come in many forms including: film laminates, liquid laminates, clearcoats, acrylic varnishes, and photo lacquers. Film laminates (hot or cold press) are the most protective but also the most visually distracting, usually resulting in a stiff, "plasticy" look. This is how restaurant menus at Denny's are coated, although John Thompson of Alpha Imaging Technologies points out that recent film-lamination advances have resulted in a very thin, very flexible overlaminate film that is only 0.5-mil thick. If it is applied correctly, it basically disappears, although this effect works only on matte or smooth surfaces. Thus, it's ruled out for canvas or textured watercolor paper.

Liquid laminates (also called *clearcoats*) are less obvious, even invisible, and there are many kinds: acrylics, solvent-based, water-based, and UV-curable in matte, luster, and gloss finishes. These types of coatings must be carefully matched to the type of inks and media used.

Ideally, you want an inert, odorless, colorless, nonyellowing, antifungal coating that's easy to apply. In addition, you want to know that the coating is not going to shorten the life of the print. This is an unresearched area at present.

Coating brands that have developed followings with digital printers include the following: Clearstar ClearShield and ClearJet (clearstarcorp.com), Superfrog Frog Juice (superfrog.com), Lyson Print Guard (lyson.com), BullDog Ultra Coating (bulldogproducts.com), Liquitex Solivar varnish, Krylon Crystal Clear, UV-Clear acrylic sprays, and Sureguard (perfectiondistributing.com) and Lacquer-Mat (lacquer-mat.com) photo lacquers. You can also use fixative sprays, which have been used for years by traditional artists to prevent smudging. Krylon and Windsor-Newton make popular ones.

How to do it: Coating a print can get messy depending on the process. There are four basic ways to put a coating onto a print: screened, brushed, rolled, or sprayed. Screening requires a setup that is beyond what most self-printers would consider. Brushing and rolling is fairly simple with the right protection in place. Aerosol spraying is easy, but it requires proper ventilation and face masks or respirators.

If using a photo lacquer spray, spray with a fixative undercoat first. Make sure any sprays or coatings are completely dry before framing or storing.

The best way to protect a print (digital or otherwise) is to frame it under glass.

Mounting and Framing

If you're at all concerned about UV fading, airborne-contaminate deterioration, and the potential for physical damage from insects, pets, or curious children, then by all means, plan on framing your (paper) prints behind glass or acrylic/plexiglass. (Canvas prints are traditionally not put under glass; hence the need to some kind of postprinting coating.) Epson's advice to "display your print in a glass frame, plastic sleeve, or a photo album" has a lot of merit.

Framing digital prints is no different from any other type of works-on-paper framing. The main advice is this: Always use acid-free materials in all phases of the framing process. That goes for mats, backing boards, and the hinging or adhesive material.

Drying: Make sure your prints are completely dry before framing. This can be anywhere from 24 hours to several days depending on the inks and media used. Still-wet prints can cause fogging inside a frame.

Sizes: Standard-sized mats and frames are the way to go for keeping costs down. Print buyers are also more likely to buy art that is either matted or framed in standard sizes. It's sometimes a little more difficult to find 13 × 19-inch-sized protective sleeves, portfolios, and mats.

Mounting: Although many photographers are successful with dry- or cold-rolled, adhesive-mounting of their prints to backing boards, others follow traditional printmaking methods where acid-free

Courtesy of Jonathan Talbot

Jonathan Talbot presents his mixed-media work, many of which contain computer-generated elements, by floating the paper (with the edges showing) inside eight-ply, all-rag mats and then framing them under glass in simple, white-washed maple frames. Shown at left is Pi Patrin, a 3-inch-square-image on 7×7" paper in a 12×12" frame. Strategic grouping on a gallery wall adds rhythm to what might otherwise be a repetitious display.

corners or archival linen hinges are preferred. The key point is to avoid nonarchival material such as rubber cement or masking tape. Use only acid-free mounting, backing, and framing materials. If dry mounting, make sure to use low heat. Some inks are affected by heat more than others.

Mats: Mats can be made with a mat cutter or bought premade in quantity. Many established photographer-artists prefer to spend their time making art instead of cutting mats and therefore buy mats from such suppliers as pictureframes.com, unitedmfrs.com, and framingsupplies.com.

A digital alternative to real mats is a "faux mat" created in an image-editing or drawing program and printed on the print itself. See Figure 9.27 for an example. Photographer-artist Konrad Poth, who makes his own frames from recycled wood from old barns and fences, actually combines faux mats with real ones to produce a double-mat effect.

Figure 9.27
A faux mat can be created in Photoshop or a drawing program and printed along with the image.

Molding: Anything goes for the type of molding or framing material— metal or wood, simple or ornate. You might want to follow JD Jarvis' advice: Break new ground and try something nontraditional. How about a frame made of empty ink cartridges glued together?

Glazing: Glazing means glass or acrylic (usually called *plexiglass*) when you're talking about framing. Both types come in plain, UV-filtering, antireflective, nonglare, or abrasion-resistant versions. With glass, the UV-filtering type is preferred except it's much more expensive than regular glass. As we've learned, even plain clear glass will block much of the UV radiation hitting a print.

Glass and plexiglass each have their followings. Plexiglass is lighter, more expensive, scratches easily, and is a magnet for dust and lint, but it's the best choice if you're shipping prints or if used in high-traffic or accident-prone areas, such as a child's room.

Canvas stretching: If you're printing on canvas, you can "stretch" the print onto the standard artist stretcher bars that painters use, complete with folded corners. Here are some canvas-stretching tips from artist and printmaker Lance Amici at Torlan Studios in San Antonio, Texas:

- Leave plenty of margin on all sides for wrapping around the wood.

- Slightly sand or round off the corners of the stretcher bars before stretching to minimize tearing or hairline cracks.

- Do not stretch or roll canvas prints in temperatures under 70 degrees F.

- If a coating seems brittle, use a hair dryer to warm up the canvas edges before stretching them.

- Do not stretch canvas prints as tight as you would an original.

Storing, Shipping, and Displaying Prints

After prints are finished, you have to store, ship, or display them.

Storing Prints

If you're not selling, giving away, or displaying your prints, then you'll be storing them. Here are some things to keep in mind.

Protective sleeves: These are a great way to store and even present digital prints to customers, clients, or colleagues. They are available in all sizes from such companies as inkjetART.com, digitalartsupplies.com, lightimpressionsdirect.com, and clearbags.com. One of the most popular types is crystal clear and has a fold-over flap with a resticking, self-adhesive strip. Don't use regular envelopes or sleeves that contain acid or polyvinyl chloride (PVC) for this purpose, and never use rubber bands, paper clips, or pressure-sensitive tapes.

Albums: Because there's no light to fade them, storing digital prints in albums can usually improve their longevity as long as the album materials are acid-free and "archival." Archival albums and individual sheet protectors are sold by the same companies as were listed above.

General Print Storage Recommendations:

- Handle all prints with great care as you would any original artwork.

- Store prints flat, but not in the open. Use dust-free cabinets, acid-free boxes, or archival sleeves.

- Because heat and humidity significantly shorten print lifespans, store your prints in a dark, dry, and cool place. Shoot for a goal temperature of 68–70 degrees F, with 30–40 percent relative humidity.

- As explained in Chapter 6, don't let prints come into contact with any objects that produce oxidizing agents, solvents, acids, or other volatile materials. Don't store prints in areas with chemicals, such as in a photographic darkroom.

Shipping Prints

The safest way to ship prints is to roll them loosely and put them inside of a strong tube. Use protective, acid-free sheets on both sides of the print, and stuff padding into each end. For a bullet-proof shipment, put the print(s) inside a tube, then put the tube inside one of those triangular boxes that courier companies like FedEx offer. Once received, rolled prints will go flat on their own or with light weights on top.

You can also ship prints flat, but it's riskier in term of potential damage. If the prints are already matted and/or framed, they will have to ship flat. Artist Jean Anne Allen uses a two-piece (inner and outer) mirror-picture carton from a moving-supply company with the artwork inside protected with bubble wrap. "My advice," business manager Michael Allen says, "is to wrap both directions with bubble wrap and use a two-part mirror box that is the largest practical size so that it fully inserts into itself giving double-walled protection."

Try to avoid shipping a print framed with glass; use plexiglass instead. Some art shows and contests will refuse artwork shipped with glass. The potential for damage and injury is too high.

Displaying Prints

Print display choices range from museum display conditions to the outside wall of your beach house. In addition, what you choose will, in large part, determine the expected life of your prints. Here are some basic display tips for prints:

- Avoid displaying or storing prints outdoors.

- Never expose prints to direct sunlight, not even for one minute a day. The lower the light levels, the better.

- Display paper prints behind glass or plexiglass. Use a protective coating on canvas prints.

- To moderate humidity fluctuations, use vapor barriers or frame desiccants like silica gel in the print frames.

- Use only acid-free, archival materials for framing prints. Never use masking tape, Scotch tape, or rubber cement for framing.

- If prints are unprotected, keep them away from sources of ozone, such as air cleaners, copying machines, or other generators of high-voltage electricity.

The Death of Prints?

There has been talk of digital displays replacing real paper prints for years (just like the predictions of the paperless office!).

Digital-Frame, Inc. makes a digital picture frame called, you guessed it, the Digi-Frame. The larger versions are targeted to commercial businesses and to wedding and other professional photographers who "shoot a wedding Saturday morning, and at the party that night have the pictures showing on the Digi-Frame ready for ordering." It can run off a computer, but it's main advantage is as a stand-alone, active matrix/LCD unit showing video or still pictures in slide-show mode. It accepts CompactFlash, SmartMedia, Memory Stick, MicroDrive, or CD media. One major problem is the cost—$2,999 for the 18-inch model and $549 for the smaller, desktop model.

The future of digital image display?

There's no doubt that, eventually, every office and home will have the equivalent of a Digi-Frame hanging in a hall or over the fireplace. However, that day, I predict, is many years away. People still love their prints.

The workflow steps and finishing points made above are meant to apply to anyone making their own inkjet prints. However, what if you want to have your printing done by an outside print provider or service? To find out about this other side to digital printing, turn the page.

PART III

Beyond
the
Basics

10

Print for Pay: Using a Professional Print Service

There are advantages and disadvantages to doing your own printing. Sometimes, it makes sense to farm out some or all of the process. Let's take a closer look at the role of printmakers and printing services.

What Printmakers Do, and Why You Might Want to Use One

The digital printing industry calls the category of outside print-service providers "print-for-pay," which is just a shorthand way to say: "You print this, and I'll pay you for it." This is a larger group than you might think, and it covers fine-art printmakers, service bureaus, imaging centers, photo labs with digital equipment, forward-thinking repro and color houses, some sign and banner shops, and even instant-print chains that are expanding their services to include art reproductions. In addition, it also includes those photographer-artists who, for whatever reason, take on outside work from others to supplement their own self-printing (a common occurrence).

Who uses printmakers? Traditional artists wanting inkjet reproductions (giclées) form a large group of buyers of digital printing services. Most have no other way to reproduce their work, especially if they're producing large prints. Photographers are a smaller group, and one reason is that many are used to doing their own lab work, and so, do their own digital printing. "Photographers tend to want complete control over their work, but artists just want to paint," is how Pennsylvania printmaker Jim Davis of The Visual Artist explains it. And finally, there are the digital artists who form another small group of users of printing services. Many (not all) frequently work at a smaller scale and like the immediate results of seeing their own prints coming out of their own printers.

Regardless of which category you might fit into, anyone who's involved with digital imaging or printing should at least consider using an outside printmaker. If you're on the fence about this, the following paragraphs provide some additional reasons for using a print service. (I'll concentrate on fine-art printing, primarily inkjet, in the first section of this chapter and then look at photographic and other commercial providers at the end.)

Knowledge, experience, and craft: Printmaking is a craft that takes years, even a lifetime, to perfect. Experienced printmakers are experts at what they do, and they usually have the best, most expensive equipment. Therefore, by using an outside printer, you shift the burden of learning the craft and of keeping up with all the latest print technology to the printmaker, which frees you up to concentrate on image-making activities.

A seasoned printing professional has seen it all and has an in-depth knowledge of materials and artistic approaches that have been tried and tested, and, accordingly, can act as your aesthetic guide and advisor. New Mexico printmaker Lynn Lown of New Media Arts explains that he has artists consistently tell him that he has helped them to take their work to the next level. "I do that by listening to them and by showing them the possible ways to go with their work."

Geoffrey Kilmer, president of Photoworks Creative Group in Charlottesville, Virginia, which offers both wide-format inkjet and photographic LightJet printing, says that "when you have a group of professionals pursuing excellence in digital output on a daily basis, it only makes sense that they have the potential to hold a much greater reservoir of knowledge in this area. In addition, an artist can learn some very valuable lessons in the process of working with such a professional provider."

I've used several inkjet printmakers in all corners of the United States, and, without exception, they have all taught me something about digital printing I hadn't known before. Each outside-printing project was an eye-opening experience that improved my own art-making process. For this reason alone, I recommend working with a professional printmaker, at least once or on an occasional basis.

Experienced printmakers are experts at what they do and can help you produce the highest-quality prints.

Quality: Unless you are an experienced, long-time self-printer, an outside printmaker will usually be able to give you higher-quality prints than you can do on your own. The fact is that first attempts at digital printing are typically not perfect. It takes a lot of trial and error as well as gallons of ink and boxes of paper before the printing process is humming along producing top-quality output.

This is why I often recommend that newcomers to digital printing start off by jobbing out their first few projects to an outside printmaker. This sets a benchmark of what is good and what can be achieved. Some photographer-artists end up being so happy using a particular printmaker that they continue to work this way, even going so far as to fly in from other locations for the printing sessions.

Time and focus: Many photographers and artists believe that their time is best spent creating their art; labs and print shops are better left to others. Printmaker Lynn Lown says, "As a commercial photographer for years, it was common wisdom that you should stay out of the darkroom. You can make much more money as a shooter if you are good at that. If you are good at the lab, you should stop shooting and open one. A pro needs a lab so he or she can spend more time shooting."

Legendary rock artist Stanley Mouse does his own printing, but he also uses outside printmakers to produce his higher-quality reproduction prints. He's shown holding The Jester *from the cover of the Grateful Dead song book.*

Other types of image makers may feel they are in the same boat. Digital artist Ileana explains that using a printmaker "allows me to focus on the creative aspects of making the picture. It would have taken me a lot of time and many trials to produce a piece that I would consider satisfying. Until I gain enough knowledge about printmaking, I can have my work printed quickly and easily."

For some, then, it comes down to a simple question: Do you want to spend the time yourself to learn about printmaking, or do you want to use someone who's already been there and back many times?

Size and practicality: If you need large prints, and you can't afford a wide-format printer or the space to house one, then your only alternative is to use a service provider with wide-format printers. "The one big factor that brings most of my print clients to the door is size," explains digital printmaker JD Jarvis. "Most of the digital artists I deal with have excellent printers that may print up to 17×22 inches, but for larger prints, they come to me. Basically, you would go to an outside printmaker when they offer services you cannot match with your own equipment, or when the cost of providing those services for a limited project outweighs the return."

Similarly, there is no practical way to use certain digital technologies *without* using an outside service. Fuji Frontiers, Océ LightJets, Durst Lambdas, and so on start at $120,000 and up, so the chances of having one of your own in the back bedroom are slim indeed. Photo labs, service bureaus, and the like are your only hope for making these kinds of prints. (See "Working with Noninkjet Providers.")

Cost effectiveness: Depending on your situation, printmakers can save you money. You can have a small print made by an outside print provider for $100 or less. This is a good way to test an image or a potential market. If the test fails, you haven't lost much. In addition, if that particular printmaker doesn't suit you, you can simply move on to someone else.

"I don't have to keep up with products, materials, and inks, or make that significant investment," says artist Ileana. "Because I currently don't sell prints in bulk, it would take me a long time before I would see any return on my initial investment if I did it all myself."

Some of the *disadvantages* of using an outside printmaker include the following:

When you need large prints, see a printmaker. Shown is a ColorSpan DisplayMaker Mach 12 inkjet printer at Harvest Productions. This 12-color printer has a maximum output size of 72" wide by unlimited length.

- Loss of some control and flexibility.
- Time delays going back and forth.
- Ongoing, per-print costs are usually higher.

Note that some photographer-artists take both approaches, doing some self-printing and farming other work out. I, myself, fall into this group.

How to Pick an Inkjet Printmaker

Selecting an outside print service is no different from choosing a lawyer. You have to do your homework and then ask the right questions. To narrow the choices of potential inkjet printmakers, interview (by phone, mail, or in person) all the candidates with the same set of questions. If you can, visit the print studios or businesses in person to get a feel for them. How they answer your questions is just as important as what they say. You are about to enter into a close, possibly long-term relationship. You want to give it the best chance of succeeding up front.

The following are several main points you should have on your questions list before you start your interviewing. (Use this list as a guide; add your own questions as needed.)

Experience?

How long have they been making digital prints? Do they understand color theory and how to manage color? Are they familiar with the kind of art output you're looking for, or are they a sign shop that figures digital printing is digital printing? "Find out if they have worked with other artists and whether or not they found that experience rewarding," says printmaker JD Jarvis. "If the printer does not realize that creating work for 'fine art' requires special attention, or if they offer that attention grudgingly, look for someone else."

Referrals?

As with any service, get referrals. How many clients or customers similar to you do they have? Can they give you any customer references? If so, absolutely follow up and contact them asking for their comments. Also, talk to other artists whose output you like and who are happy with the printing services they use. Then contact those providers.

Samples?

At a minimum, you should evaluate several samples of a printmaker's work. Most professional printmakers are glad to send out a sample packet with a price sheet and sometimes paper swatches.

An even better idea is a test print. "The best interview," explains New Media Art's Lynn Lown, "is to have them make you a small print." You'll have to pay for it, but one-quarter-size prints can be made at very reasonable prices.

Lown also advises that those searching for a printmaker "look for someone who does other work that resembles your own. This guarantees that the printmaker is aware of your sensibility. In dealing with images, most people think about 'technology' when, really, it's about 'culture.'"

Physical Space/Location?

Where are they located? Is it local, or does it require mail, courier shipments, or online interaction to reach them? (See more about online services later in this chapter.) Do they encourage artists to come in and view their work in progress or interact with the staff? Is a there a professional viewing booth?

This is the test file I had printed by Thunderbird Editions in Clearwater, Florida. I wanted to see what they could do with different types of image elements, so I made up my own composite file. I could have used a single real image just as easily, but this seemed like a better test, and it proved to be a very valuable one.

You could never confuse Harvest Productions in Anaheim Hills, California, with a garage operation (although that's exactly how they started off). Harvest is currently the largest giclée printing company in the world. Shown are some of the 12 Roland Hi-Fi JETs they use (that's in addition to the 13 IRIS printers and others).

If it's practical, take a tour and look at the printmaker's operation. Does it look like a real business, or is it a hobby in the garage?

How Long Will It Take?

What is the turnaround time from file to final print? Whatever you're told, add 50 percent to come up with a more realistic schedule. In addition, make sure you factor in shipping time, holidays, and so on.

Keep in mind that printmakers are running commercial businesses. Time is money to them, and they will want to move your project through their production flow as efficiently as possible. However, the digital print process takes time, and there's no point in short-circuiting it.

Do You Provide Printer Profiles?

The purpose of a printer-provided profile is so that the photographer-artist can soft-proof the image on the computer screen to get an idea of how it will look when printed. This reduces the likelihood of a poor print, and it becomes even more important if the photographer-artist is providing a digital file. If it's a painting or other preexisting artwork that the printmaker will scan or photograph, then a profile may not be necessary; the entire workflow is in the printmaker's hands.

More and more professional printmakers are providing their customers profiles, but not all printmakers believe in this. "I do not create printer profiles," explains JD Jarvis. "Instead, I opt to make an adjusted image file that works best for the particular circumstances. I retain this adjusted file along with my notes on how the file was created. The original image is returned to the client, and I use the adjusted file for any subsequent prints made within an edition."

On the other side of the fence is Jim Davis. "I will make soft-proof profiles for people if I'm doing the final printing," he says. "If they purchase my paper and do the printing themselves, I will also produce custom profiles. There is no charge for this service. I will even go so far as to take my calibrator to them and calibrate their whole computer system. Of course, I do make sure they are going to be a steady customer first."

Fine-art photographer Paul Eric Johnson believes that "profiles are at the heart of the matter for me. Of the six companies in the San Francisco Bay area who offer LightJet printing, only Calypso Imaging (see more about them later in the chapter) makes their profiles readily available." (See Figure 10.1)

If printer profiles are important to the way you work, you need to ask about them. (See also "Profiles for digital photoprint and photo process" later in this chapter.)

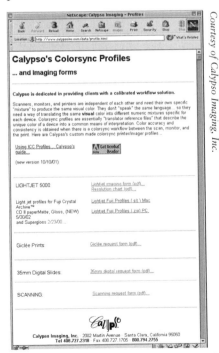

Courtesy of Calypso Imaging, Inc.

Figure 10.1
Calypso Imaging makes it easy to download their printer profiles.

Other Services?

Printmakers do more than just print. Some offer a complete range of artist support services including finishing, canvas stretching, and shipping. Lynn Lown even offers bookbinding for custom family albums and individual artist's books (see Figure 10.2).

Some print providers do printing for art publishers or are art publishers themselves, and they may be able to help you market your work. At a minimum, because they deal with so many artists, printmakers can be good sounding boards for sales and marketing ideas.

Obviously, these related services are chargeable and on top of the basic printing costs.

Photo by Dick Faller/New Media Arts

Figure 10.2
Lynn Lown of New Media Arts in Santa Fe, New Mexico, offers his own handmade rag paper for special editions.

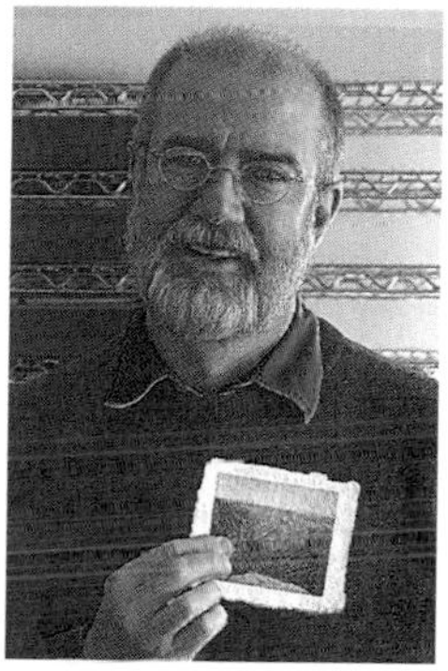

How Much?

Price is important, but even more important is *how* a printmaker charges. Per page? Per linear foot? Per square foot? Prep work additional? What is included and what is not? Here are the main issues:

Basic print cost: Digital printmakers usually charge by the output size or by the square unit measure. For inkjet, per sheet costs (a full sheet is approximately 35×45") can range from \$200–\$400 with discounts for additional sheets printed at the same time. Keep in mind that a full sheet can be divided up into multiple, smaller images to reduce the unit cost per image. In addition, certain factors such as the choice of paper will affect the costs. For example, canvas usually costs more.

Per-square-foot inkjet costs can range from \$15–\$35 per square foot with a minimum charge, and some, like Nash Editions, Duganne Ateliers, and Jim Davis' The Visual Artist even charge by the square inch. Duganne and Davis both charge \$0.10 per square inch for the first print on paper (see Figure 10.3), and Davis charges \$0.16 for canvas.

JD Jarvis charges by the linear inch, "because it matches the way frame shops have structured their services." For him, all other "value added" services are separate charges.

Courtesy of Jack Duganne

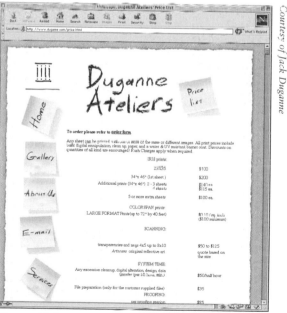

Figure 10.3
Online price list for digital printmaking studio Duganne Ateliers in Santa Monica, California

Reorders: This is one of the benefits of digital printing. Because the printmaker will store your final digital file, you can call and reorder the same print as many times as you want for as long as you want. In theory, each print will be exactly the same as the first. Because all the preliminary work has already been done, reorders cost much less than the first print.

Preprinting prep: Scans, digital retouching, extraordinary color adjustments, and so on will all incur extra charges. There is sometimes a catch-all "image file preparation" or "set-up" fee that includes basic image editing and file storage. Otherwise, image editing may be called something like "system" or "computer time" and is typically billed by the hour (figure on an average of $100 per hour).

Proofs: Proofs, usually reduced or at one-quarter-size, can make or break a printing project in terms of costs. Jack Duganne (Duganne Ateliers) charges a flat $85 per proofing session, although what constitutes a proofing session is open to interpretation. Jim Davis charges artists a one-time $150 to scan their artwork and to provide three proofs, including one at full-size. Make sure you understand what's included in a proof and how many you'll be getting.

Package prices: Some inkjet printmakers, usually only those dealing with traditional art reproductions, will offer package prices that include an image scan, basic image cleanup and color correction, up to three reduced-size proofs, and one or more final prints. For example, Staples Fine Art in Richmond, Virginia, has four packages ranging from $145 to $450 depending on the size of the print (see Figure 10.4).

Package pricing may be a good idea, or it may make more sense to price out your work *à la carte* (per item).

Guarantees: Is there one? Do you understand it?

Extras: File conversions, CDs or other archival media, shipping tubes, hand deckling, and other extra services such as special protective coatings are all charged in addition to the previously mentioned costs. Make sure you clearly understand these charges. In addition, make sure it's clear who owns the digital files—you or them?

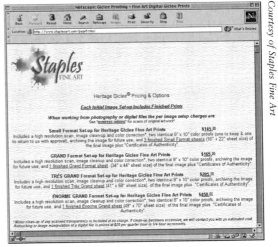

Courtesy of Staples Fine Art

Figure 10.4
Digital printmaker Staples Fine Art offers four price packages based on size.

Studio rental: If you're really feeling ambitious, some printmakers (inkjet, primarily) will even turn over and devote their entire studios to your project. Figure on about $1,500 per day for this exclusive attention.

What to Look Out For

Not only are you looking for reasons to select an inkjet printmaker, but you're also looking for any red flags for *not* choosing one. Here are a few things to watch out for:

Not Being Responsive

"One sure negative sign," explains artist Ileana, "would be a printmaker's lack of responsiveness and a rigid or negative reaction to my suggestions, especially if I'm dissatisfied with a print that shows defects. My printmaker must be receptive to my needs and want to work with me in accomplishing my vision (colors, inks, size, etc.). Not having this goes against the interdependent relationship that I think is needed."

Similarly, service provider Geoff Kilmer of Photoworks Creative Group adds, "If they won't guarantee satisfaction, then they may not have the right attitude."

I Have a Printer, Therefore I Am a Printmaker

There are printmakers, and there are printmakers. Having the equipment doesn't make you a printmaker, just like having a camera doesn't necessarily make you a photographer. Ask questions and investigate everything to satisfy yourself that they are, in fact, experienced printmakers.

The Artist as Printmaker

There are many artists who take in work to print for others. One reason is to help pay for the expensive printmaking equipment. One problem with artist-printmakers is that they sometimes don't have the well-rounded experience of doing work for many different people. Many will have printed only their own work, which may or may not be anything like yours. As I've said before, printing is a craft, and what you ideally want is an experienced craftsperson, not necessarily an artist, as your printmaker.

Disagreeing with me on this is digital artist Ileana. "Printmakers have to match the artist's vision," she says, "and that takes a lot of communication and know-how. To me, it is also important that they be digital artists themselves. This may not have anything to do with their actual printing expertise, but I think that they will be much more sensitive and understand the highs and lows of working with this medium."

So, again, it's important to carefully determine the printmaker's background.

Artist/printmaker JD Jarvis outputs a large-format edition on an HP 2500CP inkjet printer in his home studio in Las Cruces, New Mexico.

Courtesy of JD Jarvis/dunkingbirdproductions.com

The Artist/Printmaker Relationship

The ideal artist/printmaker relationship is a true collaboration. The photographer-artist provides the image, and the printmaker provides years of experience in helping the artist best realize his or her vision. To repeat the apt phrase mentioned earlier: "The artist is the eye, the printmaker is the hand."

Photographer Paul Eric Johnson sums up this idea well. "I'm all in favor of the digital revolution, but I only want to know as much technically as is necessary to produce my desired results. After several years of working with print providers, I wouldn't even think of doing this without my trusted artistic partners."

Even if you're only sending off digital files to a remote commercial business, two-way communication is vital. Are you able to explain what you want, and, conversely, are they understanding you? Print provider Geoff Kilmer adds, "The artist should realize there are limitations to what can be done and should respect the fact that the printmaker is also trying to make a living in the process of rendering the service. Generally, the same ethics that make up any mutually beneficial business relationship apply to an artist and printmaker."

Photo by Dick Faller/New Media Arts

Printmaker Lynn Lown (left) works with Santa Fe artist Barbara Bowles on her photo-based print.

"The printmaker/artist relationship is the most important factor of the whole process," adds JD Jarvis. "More important than the model type of printer being used, more important than the substrate chosen to print on. In addition, don't be impressed by the cost, size, or publicity surrounding any one make or model of inkjet print device. Look to the output of an individual printmaker. The human factor—how skilled and how willing the printmaker is to work with you—is more important than any technical factors beyond the obvious ones you need to meet in any particular project."

And that's good advice.

A Giclée Workflow

As I mentioned in Chapter 1, *giclée* is the term used to describe a digital, inkjet, reproduction print made from a work created in another medium. Prints made from paintings, watercolors, drawings, and so on are all giclées, and the process has its own workflow. Although some of the steps are similar to the ones I outlined in Chapter 9 for self-printing, the main difference is that most of the activity is the responsibility of the printmaker. This is what you pay them for.

Step 1: Planning Your Print

You still need to plan your print, and this is best done in consultation with the printmaker. Dimensions and prices will come into play to determine the perfect size, medium, inks, and method to be used. This is the preliminary step where all the issues between artist and printmaker should be laid out on the table and thoroughly discussed. If you develop a bad feeling about this particular printmaker, now is the best time to pull out, not later.

Step 2: Scanning

Each printmaker will have his or her own way of turning the original artwork into a digital file. Some prefer a traditional photograph taken on medium- or large-format transparency film and then scanned. Others will direct-scan the original artwork with a scanning back or other high-resolution scanning method (see Figure 10.5). If the piece is small enough, it could even be put on a drum (if it's flexible) or flatbed scanner. The final result is a high-resolution digital file that has faithfully captured all the details and colors of the original work of art.

Courtesy of Harvest Productions Ltd.

Figure 10.5
The ZBE Satellite digital scanning system at Harvest Productions; note artwork on riser under camera

Step 3: Image Editing and Color Correcting

Color corrections and other image editing are done on computer workstations by the printmaker's staff. Out-of-gamut colors are adjusted in comparison to the original material provided, whether that's the artwork itself or a photograph of it. The main point of this step is to match the original. Any deviations from this goal should be approved only by the artist.

Step 4: Proofing

How this is handled can vary widely among printmakers, but the purpose is to show you one or more proof prints so that you can see with your own eyes how the final prints will look. (The number of proofs will be determined by the policy of the printmaker and what level of service you've purchased.) The best scenario is for you to view the proof at a professional viewing booth at the printmaker's facility. This way, the people working on the print can be brought out to discuss any alterations or "moves" with the image.

Proofing can be the most time-delaying part of the process when working with outside print providers. Typical turnaround time is one week between proofs, and there can be more than one round of proofs depending on any problems encountered. Note that preliminary proofs are typically returned and remain the property of the printmaker.

The final, approved proof is called the BAT or *bon à tirer* ("good to pull" in French). The artist signs this print and returns it to the printmaker. It's used as the guide to which all subsequent prints are matched.

His sister gave him a whistle to wear so that if he got trapped in the wreckage he could call for help.

© 2001 Jonathan Talbot

Sometimes, one print is all you need. When artist Jonathan Talbot showed up at the November 2001 Florence Biennial in Italy, his display prints, unfortunately, did not. In a last-minute effort, he had the image shown e-mailed to him and found a local inkjet printer to output it to 35×49". The print was displayed by simply tacking it to the wall with push pins. Talbot won a medal at the show.

The Gift shows Talbot's son's ID tags and whistle from the 911 site at the World Trade Center where he worked as a rescue worker (he is alive and well). The grayscale image is simply an enlarged photocopy of actual objects with type superimposed onto the image. The gradient background was made by holding a piece of matboard at an angle while the photocopy was made. The small photocopy print was then scanned and retouched in Photoshop.

Printing

The final print or prints are then created. The advantage of digital printing is that prints can be made one at a time, and it's normal to print in small groups, depending on the discount the printmaker offers for quantity. Jim Davis does not recommend printing more than 10 prints at a time. "Unless the artist is well-known, it will take them some time to sell those 10 prints," he advises. "Financially, it's not good business to carry unsold inventory."

Curation

Curating is what happens to a print after it's output. This is the step where each print is inspected for quality (and fixed or rejected if any major imperfections are found), cleaned, and finished with any protective coatings, as needed. All trimming or special edge tearing or deckling is also done at this point. When the printmaker uses a *chop* (an embossed, identifying printer's mark), it is applied in one of the lower corners. If the prints are to be hand-embellished by the printmaker, that is also done at this stage. (See more about curating and finishing a print in Chapter 9.)

Courtesy of Jan Steinman/Bytesmiths.com

Printmaker Jan Steinman trimming prints

Shipping

The job is not complete until the prints arrive at their destination, safe and sound. Unless an artist can physically go to the printmaker's place of business for a pick-up, most prints are rolled and shipped in tubes, although they can be shipped flat, too. A good printmaker will use only the strongest tubes with plenty of slip-sheeting and end-stuffing to protect each print. There's nothing worse than to have otherwise-perfect prints ruined in shipping. It's happened to me, and that's why I always insist on the use of overnight air shipping. It's worth the extra expense.

Working with Noninkjet Providers

Many of the larger print providers now combine both inkjet and noninkjet output at one facility to cover an evolving market for digital imaging and printing. Companies like Calypso Imaging (Santa Clara, California), Photo Craft Laboratories (Boulder, Colorado), and Photoworks Creative Group (Charlottesville, Virginia) have one or more LightJets, Lambdas, Frontiers, wide-format inkjets, laser printers, film recorders, or whatever digital devices they need to satisfy their customers' imaging needs.

Digital Photoprint and Digital Photo Process

Two important noninkjet technologies that photographers are especially fond of (although non-photographic digital artists can use them as well) are digital photoprint and digital photo process (described in Chapter 3). Both of these print processes require outside service providers because the cost of the equipment is too high for self-ownership. Photo labs, service bureaus, imaging centers, and some sign shops are where you'll find this type of print service. LightJets and Frontiers are popular devices, and photographer-artists typically submit final, RGB, digital files on CD or Zip disk at 150-300 dpi at the final output size. Scans from reflective art, slides, or negatives are usually also available.

Courtesy of Océ Display Graphics Systems

Océ LightJet printers are popular digital output devices and can be found at many higher-end photo labs and imaging centers.

Wide-format LightJet, Lambda, or Chromira prints are output to regular photographic paper (only), and print prices can range from $20–$500 depending on the final size. As with some inkjet printmakers, digital photoprint providers like Calypso Imaging will allow 4-up ganging of multiple images on one sheet at no extra cost.

New Jersey based photographer Paul Eric Johnson loves his LightJet prints on Fuji Crystal Archive paper for their "sense of a pureness" in his photography. He scans his transparencies at NancyScans in New York, does the image editing on his computer, and then ships his images on CD all the way to Calypso Imaging in California for output. (Calypso also produces inkjet reproduction prints on EPSON archival printers.) Johnson explains that "although the printer is remote, the relationship hasn't been. With good technical support, I've been able to keep close to the action. There's a consistency and an understanding of just how important the work is to the art photographer. The printing itself is one thing I don't have to worry about."

© 2000 Paul Eric Johnson

Paul Eric Johnson's Grange, *available as a LightJet print in three sizes. (See more of Johnson's work in the Gallery Showcase section.)*

Digital photo process is similar to digital photoprint except it applies to smaller-format sizes and involves the use of digital minilabs that employ the Fuji Frontier or similar devices. There tends to be less customer interaction with these smaller formats because volume and lower prices are more important. However, you can still make your voice heard, and the better providers will listen. Photo Craft Laboratories' Ron Brown explains that, even though they use the Frontier as their main consumer device for smaller prints, they look at and customize every job that comes in the door. "The Frontier has an Auto mode, and a high-school student running one at the corner drugstore may be more prone to use it. However, with our qualified technicians, everything is custom."

Profiles for digital photoprint and photo process: Printer profiles (see Chapters 5 and 9) can be just as important for digital photo printing as they are for inkjet. Unfortunately, your success in finding service-provided profiles from digital photoprint and photo process shops will be hit or miss, and even an understanding of what profiles can do is scattered. My local pro photo lab, for example, doesn't provide them for either its LightJet 5000 or its Fuji Frontier. Larger providers such as Calypso Imaging and Photo Craft, however, are dedicated to providing their clients with calibrated workflows, and they make it very easy to download profiles from their Web pages. These profiles are for their LightJets and inkjets, but not for the Frontiers.

There are different ways to deal with any nonprofiled lab devices. One workaround is to do what's called *reverse proofing.* Send the lab a small target-test file to print. If you like what you get back, either adjust your monitor settings or your image file *to the print.* Yes, this is a backwards way to do color management, but it can work if you are pleased with the test prints.

You can also custom profile your lab. Simply take, or e-mail, one of the RGB profiling target files that come with your profiling software to the lab and have them make a normal print *with no color management.* Specify the size print that you need, or you may get a target print too small to work with. Back at your workstation, use your scanner- or spectro-based profiling package to build a custom printer profile for that lab printer. Convert to this ICC profile (in Photoshop: Image > Mode > Convert to Profile), and instruct the lab *not* to make any automated corrections, but to print the file just as it is.

Fujifilm has its own solution for selected labs that have Frontier printers. It's called StudioMaster PRO, and it lets professional photographers build a customer order that goes directly to their Frontier-equipped lab. The software is provided by the lab (sometimes for a fee), and it allows for color-managed, onscreen image editing.

Finally, a new way of working with minilab printers has recently become available through Oregon photographer Ethan Hansen of Dry Creek Photo (www.drycreekphoto.com). He has created a database of printer profiles for *local* Fuji Frontier, Noritsu, and Konica minilab printers. In the United States, this includes most of the Wal-Mart, Costco, and many Ritz Camera locations. If your local minilab provider is listed (160 at the time of this writing), you simply download the profile (it's free), install it on your computer, and do your image editing as described in Chapters 5 and 9. If your local operator is not on the list, and you want to profile them, download Dry Creek's profile target and print it at the minilab. You then mail the print back to Dry Creek who creates a profile at no charge and adds it to their online database. Keep in mind that the accuracy of such a profile is dependent upon how recent it is because lab conditions may change.

When 1-Hour Printing Isn't Fast Enough

If you're desperate to have a while-you-wait print made, you can always run over to your nearest drugstore, consumer electronic store, Kinko's, or mass merchant to use a self-service *photo kiosk*. Kiosks are made by manufacturers such as Kodak (PictureMaker), Fuji (Aladdin), and Olympus (TruePrint), and they offer a touch screen interface for basic image editing including cropping, red-eye removal, brightness adjustment, etc. The Olympus TruePrint kiosks come in four models with dye-sublimation printers that sit behind the counter and that can output 4×6 or 8×10 prints.

Kiosks accept CompactFlash, SmartMedia, and PCMCIA memory cards and Photo CDs, and some have optional scanners for inputting hard copy. You're not going to get a lot of expert advice or hand holding in this situation, but for a $3.99 print at my local Sam's Club in three minutes, what do you expect?

Film Recording

Film recording is a specialized digital printing service provided by photo labs and imaging centers. Film recorders (also called "film writers" and "slidemakers") are used to create slides for art show entries and for presentations, lectures, and conferences.

Film recorders are basically movie cameras loaded with bulk film (usually slide reversal) that take a picture of a CRT screen displaying a digital image. However, instead of capturing the image in its entirety, the CRT shows only a small spot of light that scans its way down the screen, one scan for each RGB color. Each color takes 15 seconds to scan; the full image is exposed in 45 seconds.

One well-known provider of film-recorded images is slides.com. In business since 1991, slides.com is run by David and Kay Sieverding in Verona, Wisconsin—although their customer base is worldwide. They use redundant Management Graphics film recorders, their own E-6 film processing, and special slide mounts with pin registration.

Because slides.com maps all images pixel-by-pixel to a 4096×2730-pixel grid, the image resolution or ppi of the file doesn't matter. It's the pixel dimensions that count, and the closer to

4096×2730, the better. "If you already have an image, it does no good to scale up the image to reach 4096×2730," explains David Sieverding. "Just leave it as it is, and our software will take care of it." In addition, you don't need to worry about cropping the image to match slide proportions (1.5:1). Their system will put the whole image on the slide and fill in any extra area with black so that only the image is projected.

You simply e-mail or upload your digital files to slides.com, and they convert them to 35mm slides and send them back within 24 hours. You pay $4–$5 each depending on the software used to create the file. Slides.com supports the widest range of programs of any slide-imaging company in the world, over 100 in all. This includes Photoshop, Illustrator, QuarkXPress, CorelDRAW, all versions of PowerPoint, and all digital camera files.

Online Printing Services

One example of the inroads that the Internet has made into our lives is the business of online processing and printing. Although this is mostly applicable to photographers, it doesn't have to be, especially now that the larger print service providers have every type of digital output device including wide-format inkjets.

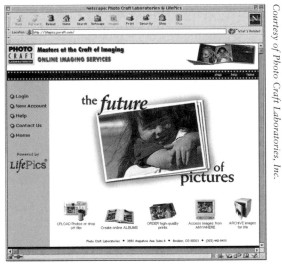

Courtesy of Photo Craft Laboratories, Inc.

More and more, the trend is for photographer-artists to work with this type of provider electronically or online. What this usually means is that image files, typically TIFFs or JPEGs, along with order forms are either sent via e-mail or uploaded to company Web sites for processing and printing. Companies like Photo Craft also offer a related service for photographers who can send in film for processing and scanning (or hard-copy artwork). The scans are then uploaded to their secure Web site (see Figure 10.6). The artist can then download them, image-edit as needed, and either send them back for printing or print them on their own desktop printers.

Figure 10.6
Photo Craft Laboratories' online printing services are accessible through their Web site.

Some image-editing software programs such as Adobe Photoshop Elements even have plug-ins to simplify the image-uploading process.

One result of all this online activity is that the physical locations of both the providers and the customers is becoming irrelevant. Miller's Professional Imaging, a specialist in portrait and wedding photography, is headquartered in Kansas, yet they have customers in all 50 states. Where before they were receiving and sending shipments by walk-in or air courier, they now receive uploaded files to their Web site and only need to return the finished prints the traditional way.

Figure 10.7
Shutterfly's Web site is well-organized and easy to use. Shown is the initial print-ordering screen and the actual prints after they arrived.

Image Sharing and Printing

If there's one thing that makes print-service providers nervous—besides the tidal wave of people doing their own printing—it's photo or image sharing. This is the process of uploading images to one of the free hosting services so they can be stored, organized, viewed, and shared. You can assign a password to your "albums," and only those you give the password to can see your images. This has become a popular way to avoid the time and trouble of e-mailing pictures and images to family, friends, and other contacts.

However, that's not all. Because most people still like to have a real print in their hands, smart companies like Shutterfly (www.shutterfly.com), Kodak's Ofoto (www.ofoto.com), and even Epson (www.photo.epson.com) not only offer image sharing, but also print ordering. After you've added images to your personal album, you can "enhance" them (crop, rotate, and add borders and effects), instruct the service which image to print and in what size, and the prints arrive a few days later. Shutterfly even has online resolution guidelines to tell you if your images are too low-res to print well on their Fuji Frontier printers (see Figure 10.7).

Apple's iPhoto software offers a more sophisticated option with its make-a-book feature. It's a layout tool that lets you use templates for designing a simple image-based book and then either printing it yourself on approved inkjet printers or uploading it to Apple, who has contracted with Kodak for having it professionally bound in a linen hardback cover. (See more about making digital books in Chapter 11.)

Apple's iPhoto software lets you create custom books and then go online to order them.

Online Image Editing

It was bound to happen. One recent development related to online printing services is online image-editing. Image-Edit & Art (www.image-edit.com) is a Web-based service for consumers to obtain custom, digital photo-editing services. Red-eye removal? Face and skin repairs? Motion effects? Color changes? All possible, remotely. The company stresses that the work is artist-executed, not automated, and performed by skilled digital artists. This is for people who don't want to do the image-editing work themselves.

How much does this kind of custom image-editing cost? As an example, Image-Edit & Art's Pro Red-Eye Repair is $3.50 for the first pair of eyes and $1.50 thereafter. Removal of glare in eyewear is only $1.50 when ordered at the same time.

Photo retailers also offer the service to their customers and receive a 15-percent commission per order.

Whether you make your own prints or have a print service do it for you, you'll eventually want to push the limits of digital printing. Read on to find out how.

11

Special Printing Techniques

Although the majority of people are content—and adequately challenged—to output a decent digital print, there are others who want to step outside the box, to go beyond the basics and to stretch their abilities. Here are some ideas for doing just that.

Beyond the Digital Print

Hybrid process, books, dye sublimation, alternative photo print process, oversized prints… these are just a few of the ways photographer-artists are experimenting with the definitions of digital printing.

Hybrid Process

For some, a digital print on a piece of paper is not the end point of a process but only the beginning. Three pioneering artists who have been pushing the digital edge the longest and the farthest are the members of Digital Atelier: Dorothy Simpson Krause, Bonny Lhotka, and Karin Schminke (see Figure 11.1). In keeping with their tagline, "a printmaking studio for the 21st Century," even the organization of the group is modern: Each member lives in a different part of the United States (Boston, Denver, and Seattle, respectively), and they come together in person only for educational forums, workshops, seminars, and artists-in-residence classes. Their work is in more than 200 corporate and museum collections, including the permanent collection of the National Museum of American Art.

Figure 11.1
Digital Atelier, from left: Dorothy Simpson Krause, Bonny Lhotka, and Karin Schminke

Krause, Lhotka, and Schminke are well known for combining traditional and digital printmaking to produce their own original digital prints. Although they each use the computer as a tool, their work and media choices are as varied as their backgrounds. It includes one-of-a-kind paintings, collages, image transfers, monotypes, and prints on all kinds of surfaces as diverse as plywood, silk, rusty metal, and handmade substrates.

"When people see our work, they don't think digital," Schminke says.

Using a digital print as a base or ground, they usually end up with something totally unique. Digigraphs, digital collages, and digital mixed media are some of the terms they've used over the years.

The wide range of their work includes these processes:

- Using a digital print as a ground and layering it with traditional media such as encaustic, paint, and collage elements.

- Transferring digital prints to paper and other substrates with a press.

- Making custom substrates for printing and transferring, including fresco, textured surfaces like spun-bonded polyester, and chine collé.

- Producing "digital decals" or "digital skins," an emulsion-type transfer for rough and irregular surfaces.

- Making hand-pulled monotypes from digital transfers.

- Using special precoats and postcoats on various media (see "inkAID Precoats").

- Exploring lenticular technology that interlaces two or more images. The images are placed under plastic lenses so that each is seen separately as the viewer moves. (See "Lenticular Printmaking" for more.)

inkAID Precoats

Digital Atelier has invented and is now marketing a remarkable set of *precoats* that give artists using inkjet printers a wider range of substrate options. inkAID can be used on papers of all kinds, aluminum, acrylic sheets, wood, and more. No special equipment is needed, just a paintbrush and rubber gloves.

Paintings, collages, and other mixed media can be coated to allow for an inkjet-printed image to be added.

Although designed to work with pigmented inks, early research by the Digital Atelier artists is showing these precoats to be compatible with at least some dye-based inks as well.

Bonny Lhotka has painted the precoats onto etched aluminum and created images on both sides of the metal. She has even coated sandblasted glass and printed on it with an ENCAD NovaJet 880 inkjet printer!

To give a feel for the varied approaches that the Digital Atelier artists take in exploring these hybrid methods, here is one step-by-step workflow from Dot Krause:

Experimental Printmaking Process: Custom Substrate
Krause Studio, Marshfield Hills, MA 2001

All images and text © 2001 Dorothy Simpson Krause

Happy Home, *inkAID "decal" transfer with encaustic, 48 × 48".*

Happy Home *was composed from two scans: a collage using a package of "Happy Home" needles and an icon, The Twelve Feasts of the Church, from The Art Complex Museum, Duxbury, MA.*

The image was printed onto film using the Mutoh Falcon printer and Wasatch RIP. A sheet of polypropylene was coated with inkAID and the print rolled onto it face down. The film was removed leaving the transferred image adhered to the inkAID emulsion.

A fresco surface was prepared by wrapping tape around a masonite panel, pouring hydrocal plaster onto the surface, and spreading and texturing it with a large spackling tool.

The emulsion layer, which can be handled like a large decal when it is dry, was glued to the hardened fresco surface and burnished down with encaustic. Touch-ups were made with oil sticks and paint.

As a separate layer, a lenticular print was added to the center of the image. The book of needles and the twelve-frame icon were "interlaced" (cut and reassembled in vertical strips by Flip! software) and printed on Rexam clear film. A Coda laminator adhered the print to a sheet of clear plastic with a series of parallel lens or lenticules embossed into the surface. When the lenses are aligned with the image, the viewer sees only one frame at a time, creating a sense

of movement as the viewing angle changes. Squares of metallic papers were added from behind to give additional luminance. The lenticular overlay, attached with brass brackets, creates both a physical and metaphorical discontinuity between the sacred and mundane.

Lenticular Prints

I couldn't do a better job of explaining lenticular prints than what's already been done by the experts themselves:

Lenticular Printmaking

by Dorothy Simpson Krause, Bonny Lhotka, and Karin Schminke of Digital Atelier, February 2002

Artists throughout the ages have worked on the problem of representing three-dimensional space on a two-dimensional plane. Several of the most effective attempts to capture realistic space rely on human stereoscopic vision, each eye sees a slightly different view. This approach, when applied to photography, made stereograph viewers a common site in parlors in the U.S. 100 years ago. In the 1950s, small novelty items in which photographic images flipped from one to another appeared in cereal boxes and on political pins. After lying dormant for half a century, advances in digital imaging allow us to create spectacular three-dimensional images using lenticular technology.

A lenticular image allows the viewer to see a series of "frames" (usually 2 to 24) sequentially. By carefully crafting these frames, the artist can create animation, depth, and/or morphing of images.

To create lenticular images, the source images are developed in image creation software like Adobe Photoshop. A series of variations on the image are saved as separate files. Each of these variations becomes a frame in the finished lenticular print.

In order to create depth in a lenticular image, the artist uses Photoshop to develop frames that use the horizontal offset of elements in the image to place these elements on different virtual planes. Elements that are designed to recede into the background are offset to the left; elements designed to project forward of the picture plane are offset to the right. Elements can also be turned on and off in sequence to give the impression of blinking. To create movement, elements are altered in form and/or position evenly across all frames.

The resultant frameset is then interlaced together in linear strips that match the lenticular lens. This lens is a piece of plastic with a series of parallel lenses or lenticules embossed into one surface. After the interlaced image is printed, it is aligned with the lens so that the viewer sees only one frame at a time. As the viewer moves by the image, all of the frames are seen in sequence, creating the illusion of movement, depth, animation, morphing, or 3-dimensional space that the artist set up in the original frames.

Specialized lenticular software like Flip! can interlace 18 or more images and create test patterns that are used to determine the proper pitch or increment (to the 1/1,000th of an inch) to interlace for a perfect match with the lens. Each lens, combined with different printers, inks, and paper may require a different pitch.

The images created can become very large as the pitch of the lens is multiplied by the number of layers, which determines the dpi of the final image. For example, an image with 10 frames interlaced for a 40-line lens creates an image with 400 ppi. To have enough computing power for the 22 × 28-inch images for a recent portfolio, the Digital Atelier artists used Intergraph's TDZ ViZual Workstation with dual Intel processors.

Sound Waves

All images and text © 2002 Karin Schminke

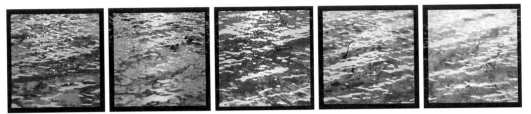

Sound Waves #1–5. *Five 36×36-inch panels.*

Figure 11.2
Permanent installation by Karin Schminke at the University of Washington, Bothel/Cascadia Community College Campus.

The hypnotizing movement of light on water was the inspiration for this installation in the library of a new college campus located just outside Seattle (see Figure 11.2). The five 36-inch-square panels utilize lenticular technology to capture movement, transformation, and depth.

Schminke began *Sound Waves* by photographing light playing on waves at various locations around Puget Sound. She created layers of water shapes based upon these photo studies (see Figure 11.3). Linear seaweed forms photographed on a beach at low tide were integrated into each panel to create a minimal focal point and help define the illusion of deep space. Hand-drawn light reflections were added in such a way that the viewer would see them for only a moment as they passed by the installation, thus mimicking the fugitive nature of light dancing on water.

Next, a series of frames (like frames of an animation) were created from the layers. The frames were interlaced into a single image using Flip! software and printed on an EPSON Stylus Pro 9500 large-format printer (see Figure 11.4).

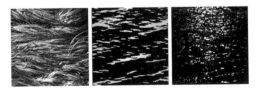

Figure 11.3
Three sample source images and layers used in creating Sound Waves #5.

Figure 11.4
EPSON 9500 printing the image (left) and the special lenticular lens.

MicroLens Technology, Inc. provided a portion of the special lenticular lens as well as the lamination of the print to the lens. As viewers pass by the finished art, each of the 24 frames is viewed in quick succession, creating an illusion of depth and movement.

A variety of lenses are created for different purposes with lenticules per inch (lpi) ranging from 10 to 300. Some have great depth for three-dimensional representation while others are designed for flip and animation. Lenses manufactured from different materials are available, including ultra-thin (4 mil) lenticular sheets, lenticular lens patterns for the billboard market, and flexible lenses for the apparel market. Companies like Microlens Technology sell a wide variety of lenses.

As little as a year ago, the only way to make a lenticular image would be to spend $5,000–10,000 to have it produced with offset lithography. Today the use of high-resolution inkjet printers like the Mutoh Falcon and the Epson 9500 make it possible for an individual to create lenticular images up to 48×96 inches, the current, maximum lens size. The higher the number of lenticules per inch (lpi), the higher the printer resolution must be. A 10–15 lpi lens can be used with lower resolution printers.

Only pigmented inks or dye-based inks with archival properties (e.g., Lysonic inks) are used for fine-art, lenticular inkjet prints. While paper may be adequate for small lenticular images, film is necessary for large ones since the shrinking, expansion, or stretching of the substrate can cause misalignment.

Because of the illusion of movement and depth in the image, there is a level of ambiguity that engages and involves the viewer. This is art that cannot be understood in a glance. However, the current convergence of software, lenses, and high-resolution inkjet printers make this emerging technology a new challenge and opportunity for artists who are interested in pushing boundaries.

Cards, Books, and More...

Printing on paper can also take nontraditional forms. Here are three examples to give you a feel for the diversity of paper-print options:

Cards

Greeting, gift, note, and promotional cards are easy to make by self-printers using inkjet or laser printers. Although you can print images on larger sheets and cut and fold them down to size, you can also use premade card blanks that are available from several paper suppliers. Digital Art Supplies, Red River paper, and Epson are three companies that carry packaged, greeting-card stock ready for inkjet or laser printing. Digital Art Supplies, for example, carries folded cards from Hahnemuhle, double-sided gloss greeting cards, and unfolded note cards. Envelopes either come with the cards in the same package or can be ordered separately.

California artist Ry Smith prints promotional folded greeting cards with images of the full-sized prints he sells on the front panel (see Figure 11.5). The insides are blank, and he has his name and Web site address on the back panel. Although he uses an EPSON 9500 to print his large prints, he prints his cards on a desktop EPSON Stylus C80. He cuts them down and folds them by hand.

Figure 11.5
Digital artist Ry Smith's promotional cards are mini versions of his full-sized prints.

You can even use outside printmakers to make cards for you. Staples Fine Art markets their own Giclée Minis, which are miniature (4×5-inch) versions of artwork they are also printing full size. Each printed master sheet yields 66 mini prints on the same paper on which the larger prints are produced. Staples suggests artists use them as promotional pieces or "leave-behinds" that feature the artist's name, title, copyright notice, and contact information in addition to the image.

Books

Making books of original digital prints for portfolios, limited editions, bios, family histories—or even as part of an art concept as artist Ed Ruscha did starting in the 1960s—is a great idea.

Books about or by artists are common, but producing books has traditionally been a complicated and expensive proposition best left to publishers and beyond the reach of most photographer-artists. Although the print-on-demand technologies now found at any Kinko's have changed that scenario somewhat, high-quality color bookmaking has remained an elusive goal for most—until now. It is possible for just about anyone to make custom books of their digital prints with inkjet or any of the other technologies we've been discussing. Here's how:

Fold-a-book: The simplest way to make a book from your own prints is to fold a single sheet of paper in half. Each sheet now becomes four book pages. (Each side of the paper is one page.) Stack all the folded sheets on top of each other, add a cover sheet, staple, sew, or otherwise hook all the pages together, and presto—you have a book (see Figure 11.6). The trick in doing all this is planning the pages. For that, make a simple mockup using office paper. Just fold a bunch of pages and start writing or sketching what goes on each page.

Figure 11.6
A simple fold-a-book, stapled at the spine

To produce this kind of book, you'll need to be able to print on both sides of the page, which, naturally, requires double-sided paper. (Be sure to let the ink dry completely between printings.) This can get expensive because if you make one mistake on one side, you've also ruined the other side as well.

One of the main drawbacks to the folded book is the fact that each sheet is folded in half. To make use of full sheets, you may need to use a commercial binding service.

Bound books: The trickiest part of bookmaking is the binding step. How are you going to collect and connect all the separate pages into a book that doesn't fall apart the moment you pick it up? The simplest solution is to take your loose pages to an instant print shop or copy center. Your local Staples, Office Depot, or Kinko's all offer the inexpensive and standard office binding methods such as comb, coil, post, Velo, tape, or other types that are typically used by businesses and students for reports. You will be limited not only by thickness but most importantly by overall page size. Don't count on binding anything larger than 11×17" at one of these places, which leaves you out of luck if you're using 13×19-inch inkjet paper. For that, you might consider a commercial binder or printer. Commercial book binderies (find them in your local Yellow Pages under "bookbinding") and printers will be able to offer more robust bindery options, including sewn, saddle-stitched, or case or perfect binding. Some of these binding techniques require pages to be printed two-up and folded as part of the binding process, so be sure your print sizes and binding techniques mesh.

One advantage of using a commercial binding method is that you could get away with printing on just one side of the paper as long as you're using an edge-binding method and not a fold-over or saddle-stitched one. The drawback is that the reverse side of every page will be blank. (An additional idea is to include a slip sheet of translucent vellum or parchment between each page. This divider sheet acts as a form of protection over the printed image and also adds an air of high-end exclusivity to the book.)

You can still use full sheets and avoid commercial binders if you're feeling creative. Some artists get a kick out of creating and fabricating their own book-binding methods. I've seen everything from rawhide cords, to steel nuts and bolts, to surgical tubing used to bind books. Sometimes a special binding method can add a lot to the overall impact of a custom book.

And, as mentioned in Chapter 10, if you're on a Mac, you can order custom, hardbound books through Apple's iPhoto system.

A few more comments about custom books:

- Because the pages of books are closed—and therefore dark—most of the time, image stability in terms of lightfastness is less important. However, dark-fading stability as well as ink smearing and rub-off still need to be taken into account.

- Consider making a book of prints and calling that book a limited edition or portfolio. Boxed portfolio sets are nothing new in the world of photography and fine art, but what is newer is the idea of making an actual book of original prints. These prints, then, are not reproductions; they are the originals, no different than if you had made the prints individually, which, in fact, you have done. The difference is that they are now bound together in some meaningful and practical way. Add a bio, artist's statement, and anything else you like, and you now have a portable, permanent art show.

- The most difficult thing about producing books is not their creation but, if you're trying to make it a commercial venture, their marketing. Distribution, sales, promotion, and all the rest of the book-marketing process is an ambitious undertaking, and I wish anyone attempting it the best of luck. However, if you're only interested in producing a few books for a close circle of friends, family, colleagues, and buyers, then you are alive at the right time in human history.

Digital Fine Art Ketubot

As a final example of digital's wide range of paper-printing options, consider the unusual niche of Jewish wedding contracts, or *ketubot*. Peggy Davis is a calligrapher who has been creating custom ketubot since 1980. These $700+ original pieces of art are hand-painted, hand-lettered legal documents (by Jewish law) that are meant to be hung and displayed on a couple's wall for a lifetime.

Courtesy of Peggy H. Davis Calligraphy

Figure 11.7
A sample Custom-Print Ketubah

Davis, and her husband Joe Kurland, who is the printmaker of the duo, recently came up with a new way to offer a less-expensive ($250) version of the marriage contract: the Custom-Print Ketubah (see Figure 11.7). Full-color, scanned art is placed as a border in a PageMaker document. Type fonts are then used to create the custom wording in Hebrew, English, or both. (The Hebrew font was created from Davis' hand lettering in Fontographer.) A CMYK RIP (Adobe PressReady) sends the finished file to an EPSON 3000 inkjet printer and onto Hawk Mountain Osprey 100-percent cotton paper with MIS pigment inks. The final prints are $17 \times 22"$, although smaller sizes and miniatures can also be ordered.

Dye Sublimation Transfers

In Chapter 3, I mentioned that dye sublimation or "dye sub" can take a couple of forms. In this section, I'm talking about the transfer dye-sub process in which an image is printed onto a medium and then transferred under heat and pressure to the final, polymer-coated surface. The variety of dye-sub transfer applications is amazing: apparel, awards, banners, carpets, flags, interior signage, promotional products, sporting goods, textiles, tile, and T-shirts. Dye sub is a substitute for silk screening, which usually requires higher quantities, and while there are plenty of businesses that provide this service, I'll focus on doing it yourself.

The simplest way to produce dye-sub transfers on your own is to buy special transfer paper and print on it with an inkjet printer using dye-based inks. Then, all you need is a hot iron to transfer the image. Epson sells packages of Iron-On Cool Peel Transfer Paper in 8.5×11-inch sizes for image-transferring to T-shirts (they even sell the T-shirts, but you can use any all-cotton or cotton/polyester-blend shirts), canvas tote bags, placemats, and other craft and decorative fabric accessories. Any *dye-based* EPSON printer will work (even non-EPSON printers may work), although Epson warns that the colors are susceptible to eventual fading, especially after frequent washing.

For a more professional approach to self-printing dye-sub transfers, you'll want to consider something like the Sawgrass Systems' Sublijet (for inkjet printers) or SubliMAX (for laser printers) process. (Sawgrass also produces ribbons for a limited number of thermal transfer ribbon printers.) SubliMAX digital toner cartridges are designed for use with specific color laser printers such as the Minolta QMS 6100. For the inkjet, patented heat-sensitive sublimation inks are printed on any coated inkjet paper. The inks come in carts for select EPSON desktop printers (C80 and 1280, and the older 3000, 800, 850, 900, 980, and 1520) and carts and bulk bottles for wide-formats including EPSON 9000 and 7000, Roland Hi-Fi JET PRO, Mimaki JV4, Encad, and Mutoh.

Note that Sawgrass even has its own bulk ink system (called QuickConnect) for a couple of printers including the EPSON 1280. QuickConnect uses modified cartridges and refillable ink bags. The printed image can then be transferred to a variety of surfaces including wood, synthetic fabric, glass, plastic, ceramics, and metal. Sublijet inks have so far only worked on polyester-blend T-shirts, but Sawgrass recently announced a way to transfer onto 100-percent cotton shirts as well.

TSS-Sublimation and Tropical Graphics are two other companies that provide dye-sub systems for inkjet printing. They sell their own sublimation inks in carts or bottles, bulk-ink systems, and special software and printer drivers for various EPSON desktops as well as Roland, Mimaki, and Mutoh wide-format printers. TSS-Sublimation also sells ingenious "mug wraps" that allow you to sublimate mugs in your home or commercial oven.

Unfortunately, transfers made with these systems cannot be transferred with a hot iron because they require a minimum temperature of 400 degrees and 35–40 psi of pressure for the inks to transfer. That's why serious producers use professional heat presses, which range from a few hundred to a few thousand dollars, depending on the design (there are special heat presses for mugs, caps, and just about anything else imaginable).

Alternative Photo Print Process

There is a mini-renaissance of antique printing methods going on in the photographic world. Cyanotypes, kallitypes, gum bichromates, bromoils, and platinum and palladium prints are popular examples. Although many of these traditional photo techniques can now be emulated or re-created digitally with image-editing software like Photoshop, purists stick to the old-fashioned methods, which many times require contact printing with full-size negatives. The modern-day twist on all this is that many of these photographer-artists are now turning to digital printing to make the digital negatives.

Digital Negatives

Fine-art photographer Dan Burkholder (see Gallery Showcase for one of his printed images) pioneered the use of digital negatives in 1992, and he helped popularize the process with the release in 1995 of his groundbreaking book *Making Digital Negatives for Contact Printing*, now in its second edition. Burkholder, who states that "a decade has passed since I made my last traditionally enlarged negative via wet processing," also maintains an active Web site (www.danburkholder.com) with updates to his custom Photoshop Curves that are crucial to the process.

There are two basic ways to print full-size digital negatives: sending a file to an imagesetter or digital photoprint device, and printing on an inkjet.

For the highest quality—for example, in printing to silver gelatin B&W paper—you can't beat a service bureau imagesetter, especially one running at 3600-dpi or even 4800-dpi resolution. Grayscale images are used to create either a *diffusion dither bitmap* in Photoshop or a traditional but high-LPI output to a full-size film negative that is then contact-printed to the final paper. Finding a service bureau that understands this process is not easy, and the negatives are not inexpensive to produce, especially at large sizes, but the quality is excellent and the result can rival the best optically made prints.

A few photographers are also experimenting with negative film output from digital photoprint devices like the LightJet. Fine-art photographer R.A. Hansen has been collaborating with Calypso Imaging to create full-size digital negatives for Hansen's 14×17-inch platinum/palladium prints.

The other main method for creating digital negatives is with your own inkjet printer. Although any inkjet can theoretically produce digital negatives, most users have settled on standard printers such as the desktop EPSONs 1200, 1160, 1270, 1280, and 2000P. One reason is surely because Burkholder provides Contrast Adjustment Curves for these printers.

Here are two alternative ways the inkjet process works: (1) For silver-gelatin printmakers, images are converted to grayscale, adjusted with Curves, inverted to negative (in Photoshop: Image > Adjust > Invert), and printed on EPSON's Glossy Film or Pictorico Hi-Gloss White Film with all four or six printer colors; or (2) for alternative process where white films would block the UV light, images are adjusted with Curves, inverted, and then *colorized* using 0/55/55/0 CMYK values to produce an orange negative (Burkholder calls them "orange, spectral-density negatives") that holds back some of the UV light used in platinum/palladium, cyanotype, and other types of photo printing. (See Figure 11.8.) This orange mask effect is needed for the heavier ink loads of printers like the EPSON 1280 when printing on Pictorico OHP film.

Figure 11.8
Dan Burkholder's method for creating colorized digital negatives includes using the correct orange Foreground color in Photoshop and then filling the image with it in Color mode. You end up with what Burkholder calls an "orange, spectral-density negative" (right).

You can also use special software like Jon Cone's PiezographyBW system and monochrome or quadtone inks (see "Monochrome Options") to print digital negatives.

Although the quality of a typical inkjet negative is not as good as one made with an imagesetter (some users report a certain graininess with inkjet negatives), this method is very adequate for alternative-process printing. Burkholder also suggests improving the tonal range by making two negatives that are pin-registered when exposing the final prints—one negative just for shadow detail and one for the highlights.

Lastly, Burkholder recommends covering the digital negative with a .002 Mylar sheet to protect it from abrasion and moisture. Alternatively, some printmakers spray the negatives with a protective coating such as McDonald's Sureguard Lustre spray or Krylon Crystal Clear Acrylic Coating.

Film Positives

Film positives are used for making photosilkscreens, photo-sensitive etching plates, photogravure prints, and other applications. Positives can also be contact-printed in a darkroom to make negatives.

Many inkjet printers, such as the wide-format Mimaki JV4, come ready to print on clear, "Artwork" film with dye-based inks. For desktop users, the ideas described in the digital negatives section of this chapter apply, but without the invert-image step. PostScript laser printers also do an excellent job of printing film positives.

Printing Big!

Sometimes, you just have to go big— panoramic prints, big blowups, banners, and super size.

There are many ways to break out of the confines of a small, rectangular page. For wide-format digital photoprint, each brand has its own maximum size. The Océ LightJet 430 can output a single image up to 50.5×120.5", and the newer 500XL model can do 76×120.5"; the Durst Lambda 130 can make one seamless print the entire length of a paper roll, or 164 feet.

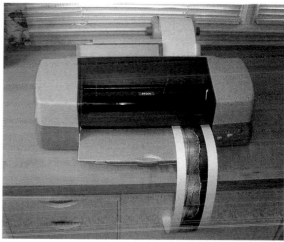

The author's digital panorama The Endless Swash *printing on 4×6-inch roll paper*

With inkjets, and this applies especially to photographer-artists printing digital panoramas on roll paper or long cut sheets, the maximum printable area is dependent on three factors: the printer driver, the operating system, and the software application.

Driver/OS Limits

The printer driver and the operating system both interact to form the printer's *maximum custom page size* (this does not include margin area, which could make the maximum image size slightly smaller). For example, with the EPSON Stylus Photo 2200, the maximum page length is 44 inches with Windows 98 and Macintosh. However, with Windows 2000, Me, or XP, the same printer can output to 129 inches. Older EPSONs have other limits (see Table 11.1).

Table 11.1

Maximum Custom Page Size Allowable
Per Operating System   (for EPSON standard drivers)

OS	5500	7600	9600	10000
Macintosh OS	44 in.	90.5 in.	90.5 in.	90.5 in.
Win 9x/Me	44 in.	90.5 in.	90.5 in.	90.5 in.
Win NT 4.0/2000/XP	44 in.	590.5 in.	590.5 in.	590.5 in.

Source: Epson America, Inc.

One way to exceed driver/OS limits is by using a PostScript RIP or application-direct export module. After you've handed off the file to the RIP or export module, it takes over by rendering the page to a potentially wider range of maximum sizes, primarily through the action of *tiling*. Tiling means breaking up the image into smaller panels that overlap seamlessly, if desired. (See more about application tiling later in this chapter.)

Cheating Pixels

When you're stuck with a given resolution of an image, but you want to blow it up and print it big, Photoshop's Bicubic Resampling function does a fair job—up to a point. It creates interpolated pixels in an attempt to trick your eyes into seeing more detail than is actually there. However, the image soon begins to break down as you increase the enlargement. There are several software products that try to improve on the basic Photoshop method; each has its own group of believers. Here are three options:

FM Stair Interpolation: Photographer Fred Miranda has developed a Photoshop *action* (automated series of commands) that breaks Photoshop's Bicubic interpolation method into small steps, which is why it's called Stair Interpolation or SI. SI is available via download (www.fredmiranda.com) for a nominal fee and works with digital camera files and scanned images including 16-bit files.

Genuine Fractals (GF): LizardTech's Genuine Fractals (GF) is not a fractal art program but, instead, a Photoshop plug-in that allows you to scale (enlarge or reduce) images using proprietary fractal technology. Although LizardTech promotes other virtues of their software, image upsampling is the significant function.

You first encode the image in GF's proprietary .STN format and save it with a choice of Lossless compression (2:1 savings) or Near Lossless (5:1 savings). You then enlarge it to 150 percent, 250 percent, or more. It comes in two versions for either RGB/Grayscale, or those formats plus CMYK and LAB.

How well it works depends on the to-from file size and the type and quality of the image involved. For example, JD Jarvis, in printing his *Guardian* image (see Figure 4.11 in Chapter 4), exported his 8×10-inch image at 150 ppi through GF and enlarged it 300 percent for printing without any problems.

VFZoom: The newcomer to this field is Celartem Technologies' VFZoom, which takes a different approach to the same problem. VFZooom (short for Vector Format Zooming) uses a vector model that they claim enables images to be enlarged up to 1200 percent without loss of clarity. There are five quality settings, and the software is available for Mac or Windows in stand-alone or Photoshop plug-in versions.

I tested VFZoom against a Photoshop Bicubic control and found a visible improvement in the quality of the enlarged image (see Figure 11.9).

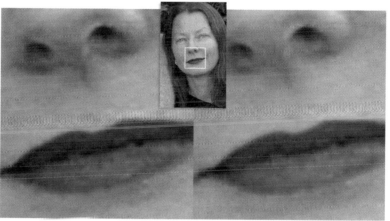

Figure 11.9
The source image is at center at 100 percent. At left is the control 1200-percent enlargement using Photoshop's Resampling in one step with the Bicubic interpolation method. At right is a 1200-percent enlargement made with VFZoom in one step using the maximum quality setting.

Application Software Limits

If you're using the *standard* printer driver, you may reach the limits of the software application before you reach the maximum printable area. (This doesn't apply to RIPs, which trump the application software limits.) Photoshop, for example, has a limit of 30,000-pixels on any one side. Because of the way EPSON drivers interface with Photoshop, the maximum page length for a wide-format EPSON printer using the standard (non-PostScript) driver is 83.33 inches (30,000 pixels/360 ppi, Epson's wide-format "input resolution"). For EPSON desktops, the maximum page length out of Photoshop is 41.67 inches (30,000 pixels/720 ppi).

The only way around these limits is either to use a PostScript RIP or to save the file to a page-layout or drawing program that does not have the 30,000-pixel limit (but which may lead to other problems with color management; you just can't have it all sometimes). QuarkXPress 4.x only goes up to a maximum page size of 48 inches. Illustrator 8.x/9.x goes up to 227 inches, and CorelDRAW 8.x/9.x can hit a whopping 1,800 inches. You are, however, still restricted by the printer's maximum custom page size—unless you do what I call *application tiling*.

Application Tiling

If you're not using a RIP, you can use application tiling to exceed the print device's maximum-page-length limit and print in banner mode up to the application's maximum. This neat trick divides the image into smaller pieces that, when laid end-to-end, form one long image without breaks. Both Corel Draw 8.x/9.x and Adobe Illustrator 8.x/9.x allow you to do this. Figure 11.10 shows how Adobe Illustrator 8.01 would be set up to print a tall banner that's 44×227" on an EPSON 10000 under a Mac/Win 9x/Me OS.

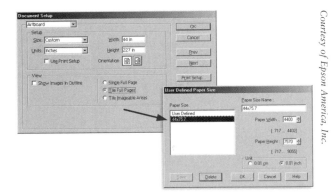

Courtesy of Epson America, Inc.

Figure 11.10
At left is the Adobe Illustrator 8.01 Document Setup screen with Tile Full Pages checked in the View section. The right screen shows the custom page size (75.7 inches), created by dividing the banner size (227 inches) by 3 to yield 75.7, which is under the printer's maximum.

A PostScript RIP, however, gives you even better control over tiling and may eliminate the need to use a page-layout or drawing program in the first place (unless you're creating your image that way).

Another way application tiling can be done is by breaking up the image into individual tiles that are printed separately and physically reassembled by either butting or slightly overlapping the edges with tape or adhesive. This is how ceramic tile murals are done. Dye-sublimation software like Tropical Graphics' Mural 7 (see Figure 11.11) make it easy to do this.

Courtesy of Tropical Graphics

Figure 11.11
A ceramic-tile wall mural is broken into 140 6×6-inch individual tiles with the help of Mural 7 imaging software.

The downside to this type of image tiling is that there will be visible seams.

One good use of this technique, as described in Chapter 9, is for making full-size mockups. This is also how super-large images (such as billboards that are meant to be viewed at a distance) are created.

Monochrome Options

In this section, I'm concentrating on inkjet applications for creating B&W or monochromatic prints. Although many of these techniques can also be used for electrophotographic, dye sub, and digital photoprint output, there are obvious differences. For example, with digital photoprint, there is no black except through the absence of light. The black you see will approximate the black on a computer monitor, and any neutral grays will remain neutral as long the RGB values are the same.

Converting Color and Printing to Monochrome

The first place to start with monochrome inkjet printing is by using the standard inks and converting or altering your color images. Here are seven ways to convert and print color to monochrome: (Note: Even if your images started out life as B&W, many of these techniques will also work. Just handle or print them as color.)

1. RGB > Grayscale

It's easy to convert a color image to a monochromatic grayscale in Photoshop (Image > Mode > Grayscale), but how you print this neutral image makes all the difference.

Print Grayscale with Black Ink Only

Most inkjet printer drivers give you a choice of "color" or "black" ink when printing (see Figure 11.12). Selecting the black-ink-only option might seem like a good way to print a monochrome image, but there are drawbacks. With the exception of printers using the smallest dot sizes, the prints usually lack detail and have a course dot pattern because you're only working with one ink. Yet, some think black-ink-only prints on certain printers and on certain papers are beautiful. A lot depends on the image characteristics. Test it for yourself.

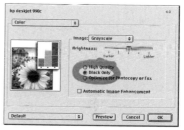

Figure 11.12

Most inkjet printer drivers like this one for an HP 990C Deskjet give you the option of using black ink only.

One advantage with black-ink-only printing is that the prints are guaranteed to be fairly neutral, with only the color of the paper and the inherent tone of the black ink (usually warm) being the variables. In addition, any concerns about metamerism with pigment inks are reduced because that problem with shifting neutral tones is caused primarily by the colored inks, not black.

Figure 11.13

The coarseness of a grayscale image printed with black ink only (top) is obvious compared to the same image printed with color inks (bottom).

Print Grayscale with Color Inks

If you print a grayscale image selecting the color-inks option in the driver, you can instantly see the difference in quality (see Figure 11.13). The image is smoother and fuller due to the added ink colors. (Even though the image is still in

Grayscale mode, all the color inks are recruited for printing.) The major drawback to this method is that you will invariably get an overall color cast (the color will vary depending on the paper and the inks), and the ways to fix that problem are limited. In Grayscale mode, color-based adjustment layers in Photoshop are unavailable, and so are the Color Control sliders in the printer driver settings. A solution is to convert the image to a duotone or back to RGB (see below).

Keep in mind that the introduction of Epson's newer seven-color, pigment inkjet printers (2200, 7600, and 9600) in the summer of 2002 changed things considerably. With these printers, you now have the option of using an additional, low-density black ink (only in color mode), which improves the print quality significantly. (See below for more about this.)

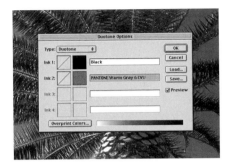

Figure 11.14
Switching from RGB to Duotone mode in Photoshop opens up interesting color possibilities for grayscale images.

2. RGB > Grayscale > Duotone

You can change the color balance of a grayscale image by converting it to Duotone mode in Photoshop (Image > Mode > Duotone) and selecting any custom color to go along with the base black (see Figure 11.14). If you then print the image with "color inks" selected, all the ink colors are used, as in the first option. The same lack of color-image-editing adjustments exists, but now you have access to the color slider adjustments in the printer driver for tweaking the overall color balance.

Using the same technique, a Photoshop Tritone or Quadtone adds even more color options to the mix.

Figure 11.15
Converting a grayscale image to RGB allows for a full range of color adjustments, such as this sepia effect with the Color Balance tool.

3. RGB > Grayscale > RGB

This is similar to the first method, but by converting the image back into RGB mode, you have access to all the other colors to increase tonal range. The result is much more color flexibility. If you don't like the overall color balance, it's easy to make it be either more or less neutral. For a sepia effect, for example, add a Color Balance adjustment layer, and move the sliders to something like -25 Magenta and -25 Yellow (see Figure 11.15). The same effect can be achieved by using the Color Control sliders in Custom > Advanced section on most inkjet printers. This is similar to darkroom photographers selecting warm or cool papers or toning chemicals to shift the overall colors of a B&W print. (You can also use canned printer presets like "sepia," but these have limited use because you typically have no ability to adjust the settings.)

You could also create a modified printer profile (see Chapter 5, "Getting the Color You Want") that automatically makes the same color shift for all your prints.

4. RGB > Desaturate

A simple way to remove color from an image is by desaturating it. Photoshop has a good tool for this: Hue/Saturation. Here's how it works:

Add a Hue/Saturation adjustment layer (Layer > New Adjustment Layer > Hue/Saturation) to the image. (I always use adjustment layers instead of making the adjustment directly to the image.) In the dialog box, and with the Edit: pull-down menu in the default "Master" position, move the Saturation slider to the left and watch the effect. A maximum saturation level of -100 is basically a grayscale image with no color. For an interesting multitoned option, you can change the saturation of the individual Edit: channels instead of the Master (see Figure 11.16). Alternatively, you can shift the colors by adding a separate Color Balance adjustment layer and playing with the sliders.

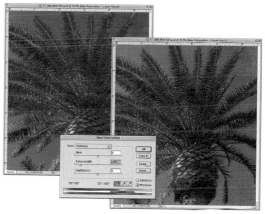

Figure 11.16
Desaturating the individual Edit: channels of an RGB image creates a muted, multitoned effect.

One drawback to this desaturation method is that you lose the distinction between some colors. To fix this, try the Channel Mixer technique.

5. RGB > Channel Mixer

This a good way to change the relationship of or to emphasize certain colors in monochrome. To do it, make a Channel Mixer adjustment layer, and in the dialog box, check "Monochrome." The image instantly changes to B&W (if Preview is checked); now the fun can start. Use the Source Channel sliders to adjust the individual Red, Green, and Blue channels while watching the image change. Make sure that the three Source Channels add up to 100 percent if you want to hold the overall lightness-to-darkness range of the image.

For my palm tree, I wanted a dark, brooding sky. To accomplish that, I adjusted my Red, Green, and Blue Source Channels in the Channel Mixer to be +55, +55, -10 (see Figure 11.17).

Figure 11.17
Photoshop's Channel Mixer with the Monochrome option checked helps change the relationship of the color values.

6. RGB > LAB

A less-flexible method for converting to monochrome is to work in LAB mode (Image > Mode > Lab Color). After opening up Channels (Window > Show Channels), get rid of the a and b color channels by simply trashing them. You'll be prompted to flatten the image, which leaves only the Lightness channel, now called Alpha 1, that contains all the light-to-dark information. You won't be able to add adjustment layers with this method, but you can still do image adjustments with Brightness/Contrast and Levels or Curves from the Image > Adjust menu.

Convert the image back to Grayscale, and then to RGB. You can then add additional adjustments to fine-tune the color, if needed, before printing.

7. The Russell Preston Brown Technique

Adobe creative director Russell Preston Brown came up with this interesting way to convert color to monochrome in Photoshop.

With a color image open, create a Hue/Saturation adjustment layer and just click OK without making any adjustments (we'll do that in a minute). With the layer active, change its blending mode to Color (see Figure 11.18). Brown likes to think of this layer in photographic terms as the Filter that lies between the base color image and the Film layer, which needs to be created next.

To make the Film layer, add a new Hue/Saturation adjustment layer, but this time do the normal desaturating by putting the Saturation slider all the way to the left to -100. If it isn't already, make sure that this adjustment layer is on top of the stack above the first one (see Figure 11.19). (Brown likes to change the adjustment layers' names to Filter and Film.)

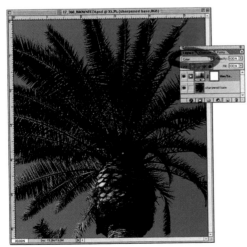

Figure 11.18
First, add a Hue/Saturation adjustment layer and change its blending mode to Color.

Figure 11.19
Next, add another Hue/Saturation layer, and desaturate the image all the way to make it monochrome. Rename the adjustment layers Filter and Film, as Brown does.

Open up the middle Filter layer by double-clicking it. Make adjustments by moving the Hue, Saturation, and Lightness sliders until you like what you see (see Figure 11.20). This allows you to change the emphasis of the different colors that contribute to the desaturated image.

To go even further with this technique, open the same Filter layer and move past Master to the individual colors in the Edit: pull-down menu. You can now adjust *only* the blues, reds, or whatever you like.

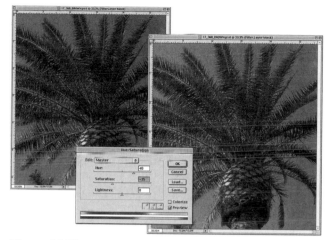

Figure 11.20
Finally, adjust the middle layer's (Filter) sliders to fine-tune the image.

Using Specialized Monochrome Inksets

A recent improvement in the digital printing of B&W images is the development of multitoned, monochromatic inks that replace the color inks in inkjet printers. This is also called quadtone or hextone printing; the printer thinks it's printing in color, but the inks that come out are all shades of black (or small-gamut color inks as described later in this section).

Some monochrome printmakers who use these special inks like to dedicate a separate printer for the job. That way, they don't have to continually switch back and forth between color and monochrome inks, which is a lot of trouble. It also wastes ink. The older EPSON 1160 and also the 3000, both four-color printers, are popular choices, although just about any inkjet printer will do, taking the restrictions of chipped-ink cartridges into account. If you have a thermal inkjet printer with replaceable heads, you could have one set for color and another for monochrome. Bulk ink systems are also popular add-ons for more efficient ink use.

Quadtone and Hextone Black Inks

If using all four or six colors to make monochrome prints yields smoother prints with subtler tones, then it stands to reason that using four or six black inks of varying densities would be even better. And so it is. With "quads," carbon or pigment particles are suspended in different concentrations in a transparent base to produce four different shades or dilutions of black. With "hex," it's six shades. For example, with the MIS Quadtones for four- or six-color printers, the light cyan position contains 15 percent black concentration; the cyan is 25 percent black. The light magenta is 45 percent, the yellow is 50 percent, the magenta is 75 percent, and the black is 100 percent. Whether six blacks is appreciably better than four is debatable; many believe not.

Because many of the inksets are either carbon- or pigment-based, the resulting image stability is excellent. Here are some top monochrome inksets and what they do:

Lysonic Quad Black: One of the original quad-black inksets, Lysonics come in three different types to match three looks: *Quad Black Cool Tone, Neutral Tone,* and *Warm Tone.* Each tone is a complete cartridge (only) set (see Figure 11.21); a different tone requires a new set. Lyson claims excellent image stability with display life exceeding that of most photographic silver-halide prints.

Lysonic Quad Blacks work with RGB images and require no special profiles or custom curves. The inks come in new, compatible cartridges for many four- or six-color EPSON printers with their own chips as needed. The inks also work on certain wide-format Canons and the Mutoh Falcon. Lyson recommends the use of cleaning cartridges between color ink to quad-black changes to eliminate any cross-contamination of the inks. They also sell matching Quad Black media.

Courtesy of Lyson, Inc.

Figure 11.21
Lyson's Quad Black inks come in cartridges that replace the color ones on selected inkjet printers.

MIS Quadtones: The original *Archival Quadtones* product was introduced in 1998 by mixing black archival ink with clear EPSON base stock. The newer *MIS Full Spectrum (FS) Quadtones* include an improved, higher-density black. Both of these quadsets are neutral in color, although they tend to produce a warm-toned print. These inks come in both bulk bottles and prefilled, replacement cartridges. MIS Quadtones should be used with custom workflows and Photoshop Curves (created by enthusiastic users and posted on the MIS Web site), and they can be used with either the OEM EPSON drivers or with the specialized Cone Piezography driver (see below).

InkjetMall's PiezoTones: New in 2002 from Jon Cone's InkjetMall are PiezoTone black/gray inks (quads and hex). These are improved, carbon-pigment inks meant to be used in the PiezographyBW system (see below), although they can also be used with EPSON printer drivers and other monochromatic workflows. There are four tone sets: *Warm Neutral, Selenium Tone, Cool Neutral,* and *Carbon Sepia,* and they are reported to have good longevity with very deep blacks (high Dmax). PiezoTones come in cartridges and bulk bottles for select EPSON (only) printers and, because they are *not* compatible with the original PiezographyBW inks, they may require old-ink purging before use. (The original *PiezographyBW* inks, now called *Sundance Neutral Warm Tone Quad Black* inks, are still available from both InkjetMall and other suppliers, including Digital Art Supplies.)

ILFORD Archiva Monokrome: Aimed at the wide-format market, this pigmented inkset has four dilutions of black. The inks are designed to be used with the ILFORD ILFOSTAR NovaJet range of printers, RIPSTAR R Series RIPs, and ILFORD media, although they'll work with others, too. Indoor permanence based on 200-lux conditions is projected to be at least 100 years. It comes in 500-ml bottles or in bottle/cart kits.

Variable Tones

Variable-toned, multi-monochromatic inks are designed to offer a range of subtle color effects by making adjustments to the image instead of having to change inks for each effect.

Lysonic Small Gamut (SG): SG inks are actually color inks with a very small gamut or color range. This makes it easy to maintain image neutrality when needed. However, it also helps produce a wide variety of monochrome effects without the need to switch inks, as with the Lysonic Quad Blacks, which have a zero gamut. SG inks don't require any custom curves, but they can take advantage of ICC printer profiles. The mild color effects can be made by using either printer driver settings or Photoshop adjustment layers, especially the Hue/Saturation tool. The full spectrum of SG colors is available through this adjustment. Available in carts and bulk (for six-ink printers only), SG inks are dye-based and designed for many EPSON and also the latest Canon desktop printers.

MIS Variable Mix (VM) Quadtones: This is a newer product for MIS, and it answers many requests from customers for prints that can vary from warm to neutral to cool. Photographer Paul Roark helped MIS develop this system by adding a blue-shaded ink to the mix. When Roark's custom

Courtesy of Paul Roark

Figure 11.22
The same Paul Roark image (The Dunes at Oceano) was printed with MIS Variable Mix Quadtone inks and two different adjustment curves applied (warm on the left, cool at right).

Photoshop Curves are loaded, they allow the blue ink to come in with the other blacks in a variable way. Where there's no blue, the print looks warm. With some blue, it's neutral. A full-strength blue produces a cool print (see Figure 11.22). The relative warmness or coolness is completely dependent on which Roark workflow curve is applied (they're available for free downloading from the MIS Web site, www.inksupply.com).

For those who want to do their own experimenting with custom tinting, MIS also sells bottles of clear EPSON base stock and the primary colors.

Lumijet Monochrome Plus: These six-color variable-tone inks are available for the EPSON 870, 890, 1270, and 1280. These variable-tone inks come only in Lumijet's bulk ink system (no cartridges). No special workflows or custom curves are required. The company claims that the inks have the same values as the color inks they're replacing, so any color management settings can still be used, even though you're printing in monochrome.

Figure 11.23

Enlargement detail from prints made with the standard EPSON (Stylus 1160) printer driver (left) and the PiezographyBW plug-in (right)

Using Specialized Drivers and Printers

Some of the highest-quality B&W digital prints being made today are the result of specialized printer drivers or printers.

Jon Cone's PiezographyBW System

The first time I saw a Piezography B&W print, I was floored. The richness of the tones, the smoothness of the gradations, the lack of a visible dot structure—it was continuous-tone and breathtaking.

Here's what PiezographyBW is: (1) a Photoshop plug-in that increases the optical resolution of EPSON printers by replacing the EPSON driver with its own proprietary RIP software, (2) 40+ popular paper profiles, and (3) the ability to use specially designed inks (PiezoTones, Sundance Quad Blacks, and MIS Full Spectrum) to take advantage of the driver's capabilities.

The key to this system is the printer driver, which not only creates deep, detailed blacks, but also increases EPSON printer resolutions up to 2160 dpi (see Figure 11.23). It does this with adaptive, stochastic, error-diffusion algorithms that allow the printer to lay down a much higher density of printing dots. Even the venerable EPSON 3000, with its huge 11-picoliter droplet sizes is rendered dotless with this driver. Developer Jon Cone says that "images printed with this system exceed the quality produced by any other digital printer and rival that made by traditional darkroom-produced, fine silver and palladium prints." It's hard to disagree.

The software plug-in was recently unbundled from the larger package that included ink and can now be purchased separately for about $150 from various suppliers (Digital Art Supplies and Inkjet Goodies) in addition to Cone's InkjetMall. Starter cartridge kits complete with plug-in and inks are also available. This is for select EPSON printers only, Mac or Windows.

The EPSON Stylus Photo 2100/2200 uses seven ink tanks for seven colors including two blacks (far left).

EPSON's Seven-Color Printers

Epson really raised some eyebrows with the introduction of its new printer line in the summer of 2002. The EPSON Stylus Photo 2200 and Stylus Pro 7600/9600 with the new UltraChrome pigment inks were groundbreaking in several ways, including the first use of seven ink colors (in separate tanks) outside of Japan. The story for this section is the two blacks—one full-strength, one diluted— that are designed for "improved B&W photographic printing."

Although I hadn't seen the printers or sample prints at the time of this writing (Summer 2002), reports were coming in from all sides that Epson was able to significantly improve the printers' gray balance, although maybe not to the satisfaction of the most serious of the B&W crowd. (Epson did get into some hot water when it was revealed that the North American models of these printers would *not* include the GrayBalancer software available in Europe and elsewhere. The ability to print directly onto CDs was also scuttled for the U.S. and Canadian markets.)

The light black ink, which is a diluted black similar to the quad blacks previously discussed, is designed to reduce graininess in the lighter tones, help the quality of gradations, and improve the neutrality of gray areas. One way it does the latter is by replacing some of the yellow, light cyan, and light magenta inks in the midtones of color images. This is called gray component replacement (GCR), or replacing the color components that make up a neutral gray with black. The more black or light black and the less color, the better your chances of staying neutral. The downside to GCR handling in earlier pigmented EPSONs was the graininess in highlight areas where black dots "peppered" the light tones. The light black ink reduces this problem because the light black dots are harder to see.

The light black is also meant to replace some of the regular black ink in the darker shadow tones, which should provide more detail there. A tinted, monochrome effect is also possible by adjusting the color inks in relation to the blacks.

In addition, these new inks are said to reduce the metamerism effect of pigment inks when using all seven colors to print B&W. Many owners of the EPSON 2000P printer had a hard time getting a neutral monochrome image that stayed that way in different lighting conditions. This is one reason photographer-artists were anxiously awaiting the 2200, which replaced the 2000P, in 2002.

The two blacks give users a choice of three black-ink printing modes for various media types and printing applications. For example:

- Photo Black + Light Black + CMYKcm for traditional photographic and inkjet coated media

- Matte Black + Light Black + CMYKcm for matte or fine-art media

- Matte Black + Matte Black + CMYKcm for matte or plain media, such as newsprint or bond paper

CMYK Proof Printing

This section applies primarily to graphic artists and designers, those "creatives" who usually work in the world of commercial printing and pre-press, although many photographer-artists now find themselves in that role as they try to market their art. If you don't understand what the word "pre-press" means, don't feel badly. Even people who work in that field every day are becoming more puzzled by its meaning and application. Many are looking for new jobs.

Time for a history lesson. In the "old days" of commercial printing, say five to ten years ago, there were separate companies who did nothing but pre-press: *scanning*, *separations*, and *proofing*. All this work was in preparation for the final step: printing. The workflow was complicated, but not hard to understand in its basic form. A designer or art director assembled the images, type, and overall concept for an advertisement, brochure, or other type of marketing piece. The color separation house or pre-press shop would then take these elements, more recently in the form of a page-layout digital file, and produce films or hard proofs on their expensive equipment that included scanners, imagesetters, and proofing devices. The best proofs—apart from running a *press proof* on a real press—were made from the actual film negatives (film positives in Europe) that would go to the printer. Because of this, these "contract" proofs—*Chromalins* or *MatchPrints*—were very accurate in predicting what might happen at the printing stage, and after being signed off by the designer and/or client (this is the "contract"), they ended up at the side of the press where they were used as quality-control guides. However, these proofs were also expensive, and they added extra time to the process. Extra time in the printing business is the enemy. The printer, who might have run another internal proof to verify that things were as they should be, was only interested in putting ink on paper in a way that matched the provided proofs.

Then, a paradigm shift occurred. The commercial printing industry, in its search to become ever-more lean and mean, started squeezing out the middle step: pre-press. Designers, who had already taken over the function of the typesetter by using page-layout software programs, now had lots of digital tools like Adobe Photoshop to play with. Suddenly, they could do their own scans, retouching, and color separations, especially as color management came into being. They could control more of the image-to-print process. At the other end, the printers, who saw their business dwindling with the onslaught of the Internet, realized that they needed to offer more services, so they bought the imagesetters to make the film themselves. Some of them even skipped that step, pulled the plug on film, and moved into CtP (computer-to-plate) technologies or DI (direct-imaging) presses.

But what about the proofing? In most cases, there needs to be a way to see in advance what a printed piece is going to look like; soft-proofing on a computer monitor can only go so far. A

Figure 11.24
The HP Designjet 10ps/20ps/50ps with software PostScript RIP is primarily used as a graphics-proofing printer.

hard proof is still necessary to show a client and to get an approval signature. In addition, because the designers are doing all the up-front, image-preparation work, it makes sense that they have now also taken on at least the preliminary proofing responsibility.

Hard Proofing to Inkjet

The main challenge for using inkjet printers to proof commercial printing jobs is this: Inkjets are very different from commercial presses. First, inkjets want RGB data, but the commercial printing world works in CMYK. This can be fixed with a Mode change in Photoshop or by the use of a CMYK RIP. Second, inkjet inks are nothing like the process inks typically used on offset presses. Inkjet inks are much more saturated and brilliant in comparison, which is fine if you're printing a colorful photo, but not if you're trying to accurately match what a specific four-color press will produce.

The best way to have an inkjet printer make a print from a page-layout program that accurately matches a commercial press is to use a PostScript RIP and a press simulation profile. The RIP converts the file to CMYK (or you can do it through Photoshop) and handles any PostScript elements and PANTONE spot colors. The press simulation profile, ideally based on the specific press, ink, and paper combination ultimately being used, is selected in the RIP so that the inkjet printer's wide color gamut can be reduced and more closely mimic the gamut of the final press inks. If no specific profile is available, the standard SWOP Coated profiles will get you close. (If you're printing only from Photoshop, and not a page-layout program, the RIP is not required; it's the ICC printer profile that does the main work as you "print the proof"—in Photoshop: Source Space > Proof Setup.)

The final requirement of accurate proofing is the paper selection. The point is to match as closely as possible the actual paper that will run on the press. Mitsubishi, HP, Epson, and others make several varieties of inkjet proofing media that simulate standard, coated press sheets. Alternatively, you can run a glossy white proofing stock and use the Absolute Colorimetric intent to "paint" the proofing stock the color of less white press media, such as newsprint.

EPSONs, especially the non-ink-chipped Pro-line variety, are the most popular choice for inkjet proofing printers, although other PostScript-enabled brands like the HP Designjet 10ps/20ps/50ps (see Figure 11.24), which were designed specifically for this purpose, also do a good job. Because there is no need for image stability with short-lived proofs, dye-based inks are most often used.

The benefit and ease of making my own press-simulated, inkjet proofs was brought home to me recently with an advertisement I had designed that was to be printed in a magazine on a web offset press (see Figure 11.25).

Figure 11.25
This magazine ad was proofed on a desktop inkjet printer using a PostScript RIP and a press-simulation profile.

My service bureau had experienced a power outage, and all the normal proofing options were suddenly unavailable to me with a looming deadline. Because I had worked on and printed this ad before and had several earlier proofs (both analog MatchPrints and digital Rainbow proofs), I decided to try my trusty EPSON 1280 and the EPSON StylusRIP, an inexpensive software RIP for selected desktop printers. Although EPSON does not recommend this RIP for accurate color proofing, I was in a bind and willing to take a chance.

The whole process was very simple. After I loaded a glossy, white proofing stock into the printer, I opened the file in QuarkXPress, my page-layout program, and sent it to the StylusRIP server, which processed the PostScript file into a raster image. I selected the PostScript Color Matching method and chose for my press simulation setting the SWOP/EPSON profile for web offset publications (see Figure 11.25). (The StylusRIP works only with a limited number of stock profiles; luckily, one of them was the one I needed.)

The results? Apart from the fact that the StylusRIP prints only at 720×720 dpi and that some of the ad's finer details were a little ragged, the proof was surprisingly good. When I compared it to the older, service-bureau proofs and also with the actual printed press sheets of earlier versions of the ad, and I was amazed at how close the match was. I had no hesitation sending this inkjet proof to the printer with the digital files, and the job printed beautifully.

Although it's true that there are still a few printers and publications that refuse to accept inkjet proofs, their numbers are dwindling in the face of knowledgeable designers and imaging professionals who are learning the ins and outs of inkjet proofing.

— ■ ■ ■ —

You have now reached the end of this book's regular chapters. However, we're not done yet. Be prepared to be stunned by the inspiring images and techniques that follow in Part IV's Gallery Showcase.

PART IV

Gallery Showcase

Gallery Showcase

I've selected these 18 artists and images to showcase the variety of digital imaging and printing being done today. (For a complete alphabetical listing of photographer-artists featured in this book, including these Gallery Showcase participants, see the Appendix.)

These examples, along with the descriptions of how they were produced, are divided into five categories or types. As mentioned in Chapter 1, digital categories and classifications are a risky undertaking because they are constantly changing and inherently blurry around the edges. However, there are some basic differences, and these divisions act as a kind of road map to help us find our way along the digital highway. Consider the categories only as rough sign posts to the digital methods available to photographer-artists.

The five categories are as follows:

Photography

Images are created by means of a camera (traditional or digital). There is often some digital intervention and definitely digital output, but the focus is to be true to the image as originally captured.

Enhanced Photography

Here, the digital process flexes its muscles, altering the image, usually significantly, and sometimes to the point that it cannot be recognized as originally starting out as a photograph. This is also where photo-based digital montages and collages fit.

Digital Drawing/Painting

Artists creatively input their ideas directly into the computer, typically with an electronic stylus or graphics tablet and related painting software.

Hybrid Process

This category starts where digital drawing/painting leaves off and can combine all the previous groups. It also includes digital imagery that takes advantage of 3-D modeling software, fractal mathematics, "machine art," algorithmic art, automatic filters, and alternative photo process and mixed-media when the digital print is only one step in the process.

Reproduction from Another Medium (Giclée)

These are digital reproductions that come from other media: painting, drawing, watercolor, and so on. The original already exists in tangible form outside the computer. This is what *giclées* are, and they can either be self-printed or output with the help of a print-for-pay service. (Note that some artists featured here disagree with my definition and call their original prints *giclées*.)

Enjoy the show!

Photography

Grant Peterson's 9/11 prints were on display at the New York Historical Society, February–May, 2002.

Grant Peterson

On the morning of September 11, 2001, advertising photographer Grant Peterson was setting up for a shoot in an eighth-floor New York City studio with a clear view of the Twin Towers. Instead of concentrating on his assignment, he turned his camera around and started documenting the horrifying events outside. He shot a total of sixteen 4×5-inch transparencies during the course of that morning, and he quickly pulled together a team that would help him to produce some of the most extraordinary pictures of that day and to present them to the public.

With the coordination of Improved Technologies' Steve Boulter, the photos were converted to digital on a drum scanner and retouched by digital guru Leo Chapman. The resulting 1.5-GB files were then sent to Autograph in Farmington, Connecticut, for printing. Autograph, which specializes in large trade show graphics, used a Mimaki JV4 wide-format inkjet running dye inks to print the 58×108-inch images on ChromaZone glossy film. The prints were float-mounted to Sintra board, and a nonreflective laminate coating was applied as a last step.

How did Peterson pick the dimensions of these mural-size photos? "They were supposed to be 6 ft. $\times$ 10 ft., but we ended up with 5 ft. $\times$ 9 ft. out of the printer due to the substrates available. We also maxed out Photoshop with the image at 30,000 pixels across. This then determined the overall proportion and scale." The result is some of the most riveting and amazingly detailed imagery to be created from that fateful day.

Photography

© 2000 Seth Rossman

Blue Chairs, *2000, color laser print,*
8.5 × 11" and 11 × 17"

Seth Rossman

Indiana photographer Seth Rossman shot this photo on the island of Crete while on assignment for the Navy with a Nikon D1 digital camera. "That blue is very typical for the area," he says. After converting the file from NEF to TIFF format, Rossman went into Photoshop to adjust Curves, Levels (gamma only), and Saturation. The image was finally saved as a .STN file in Genuine Fractals for sizes 11 × 17" and up. Prints are output on a Xerox Docucolor 50, and he also prints small versions of the image on an EPSON 740 and a C80 on EPSON Matte Paper-Heavyweight.

Rossman likes working with color laser output because of the costs (inexpensive!) and the quality, which he finds excellent. "The downside is that white areas are just that—the white of the paper," he explains. "It shows because there is no toner there; thus the Xerox-raised-relief look. It is not so obvious on matte stock. For those who don't insist on gloss prints, color laser is a great medium."

Photography

© 2001 Chris Maher—www.IRDreams.com

Rolling Hills, 2001, Noritsu minilab print, 8 × 10"

Chris Maher

Photographer, writer, and Web designer Chris Maher has been selling his work at art shows since 1978, and it was on a rainy day at one of those shows when he went looking for digital infrared pictures. *Rolling Hills* was shot with a Nikon Coolpix 950 with the fisheye (FC-E8) zoomed in to full frame. The lens was rear-filtered with a gel 87c infrared filter.

Maher uses different printing technologies (inkjet, LightJet, and Noritsu minilab) depending on the situation and whether a particular art show is "digital adverse." "Lately, I've been printing on Kodak Royal paper through a Noritsu SMP 1700 digital printer," he explains. "I do quite a bit of work in Photoshop to balance my tones and place them where I want them. Then, I insist that the folks running the printer do no further 'corrections.' I like the neutral tones and known archival aspects of the paper, although the highlights are not as pure as my inkjet prints."

Photography

Mudflat, 2000, LightJet print, 20×24", 20×30", and 24×36"

Paul Eric Johnson

Fine-art photographer Paul Eric Johnson, whose latest project is a book with author Elinor DeWire, *Lighthouses of the Mid-Atlantic Coast* (Voyageur Press, 2002), has a work-in-progress titled *Re-imagine New England*. "Entering the fifth century after its settlement," Johnson explains, "New England approaches final buildout of the natural setting that will determine the essential character of its future. The purpose here is to re-imagine New England and its relationship with nature to see more clearly the choices for the region." The current portfolio comprises 12 prints, one of which is *Mudflat*, which was shot on the bayside of the outer reaches of Cape Cod.

Johnson has his original 35mm transparencies drum scanned, and then he works in Photoshop, "spending up to five days preparing each image," he says. "*Mudflat* was one of the first LightJet prints I attempted, and I couldn't know what a learning experience it would be! This image's saturation, deep blues, and fine transitions create problems for banding and color crossover at the edges of the gamut. I first learned the intricacies of RGB curves and hand-blurring. Then, I fine-tuned the highlights, shadows, and reflections with a total of seven color-selection layers for color balance and more curve and level tweaks. Finally, I used saturation and contrast gradient layers to enhance depth perception along with a bit of blur and noise gradients to preserve the wispiness of the remaining fog. The result is accurate to my experience of the event." Final prints are made on a LightJet digital photoprinter onto Fuji Crystal Archive paper.

Enhanced Photography

The Chair, 2002, Frontier/Lambda prints, various sizes

Larry Berman

Photographer Larry Berman is a veteran of 25 years on the art show circuit selling his fine-art photography. He recently added a new technique: color infrared. Using a Nikon Coolpix 950 camera and combinations of color filters to block all but narrow-band spikes of visible light while letting all infrared radiation pass, Berman captured his *The Chair* image on a trip to Miami Beach, Florida. "Unlike the old days of shooting infrared in 35mm where you never knew what you got until you developed the film," he says, "digital cameras let you see the results instantly on the LCD screen. The different colors are a result of the quality of light and shadows hitting the subject." Berman then takes the next step by opening up the images on his computer and running his own Photoshop actions that he has developed through experimentation. "Infrared images have a strange color and tonal balance to them right out of the camera. Some go red; others have a cyan sheen. Rarely will they have a full tonal range."

Berman makes 8 × 10-inch and 10 × 14-inch Fuji Frontier prints for art-show sales, and when he needs large prints for a corporate art consultant, he has a lab make 24 × 30-inch Durst Lambda prints at 200 ppi on Fuji Crystal Archive paper. "I like the Frontier and Lambda prints for the intense colors and the glossy look."

Enhanced Photography

© 2000 James G. Respess

Souvenir of Mexico, 2000, *pigment ink print on archival paper, sizes up to 30×41"*

James Respess

A former molecular biologist, James Respess has devoted full time to fine-art photography since 1996. Well-schooled in traditional photo techniques, he has made the switch to digital printing and composing, and is the Best of Show winner of the March 2002 Photoshop World's Guru Awards.

Souvenir of Mexico, which won Best in Show, Second Grand Prize in the 2001 Museum of Computer Art digital art contest, is what Respess calls a digital composition. "The window sill and tequila bottle were photographed separately and specifically for this," he says. "The snow scene was shot in Ann Arbor, Michigan, and the scene inside the bottle was shot in Cozumel, Mexico. I shot the bottle with a white background and positioned the Mexico image into it in Photoshop. With the history brush, I painted some of the bottle back in over the scene at low opacity. The snow scene was placed behind the window, and the bottle was put on the sill with a shadow added by using the burn tool. I made sure that some of the snow scene could be seen through the bottle, and I adjusted the color in all layers to match, with the Mexico scene a little more vivid."

Respess outputs his own prints (and those of other artists) using an EPSON Stylus Pro 9600 and a pair of EPSON Stylus Photo 1200s. One is loaded with MIS color archival inks, and the other is loaded with MIS Variable Mix Quadtone inks. Papers used are Schoellershammer Velvet and Hahnemuhle William Turner.

Enhanced Photography

Fabrication of Congruence, *2000, digital illustration/LightJet print, 20 × 20"*

Julieanne Kost

In this self-portrait of the artist, the central figure, surrounded by words and roots, has no eyes. "It's really about how we relate to nature and to the world," explains Julieanne Kost, a senior graphic evangelist at Adobe Systems.

"Creating digital images has completely changed the way I shoot and think about images," she says. "I use multiple images in an attempt to convey an emotion or to create a reaction or some kind of sensation. I use compositing and layering to hide or reveal what I want to do in an image. I found that I couldn't say what I wanted with just one photo. Now, I take multiple photos that provoke the same reaction, then layer them to tell a more complete story. For me, the images I'm creating on the computer have much more depth and tell more than my 'straight' photos do."

As for printing, "I use the LightJet for my more traditional photographic (non-manipulated) images, but I like the softer look of inkjet on watercolor paper for my fine-art images." For her inkjets, Kost prints in her studio with EPSON 2000P, 1280, and 1270 printers.

Enhanced Photography

© 2001 Bobbi Doyle-Maher

Katy's Flower, *2001, inkjet print, 12×18"*

Bobbi Doyle-Maher

Self-taught artist Bobbi Doyle-Maher changed her approach to art after receiving a digital camera as a gift. Formerly a traditional painter, she quickly embraced the digital world. She feels that her art experience has come together to form a perfect union of paint and pixels.

With *Katy's Flower*, the source photo was taken with a Nikon Coolpix 950. "The original photo was a still-life setup of a green cup with white flowers and a single flower lying on the table," explains Doyle-Maher. "The image was then brought into Corel/Procreate Painter where I painted away the cup and white flowers and left the red flower as the focal point. When using Painter with brushes that blend existing color the tendency is to go too soft, so color was painted back into this image and softened when needed, while making sure to leave some texture. The blending and painting-in of color was repeated many times to get the final result. The file was then brought back into Photoshop for final adjustments."

Doyle-Maher outputs her own prints on an EPSON 2000P (at this writing she's just added the EPSON Stylus Photo 2200). After a difficult trial-and-error period, she is happy with her current workflow that includes ColorVision's PhotoCAL and ConeStudio printer profiles. "I prefer the look of EPSON Archival Matte and Watercolor papers, but the Semigloss and Luster give a bit richer color and detail. When I use these last two papers, I spray the dry print with a coating to get rid of the photographic look."

Digital Drawing/Painting

Anza-Borrego Oak, 2001, *digital drawing/IRIS print, 30×45"*

Martha Jane Bradford

Digital artist Martha Jane Bradford is known for her large-scale, photorealist "digital charcoal drawings." She uses a Wacom Intuos2 graphics tablet and Painter software. "*Anza-Borrego Oak* was the first drawing where I had enough memory to take advantage of Painter's Layers features," says Bradford. "I found that it really expanded my creative freedom to be able to put highlights, tones, and paper textures on different layers and to, for example, change the tree without messing up the sky. You can fine tune much more freely with layers and try things you might not be willing to risk otherwise."

Bradford uses desktop EPSON printers for proofing, but because the final images are so large, she makes proofs in tiled sections using 8.5×11-inch paper taped together. Matching these preliminary proofs to the IRIS proofs she gets from printmaker Jonathan Singer at Singer Editions was a challenge until she calibrated her monitor with the ColorVision Spyder. "Now, my images come out almost perfect on the first proof." Even though Bradford's drawings are B&W, final prints are output on the IRIS in four CMYK colors on Somerset Radiant White Textured or Natural Textured stock.

Digital Drawing/Painting

© 2001 Ry Smith

French Farm 1, 2001, limited edition giclée print, 22 × 17"

Ry Smith

Northern-California artist Ry Smith is a former inventor and entrepreneur who now takes advantage of his background to combine technology and art. Frequently using his own photos as preliminary references, he creates his own brushes to paint the image in Painter. After painting, he opens the image in Photoshop where he performs additional Curves, Levels, and Saturation adjustments. Smith then saves out different versions of the file for different purposes: smaller sizes for his Web site and for spec sheets, and one for printing using Genuine Fractals, which he finds very useful for enlargements.

"It usually takes me between 10 to 30 variations of the painting before I am done with it," explains Smith. "I first print on 8.5 × 11-inch paper on my EPSON C80 desktop printer. I review and rework as needed. After I get something I'm satisfied with, I move to my wide-format EPSON 9500 pigment printer and print on 17 × 22-inch Semigloss paper. I typically end up making more changes at this point. Once I'm satisfied, I print a "final" on Somerset art paper. That print becomes No. 1 of the limited edition; 60–225 is my current edition range."

Smith also produces one-of-a-kind prints for some images like *French Farm 1*. In this case, he prints the same image on canvas and embellishes it with oil paint after it is mounted on stretcher bars. Only one unique print is offered.

Digital Drawing/Painting

Contemplation, 1998, inkjet print on canvas, 26×22"
(also in other sizes)

Jeremy Sutton

Digital artist, portraitist, educator, and author Jeremy Sutton is a digital-painting aficionado and expert. Using a Mac, a Wacom graphics tablet, and Corel/Procreate Painter software, "I can flow seamlessly and effortlessly from painting with broad washes of watercolor one moment to applying thick, viscous, impasto oil paint the next," he says. "I find the level of control I have exceeds that of working in traditional media."

Sutton has also developed a unique niche: live digital portraiture at trade shows and special events. Always attracting a crowd, he paints subjects who can watch their portraits unfold on a large display screen. Each portrait subject leaves with a signed color print output on the spot on a desktop, color inkjet printer. Back at his San Francisco studio, Sutton focuses his drawing talents on design, animation, and illustration. His portrait of Albert Einstein (shown) was originally created for Apple Computer. He also offers limited-edition, fine-art prints of all his images. "I like to print my images on canvas. I usually use a local service bureau that has HP and EPSON wide-format printers. I then stretch the canvas and frame the work myself."

Sutton's two latest book projects are *Secrets of Award-Winning Digital Artists*, with Daryl Wise (2002), and *Painter Creativity: Digital Artist's Handbook* (2002).

Hybrid Process

Grace Under Fire, *2001, giclée on canvas, 24×30"*

Ileana

Born in Venezuela and raised in the lush beauty of the Caribbean, Ileana integrates digital painting and photography to create her dynamic and colorful images and prints. She starts off by creating a line drawing with the major elements of her composition. Next, she adds shape, color, and texture to the central figures using a Wacom graphics tablet. Finally, she prepares the background from images captured with her digital camera—enhancing and arranging them until the piece is complete.

Grace Under Fire, in a signed and numbered edition of 50, is printed by JD Jarvis of Dunking Bird Productions using an HP 2500CP inkjet printer with pigmented inks on canvas. "Choosing an outside printer has allowed me to focus on the creative process of making images," Ileana explains. "With my input and the printer's expertise, I can come up with a product that matches what I had originally envisioned."

Hybrid Process

© 2000 Dan Burkholder

Pines and Palace, *Versailles, 2000–2001, pigment-over platinum print,* 6×9"

Dan Burkholder

Fine-art photographer, educator, and author Dan Burkholder is a true innovator when it comes to alternative photo process (see Chapter 11), and his latest technique is what he calls Pigment-Over-Platinum prints. He is the first to combine a hand-coated platinum/palladium print with digitally applied, archival color pigments.

Here's how it works, in Burkholder's own words: "*Pines and Palace* was shot in France with an Olympus E-10 digital camera; I've pretty much retired film from my shooting life. I then stylized the image to give it the desired look and feel. The tricky part is segregating the color information from the platinum component—it's never the same for any two images."

"First, the pigment is applied with an EPSON 7000 running Indelible archival pigmented inks. The pigment image is fairly faint and desaturated; the platinum step is responsible for most of the contrast and density. I then coat the pigment print with platinum/palladium sensitizer. This coating is dried and flattened, and the digital negative (produced on desktop with an EPSON inkjet printer) is registered with the pigment image. The neg/print sandwich is then exposed under a UV light, and the final print is developed in hot developer and cleared and washed traditionally."

Hybrid Process

12:6:65, 2000, inkjet print on canvas, 22 × 22"

Fred Casselman

Artist Fred Casselman directs Earth Echo, "a gallery of peace, love, and light on the Internet." To create his ethereal art, he works mainly in Photoshop, using several third-party, plug-in filters. The image *12:6:65* started out as a lens flare effect created in Knoll Lens Flare Pro. "Then, I did some playing around with the colors, including shifting the cyans to orange. The next step involved a series of geometric distortions with the main filter being Xaos Tools Terrazzo."

Instead of offering prints for sale in the normal fashion, Casselman has a unique three-tiered distribution system. Option 1 allows anyone to download and print out high-resolution images for personal noncommercial use. There is no charge although a donation is suggested. For the second option, Casselman recommends taking the high-resolution files to a local printmaker for output. Again, there is no charge. Finally, you can purchase prints directly from Casselman who prints them on a wide-format EPSON 7000 using Indelible pigment inks on canvas. Charges are negotiable.

Hybrid Process

FlyFree, 2001, lenticular print or fresco transfer, 35×44"

Bonny Lhotka

Digital art pioneer and a founding member of Digital Atelier, Bonny Lhotka includes *FlyFree* in her *Singular* collection, which combines fragments of objects, dreams, and reality to illuminate the connection between life and death, technology, and the human spirit. It is available both as a lenticular print ("my favorite art medium") and as a fresco transfer. (See more about Digital Atelier's experimental printmaking methods in Chapter 11.) Lhotka used an Olympus E-10 digital camera to capture the American flag, the birds, and the clouds. The rope and frame were scanned on a large-format, flatbed scanner. "I collaged the parts in Photoshop to compose the image," says Lhotka. "For the lenticular prints, objects were kept on different layers for creating the lenticular frames."

FlyFree is also available as a fresco transfer. "I make a solution of glue and calcium carbonate that is applied to a sheet of Gatorfoam. The calcium carbonate is what makes the surface resemble a fresco. When it sets up like jello, a print imaged on the Mutoh Falcon is printed with pigment inks onto clear film that's rolled down on the surface of the medium. After a few minutes, the film is removed, leaving the print on the surface. After drying, the result is a pigment image that looks like plaster."

Hybrid Process

© 2001 Mel Strawn

Bamboocut *(Coins of the Realm series), 2001,*
inkjet print, 30×33"

Mel Strawn

Mel Strawn, Professor Emeritus at the University of Denver, is a longtime painter, printmaker, and art educator. He started working with home computers in 1981 and has used digital technology as a creative tool ever since. His recent *Coins of the Realm* series is based on bottle caps or similar round artifacts. "I'm not really interested in the social message but in the unique visual qualities, configurations, and juxtapositions abandoned things present," he says.

Bamboocut combines an ink drawing of bamboo root and a scanned, red bottle cap. Another bottle cap is enlarged digitally and cut into slices and reassembled. Strawn uses an Olympus 3030 digital camera and a UMAX PowerlookIII scanner. All image-editing work is done in Photoshop. He makes prints with an ENCAD Pro36 inkjet printer (he also has an EPSON 9000) on Hawk Mountain Osprey paper with Lysonic inks. "The typical printing challenge is maintaining the color range/gamut and full saturation while holding detail," Strawn explains. "In my work, which is closer to 'hand-done' painting, drawing, or printmaking, photo detail is not the same problem faced by photographers with a traditional expectation. The ENCAD printer outputs only at 300 dpi from a file encoded at 100 ppi at full-expected size. On the ENCAD, I use a Cactus RIP to handle output resolution."

Reproduction from Another Medium (Giclée)

10-10-10, original: 1982, watercolor and drybrush, 14 × 21", prints: 2001, limited-edition giclée, 13 × 19"

Craig Forrest

Rural-realist painter Craig Forrest starts his painting process with pencil drawings to quickly discover potential compositions and to explore contrasts and values along with texture. He then applies watercolor washes. When a subject lends itself to further effort, as *10-10-10* (named after the fertilizer bags stored in the barn) did, Forrest next turns to drybrush, which is a watercolor style that involves squeezing most of the water from the brush and working primarily with the watercolor paint alone.

To reproduce his originals, Forrest scans them in pieces and stitches them together in Photoshop. Using an EPSON 2000P, he prints his own limited-edition giclées (editions of 400) on either EPSON Archival Matte or Watercolor papers. "When I first started printing with the 2000P," says Forrest, "the prints were terrible. Then I learned about color matching and, after adding the Monaco EZcolor system, I refined my workflow to where I'm now getting excellent results. The only improvement I can see is possibly moving up to an EPSON 7600 so I can output a larger size."

Reproduction from Another Medium (Giclée)

© 2001 Blazing Publications

Romantic Melody, *2001, embellished edition on canvas, 38 × 50"*

Tatyana Eliseeva

Russian artist Tatyana Eliseeva received a classical education at the prestigious Leningrad Academy of Arts with countless hours devoted to drawing anatomy and with many visits to the Hermitage to copy works of the Renaissance Masters. Eliseeva loves theater, especially Shakespearean tragedy, and this love is reflected in her canvases where she provides a nostalgic glimpse of the Renaissance with its elaborate costumes and colorful pageantry.

Blazing Publications, a sister company to fine-art digital printmaking studio Blazing Editions, is Eliseeva's exclusive representative and art publisher. Her work is available either as a canvas giclée edition or as a signed and numbered edition on paper, but not both. *Romantic Melody* was photographed to 4 × 5-inch film, scanned, and printed on canvas on a Mutoh/I-Jet inkjet printer in an edition of 100. Prints are hand-embellished by staff artists at Blazing Editions, and the final prints, which are shipped pre-stretched, sell for $2,250 each.

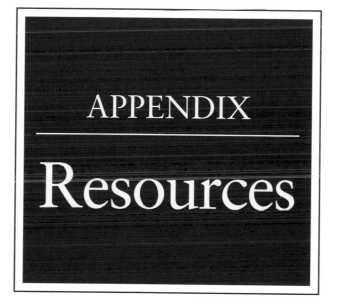

Appendix: Resources

Consider this book the base camp for your digital explorations. If you want to go further afield in search of more in-depth information, here are some resources that I have found useful and that might help you as well. I've tried to list only those companies, groups, and individuals who are digital-friendly, and, of course, all information is current only as of this writing.

Make special note of my companion Web site (DP&I.com—www.dpandi.com) and the digital-fine-art discussion list I run (http://groups.yahoo.com/group/digital-fineart/) if you want the latest information or to make contact with me directly. For updates, corrections, and other information about the content of this book, go to: www.muskalipman.com/digital printing.

Photographer-Artists

These are the photographers and artists featured or mentioned in this book.

Jean Anne Allen
http://www.watercoloronline.com

Tom Andrews
http://www.wildlandart.com

Diane Clapp Bartz
http://www.bartz.com/studio

Howard Berdach
http://www.howardberdach.com

Larry Berman
http://BermanGraphics.com,
http://www.AlternatePhoto.com

Martha Jane Bradford
http://www.marthavista.com,
marthabradford@mindspring.com

Teri Brudnak
tbrudnak@cox.net

Dan Burkholder
http://www.danburkholder.com

John Paul Caponigro
http://www.johnpaulcaponigro.com

Fred Casselman
http://www.earthecho.com

Marilyn Culler
http://www.msrphoto.com

Peggy Davis Calligraphy/Jewish Ketubot
http:// www.HebrewLettering.com/ketuba.html

Gary Dorothy
http://www.garydorothy.com

Bobbi Doyle-Maher
http://www.rabbittwilight.com

Tatyana Eliseeva
c/o Blazing Editions (*see below*)

Craig Forrest
http://www.sleepyhollowstudio.net,
sleepyhollo1@earthlink.net

Gregory Georges
http://www.reallyusefulpage.com

Robert A. Hansen
http://www.roberthansen.com

Jean-Pierre Hébert
http://www.solo.com

Ileana
http://www.ileanaspage.com

JD Jarvis
http://www.dunkingbirdproductions.com

Diana Jeon
diana.jp@verizon.net

Paul Eric Johnson
http://www.paulericjohnson.com,
pejohnson@pauleriçjohnson.com

Julieanne Kost
http://www.adobeevangelists.com

Dorothy Simpson Krause
http://www.dotkrause.com

Sally Larsen
sally@solozone.com

Bonny Lhotka
http://www.Lhotka.com

John Livsey
http://www.livzey.com

Joy Turner Luke
(540) 987-3353 fax

Chris Maher
http://www.IRDreams.com

Bob Meyer
http://www.meyerweb.net/epson

Stanley Mouse
http://www.mousestudios.com

Carol Pentleton
http://www.thedigitalartist.com

Grant Peterson
gpet@rcn.com

Konrad Poth
kpoth@bellsouth.net

C.J. Pressma
cjp@rosewood.win.net

James Respess
http://www.greenflashphotography.com

Ray Bliss Rich
http://www.conknet.com/~r_rich

Paul Roark
http://www.PaulRoark.com

Seth Rossman
http://www.msrphoto.com

Alan Scharf
ascharf@sk.sympatico.ca

Karin Schminke
http://www.schminke.com

Roger Smith
rsmith@unb.ca

Ry Smith
http://arthill.com,
rysmith@arthill.com

Barry Stein
http://www.BSteinArt.com,
bstein@tntech.edu

Jeremy Sutton
http://www.portrayals.com,
jeremy@portrayals.com

Mel Strawn
http://www.911gallery.org/mels/mel.htm,
http://www.worldprintmakers.com/english/
strawn/melmain.htm

Jonathan Talbot
http://www.talbot1.com

Print Service Providers

These are all the printmakers and digital print-
service providers mentioned in the book plus a
few more.

David Adamson Editions
Washington, DC USA
(202) 347-0090

Bair Art Editions
Salt Lake City, UT USA
http://www.inkjetart.com/bae/index.html

Blazing Editions (& Publications)
East Greenwich, RI USA
http://www.blazing.com

Bytesmiths (Jan Steinman)
West Linn, OR USA
http://www.bytesmiths.com

Calypso Imaging
Santa Clara, CA USA
http://www.calypsoinc.com

Cone Editions
East Topsham, VT USA
http://www.cone-editions.com

Duganne Ateliers
Santa Monica, CA USA
http://www.duganne.com

Dunking Bird Productions (JD Jarvis)
Las Cruces, NM USA
http://www.dunkingbirdproductions.com

Greencastle Photo Service (Lester Wilson)
Greencastle, IN USA
(765) 653-6418

Harvest Productions
Anaheim Hills, CA USA
http://www.harvestpro.com

Hawk Mountain Editions
Leesport, PA USA
http://www.hawkmtneditions.com

Kolibri Art Studio
Torrance, CA USA
http://www.kolibriartstudio.com

Miller's Professional Imaging
headquartered in Kansas, USA
http://www.millerslab.com

Nash Editions
Manhattan Beach, CA USA
http://www.nasheditions.com

New Media Arts (Lynn Lown)
Santa Fe, NM USA
http://www.nmarts.com, (800) 662-9194

Old Town Editions
Alexandria, VA USA
http://www.oldtowneditions.com

Pamplemousse Press
New York, NY USA
(212) 243-0439

Photo Craft Laboratories
Boulder, CO USA
http://www.pcraft.com

Photoworks Creative Group
Charlottesville, VA USA
http://www.photoworksgroup.com

Renaissance Art Editions
West Palm Beach, FL USA
finalproof@earthlink.net

Shutterfly
Hayward, CA USA
http://www.shutterfly.com

Singer Editions
Boston, MA USA
http://www.singereditions.com

Staples Fine Art
Richmond, VA USA
http://www.staplesart.com

Talon Graphics
San Clemente, CA USA
http://www.talongraphics.com

Thunderbird Editions
Clearwater, FL USA
http://www.motors.com

Torlan Studios
San Antonio, TX USA
http://www.torlanstudios.com

The Visual Artist (Jim Davis)
Hummelstown, PA USA
http://www.visual-artists.com

Equipment, Supplies, Software, and Related Services

Here is just about every product and services provider mentioned in the book and more.

Printers, Supplies, and Software

3P Inkjet Textiles
Textiles for inkjet printing.
http://www.3P-inktextiles.com

ACD Systems
ACDSee picture viewer and other software.
http://www.acdsystems.com

Adobe Systems
Photoshop, Elements, Illustrator, InDesign, Acrobat, GoLive, and more.
http://www.adobe.com

Agfa
Scanners, cameras, mini-lab systems.
http://www.agfa.com

Alien Skin Software
Special-effects software including Eye Candy.
http://www.alienskin.com

Alpha Imaging Technologies
Digital imaging systems and supplies.
http://www.alphaimaging.com

All-Square Computer Technologies
Online digital printing supplies.
http://www.allsquare.com

American Imaging Corporation
Symphonic inks, digital printing systems, and supplies.
http://www.inkjetcolorsystems.com

American Ink Jet
Inkjet inks.
http://www.amjet.com

Andromeda Software
Visual enhancement plug-ins.
http://www.andromeda.com

Apple Computer
Computers, peripherals, software, and services.
http://www.apple.com

ArcSoft
Digital imaging software.
http://www.arcsoft.com

Atlantic Exhange
Discount printer supplies.
http://www.atlex.com

ArtScans Studio
Specialty fine-art scanning service.
http://www.artscans.com

Auto FX Software
Photo/Graphic Edges and other visual imaging software.
http://www.autofx.com/

Azon
Digital printing supplies.
http://www.azon.com

Better Light
Digital scanning camera systems.
http://www.betterlight.com

BrightCube
Digital printing papers and turnkey imaging systems.
http://www.brightcube.com

BullDog Products
Digital printing supplies.
http://www.bulldogproducts.com

Canon
Cameras, scanners, printers, and printing supplies.
http://www.canon.com

Canto Software
Cumulus and other software.
http://www.canto.com

Celartem Technology
VFZoom and other software.
http://www.celartem.com

Cerious Software
ThumbsPlus image database and graphics editor.
http://www.cerious.com

CHROMiX
Color management systems and profiles.
http://www.chromix.com/

ColorByte Software
Makers of the ImagePrint RIP.
http://www.colorbyte.com

ColorMall
Color management products.
http://www.colormall.com

ColorVision
Color management systems.
http://www.colorvision.com

Continuous Ink Systems
NoMoreCarts CIS.
www.NoMoreCarts.com

Corel/Procreate
Painter and other imaging software.
http://www.procreate.com

Crane & Co.
Museo fine-art paper.
http://www.crane.com

Creo
Scanning systems and Leaf digital cameras.
http://www.creoscitex.com

DigiFab
Pre-treated fabrics and digital textile printing.
http://www.digifab.com

Digi-Frame
Digital picture frames.
http://www.digi-frame.com

Digital Atelier
inkAID precoats.
http://www.inkaid.com

Digital Art Supplies
Inkjet printing papers and archival inks.
http://www.digitalartsupplies.com

Digital Domain
Profile Prism and other software.
http://www.ddisoftware.com

Durst Phototechnik AG
Durst-Dice America
Image-reproduction devices; Durst Lambda.
http://www.durst-online.com
http://www.durstdice.com

Digital Pulse
Digital printing systems integrator.
http://www.digitalpulseinc.com

Dotworks
Inkjet printing papers.
http://www.dotinkjet.com

Dry Creek Photo
Minilab profiles.
http://www.drycreekphoto.com

ENCAD (Kodak)
Wide-format inkjet printers.
http://www.encad.com

Epson
Printers, scanners, cameras, media, RIPs, and more.
http://www.epson.com

ErgoSoft
RIPs and digital printing software.
http://www.ergosoftus.com

Extensis
Extensis Portfolio and other imaging/printing software.
http://www.extensis.com

Fredrix
Canvas for digital printing.
http://www.fredrixprintcanvas.com

Fuji Photo Film USA
Printers, scanners, cameras, and more.
http://www.fujifilm.com

GretagMacbeth
Color management and software.
http://www.gretagmacbeth.com

GTI Graphic Technology
Viewing booths and systems.
http://www.gtilite.com

Hahnemuhle FineArt
Digital fine-art papers.
http://www.hahnemuhle.com

Hawk Mountain Art Papers
Fine-art papers for inkjet printing.
http://www.hawkmtnartpapers.com

Hewlett-Packard Company (HP)
Printers, scanners, cameras, and supplies.
http://www.hp.com

Ilford Imaging
Inkjet printing media, inks, and systems.
http://www.ilford.com

Imacon
FlexTight scanners.
http://www.imacon.dk

Image-Edit & Art
Online image editing.
http://www.image-edit.com

Image Permanence Institute (IPI) at the Rochester Institute of Technology (RIT)
Image permanence testing and research.
http://www.rit.edu/~661www1/sub_pages/8contents.htm

Imaging Technologies Corp.
ColorBlind color-management software.
http://www.color.com

Improved Technologies (IRIS/IXIA)
Printer manufacturer and digital printings integrator.
http://www.itnh.com

inkjetART.com
Online resellers of printers, consumables, and more.
http://www.inkjetART.com

inkjetgoodies.com
Photographic and fine-art inkjet supplies.
http://www.inkjetgoodies.com

InkjetMall.com
Jon Cone's inkjet printing systems, inks, and media.
http://www.InkjetMall.com

Iomega Corporation
Portable data storage devices.
http://www.iomega.com

iProof Systems
RIPs and proofing software.
http://www.iproofsystems.com

IrfanView
Freeware graphic viewer.
http://www.irfanview.com

Jasc Software
Paint Shop Pro and other digital imaging software.
http://www.jasc.com

Kodak
Printers, cameras, scanners, media, software, services.
http://www.kodak.com

LaCie
Monitors.
http://www.lacie.com

Legion Paper
Fine-art paper.
http://www.legionpaper.com

LexJet Direct
Inkjet digital printing supplies.
http://www.lexjetdirect.com

Lexmark
Inkjet printers.
http://www.lexmark.com

Lincoln Ink & Paper
Digital printing inks and media.
http://www.lincolninks.com

LizardTech
Genuine Fractals and other imaging software.
http://www.lizardtech.com

Luminos/Lumijet
Inkjet media and inks.
http://www.lumijet.com

Lyson
Digital printing inks and media.
http://www.lyson.com

M&M Studios
Indelible fine-art inks.
http://www.mandmstudios.com/inks

MacDermid ColorSpan
Wide-format inkjet printers.
http://www.colorspan.com

Macromedia
Freehand, Dreamweaver, Fireworks, Director, Flash, and more.
http://www.macromedia.com

MediaStreet.com
Online digital imaging and printing supplies.
http://www.mediastreet.com

Microtek
Scanners, monitors, and cameras.
http://www.microtek.com

Mimaki
Wide-format printers, plotters, and cutters.
http://www.mimakiusa.com

Minolta Co.
Laser printers, cameras, and scanners.
http://www.minolta.com

MIS Associates
Inkjet supplies, inks, and media.
http://www.inksupply.com

Monaco Systems
Color management systems.
http://www.monacosys.com

Mutoh
Wide-format printers.
http://www.mutoh.com

NancyScans
Scanning service.
http://www.nancyscans.com

NEC/Mitsubishi
Monitors.
http://www.nec-mitsubishi.com

Nikon
Digital cameras and scanners.
http://www.nikon.com

Noritsu
Digital printers and minilabs.
http://www.noritsu.com

Océ (LightJet)
Wide-format, digital photo printers.
http://cymbolic.com

Olympus
Digital cameras, printers, and scanners.
http://www.olympus.com

Onyx Graphics
RIP products for wide-format printing.
http://www.onyxgfx.com

Parrot Digigraphic
Imaging-systems, color management,
consumables, and support.
http://www.parrotcolor.com

Pictorico
Digital printing media.
http://www.pictorico.com

Polaroid
Digital scanners, cameras, and photo printers.
http://www.polaroid.com/polaroiddigital

ProfileCity
Color management systems and profiles.
http://www.profilecity.com

Q-Panel Lab Products
Q-Lab Weathering Research
Image-permanence equipment and
testing services.
http://www.q-panel.com

Quark
QuarkXpress page-layout software.
http://www.quark.com

Red River Paper
Inkjet papers.
http://www.redriverpaper.com

Right Hemisphere
Deep Paint and 3-D graphic software.
http://www.righthemisphere.com

Roland DGA Corporation
Wide-format digital printers.
http://www.rolanddga.com

Sawgrass Systems
Dye-sublimation equipment and supplies.
http://www.sublimation.com

Schoellershammer
Fine-art printing paper.
http://www.schoellershammer.de/eng/
index_de.html

Segmentis
Developers of the buZZ image-editing plug-in.
http://www.segmentis.com

Sinar Bron Imaging
Digital and conventional photo equipment.
http://www.sinarbron.com

Sony
Digital cameras, dye-sub printers.
http://www.sony.com

Synthetik Software
Studio Artist software.
http://www.synthetik.com

Talas
Blue Wool References and other
conservation/preservation supplies.
http://www.talasonline.com

Tropical Graphics
Dye-sublimation equipment and supplies.
http://www.tropicalgraphics.com

TSS-Sublimation
Dye-sublimation equipment and supplies.
http://www.tss-sublimation.com

Ulead Systems
Photo Impact and other software.
http://www.ulead.com

Umax
Scanners.
http://www.UMAX.com

Wacom Technology
Graphics tablets.
http://www.wacom.com

Xerox Network Printers
Laser and solid-ink printers.
http://www.officeprinting.xerox.com

X-Rite
Color measurement devices.
http://www.xrite.com

Wasatch Computer Technology
RIPs and printing software.
http://www.wasatchinc.com

WeInk (Camel Ultra-FLO)
Inks, ink supplies, and media.
http://www.weink.com

Wilhelm Imaging Research
Image permanence testing.
http://www.wilhelm-research.com

ZBE (Chromira)
Chromira digital photo printer.
http://www.zbe.com

Researchers & Consultants

Andrew Behla
Digital printing and color
management consultant.
andrew@behladesign.com

Steve Boulter
Digital imaging consultant.
srboulter@attbi.com

Martin Juergens
Conservator of Photographs,
Hamburg, Germany.
http://aic.stanford.edu/conspec/emg/juergens,
post@martinjuergens.net

David J. Matz, Ph.D.
Technical Consultant,
E.I. du Pont de Nemours & Co.
David.J.Matz@usa.DuPont.com

Mark McCormick-Goodhart
Image quality and preservation research
and consulting.
mccgresearch@aol.com

C. David Tobie
Color workflow and profiling consultant.
CDTobie@designcoop.com

Barbara Vogt
R&D engineer.
barbara.vogt@boettcher.de

Charles Wehrenberg
Art consultant and publicist.
charlie@solozone.com

Ray A. Work, III, Ph.D.
Inkjet applications, markets, and
technology consultant.
http://www.workassoc.com

Suggested Reading and Information Sources

Not a complete list by any means, but here are
additional sources of information for those
who want to learn more.

Online Discussion Groups and Web Sites

Web sites and online discussion lists are
excellent resources for instant feedback,
information, and gossip. Here are my favorites
that I regularly contribute to or look in on:

Online Discussion Lists
archivalcolor
Archival color inkjet printing.
Run by Antonis Ricos.
http://groups.yahoo.com/group/archivalcolor

colortheory
Discussion of color theory and retouching in
Photoshop. Run by Dan Margulis.
http://groups.yahoo.com/group/colortheory

DigitalBlackandWhiteThePrint
Produce quality B&W prints from digital
sources. Run by Martin Wesley and
Antonis Ricos.
http://groups.yahoo.com/group/
DigitalBlackandWhiteThePrint

digital-darkroom
Just like it sounds. Moderated by
AlwaysPhotographing.com.
http://www.groups.yahoo.com/group/
digital-darkroom

digital-fineart
Making... Printing... Marketing. Run by
Harald Johnson.
http://www.groups.yahoo.com/group/
digital-fineart

digital-photo-editing
Editing digital photos with Photoshop. Run by
Gregory Georges.
http://groups.yahoo.com/group/
digital-photo-editing

epson-inkjet
The granddaddy of all inkjet lists. Run by
Mitch Leben. Mysteriously stopped operation
June, 2002, in process of being replaced by:

inkjetepson–Epson Inkjet
A successor to Mitch Leben's epson inkjet list.
Run by Diana York.
http://groups.yahoo.com/group/inkjetepson

Epson2000P
Dedicated to the Epson 2000P, 2100, and
2200 printers. Run by Fritz Meijer.
http://groups.yahoo.com/group/Epson2000P

Epson9000
For all wide-format EPSON inkjet printers and associated hardware, software, supplies, and consumables. Run by Diana York.
http://www.groups.yahoo.com/group/Epson9000

EPSONx7x_Printers
Covers all aspects of using these printers. Run by Keith Krebs.
http://groups.yahoo.com/group/EPSONx7x_Printers

HPDesignJet_Printers
The place to swap tips, hints, and troubleshoot your HP DesignJet problems. Run by Tony Parker.
http://groups.yahoo.com/group/HPDesignJet_Printers

macepsonlist
Macintosh Epson users list. Run by Bill Gore.
http://groups.yahoo.com/group/macepsonlist

Web sites

DP&I.com
The author's digital printing and imaging resource for photographers and artists.
http://www.dpandi.com

Computer Darkroom
Ian Lyon's Web site devoted to the art and technique of photography and digital imaging.
http://welcome.to/computerdarkroom

Digital Outback Photo
Fine Art Outdoor Photography using Digital Cameras
http://www.outbackphoto.com

FLAAR
Nicholas Hellmuth's FLAAR provides recommendations on wide-format printer hardware and software.
http://www.wide-format-printers.org

FredMiranda.com
Photographer Fred Miranda's site with Actions (including SI) and more.
http://www.fredmiranda.com

Imaging Resource Digital Photography
Dave Etchell's digital camera information and resource.
http://www.imaging-resource.com

The Luminous Landscape
Michael Reichman's site devoted to the art of landscape, nature, and documentary photography using traditional and digital image processing techniques.
http://www.luminous-landscape.com

Welcome.to/epson-inkjet
Alan Womack's resources for EPSON inkjet printers.
http://home.att.net/~arwomack01

Books and Magazines

For additional reading on related subjects...

Books

50 Fast Photoshop 7 Techniques
by Gregory Georges
(John Wiley & Sons, 2002)

Making Digital Negatives for Contact Printing
Second Edition
by Dan Burkholder
(Bladed Iris Press, 1999)

Painter Creativity: Digital Artist's Handbook
by Jeremy Sutton
(Focal Press, 2002)

Professional Photoshop 7: The Classic Guide to Color Correction
by Dan Margulis
(John Wiley & Sons, 2002)

Real World Color Management
by Bruce Fraser, Fred Bunting, and
Chris Murphy
(Peachpit Press, 2002)

**Secrets of Award-winning Digital Artists:
Creative Techniques and Insights for
Photoshop, Painter and More**
by Jeremy Sutton and Daryl Wise
(John Wiley & Sons, 2002)

Consumer Magazines

Design Graphics (Australia)
Digital publishing and design graphics.
http://www.designgraphics.com.au

Digital Imagemakers International Magazine
Official magazine of Digital ImageMakers
International. For members only.
http://www.dimagemaker.com/magazine/
magazine.html

eDIGITALPHOTO
The digital version of Shutterbug magazine.
http://www.edigitalphoto.com

EFX: Art & Design
Publication for cutting-edge digital artists and
designers. Published from Sweden.
http://macartdesign.matchbox.se

Kelvin Magazine
An independent print and online publication
featuring emerging artists.
http://www.kelvinmagazine.com

PEI
PHOTO > Electronic Imaging
http://www.peimag.com

More Digital-Friendly Art Resources

Here are some useful contacts and
information assets.

Organizations, Galleries, Showcases, Art Shows, Festivals, and Contests

Groups and events that cater to the
digitally inclined.

Organizations

American Print Alliance
A consortium of nonprofit printmakers'
councils in the United States and Canada.
http://printalliance.org

Digital Art Museum
Electronic archive of computer art.
http://www.dam.org

Digital ImageMakers International
Paid member organization for professional
and amateur digital imagemakers working in
all mediums.
http://www.dimagemaker.com

Digital Printing & Imaging Association
Paid member organization for digital printing
and imaging applied to the commercial
graphics industry.
http://www.dpia.org

Giclée Printers Association
Member organization for Tru Giclée
certification.
http://www.trugiclee.org

Graphic Artists Guild
Union of graphic artists. Publishes the
Graphic Artists Guild Handbook: Pricing &
Ethical Guidelines.
http://www.gag.org

International Association of
Computer Graphics
Accepts juried, nonpaid applications
for membership from organizations
and individuals.
http://www.iacgr.com

Photo Marketing Association International
Digital Imaging Marketing Association
Member organizations of the photo
imaging industry.
http://www.pmai.org

STANDARDS ORGANIZATIONS

American Society for Testing and
Materials (ASTM)
Standards-developing organization.
http://www.astm.org

American National Standards Institute (ANSI)
U.S. standards administration.
http://www.ansi.org

International Organization for
Standardization (ISO)
The main international standards group.
http://www.iso.ch/iso/en/ISOOnline.frontpage

Digital Galleries and Showcases

911 Gallery
In April, 2002, 911 Gallery celebrated 10
years of specializing exclusively in digital art.
http://www.911gallery.org

Artists Own Registry
Visual arts showcase.
http://artistsownregistry.com

Boston Cyberarts Online Gallery
http://gallery.bostoncyberarts.org

The Digital Artist
Where artists, designers, and artisans display
their work to buyers around the world,
around the clock.
http://www.thedigitalartist.com

Digital Art Museum.com
Promoting digital art culture.
http://www.digitalartmuseum.com

Digital Arts Group
Nonprofit organization dedicated to
supporting the advancement of digital fine art
and the artists that create it.
http://www.digitalartsgroup.com

Digital Fine Art.org
A nonprofit organization committed to
presenting the creative accomplishments of
digital artists who excel in their field.
http://www.digitalfineart.org

DigitalSalon.com
A private, pro-artist organization dedicated
to showcasing visual art produced using
digital media.
http://www.digitalsalon.com

The IDEA
The Indian Documentary of Electronic Arts
semiannual CD-gazettes.
http://geocities.com/shankarb.geo/idea.htm

Museum of Computer Art (MOCA)
A nonprofit computer art museum that
promotes computer art.
http://www.museumofcomputerart.com

PODgallery
An online art store for offering fine-art prints.
http://www.podgallery.com

Sciartists Online
Guest artist exhibitions.
http://sciartists-online.com

Studio Matchbox/Agosto
Publications and Web sites for digital artists.
http://macartdesign.matchbox.se

World Printmakers & Fine Art Print Sales
Worldwide showcase for contemporary
fine-art printmakers.
http://www.worldprintmakers.com

Art Shows, Festivals, & Contests

**Top American Art Shows and Festivals
Accepting Digital:**

(thanks to Larry Berman,
http://bermangraphics.com/contents.htm)

Ann Arbor Street Fair
(http://www.artfair.org)

Cherry Creek Arts Festival
(http://www.cherryarts.org/asp/users)

Coconut Grove Arts Festival
(http://www.coconutgroveartsfest.com)

Lakefront Festival of the Arts
(http://168.215.58.111)

International Computer Art Festival
The festival that gathers artists, students, and
enthusiasts of computer art. Free entry.
http://www.pixxelpoint.org

Museum of Computer Art (MOCA)
The annual MOCA Digital Art Contest.
(Donnie Awards). Free entry.
http://www.museumofcomputerart.com

And...

http://www.absolutearts.com
Dedicated arts news service covering
important and qualitative arts news from all
over the world.

http://artdeadlineslist.com
A monthly e-mail newsletter listing art
contests and competitions, art scholarships
and grants, juried exhibitions, et al. for artists,
art educators, and art students of all ages.

Workshops, Seminars, and Tutorials

Continuing education at its best.

Workshops, Seminars, and Classes

Dan Burkholder
Platinum printing and digital techniques
including making digital negatives.
http://www.danburkholder.com

Cone Editions Digital Print Workshops
Digital Darkroom Studio, Creative Studio, and
Professional Development Studio Courses.
East Topsham, VT.
http://216.71.143.81/store/workshops.html

Andrew Darlow Images Intl.
Two-day inkjet printing and color correction
workshops in New York City.
http://www.andydarlow.com/workshops

Dan Jahn
Based in Denver, CO, offers training
regionally, nationally, internationally.
http://www.danjahn.com

Palm Beach Photographic Centre
A nonprofit visual arts organization dedicated
to promoting the arts of photography and
digital imaging.
http://www.workshop.org

Santa Fe Workshops
Committed to providing a positive,
challenging, and experiential photographic and
digital learning environment.

http://www.sfworkshop.com

Professional Photoshop Training with Dan Margulis
An intensive, small group, hands-on, three-day color correction class with Dan Margulis.
http://www.ledet.com/margulis

Painter Creativity Workshops with Jeremy Sutton
Various locations.
http://www.portrayals.com/classes.html

CDs and Tutorials

Artistry Online (Karen Sperling)
Corel/Procreate Painter tutorial CDs and training classes.
http://www.artistrymag.com

Creating Digital Imagery (Steve Friedman)
CD tutorials, mostly Corel/Procreate Painter.
http://www.digitalartmasterworks.com

Print Exchanges

A traditional form of freely exchanging prints among artists/printmakers—but with a digital twist. There's even a Print Exchange Central ("The Printmaking junkie's guide to fine print exchanges") at http://www.printmakingstudio.com/printexchanges.html.

Discussion Group Print Exchanges
http://groups.yahoo.com/group/epson9000
http://groups.yahoo.com/group/piezography3000
http://groups.yahoo.com/group/DigitalBlackandWhiteThePrint
http://groups.yahoo.com/group/digital-fineart

Print Exchanges
Co-sponsored by inkjetgoodies.com and EPSONx7x_Printers discussion list. Quarterly, U.S. print exchanges.

International Exchange of Prints and Digital Images
Prints or CDs accepted.
http://www.estampe.be/exchange/en.html

Index